T0344843

READ THE REVIEWS

"*The Procurement Game Plan* is an impressive collection of key topics that provides essential knowledge for the contemporary supply chain management professional. Real-world insights and proven strategies, presented with intentionality and a balanced perspective, make for an easy-to-read book from which every reader can gain significant value. Of particular note are the chapters on talent management and socially responsible procurement which deliver exhaustive and multi-faceted content that should be required reading for today's procurement leaders."

—David A. Hargraves,
Senior Vice President Supply Chain, Premier Inc.

"I read a lot of business and textbooks for training every year with most being repetitive and quite a slog to get through. I cannot tell you how many times I am halfway down a page when I realize that I have no idea what I just read. I did not have that problem with *The Procurement Game Plan*. This fast, easy read is complete with both real-world examples and specific implementation recommendations. Many procurement books say what should be done with no recommendation or roadmap on how to actually implement. The interviews with senior practitioners in Chapter 15 also differentiate this book from others. The authors do not reference big name consultants that never ran a procurement organization in their careers; they call on experienced senior procurement executives that have scars.

Procurement/Supply management does not have a published body of knowledge like management accounting, internal audit, or project management so *The Procurement Game Plan* can help provide a foundation for those new to the profession and a solid reference for those of us with experience."

—Robert Semethy,
CPOE, CPSM, FCIPS ExDip-Chartered,
Chief Procurement Officer,
Erste Group Bank AG, Vienna, Austria

"Whether you are just getting started or an experienced procurement/supply chain executive, I recommend this book to any professional seeking to learn successful strategies for a high-performing procurement organization. It's a fun, practical guide (or game plan) that if executed will add value to your organization's bottom line! As a former pro athlete and long-time procurement professional, I assure you this book does an amazing job of relating common sports strategies to the business environment. You'll find yourself not only enjoying the book front to back initially, but also keeping it nearby as a reference guide to continuously support you in executing best-in-class-procurement strategies!"

—Matt Mehler,
VP of Procurement,
Madison Square Garden Entertainment

"I found this book well written and easy to read with down-to-earth language not often found regarding technical subjects. The chapters are a recipe for success in a modern purchasing concern with many good lists of do's and don'ts, checklists, and strategies throughout the book.

It checks all the boxes of functions that can make a procurement department run well: sourcing strategies, contracts, negotiations, quoting, outsourcing, supplier scorecards, talent management, social responsibility, strategic sourcing, collaborative sourcing, supplier relationship management, qualifying suppliers, risk hedging, e-sourcing and reverse auctions, and global sourcing. The book is beneficial to big and small companies looking to improve their procurement processes.

This guide is for the corporate world—both executives and procurement personnel—to review their own purchasing practices and improve them. It's a resource for developing your specific procurement game plan, so don't just read it— act upon its teachings!"

—John Russo,
Associate Director, Center for Excellence,
Supply Chain Management, Duquesne University

"This book's clarity and comprehensive coverage make it one of the best procurement practitioners' guides on the market. It will successfully serve the needs of the purchasing professional who wants to do some serious thinking about what really does contribute value to his/her firm and why."

—Paulo Moretti,
Principal, PM2Consult

THE PROCUREMENT GAME PLAN

Winning Strategies and Techniques for
Supply Management Professionals

SECOND EDITION

CHARLES DOMINICK, SPSM3
SOHEILA R. LUNNEY, Ph.D.

J.ROSS
PUBLISHING

Copyright © 2022 by Charles Dominick and Soheila Lunney

ISBN-13: 978-1-60427-182-9

Printed and bound in the U.S.A. Printed on acid-free paper.

Cover design by Sharon Dominick

10 9 8 7 6 5 4 3 2 1

For Library of Congress Cataloging-in-Publication Data, please visit the WAV section of the publisher's website at www.jrosspub.com/wav.

Phone: (954) 727-9333
Fax: (561) 892-0700
Web: www.jrosspub.com

CONTENTS

PREFACE

Why another procurement/supply management book? We raised this question when first entertaining the idea of coauthoring a book. There are many books in the marketplace related to procurement that focus on a variety of issues, ranging from customer-centric demand management to basic principles of managing suppliers' suppliers for highly effective and efficient supply chain management operations. Although these books are credible and provide valuable, up-to-date information, we did not want to write a book that would be hard to read or difficult to comprehend. To sum it up, we wanted to write a book that would be *exciting*! While many books and publications offer best practices and new methodologies in the world of procurement and supply management, they lack easy-to-follow approaches in implementing those best practices and methodologies. In other words, they offer the *what*, but lack the *how to*. We wanted to address this nagging need of procurement and supply management professionals.

As educators who have provided procurement training to professionals throughout the world, we believe in the power of using real-life examples to convey our messages and simplify complex concepts. As a result, we use many real-world examples. We have both provided consulting services for a variety of industries and gained extensive procurement experience by working in different organizations, including a small manufacturer, two educational institutions, a Fortune 500 airline, and a Fortune 100 pharmaceutical/life sciences company. Examples from consulting and work experiences are shared in this book so that readers can apply recommended, winning strategies and techniques to achieve results and be successful in their roles as procurement professionals.

Best of all, we wanted to introduce a new twist to books on procurement and supply management by drawing similarities and contrasts to real-world sports. This is due to the fact that both authors are avid sport fans who have found that many principles that victorious sports teams apply to make themselves *champions* can also be applied to the business world. We want the procurement professional, like yourself, to achieve results, prove their value to their employers, and have rewarding careers.

The topics presented in this book were deliberately selected to prepare procurement and supply management professionals to be successful, given the complexity of changes that have occurred in the past 10–15 years and what will lie ahead for the profession. As a result, this book focuses on topics of utmost importance, from the fundamentals of procurement/supply management to emerging trends that are likely to revolutionize the way procurement is done in the future. The first chapter highlights the role of procurement in an extended enterprise and explains how this role has recently evolved. In addition to setting a procurement strategy, developing a business case, and paying attention to organizational structure (Chapter 2), a well-planned talent management approach (Chapter 3) emerges as an important strategic consideration. Once social responsibility (Chapter 4) as a higher standard of procurement behavior is explored, we'll cover how to demand a higher standard of supplier behavior by discussing preventing and managing back-door selling (Chapter 5). Once back-door selling is prevented, we can walk through the better alternative to back-door selling—the strategic sourcing process (Chapter 6), and cover supplier evaluation and selection (Chapter 7). We also address negotiation in general (Chapter 8), negotiation techniques used in specialized situations (Chapter 9), and ongoing supplier relationship management (Chapter 10). Achieving supply chain resilience through contingency planning (Chapter 11) highlights the important role that procurement plays in continuous business performance in the face of adversity. Measuring procurement performance (Chapter 12) provides insight into how to maintain a scorecard on procurement performance that is credible. Technologies and services (Chapter 13) are presented as overarching factors for improving supply management performance. Specialized areas of procurement (Chapter 14), such as global sourcing and procurement of services, play an important role in today's procurement world. You will hear directly from *superstars of the game* in our penultimate chapter dedicated to interviews that we've conducted with incredible procurement thought leaders (Chapter 15). And, we'll close out this tome with a chapter on managing what we hope is a long and successful procurement career for you (Chapter 16).

This book is of interest to professionals who are engaged in or considering procurement and supply management, particularly readers who are seeking the answers to the challenges of proving their value and braving the criticism cast by nonbelievers. It will have meaning for vice presidents and directors who are looking for ways to get to the next level of performance improvement, as well as managers charged with getting the intended results and returns on assets or investments. Academics will value the content as a guide for preparing students for future work in the field of procurement/supply management.

Procurement and supply chain management continue to be hot topics as more executives realize the value of these functions. Although companies from small businesses to large enterprises are paying more attention to these disciplines, much more remains to be accomplished. We hope that this book assists procurement and supply chain management professionals and their organizations in their quest for mastering best practices, achieving results, and making measurable contributions to the bottom line.

Charles Dominick, SPSM3
Soheila Lunney, Ph.D.

ACKNOWLEDGMENTS

To Sharon, Maleena, and Carson. Of all my dreams that have become reality, having you in my life is the best dream and the biggest blessing.

—Charles Dominick, SPSM3

To the memory of my mother and to all my loved ones who have always supported me in every endeavor and have never doubted my dreams.

—Soheila Lunney, Ph.D.

ABOUT THE AUTHORS

CHARLES DOMINICK, SPSM3

Charles Dominick, SPSM, is a serial entrepreneur who spent decades of his career as a successful procurement practitioner and thought leader. He founded Next Level Purchasing, Inc., where he created educational content that benefited procurement professionals from over 100 countries around the world. During his time at the helm of Next Level Purchasing, he guided the organization to several awards and honors, was the mastermind behind the organization's globally recognized Senior Professional in Supply Management (SPSM) Certification family, and led the company to an acquisition in 2016 at which time he successfully completed his personal exit strategy from the business. He has spoken at procurement events internationally where he earned rave reviews.

Prior to founding Next Level Purchasing, Charles acquired nearly a decade of results-producing experience in procurement at the University of Pittsburgh, US Airways (now American Airlines), and Kurt J. Lesker Company. He is currently CEO of Before and After Music Group.

A lifelong learner, Charles holds degrees in General Studies, Business Management, and Music Technology. He lives in Moon Township, Pennsylvania, with his wife and two children.

Charles can be reached at cdmnck@gmail.com.

SOHEILA LUNNEY, PH.D.

Soheila Lunney, Ph.D., is a lifetime educator, an inventor, and an accomplished procurement executive with a demonstrated history of achieving significant results as a practitioner and consultant. Presently, she is enjoying retirement while conducting highly rated negotiation seminars and serving on the Board of Directors of several nonprofit organizations.

In 2007, she founded Lunney Advisory Group LLC, a firm that provided procurement and supply chain management coaching, mentoring, and training services for both domestic and international (Far East, Europe, and Russia) clients. She also served on the Board of Directors of the Pittsburgh Chapter of the Institute for Supply Management (ISM), and the Supply Management Advisory Board of Duquesne and Chatham Universities in Pittsburgh, Pennsylvania.

Soheila was previously Vice President of Procurement for Education Management Corporation (EDMC). Prior to that position, she was the Director/Deputy to the Chief Procurement Officer at Bayer Corporation, where she held various positions with increasing responsibilities in research and development, logistics, customer service, materials management, and procurement.

Dr. Lunney obtained her Bachelor of Science (BS) in Chemistry from the National University of Iran, and an MS and Ph.D. from the University of East Anglia in Norwich, Great Britain. After a postdoctoral assignment at Clemson University, she joined the faculty as a lecturer. In 1983, she joined the University of Arkansas as an associate professor, prior to joining Bayer in 1986.

Dr. Lunney is the author of several publications, a sole holder of a U.S. Patent related to polyurethane technology, and has successfully spoken at supply chain management professional organizations and conferences.

Dr. Lunney can be reached at soheila.lunney@gmail.com.

 Web
Added
Value™

This book has free material available for download from the
Web Added Value™ resource center at *www.jrosspub.com*

At J. Ross Publishing we are committed to providing today's professional with practical, hands-on tools that enhance the learning experience and give readers an opportunity to apply what they have learned. That is why we offer free ancillary materials available for download on this book and all participating Web Added Value™ publications. These online resources may include interactive versions of the material that appears in the book or supplemental templates, worksheets, models, plans, case studies, proposals, spreadsheets and assessment tools, among other things. Whenever you see the WAV™ symbol in any of our publications, it means bonus materials accompany the book and are available from the Web Added Value Download Resource Center at www.jrosspub.com.

Downloads for *The Procurement Game Plan, 2nd Edition,* include instructor material for professors, a spreadsheet for calculating The Dominick Formula and using it in proposal evaluations, a 13-point procurement ethics checklist, a 20-point proposal evaluation checklist, a 21-point negotiation checklist, and a case study on "Business Process Re-engineering and e-Procurement Implementation at ASSET, Inc."

CHAPTER

PROCUREMENT'S PLACE IN THE ORGANIZATION: WHAT POSITION DOES SUPPLY MANAGEMENT PLAY?

Procurement—Except for perhaps sales, it is arguably the department within an organization that has the most impact on that organization's bottom line. Unfortunately, the leaders and top management of many organizations have not discovered that, yet.

Imagine a sports team. That sports team has players for every position, just like every other team in their league. But picture the coach having no idea how one of those positions can contribute to victory.

That sounds ludicrous, right? It is ludicrous. Yet, that scenario has parallels to the way that procurement is perceived in many organizations throughout the world. The management teams of those organizations are just not aware of the value that procurement can contribute.

PROCUREMENT IS AN IMPORTANT PLAYER ON ANY BUSINESS TEAM

We have a fond memory from a business conference that we attended. At one point, we spoke to another attendee, who was a senior manager for a government contractor. Out of curiosity and to make conversation, we asked him about how his procurement department operated and what improvement initiatives they were pursuing. He replied nonchalantly that his company really didn't do much in terms of procurement training or process improvement, and he wasn't concerned. They were a *small company* and didn't spend much, relatively speaking.

We then learned that his company spends about $20 million per year on goods and services, so we asked if the company could save 5% of that—in other words, if pre-tax profit increased by $1 million—would the owners care? Would that be too small to matter? We could see by the look in the manager's eyes that he had an epiphany at that very moment.

The coach came to a dramatic realization of how one of his players can contribute to victory.

Saving money is just one of the numerous ways that procurement can contribute to corporate victory. In American football terms, if saving money is *blocking and tackling*, achieving supply continuity in even the most challenging of times is *passing*. Implementing a supplier diversity and inclusion program that earns favorable press coverage for your organization is *running*. Being environmentally responsible is *kicking*. You get the idea. There's a lot that procurement can do to contribute to corporate victory.

Corporate victory through smart procurement is what this book is about. It is literally a *game plan* for supply management success, providing play-by-play descriptions of how to achieve measurable results for your organization.

MANAGEMENT'S EXPECTATIONS OF MODERN PROCUREMENT

As stated earlier, some management teams have no clue about the value that procurement can deliver to the organization. It is up to you to demonstrate that value.

The best way to demonstrate value is by performing well and delivering real, measurable results. If you are in a procurement department that has not gotten much respect or attention over the years, you may need help in the form of new staff, technology, or training. You may need to ask management to make an investment in improving procurement performance.

You may also find yourself asking a question similar to the one we asked of the government contractor's senior manager, as described earlier in this chapter: "If you could have $x more in profit, would that matter to the owners/investors/stockholders?"

What else can a reasonable person say? Saving, say, 5% of spend may be tough in an inflationary market if you already squeezed out cost savings in the past few years. But if the company hasn't been historically concerned with procurement, there is likely a lot of *low-hanging fruit*, a common phrase used to describe easy and obvious decisions that you can make quickly to achieve positive results.

On the other hand, management may have had its *procurement epiphany* a while ago. If so, they may have high expectations of you and they will challenge you to deliver more aggressive results. So, what does management want from procurement? Here are a few common expectations:

- **Cost savings**—Management wants procurement to save money and reduce overall costs. Please note that the previous sentence is not synonymous with management wants procurement to get lower prices. You need to focus on the reduction of total cost of ownership, not just price reduction at any cost. Upcoming chapters will teach you more about total cost of ownership.

- **Supply continuity and risk management**—Attaining the lowest price on a product or service is absolutely meaningless if the product doesn't get delivered or the service doesn't get performed when needed. Organizations depend on an uninterrupted flow of goods, services, and information—both into the organization as well as out of the organization—to accomplish what they are in business to do. Procurement plays a vital role in ensuring that the incoming flow of goods, services, and information is happening at a rate that is optimal for the organization. This means being able to overcome foreseeable and unforeseeable challenges by maintaining a resilient supply chain. It also means being proactive in predicting demand fluctuations and mitigating any negative impact, as well as being agile and seamlessly responding to any surprising changes in the market that could pose a risk to supply continuity.

- **Productivity improvements**—Management will always expect you to do more work with fewer resources. No matter whether you are in a tactical or strategic procurement organization, there are many productivity metrics that you can choose from to track productivity gains: contracts executed per buyer per month/quarter/year, average length of sourcing cycle, man-hours per dollar saved, etc.

- **Brand/differentiation support**—Your organization's mission or vision statement should give you some clues as to how your organization wants to be perceived in the marketplace and how it wants to be differentiated from its competition, such as offering higher quality, faster cycle time, better service, lower cost, or something similar. Make sure that your decisions and metrics support your management's brand and differentiation strategy. As logical as this may sound, you would be surprised by how many organizations have a mission of being the *highest quality provider* in their industry, yet their procurement departments measure only cost savings.

- **Customer satisfaction**—Sometimes, being in procurement can make you feel separated from your organization's customers. But management relies on things that you're responsible for, like assuring continuity of supply, to keep its promises to its customers. Realize that you can personally be responsible for your organization's failure to meet customer expectations. In this era of tough competition, organizations have to meet or exceed customer expectations simply to survive, and you have a critical role in that survival.

- **Positive cash flow**—In some organizations, the timing of monetary receipts and payments is critical. Those organizations cannot afford to have more cash leaving the company than coming in during certain periods. Be aware of that limitation and negotiate appropriate terms with your suppliers. Never pay them late and hope that they don't notice!

- **To be the best**—While some senior managers may have no real understanding of exactly what some of their departments do, most want the best performance possible out of each and every one of those departments. Whether they push for benchmarking or expect the individual departments to benchmark on their own, management teams want to know that departments, such as procurement, are promoting and adopting the latest best practices.

- **Efficient service to internal customers**—Every department within an organization is tasked to get something done to contribute to the success of the organization. Procurement can facilitate the timely contributions of other departments. Often, procurement is blamed for being an obstacle to timely contributions. So, management expects procurement to continually improve processes in order to better serve those who are making their own contributions to the organization's success.

- **Generating revenue**—It is no longer a secret that procurement's cost saving efforts can help an organization's bottom line get bigger. But the fact that procurement can actually generate revenue too is still in the early stages of discovery among many organizations. Through supplier rebates on employee and customer purchases, along with other innovative practices discussed later, procurement can actually bring cash into an organization. Later in this chapter, we'll talk about the emergence of the *Procurement as a Profit Center* view. The management teams that have learned about this concept and other creative approaches now have revenue-generating expectations of their procurement groups.

- **Competitive advantage**—Why do your organization's customers do business with your organization? They do business with your organization because it offers something that the customers view as being more beneficial than other organizations. Collectively, the aspects of your organization that are more beneficial in the eyes of the customer are referred to as your organization's *competitive advantage*. These days, with more functions being outsourced, the marketplace is not a war of company versus company—it is a war of supply chain versus supply chain. So, the suppliers that you select and manage often determine the relative strength of your organization, compared to its competitors. Therefore, management expects procurement to develop a stronger supply chain and, thus, for procurement to be its competitive advantage.

Experienced procurement professionals know the traditional contributions expected of them—such as faster and more reliable supplier delivery, quality approaching perfection, and collaborative supplier relationships focused on continuous improvement—but, it is important to know how those contributions fit into the big scheme of things from senior management's perspective. Procurement professionals who do understand senior management's point of view find themselves leading *modern procurement departments*. How do you know if your organization qualifies as a modern procurement department? If you are working in a modern procurement department, your department will have all 12 of these characteristics:

1. The head of procurement reports directly to the CEO of your company.
2. Procurement is actively involved in senior management level, long-term strategic planning.
3. Procurement has established a senior-management endorsed Procurement Governance Council.
4. Procurement is involved in the early stages of new product/service development.
5. Your department is responsible for procurement in *nontraditional* spend areas, such as healthcare benefits, fleet management, facilities and construction, temporary labor, and travel.
6. The procurement staff is responsible for placing only a small percentage of your organization's purchase orders, if any at all.
7. Contract management, logistics, and inventory functions either fall under procurement or supply management on the organizational chart, or are integrated into the work of procurement or supply management staff.
8. Maverick buying—when an end user orders from a noncontracted supplier despite the organization having a contract with another supplier—is a thing of the past.
9. When dealing with large, frequently used suppliers, no paper is exchanged between the time that a need for a product or service is defined until the time that the supplier receives payment.
10. No major sourcing process is conducted without the use of a cross-functional team.
11. You are buying from a large list of global sources and measuring non-domestic spend as a percentage of total spend.
12. Your department has social responsibility goals and measurements in place.

While most procurement leaders consider their departments to be *modern*, when they compare their departments with this list, they often realize how far they still have to go to truly earn that *modern* distinction.

TYPES OF GOALS THAT PROCUREMENT TEAMS HAVE

In analyzing procurement departments across many different industries and geographies, one thing is clear—goals can vary wildly! While this book draws comparisons between procurement and sports, the topic of goals is where procurement and sports are dramatically different. In sports, the goal is generally simple—win the game. In procurement, goals are not that easily summarized.

Let's characterize the types of goals in procurement departments across a wide continuum that spans from good, to bad, to ugly. We'll go from worst to best in a discussion of the objectives that procurement departments set for themselves:

The ugly: no goals—Procurement departments who have no documented goals are moving in many directions without clear focus. Their value is not measured nor communicated to management. These procurement departments are likely to find themselves being downsized or outsourced.

The bad: vague goals—Having goals that fail to state exactly what needs to be accomplished is almost as futile as having no goals. These types of goals make a subjective process out of distinguishing good performance from bad. An example would be: *improve control of spending*. What does that mean? Does it mean that requiring 25 signatures to make a purchase will be doing a *good job*? Could a procurement specialist think that control was sufficiently improved, yet an executive would disagree?

The good: SMART goals—A timeless buzzword relative to goals is *SMART*. SMART goals are specific, measurable, attainable, relevant, and time-bound. Simply being specific and using numbers makes goals infinitely more effective than vague or immeasurable goals. Let's modify the last example: *Improve control over spending by increasing expenses under contract by 25 percent over the previous year*. Now that's better. You know what is meant by *improve control over spending*. The numbers enable you to determine whether you exceeded, met, or failed to meet your goal. If you increased the expenses under contract by only 20 percent, you came up short. If you achieved a 30 percent increase, you performed very well. A goal like this gives you a clear target to shoot at.

The great: money-based goals—While SMART goals are good, there is the opportunity to set even better goals. *Great* goals are not only specific, measurable, attainable, relevant, and time-bound, but they are expressed in the language of business—money! The reason you reduce inventory, increase contract coverage, or reduce lead time is to put your organization in a better financial position. So, translate other statistics into money. Continuing with the example—*improve control over spending by increasing expenses under contract by $3 million*.

The best: organizational strategy-based goals—The best goals go a step beyond great goals, and are tied to the strategy and goals of the overall organization. *Improve control over spending by increasing expenses under contract by $3 million* is a great goal, and may be the best goal if the organization's goal is to maintain or increase profitability. But what if the organization's number one goal is to be the first to market a new item? There is a fatal disconnect between executive management and procurement management. Speed, rather than expense control, should be the priority. The best goals facilitate the accomplishment of organizational goals, are expressed in monetary terms, and possess all the characteristics of SMART goals (Figure 1.1).

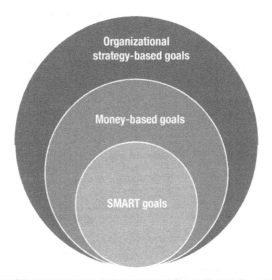

Figure 1.1   Components of the *best* goals

THE EXPANDING ROLE OF PROCUREMENT

Because the best goals facilitate the accomplishment of organizational goals, there needs to be an alignment between procurement objectives and organizational goals with a clear channel of communication linking procurement to the highest levels within the organization. Though earlier in this chapter we said that the head of a modern procurement department reports directly to the CEO, sometimes this direct reporting can only be accomplished after a successful transformation of the procurement department into a world-class department.

So, the question in the interim is, "To whom should procurement report?"

Our answer, "It depends." To whom the procurement function reports can be different from company to company, and that's okay. To simplify it, if the company sees procurement's primary role as delivering cost savings, the company generally positions procurement under finance, reporting up to the Chief Financial Officer (Figure 1.2). If the company sees procurement's primary role as supporting operations (through assuring continuity of supply, reducing risk, and the like), then the company generally positions procurement under operations/supply chain management, reporting up to the Chief Operations Officer or Vice President of Supply Chain Management (Figure 1.3).

As another generalization, in manufacturing, procurement commonly reports to operations/supply chain management; in service industries, procurement commonly reports to finance. Regardless of the reporting hierarchy, there needs to be the full support of top-level management in order for procurement to succeed and secure quantifiable results.

The need for alignment with other parts of the organization has changed the qualifications for procurement leaders and those who report to them. Because of the higher-level responsibilities of modern purchasers, they must have solid fundamental procurement capabilities, analytical skills (particularly in financial analysis), advanced computer expertise, along with skills in contract execution and

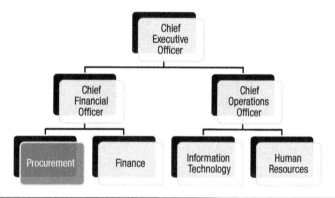

Figure 1.2   Organizational chart with procurement reporting to CFO

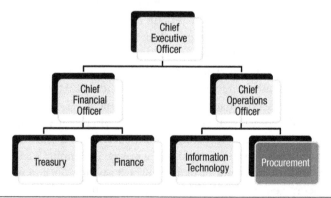

Figure 1.3   Organizational chart with procurement reporting to COO

laws, project management, relationship building, strategy development, and negotiation. The manager needs to have all of the skills of his or her employees, plus the ability to:

- Align the procurement department's objectives with the mission and vision of the overall organization
- Implement initiatives and best practices that support the mission and vision of the overall organization
- Provide effective leadership for their staff and the procurement function in general
- Be a change agent

So, it is clear that procurement is moving in a direction toward a destination, moving the ball down the field toward the end zone, as is done in American football, if you will. But where is that end zone? Does it have a name? How does one know when they've reached it?

STRATEGIC VERSUS TACTICAL PROCUREMENT

Many consider a transformation to *strategic* procurement to be the desired end state. Most procurement departments aspire to be strategic. But what does a *strategic* procurement department look like?

A common thread of strategic procurement departments is the fact that they seek to minimize their tactical duties and spend more time on initiatives that are more closely aligned to the long-term goals of the organization, in order to produce measurable, positive results. Here are 12 characteristics of strategic, in contrast to tactical, procurement:

1. **Spend analysis**—Strategic procurement departments examine the amount of money they spend in each category of goods and services with different suppliers and use this analysis to identify opportunities for improvement in *traditional* and *nontraditional* areas of buy.
2. **Strategic sourcing process**—Strategic procurement departments have a systematic approach of building cross-functional teams and applying the principles of strategic sourcing for selecting suppliers.
3. **Supplier relationship management**—Strategic procurement departments monitor and measure supplier performance and regularly spend time meeting with their key suppliers to review their scorecard and plan for improvement initiatives.
4. **Technology implementation**—Strategic procurement departments frequently update and add technologies that measurably reduce costs, decrease cycle time, and make the procurement process more efficient.

5. **Developing project plans**—Strategic procurement departments use project management techniques to map out both recurring activities and one-time projects. Project timelines are well defined to assure timely completion of different initiatives.

6. **Enterprise-wide contracts**—Strategic procurement departments consolidate spend across all parts of their organizations and enter into contracts with a limited supply base to serve the needs of the entire organization.

7. **Forecasting**—Strategic procurement departments regularly document changes that they foresee in price levels, availability, and markets to ensure a competitive advantage for their organizations.

8. **Involvement in spec development**—Strategic procurement departments are involved at the early stages of product and specification development, lending specialized knowledge in material availability, cost drivers, standard parts, and reliability of supply.

9. **Process optimization**—Strategic procurement departments analyze existing processes and then optimize them for maximum efficiency and effectiveness. Part of this involves developing tools (e.g., request for proposal and contract templates) so that repetitive tasks can be done more quickly and error free.

10. **Supplier development**—Strategic procurement departments don't blindly accept the suppliers and products that are currently available. They work with suppliers to develop new capabilities or products that will improve cost or quality.

11. **Work responsibility refinement**—Strategic procurement departments constantly identify ways to automate, delegate, or eliminate tactical, non-value-added work.

12. **Garner stakeholder support**—*Stakeholder* refers to anyone who has a vested interest in a product or service being procured. Stakeholders can include end users all the way up to senior executives. Strategic procurement departments secure stakeholder support. Procurement strategic targets, cost reduction goals, and initiatives are routinely communicated with internal customers for their participation and buy-in. Best-in-class strategic procurement teams use an intranet site within their company network to communicate and reach out to stakeholders.

You can see that there are quite a few characteristics of strategic procurement, not just one or two. If you want your procurement department to be more strategic—and who doesn't?—you can work on steadily adding more of these characteristics over time.

PROCUREMENT AS A PROFIT CENTER

With procurement focusing on strategic initiatives, delivering results, and demonstrating value, its legacy as being considered a cost to the organization is being shed. Procurement is increasingly recognized as a contributor to the profit of an organization. This transformation has resulted in some individuals referring to old-fashioned procurement departments as *cost centers*, and modern procurement departments as *profit centers*.

The *profit center* term sounds great, but is somewhat ambiguous. We've seen procurement departments with different approaches from each other all called profit centers. Here are four distinct procurement profit-center models used today:

- **Model 1:** This most simplistic model merely recognizes the fact that procurement savings contributes to higher profits. The procurement department may report corporate net income and illustrate how it would have been lower if it were not for procurement's actions.
- **Model 2:** This model also recognizes savings but, in addition, sets procurement's budget (for supplies, equipment, salaries, etc.) based on savings per year. In addition, procurement may negotiate volume rebates from suppliers and use those rebates toward its budget.
- **Model 3:** This model is used where a parent company has several subsidiaries or franchises. The parent company's procurement department *markets* itself to the subsidiaries or franchisees who pay for the procurement department to execute projects such as spend analyses, requests for proposals, negotiations, and so forth. The subsidiaries or franchisees have a customer/supplier relationship with procurement and are not obligated to use their services.
- **Model 4:** This is the most controversial model. A procurement department will work on initiatives for the success of its own organization, and develop techniques, tools, and technologies in the process. Then, after successful internal implementation, it will sell to other companies those techniques, tools, and technologies in the form of training, software, or consulting services.

Why is Model 4 controversial? First of all, organizations have been following a trend to focus on core competencies and divest the rest. Therefore, if a pharmaceutical company wants to focus on selling medications, it may choose to abandon the selling of procurement software. Second, if your responsibilities are split between executing the procurement function and developing and selling services, your interest in doing an excellent job at procurement may be diluted to the point of being dispensable. Third, can you imagine the result if you taught your suppliers your own negotiating secrets?

Model 4 may work for some. Our advice? Don't try Model 4 *at home* unless you have an inseparable relationship with your organization's top management.

PROCUREMENT'S PIECE OF THE SUPPLY CHAIN

We get asked the following question a lot. "What is the difference between procurement and supply chain management?" Though many different and conflicting definitions of supply chain management abound, in our definition, procurement is a subset of supply chain management. Procurement deals primarily with managing all aspects related to the inputs to an organization (i.e., purchased goods, materials, and services), while supply chain management deals with inputs, conversion, and outputs.

A supply chain consists of three types of entities: customers, a producer, and the producer's suppliers. The extended supply chain includes customers' customers and suppliers' suppliers (Figure 1.4). Supply chain management oversees and optimizes the processes of acquiring inputs from suppliers (procurement), converting inputs into a finished product (production), and delivering those products—or outputs—to customers (fulfillment).

Under this definition, supply chain managers decide where to locate manufacturing and distribution facilities, how to route goods and materials among those facilities, and from which parts of the world to source the inputs. Supply chain management organizations unite disparate functions that historically reported to different executive positions with different, and sometimes conflicting, priorities.

What does this mean for individuals who have a procurement-related title? One myth is that procurement will become less important. To the contrary, analyzing spend information for cost savings opportunities, negotiating, and selecting reliable sources of supply will always be critical. These functions fuel profit and provide competitive advantage for the organization.

However, the procurement professional can expect to see his or her role expand to include the management of functions that were separate in the past. These functions include inventory management, internal logistics, warehousing, and other functions that are more related to the *input* or *preproduction* side of the supply chain. In some cutting-edge cases, procurement is even being invited to be a significant part of a customer collaboration team.

Figure 1.4   The extended supply chain

PROCUREMENT AS A SERVICE TO THE ORGANIZATION

In talking about procurement's expansion, it is clear that today's procurement department interfaces with other departments more than ever. Unfortunately, procurement's new involvement is not always greeted with open arms.

The Procurement Manifesto

Because it can be difficult to gain *buy-in* from functional departments when trying to get them to accept procurement's involvement, it is important to have a list of reasons why it will benefit them to work with procurement. We encourage you to develop such a list—a Procurement Manifesto, if you will—to aid in your efforts to *sell* the value of working with procurement.

Here is an example of four points you can include in the Procurement Manifesto. Because the Procurement Manifesto is a document that you will provide to your stakeholders, *you* refers to those stakeholders—the readers of the document:

1. **Procurement's involvement allows you to focus on your core competency**—You have an important role in the organization. Your expertise in your function makes you valuable. With procurement handling your purchasing activities, you will be able to spend more of your time on what you do best.

2. **Procurement's involvement helps you avoid last minute crises**—Your department is busy with numerous competing priorities. In many departments that meet the same description, purchasing activities are often put off until the last minute. This results in a failure to find the best value in the market, paying expediting shipping charges, or, worst of all, not obtaining goods and services on time. Procurement can help you avoid these headaches.

3. **Procurement's involvement gets the most out of your budget**—Unless your department invests in negotiation training for its staff and gives them the daily opportunity to negotiate with suppliers, suppliers may have an advantage in bargaining. Because the procurement staff regularly receives negotiation training, negotiates daily, and keeps up to date with the latest market trends and cost saving techniques, procurement can help save your department money and alleviate some of your budget constraints.

4. **Procurement's involvement can uncover unforeseen obstacles**—Whether noticing the warning signs of a supplier in financial trouble, identifying a material in short supply, or just knowing the typical timelines associated with getting the goods or services you need, procurement reduces risks to your department's operations.

A key takeaway of the Procurement Manifesto concept is that you have to communicate to your stakeholders what is in it for them; and saving money is not always at the top of their list.

You see, stakeholders often scoff at the notion of saving money because they (rightly or wrongly) feel that you are going to sacrifice quality, service, delivery, and the like by finding the lowest price. It is up to you to explain to them how they will benefit by working with you. More than anything, you must have credibility in the eyes of all stakeholders. It will take time to gain trust and become credible in the eyes of your counterparts. However, the outcomes are rewarding for you personally as well as for your organization.

Careless procurement professionals don't spend much time trying to gain or sustain credibility. Yet, they constantly wonder why procurement gets no respect.

Service Principles for Procurement

In the procurement world, another term for stakeholders is *internal customers.* End users of the products you buy—management, engineers, the shop floor—these are all examples of your customers, and they want good service. They expect to be treated like patrons at a restaurant, guests at a hotel, or shoppers at a store.

Rather than being reactionary, procurement professionals need to reach out to their internal customers in a proactive manner. Meeting regularly, sharing information, and discussing goals, requirements, and concerns can help procurement professionals to plan ahead and proactively address the needs of their customers. When you are in a proactive mode, you have more time for doing your job more efficiently.

Sometimes, procurement professionals find benefit in being *tough* with their suppliers. Thus, it is difficult for them to turn around and exhibit a customer-friendly persona to their internal customers. However, remembering the following seven service principles will help you delight your internal customers.

Principle 1—Involve your internal customers

Involving internal customers from the beginning of a project and soliciting their input as part of your regular communication is invaluable. Involved internal customers will be valuable partners and resources for implementing new agreements. They can champion the roll out of a new agreement or program which, ultimately, makes your job easier.

Principle 2—Document and share your action plan

After involving your internal customers and getting an understanding of the outcome desired, communicate, in writing, what you are going to do, what is expected from them, and when you will be done. This helps customers understand all of the work involved in meeting their needs and sets their expectations for what constitutes a timely completion.

Principle 3—Under-promise and over-deliver

Imagine this scenario: A pizza shop promised to deliver your pizza in 30 minutes, but delivered it in 40 minutes. Another pizza shop promised to deliver your pizza in 45 minutes, but actually delivered it in 40 minutes. Which pizza shop would you be upset with? Certainly not the one who performed better than the expectations that it set.

When you communicate timelines to your customers, you should under-promise. Give them a date that you can not only meet, but beat. They will think you're excellent when you over-deliver (i.e., perform better than expected). If you do the opposite—over-promising and under-delivering—you'll quickly gain a reputation of incompetence.

Sometimes, internal customers are impatient, and their impatience may negatively impact your quality. While you do need to learn how to work both quickly and effectively, you don't want to allow an artificial deadline to dilute your ability to contribute to the organization's success. You may need to negotiate for the appropriate amount of time.

To ensure that internal customers give you enough time to do your job well, you must communicate:

1. What you actually do after getting a request for your action
2. Why your work is valuable and has measurable benefit to the organization
3. How you do care about productivity and how you've improved your productivity/cycle time over the past few months/years
4. What the consequences are if you are not given enough time

Principle 4—Update customers regularly

When there is a significant amount of time between the communication of your action plan and completion of your work, give your customers regular updates of your progress. Without periodic communication, your customers will fear that you have forgotten their needs. Simply sending your customers a brief weekly email will give them comfort in planning their work, while avoiding any impatient, ill-timed calls to you.

Those first four principles were designed to be followed at the beginning of a project in order to deliver excellent service to your internal customers. If you follow those tips and all goes as planned, you have provided excellent service. But what if things do not go as planned? You could have a customer relations disaster if you're not careful. The next three principles will help you handle adversity when serving an internal customer.

Principle 5—Express concerns immediately

Sometimes it may not look like you're going to meet a deadline. Don't avoid speaking with your internal customer, fearing their wrath and hoping a miracle will turn things around. Be honest. Give them time to plan in case things don't turn around. They may be upset that their project is not on schedule, but their fury will be minor compared to the anger they would feel if they found out *at the last minute* as opposed to well in advance. Assure them that you will stay on top of the project to try to get it back on track.

Principle 6—Don't make excuses

If something negative happens with the project, accept responsibility. Tell your customer what you are going to do to minimize the impact of the issues. Don't displace blame by saying that your supplier is incompetent or that your boss took too long to review your work. People don't like to hear about problems. They like to hear about solutions. Take responsibility for whatever actions are required to satisfy your internal customer. Let them know you have something personal at stake.

Principle 7—Follow up

After you've met the project goal, touch base with your internal customer. Find out how your work is affecting them after the fact, and ask them about your service. It is rewarding to hear someone compliment your efforts—it doesn't happen too often for many of us! Plus, their words may give you ideas on how to improve your service for them and other internal customers in the future. It will be best to solicit feedback in writing, such as a simple email, when projects go smoothly and they get completed on time. Such positive feedback from internal customers can come in handy when you have your performance reviews, or when you hear the question, "What is procurement doing?" Testimonials from happy customers are the best justification for procurement's existence.

Procurement's Role in Specification Writing

An underlying theme to good service is that the walls separating procurement from its internal customers need to be taken down. No longer is it acceptable for either the customer or procurement to blame the other. Procurement perfection is a team sport and both sides need to work together for success. We will close this chapter with one more example of how the team concept can apply.

A requisitioner sends you a requisition describing an item that he needs. You get bids from the major suppliers of that item, qualify the most attractive ones, and collaborate with the requisitioner on a mutually agreed supplier selection. You place the order; the item arrives. The requisitioner refuses it, says it isn't what he wanted (though it matched the description on the requisition), and behaves like a disgruntled fan booing the home team.

Sound familiar? It's a common procurement situation. The problem is clear—the specifications were poor. So that's the requisitioner's fault, right? Not completely. Requisitioners have their areas of specialty, and specification writing usually isn't one of them. Procurement deals with specs daily. It's not your job to write specs, but helping requisitioners write them well is.

The first step in helping them is to add a questionnaire to your requisition template, whether that template is paper or electronic. This questionnaire should help requisitioners provide commonly omitted information. For a sample 14-question requisition questionnaire, see Exhibit A in the back of this book.

The detail harvested through the questionnaire should be built into the specifications provided to bidders. Then, before awarding an order to the top bidder, review those details with that supplier and the requisitioner. Obtaining the requisitioner's sign-off on the specifications will eliminate finger-pointing and blaming procurement for ordering the wrong item.

These additional steps will decrease the risk of buying the wrong thing, and you won't have to fear being booed by your internal customers!

CLOSING REMARKS

Procurement is an important department in any organization, large or small, and can have a dramatic impact on the financial performance of an organization and the efficiency of its internal operations. The moral of this chapter is: *Procurement has to take a total strategic approach to exceeding management's expectations, embracing a broader supply chain role, and delighting its internal customers.*

$$2$$

CHAPTER

SETTING A SUPPLY MANAGEMENT STRATEGY: THE FOUNDATION FOR PROCUREMENT VICTORY

Every sports team has a strategy and a playbook, together serving as a foundation for how it will play the game and setting forth what it will do in the various situations that it will face throughout the season. Likewise, every procurement department should have its own strategy and playbook, of sorts, to help it focus on why it exists and what it must accomplish.

What should a supply management strategy address? A supply management strategy may vary from organization to organization but, at a minimum, it should address these five topics:

1. A business plan for contributing to success
2. Procurement organizational structure
3. Cost control
4. Risk management
5. Playing within a system

We will now discuss each of these topics individually.

A BUSINESS PLAN FOR CONTRIBUTING TO SUCCESS

Business planning is not just about producing a document. The work of writing and thinking things through is as important as the final document. A business plan is a tool for understanding how your procurement organization is put together, and you use it to chart the direction you want your team to take. The process of creating a business plan—which we will call your *Procurement Game Plan*—will help you coach your team while you and the members of your team become more sophisticated in introducing and implementing best-in-class practices. It creates a framework for you to lead and grow your department in various aspects and contribute to the success of your organization. Well-prepared business plans are dynamic. Each organization and its culture are different and your business plan should reflect this.

As a procurement professional, you may ask, "Why do I need to prepare a business plan?" Here are some reasons:

- It brings credibility to your work and your department
- It helps you think long term
- It provides justification for securing funding and the needed resources
- It helps you anticipate problems and proactively plan for avoiding or overcoming them
- Gathering information for your plan will increase your knowledge of your industry, suppliers, best practices, and opportunities, thereby assisting you in making better informed decisions
- It helps you to know what is expected of you as the leader of your team
- It keeps you and your team motivated

While we think that this chapter alone can help you produce a winning Procurement Game Plan, we also encourage you to look beyond the covers of this book for business planning ideas. By devoting a small amount of time searching on the web, you should be able to find good examples of effective business plans. You should also adopt and practice benchmarking if you have not done so already. Colleagues from other industries may have already developed business plans that are helping them to successfully manage productive procurement departments. Contact them, and you may be pleasantly surprised at how eagerly they will share their plan with you. Avoid reinventing the wheel, and do not shy away from asking for help and learning from others; it will save you valuable time.

An important step in preparing a winning Procurement Game Plan is defining your objectives and action plans. This will help you and your team focus on what is of high priority and importance for your department, while not getting distracted. As stated in Chapter 1, your objectives should be in line with the strategic goals of your organization. Failure to pay attention to this important aspect of setting objectives may take you on the wrong path, and place you in conflict with your organization's executives. Another important aspect to take into consideration is developing a timeline for your plan, whereby all objectives will be completed and addressed. Again, your timeline should closely correlate with your organization's strategic plan and timeline. The time-consuming step in preparing your business plan is conducting research and gathering information. Obtaining internal and external data/information, learning about best practices, finding out what you need to do to meet the expectations of your internal customer, and learning about how your procurement work can become a competitive advantage for your organization are aspects of your research and information gathering process.

A powerful tool that Soheila has successfully promoted and used to assist her clients when they begin gathering information to develop their business plan is a SWOT analysis. Conducting a SWOT analysis is a veritable prerequisite to starting your Procurement Game Plan. It is necessary that your Procurement Game Plan contains all the essential information of a SWOT analysis, based on your research and findings.

SWOT Analysis

A SWOT analysis may sound like a form of mission planning for action movie characters like Rambo, James Bond, or John Wick. However, SWOT simply stands for strengths, weaknesses, opportunities, and threats. Assessing your procurement department's strengths, weaknesses, opportunities, and threats through a SWOT analysis is a simple process that can offer powerful insight into the potential and critical issues affecting your team's performance (Figure 2.1).

A SWOT analysis is the starting point of strategic planning. Once you have a SWOT analysis completed, you may want to try a more advanced analysis, such as Porter's Five Forces.[1]

Strengths and weaknesses provide a focus for you to look internally at what you are doing and what you can do. It is the tendency of many procurement professionals to look inward, but they fail to look outside their organization. Threats and opportunities are external, focusing on the conditions of the real world. This is where a SWOT analysis is helpful. It challenges you to see beyond the company walls in order to determine what opportunities are available for your team in securing meaningful cost reductions, successfully managing your supplier relationships, and capitalizing on your strengths.

You may want to consider outlining the external opportunities and threats before the strengths and weaknesses. Regardless of the order in which you complete your SWOT analysis, per experience in working with various clients, it is best to include the members of your procurement team and your stakeholders (internal customers) in a brainstorming session to obtain comprehensive and nonbiased

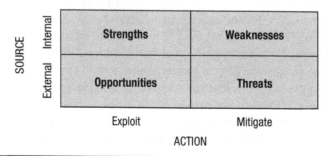

Figure 2.1 SWOT analysis matrix

information. Having a facilitator who conducts the brainstorming session and keeps participants focused can save valuable time. But, who should be the facilitator? Be creative. If you have an internal quality department, an organization efficiency team, or a training department, do not be shy about asking for their help. Often, the members of these departments are well-trained in facilitating meetings.

Strengths

Strengths describe the positive attributes, tangible and intangible, that are internal to your department. They are within your control. What do you do well? What resources do you have? What services do you perform well? What benefits do you bring to your company? How many new and additional value-added services have you introduced in the past year? The answers to these questions will reveal your strengths.

You may want to evaluate your strengths by area, such as commodities, supplier base, or organizational structure. Strengths include positive attributes of the people involved in your team, including their knowledge, backgrounds, education, credentials, reputation, or the skills they bring. Strengths also include tangible assets, such as available funds/budget, equipment, technology and processing systems, and other valuable resources within the organization.

Strengths capture the positive aspects internal to your team that add value or offer your organization a competitive advantage. This is your opportunity to remind yourself and the members of your team of the value existing within your procurement department.

Weaknesses

Capture the weaknesses within your team and your department. *Weaknesses* are factors that are within your control that detract from your ability to obtain or maintain a high-performing team. Which areas might you improve?

Weaknesses might include, but are not limited to: lack of expertise; limited resources; team members with substandard procurement skills; lack of access to advanced technology; lack of funds for training staff; and poor relationships with accounting, finance, audit, and other internal service providers. Addressing weaknesses is within your control, but for a variety of reasons, may be in need of improvement to effectively accomplish your short- and long-term objectives.

Weaknesses capture the negative aspects internal to your department that detract from the potential value that you can offer or that place you at a disadvantage. These are areas you need to improve upon, in order to gain the trust and respect of your internal customers and executives. The more you and your team identify your department's weaknesses, the more valuable the SWOT analysis will be for your business plan.

Opportunities

In sports, the big opportunity is always the championship, like winning the World Cup or being named best in your league by your peers. But, in your business plan, analyzing opportunities involves assessing the external factors that represent the reason that you and your team members work. These are external to your organization. What opportunities exist in your industry, the environment, or the supplier community from which you can benefit? Where can your team receive their reward or acclaim? How can they be champions?

These opportunities reflect the potential that you and your team can realize through implementing your strategies. Opportunities may be the result of regulatory or economic changes, the resolution of problems associated with current practices, or the ability to offer greater value that will create a higher demand for your team's services. If relevant, place time frames around the opportunities. Is an opportunity ongoing or a brief window of opportunity? How critical is your timing?

Again, opportunities are external to your team. If you identified *opportunities* that are internal to your organization and within your control, you will want to reclassify them as your strengths.

Threats

What factors are potential threats to your team? *Threats* include factors beyond your control that could place your department at risk. These are also external—you have no control over them, but you may benefit by having game plans ready to address them if they occur.

A threat is a challenge created by an unfavorable trend or development—or potential trend or development—that may lead to the deterioration of your hard work in generating positive procurement results. Threats may include intolerable price increases by suppliers, government regulations, economic downturns, devastating natural disasters, a shift in consumer behavior that impacts your company's products, or the introduction of new technology that may make your services obsolete. What situations might threaten your team's existence? Get your worst fears on the table. Many threats on your list may be speculative in nature, yet still add value to your SWOT analysis and thus your business plan.

Once identified, it is valuable to classify threats according to their *seriousness* and *probability of occurrence*. The better you are at identifying potential threats, the more likely that you and your team can position yourselves to proactively plan for and respond to them.

The internal strengths and weaknesses, compared to the external opportunities and threats, can offer additional insight into the current condition and potential for your procurement team and department. How can you use the strengths to better take advantage of the opportunities ahead and minimize the harm that threats may introduce if they become reality? How can weaknesses be minimized or eliminated? The true value of the SWOT analysis is in bringing this information together to assess the most promising opportunities and the most crucial issues.

IDENTIFYING THE MAJOR PROBLEMS TO SOLVE AND THE OPENINGS ON WHICH TO CAPITALIZE

The SWOT analysis is a means to an end, not an end in itself. A well-done SWOT analysis will not just reveal your strengths, weaknesses, opportunities, and threats; it should also open your eyes to what you need to do to drive organizational performance improvement through procurement performance improvement. In general, your SWOT analysis should reveal either a major *problem* that needs to be solved or a major *opening* on which you can capitalize.

Just to be clear, let's explain the difference between a problem and an opening. A problem exists when your organization is underperforming. Your SWOT analysis may reveal situations like these:

- Your organization's supply continuity is behind that of other organizations in your industry
- Your organization's supply costs are higher than those of other organizations in your industry
- Your procurement department is not as productive or efficient as others in your industry

If the most significant finding from your SWOT analysis is that your procurement department is underperforming, your Procurement Game Plan will be focused on solving a problem.

An opening exists when your procurement department is performing well, but there is potential for you to elevate performance to an even higher echelon through specific changes. Your SWOT analysis may reveal situations like these:

- Your organization could become fastest-to-market for new products with a tweaked procurement approach
- Your organization could be the first in your industry to appeal to environmentally conscious customers and gain market share with modifications to its procurement approach
- Your organization could undercut competition by leveraging procurement's expertise with cost reduction
- Your organization could be more profitable by adopting a procurement technique that has been used in another industry but has not been used in your industry

If the most significant finding from your SWOT analysis is that good performance can be elevated to great performance by doing something that hasn't been done before, your Procurement Game Plan will be focused on capitalizing on an opening.

YOUR PROCUREMENT GAME PLAN IS ACTUALLY A SELLING DOCUMENT

There has been a traditional mind-set that procurement and sales are polar-opposite disciplines. That's not a healthy mind-set! In procurement, we often have to persuade others to embrace an idea that they normally would not have embraced. Do you know what that is, essentially? *Selling!*

Your Procurement Game Plan is likely going to be a document that you will use for persuasion. You may use it to persuade top management to fund your solution or ideas. You may use it to persuade your direct management to authorize you to utilize your time and your team differently. You may use it to persuade your procurement team members to perform the tasks you have planned out. As such, your Procurement Game Plan is a selling document.

Before you type the first character into your Procurement Game Plan, you need to acknowledge that it is a selling document and craft it accordingly right out of the gate. It's easy to get caught up in facts and figures, benchmarking and best practices, and tactics and techniques, but those alone won't guarantee a successful Procurement Game Plan. You have to construct your Procurement Game Plan such that it persuades its readers to say an emphatic "yes" to everything you are proposing. This means that your Procurement Game Plan must have a tangible, measurable, financial benefit to executing the plan and it must convince readers that the person who wrote it—you—is the perfect person to deliver the results that the plan is promising.

FORMATTING YOUR PROCUREMENT GAME PLAN

Now that you have completed your research, conducted a SWOT analysis, determined if you need to solve a problem or capitalize on an opening, and are prepared to sell your solution or idea, the time has come to organize your findings into business plan components and begin developing your Procurement Game Plan. What format do you use? The layout may vary depending on the purpose of your business plan and the readership. Regardless of the purpose, a well-documented Procurement Game Plan may contain the following sections:

- Table of Contents
- Executive Summary

- Problem and Solution or Opening and Idea
- Operational Plan
- Team
- Financial Plan
- Return on Investment and Conclusions

Table of Contents and Executive Summary

You should prepare the Table of Contents last and the Executive Summary next-to-last, when all of the other components are completed. The Executive Summary is a one- or two-page section that includes the most salient points from each section that follows. It is important to develop a concise representation of your plan to capture the interest and support of the reader, such as the CPO, CFO, or other executives within your organization. Your boss or a C-level member of your organization may read the Executive Summary in order to decide if they should read the remainder of the plan. It must create excitement to entice the reader to continue reading.

Problem and Solution or Opening and Idea

The next section will be entitled either *Problem and Solution* or *Opening and Idea*, depending on whether your SWOT analysis revealed that you need to solve a problem or capitalize on an opening. This section can have as few as two paragraphs.

The first paragraph of this section is probably the most important paragraph in your entire Procurement Game Plan. That's such an important point that we are going to say it again, a little louder: THE FIRST PARAGRAPH OF THIS SECTION IS PROBABLY THE MOST IMPORTANT PARAGRAPH IN YOUR ENTIRE PROCUREMENT GAME PLAN.

If your Procurement Game Plan is aimed at solving a problem, this paragraph must convince the reader that the problem is real, the problem is costly, the problem is worth solving, and the time to solve the problem is now.

If your Procurement Game Plan is aimed at capitalizing on an opening, this paragraph must convince the reader that the opening is desirable, that capitalizing on the opening is feasible, that capitalizing on the opening is worth doing, and that the time to capitalize is now.

If your first paragraph does not convince the reader of the aforementioned things, the likelihood of the rest of your plan being read goes way down. And, if your plan isn't read, do you know how likely it is that your plan will be approved? Very unlikely! So, let's consider some examples of how to start strong.

We will start with an example of a problem-based paragraph for the fictitious ABC Company:

"In the past year, ABC Company's market share has slipped from second in the industry to third. This is largely due to a decrease in on-time delivery to customers, which itself was due to disruptions in supply continuity. This has cost the company an estimated $8 million in revenue and $2 million in profits in the past year. If not mitigated, these problems could worsen in the year ahead, drastically degrading ABC's competitiveness and causing further financial losses."

Let's dissect this paragraph a bit and point out why it is good. First, it starts off talking about problems within the organization: slips in market share, revenue, and profits. It does not start off by talking about procurement problems. In the mind of a CEO, procurement problems could be perceived as *little problems*. But problems within the organization—even if they are really the direct results of procurement problems—are viewed as big or strategic problems. Slips in market share, revenue, and profits are strategic problems. Organization-wide problems command attention.

Second, it addresses what's referred to as *the cost of doing nothing*. In some organizations, getting executives to free up money for new initiatives is like a nine-year-old child sumo wrestling against champions of that sport—there's just no way to move them. They are comfortable with the status quo. They unconsciously may think something like, "Our situation can't be that bad; we've dealt with it all of these years and we're still here." Sometimes, in order to convince these executives to free up money to invest in an improvement, you not only have to focus on how valuable the future possibilities could be, but how bad things are right now or how bad they could be in the years ahead. By mentioning that there could be *further financial losses*, this communicates that not approving the plan to move forward (i.e., doing nothing) has a cost to it.

Remember this: the more painful the pain or the bigger the cost of the current situation, the more likely it is that a solution would be embraced. So, use an adequate amount of ammunition in communicating how painful or costly the problem is to increase the chances of your Procurement Game Plan getting approved.

Now, we will continue with an example of an opening-based approach for the fictitious XYZ Company.

"According to research, companies that are first-to-market with a more environmentally sustainable version of a legacy product increase annual revenues by an average of 12% within two years and 24% within five years. If XYZ Company achieves these results, this could mean annual revenue growth of $360 million and annual profit growth of $60 million within two years—and double those numbers within five years."

Again, this paragraph focuses on organization-level issues and numbers, not procurement-level issues and numbers, which is why it would be likely to get attention.

After your first paragraph, it's time to introduce your solution to the problem you described or your idea for the opening you described. This is where this section can get a little more procurement centric.

Here's an example of how you might introduce your solution to the previously described ABC Company's problem.

> *"Ninety-eight percent of ABC Company's late deliveries were due to waiting on materials from suppliers. So, solving supply-side problems would mitigate most of ABC Company's on-time delivery challenges. There are three root causes of the supply side problems: unacceptably long cycle time between recognized need and order placement, lack of visibility into supplier capacity, and a small number of underperforming suppliers. This plan will describe how affordable technology, process improvement (including training), and a strategic sourcing initiative can address these root causes, eradicate the problems, and help ABC Company reclaim its lost market share."*

Here's an example of how you might introduce your idea to the previously described opening for XYZ Company.

> *"In the past three years, three ingredients have emerged that serve as more environmentally sustainable substitutes for ingredients that XYZ Company uses in its products. Preliminary research among the supply base for these ingredients indicates that only a small premium would be paid for these ingredients and that creative procurement techniques could eliminate the premium or even facilitate paying lower prices than XYZ Company is paying for the current ingredients. This could enable XYZ Company to be first-to-market with a more environmentally sustainable version of our products, establish XYZ Company's brand as the environmentally friendly leader in our industry, and increase revenue and profits in a short period of time."*

There are a couple of keys to notice in these second paragraphs. First, notice how they describe procurement solutions and ideas, but they solve organization-level problems or capitalize on organization-level openings. It's important to always tie in what procurement efforts mean to the bigger picture. Second, notice how they don't go overboard describing the details of the solution or idea. That's what the next section is for. And, let's face it, executives may not want to know—or be able to digest—all of the granular details of a procurement task list. They may be comfortable enough with your solution or idea to be sold on it just by reading the second paragraph of this section.

While it would be great if this section was all your reader would need to read to approve your plan, you still need to provide the details in case they need them. That's what the next section is for.

Operational Plan

In this section of your Procurement Game Plan, you will get into the specifics of how you will solve the problem or capitalize on the opening. It will list the tasks that will be done, when they will be done, how many people in each role will do them, milestones and metrics to measure success, and so forth. One of the examples we shared in the previous section talked about a strategic sourcing initiative. This section is where you can add details about such things, such as which categories would be sourced, how much money is currently spent in those categories, how many suppliers serve those markets, which buyers on your team will lead the different sourcing projects, and so forth. That's the level of detail you can provide in this section.

So far, we have focused on the *reader* of this document being a senior executive or team of senior executives who have the authority to approve or deny your plan. This section will help to show them how thoroughly you have thought through the work that your procurement department will do, but it also can be used by the procurement team itself. It can serve as a veritable playbook that includes all of the projects, all of the tasks, all of the resources needed, all of the timelines, etc. You can also discuss any risks associated with your plan, potential barriers to success, assumptions, and all of the other contingencies on which your plan hinges in this section.

The end of this chapter and the following chapters of this book will arm you with the knowledge of the types of tasks, tools, techniques, tips, and best practices you can incorporate into your operational plan/playbook. Whether it's restructuring or transforming your procurement department, expanding your procurement social responsibility, engaging in strategic sourcing, implementing a new technology, or making virtually any procurement performance improvement, you will find many helpful components for developing and executing your operational plan in the pages ahead.

Team

The Team section of the business plan should indicate the total number of employees that will be executing the operational plan. It can break down the total number into discrete roles, if helpful (e.g., 25 buyers, four purchasing managers, and one director). It should include employees from outside of procurement if their efforts—even if part-time—will be required. And, depending on how important it may be to have detailed descriptions of the various people involved, you may want to have three subsections to the Team section: one each for Management, Staff, and Advisors, where advisors may be outside consultants who may need to be hired in order to maximize the probability of success for the plan.

If you employ these subsections, it is particularly important for you to provide the names of the procurement management members who are in charge and their qualifications. Educational background, professional experience, certifications, awards and accomplishments, and success in similar initiatives are critical things to include. These things will help to sell readers on the fact that these are the best people to be leading the execution of the Procurement Game Plan.

Financial Plan

This section of your Procurement Game Plan should detail all financial implications of the plan. You should cover outlays of funds, such as up-front investments and ongoing costs. You should cover financial benefits of the plan, such as cost savings and incremental revenue that can be generated as a result of the plan.

Do not combine all figures together in one lump sum in this section. There will be an appropriate place to summarize the financial implications later. This section is for all the details that a reader may need to see to be convinced that you've thoroughly thought your plan through. If you're investing in products or services as part of your plan, disclose each one along with its cost.

All financial outlays and benefits should be assigned to a timeline. Maybe for your plan, $500,000 would be required up front to acquire a technology platform and an additional $25,000 would need to be spent monthly for new staff. And maybe the financial benefits wouldn't start to be realized until 18 months later. Describe those things thoroughly and demonstrate them with visuals.

If you are including estimates, share your rationale for your estimates. What research did you do? What assumptions went into them? How certain are they?

For example, if you are proposing that switching to a more environmentally friendly ingredient will enable your organization to grow its revenue by 10%, where did you come up with that number? What sources support that estimate? Is it a number that can be relied upon to the penny? Or, is your estimate better expressed as a range, such as 8 to 12%?

These are the types of financial questions executives will ask, whether directly to you or simply in their own heads. Your goal is to make sure that your Procurement Game Plan answers these types of financial questions before readers can even ask them.

Return on Investment and Conclusions

Where the Financial Plan section was deep with details, this section is where summaries are appropriate. Return on investment (ROI) is a calculation of how much financial gain is realized after recouping an investment. So, if the financial benefits such as cost savings and incremental revenue amount to $3 million and the investment required to achieve those benefits was $2 million, the return is $1 million. A $1 million return on a $2 million investment can be expressed as a 50% ROI.

When communicating ROI, always specify the monetary amount and/or ROI percentage along with a time frame. For example, you might write that "This plan is estimated to produce a 50% ROI over just two years." This is important, because a plan promising a 50% ROI in two years is much more likely to earn senior management approval than one promising a 50% ROI in 20 years.

Make sure that you close your Procurement Game Plan with a strong conclusion or set of conclusions. First, you should hammer home the point that, by moving forward with the plan as proposed, your organization stands to gain financially as well as in other ways. The monetary value of the financial gain matters, so use it.

Second, you can outline the consequences of not moving forward with the plan. The type of consequences that executives would love to avoid include lower profits, lost market share, barriers to revenue growth, risk of any sort, and a declining brand perception. So, you can follow up your conclusion about financial benefits for executing the plan with a conclusion about what might happen if the plan does not move forward.

Finally, if there is a next step such as formally granting approval for the plan to move forward, state what the next step is and how soon you can begin executing the plan after that step is completed. That's it! By following these steps, you will have your very own Procurement Game Plan!

Let's continue this chapter by covering some of the foundational and structural decisions that may work their way into your operational plan/playbook.

PROCUREMENT ORGANIZATIONAL STRUCTURE

In terms of organizational structure, there are variations on where procurement is placed within the organization—as discussed in Chapter 1—and variations as to how the procurement department itself is structured. Modern procurement departments often structure themselves according to a *center-led procurement* model to achieve the perfect mix of centralized and decentralized buying.

In the center-led procurement model, end users—not procurement professionals—place orders for low-value items, using contracts set up by a centralized procurement staff. Thus, transaction processing is decentralized, not decision making and strategic goal setting. The centralized procurement staff is concerned not with order placement, but more importantly with strategic sourcing, establishing enterprise-wide contracts, managing relationships with suppliers, and providing optimized processes for decentralized transactions.

While the centralized versus decentralized balance is critical, it is equally important to align your procurement department properly with other departments within the organization. There is no one-size-fits-all alignment of a procurement department. Some organizations align their procurement staff according to internal customer (Figure 2.2). Others align according to commodity or category (Figure 2.3). Still others align by supplier (Figure 2.4). The *best* way depends on the goals of the company. As in sports, every team requires all the same supporting departments to function. Whether it's equipment management or health coaching, all supporting departments are key to the end results expected. That being said, each team in every sport has completely different individuals, different priorities, and different assessed strengths/weaknesses. There is no one perfect structure that assures an automatic championship.

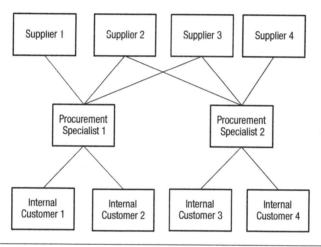

Figure 2.2   Procurement department aligned by internal customer

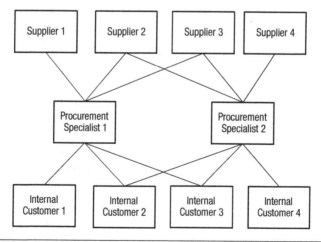

Figure 2.3   Procurement department aligned by category

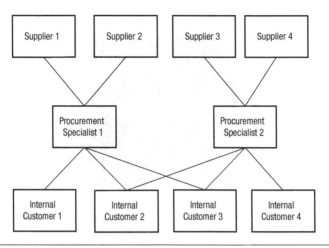

Figure 2.4   Procurement department aligned by supplier

COST CONTROL

In most team sports, the object of the game is to score more points than your opponent. The bigger the difference between your score and the opponent's score, the better the victory.

There is a parallel object of the game in business—to earn more money than you spend. The bigger the difference between revenue and expenses, the more successful the business is.

Procurement departments often spend an amount of money that can equal more than half of an organization's revenue. If procurement costs are not controlled, it can be the difference between the organization making a profit and the organization incurring a loss. That's a significant risk, so controlling the costs of purchased goods and services should be a high priority in a procurement department's game plan.

Conversely, procurement has the opportunity to dramatically increase the *margin of victory*, if you will, by doing a good job of controlling costs. While we will get into the specific techniques for minimizing costs in later chapters, the foundation for these techniques rests on the four cornerstones of procurement cost control.

In strategic planning and while developing its playbook, a procurement department should ask itself how it can increase the use of each of these four cornerstones to deliver improved results. The four cornerstones—or *four C's*—of procurement cost control are consolidation, competition, contracting, and collaboration (Figure 2.5).

Figure 2.5   Four C's of procurement cost control

Consolidation

A timeless principle of cost-effective procurement is that the more you buy, the less you pay per unit. So, you should consolidate your enterprise-wide spend in a category or combination of categories into a large *market basket* that you will entice suppliers to bid on. Leveraging your volume in this way helps to maximize the cost savings available to you.

In working toward better consolidation, your playbook should address whether the visibility into the suppliers you are using in each category of purchased goods and services is sufficient or if it could be improved. Then, it should address how adequately consolidated your spend is in each category and in which categories you are using too many suppliers.

Competition

Competition between suppliers is a powerful tool for reducing costs. After you have developed your market baskets, you should identify a healthy number of suppliers to bid on your requirements, perhaps even using a reverse auction (described in Chapter 13), if appropriate. The less certainty that suppliers have about earning a valuable portion of your business, the more aggressive their pricing will be.

In working toward increased competition, your playbook should address whether you had a large number of bidders and if you allowed newer, less familiar suppliers to be considered the last time you sourced in each high-spend category. Those sourcing initiatives where you involved only the same cast of characters consisting of only three or four suppliers represent areas where increased competition can lead to improved cost control, if not more innovation.

Contracting

What gives suppliers a huge incentive to win your business? A long-term guarantee of a certain volume of business does! If you are able to promise a forecasted quantity to the successful supplier via a contract that lasts three or more years, you will likely inspire in suppliers a keen interest in helping you achieve your cost-control goals.

In working toward increased use of contracting, your playbook should address whether you have long-term contracts in place and how much of your spend is covered under contract. Then, it should address what statistics would reflect a better use of contracting and a plan for achieving those better statistics.

Collaboration

Your cost-control work with suppliers does not have to end when contracts are signed. You can collaborate with suppliers to identify waste, inefficiencies, and other opportunities to take cost out of the supply chain in a manner from which your organization and the suppliers can financially benefit. Agree to meet regularly during the terms of the contracts with the goal to discuss supplier performance, review compliance against contract terms, and exchange ideas that can result in measurable cost-control activities.

How closely do you work with your suppliers to measure their performance against contract terms and to identify improvement opportunities? Do you just place orders and expect to get them in without any further expectations on your suppliers? Your playbook should reflect how you plan to increase collaboration with suppliers over current levels.

RISK MANAGEMENT

In the previous section on cost control, we talked about the risk associated with costs getting out of control. However, cost risk is not the only major procurement risk you'll have to face. There are actually many. Three of them that we will touch on here are: supply continuity risk, public relations risk, and legal risk.

Supply Continuity Risk

While the risk of out-of-control costs is of seemingly daily concern to procurement professionals and their executive management, the risk of supply disruption is equally—or perhaps more—significant. So, for every significant category of goods or services that your organization purchases, you will need a contingency plan to assure continuity of supply.

In recent years, the criticality of contingency planning and the desire for supply chain resilience has exploded into one of the hottest procurement topics. Therefore, we have dedicated an entire chapter (Chapter 11) to supply chain resilience and contingency planning.

One should never assume that a supplier's performance, business conditions, or any type of predictability or stability that has been experienced is permanent. A thorough procurement contingency plan can help your organization perform in a predictable, stable way even if the rest of the world doesn't.

Public Relations Risk

While disruption of supply continuity often gets the most attention in risk assessment, you also must consider that procurement approaches can involve a different type of risk. Consider what these three scenarios have in common:

- **Scenario 1:** In recent years, activist groups have encouraged parents of children in the United States to return their Halloween candy to certain candy manufacturers. They do this to protest the manufacturers' purchase of cocoa from sources that allegedly use child or slave labor.[2,3]
- **Scenario 2:** Over 600 people became ill and four people died after eating at a restaurant during a one-month span. All of them were diagnosed with Hepatitis A. Experts believe that the disease was carried by green onions used by the restaurant.[4,5]
- **Scenario 3:** A commercial airliner crashed, killing 110 people. Investigators attributed the crash to oxygen generators that caught fire during the flight. A supplier of the airline improperly prepared these generators for shipment. A United States' court ruled that the supplier recklessly failed to comply with hazardous materials regulations, and willingly failed to properly train its employees in handling hazardous materials.[6]

These three real-life scenarios share one theme—they are public relations nightmares that have a root cause of a questionable procurement decision.

Now, you may not buy cocoa, or green onions, or airline maintenance services, but the decisions that you make daily could be the cause of a highly-publicized scandal that hurts your organization. The keys to avoiding a public relations nightmare are to consider all of the possible problems in advance, and take preventative measures to ensure that those problems never arise. Ask yourself these types of questions:

- What do I buy that could cause illness, injury, or death?
- What do I buy that could raise the attention of special interest groups (e.g., environmental, child labor, ethnic, etc.)?
- What do I buy that could be perceived as a conflict of interest or misuse of funds?

Then, devise a strategy to mitigate all risks of being mentioned in a future negative news headline.

A documented approach to managing all potential risks, a process described in this section, is mandatory for having a truly thorough playbook.

Legal Risk

It's somewhat obvious that an organization is legally responsible for the actions of its employees and any harm they may cause while conducting business on behalf of the organization. And, a single employer may have tens of thousands of employees, so that's a lot of legal responsibility.

But, it's not so obvious that an organization could be legally responsible for the actions of its suppliers and any harm they may cause while conducting business on behalf of the organization. If you think about the size of the employee base of just your employer, imagine how much bigger an employee base is when it also includes all of the employees of your suppliers! That is a potentially gargantuan amount of legal responsibility!

We use the term *potentially* because procurement professionals have a great deal of control over how the risk between a buying organization and its suppliers is allocated. Risk is generally allocated by the law or—where they exist—contracts. Contracts include those big documents bearing the signatures of buyer and seller representatives. But, *contracts* technically also include the terms and conditions that may apply to a buyer-seller relationship as a result of the exchange of forms such as quotes, purchase orders, and order acknowledgments—even ones exchanged electronically.

So, it is advisable to have an attorney work with your procurement department to ensure that you have contracts, purchase order terms and conditions, and related processes in place that will adequately protect your organization. Depending on what your organization does, some or all of these questions may help you and an attorney craft the most appropriate language for your contractual terms and conditions:

- Who is responsible if a purchased product is responsible for property damage, injury, or death to an employee or customer of the buying organization?
- Who is responsible if a supplier's performance of service causes property damage, injury, or death to an employee or customer of the buying organization or a member of the public?
- What types of insurance should a supplier have and how much coverage is necessary?
- What limits of liability, if any, should there be for the organization and its suppliers?
- Under what circumstances would the buying organization or supplier have to indemnify the other?

- What state or country laws should apply to the relationship between the buying organization and a supplier and what court system would be used in the event of litigation?
- What type of dispute resolution methodology (e.g., mediation, arbitration, etc.) should apply between the buying organization and a supplier?
- What type of damages (e.g., consequential, cover, etc.) should be available to recoup in the event of a supplier failure?

Reading through these questions may make you realize how much potential risk is actually present in a single buyer-seller relationship. These types of questions only begin to scratch the surface of all of the legal ramifications involved in procurement. If we dedicated all of the pages to this book to writing about nothing but procurement-related legal matters, we would run out of pages before we ran out of topics to cover adequately. So, our best advice is to collaborate with an attorney to craft the optimal strategy for managing legal risk in your organization.

PLAYING WITHIN A SYSTEM

In many sports, there are regulations, such as salary caps, that prevent teams from hiring all of the best (and most expensive) players and thus dominating their leagues. So, instead of a team fielding the best players in the world and then winning based on sheer skill, teams often rely on *playing within a system* as much as or more than they rely on talent. If a team plays *within a system*, it can defeat a team that has more skilled players.

Playing within a system—or performing in accordance with documented guidelines and with certain tools—is critical to success in procurement as well. What might such guidelines and tools include? Consider the following:

- Documented processes with checks and balances
- Standard supplier selection criteria
- All-hands meetings
- A procurement library
- Supplier guides

A procurement playbook should include descriptions of how most, if not all, of these guidelines and tools will be deployed in the organization. We will now talk about each of these guidelines and tools individually.

Documented Processes with Checks and Balances

If you want order and not chaos, you absolutely need to have documented procurement procedures and good processes. If you do not have documented procurement procedures at this time, you need to have them written sooner rather than later. Here are some key thoughts about procurement procedure writing.

First, it is essential to understand the importance of procedures. Procedures should be put in place to ensure quality and continuity. What we mean by *quality* is that your procedures should be written so that, irrespective of who executes a certain process, the quality will still be good and the result will be the same. With regard to continuity, your procedures should be written so that if you lose an employee for a vacation, a medical leave, or even if that employee leaves the company, you will feel covered by the fact that another employee can come in, follow the procedure, and do a reasonably good job of executing the related process.

Second, it is important to realize that, unless you do a good job of selling your procedure-writing initiative to the employees responsible for writing the procedures, there will likely be a lot of resistance. Procedure writing can make an employee feel dispensable if the manager is not careful with positioning the assignment. We can't help but recall a funny anecdote from a consulting engagement in this regard. When we began the engagement, the management talked about their procedure-writing initiative, and they referred to their procedures as standard operating procedures (SOPs). The nonmanagement employees also referred to the procedures as SOPs, but their definition of SOP was slightly different. They referred to them as *something on paper*, only they substituted another word for *something*. We'll let your imagination tell you what that *something* stood for. So, do a good job of selling the initiative, communicating why it's important, and getting people on board with it.

Third, it is beneficial to utilize something that we call the *Powerball Principle* of procedure writing. This is something we use at our companies. We always say that if all of the employees played Powerball (the lottery) and won $100 million or more, and then decided not to come back to work, we want to be able to take our procedures, get some folks off the street who are intelligent and computer literate, and have them be able to step in and do a good job in as short a time as possible. That principle requires the procedures to be very detailed. When employees write procedures, sometimes they have been doing the same work for so long that they forget all of the little details they instinctively address in that work. But we like to break procedures down as granularly as possible, and document those details as part of this Powerball Principle.

Now, let's move on to processes. While it would be nice to think that all human beings are honest, there are invariably some individuals in the world who stray from legal, ethical, and moral behavior. Unfortunately, procurement is an area where fraud can occur.

To prevent fraud, a procurement department must structure its processes to incorporate checks and balances to ensure that no fraud has occurred. While each organization will have different specifics of its processes, answers to the following questions should be documented and made available to all employees:

- How will spending against a department budget be approved?
- How will authorization to spend against a budget be confirmed?
- When is supplier competition for an order mandatory, and under what circumstances can this competition requirement be waived?
- Who has the authority to approve suppliers?
- How are suppliers set up in the organization's computer system and by whom?
- Who has the authority to contract with suppliers?
- What criteria must be satisfied to make an authorized payment to suppliers?
- Who has the authority to release payment to a supplier?
- How will orders and payments be audited to ensure against fraud?

Answering each of these questions is a good place to start in gaining and maintaining control over purchases.

Standard Supplier Selection Criteria

You should use a *Hierarchy of Constraints and Criteria* every time that you select a supplier. A Hierarchy of Constraints and Criteria is probably best explained by defining its components.

Criteria are attributes that a procurement department values in its arrangements with suppliers. There are eight common supplier selection criteria, in no formal order:

1. Cost and value
2. Quality and safety
3. Delivery
4. Service
5. Social responsibility
6. Convenience/Simplicity
7. Risk
8. Agility

Depending on the situation, you may use the criteria as-is, use more or fewer criteria, or use a different combination. Often, members of a supplier selection team will want some criteria to be treated as *constraints*—unbreakable rules in the supplier selection process. Examples of constraints might include criteria that there can only be one supplier, we must select the low bidder, or delivery must be within six weeks, and so on.

Your job as leader of a supplier selection team is to determine whether a proposed constraint is truly warranted or simply an important criterion. You can do so by asking questions, such as, "If we had to choose between (a) having the best quality for all items by using two suppliers, and (b) having the best quality for only half the items by using one supplier, would we still insist on using one supplier?" Or ask, "If we could save 34 percent by accepting a seven-week lead time instead, would we choose to save the money, or would we still need to insist on the six-week lead time?" The fewer constraints, the more flexibility the team has in its decision making.

After agreeing on constraints and criteria, the supplier selection team must agree on a *hierarchy*—an order of these attributes ranked from most important to least important, with constraints preceding criteria. In most cases, supplier offerings will differ and there will be trade-offs involving the criteria; you may get a better price from one supplier (cost and value), but that supplier insists on contract terms less favorable to you (risk). Creating a *Hierarchy of Constraints and Criteria* in advance will help your supplier selection team remain focused on what is most important to help make balanced decisions.

All-Hands Meetings

All-hands meetings are attended by all staff in the procurement department, not just people in a particular group. These meetings should be scheduled regularly, and can be used to report progress on key goals, or give an opportunity for selected staff members to present case studies of successful projects they've managed or solutions that they implemented.

Procurement Library

Whether you need a tactic to kick-start a plodding negotiation or a definition for a term that you've read in a supplier's correspondence, it is helpful to have easily accessible literature in your department. Pick up a few magazines and books, curate a collection of web articles and digital resources, and make them available to the staff. While the Internet has no shortage of material available on procurement topics, having authoritative, carefully vetted literature that is easily accessible can prove to be a more reliable alternative than leaving buyers at the mercy of Google searches.

Supplier Guides

The most professional procurement departments have a brochure, folder, hardcopy booklet, and/or website that educates suppliers on how to do business with the procurement organization. In just a few hours, and with the help of your IT department, you can create something that is not only useful, but looks good to senior managers who are concerned about projecting a professional image in the business community. If you follow the ten steps illustrated in Figure 2.6, and described as follows, you can create a great Suppliers' Guide in one day!

Figure 2.6 Supplier guide development process

Step 1: Define the purpose of the suppliers' guide. The purpose can differ dramatically among organizations. Ask yourself, "What problem am I trying to solve?" Is it preventing the wasting of everyone's time with untargeted supplier phone calls? Is it eliminating the struggle of reviewing supplier materials that all look different? Is it avoiding breaches of your ethics policy?

Step 2: Develop a theme and tagline. What theme do you want to communicate to the supplier community? An interest in good relationships? Diversity in supplier selections? Once you know your theme, it is nice to use a *tagline*—a phrase that memorably captures the essence of your theme. Taglines that we have seen include *Alliance For Excellence, The Right Combination,* and *Collaboration. Synergy. Success.*

Step 3: Choose a format. Formats range from trifold brochures, to folders with multi-tiered pockets, to other simple formats for your Suppliers' Guide. Consider the cost and your budget when selecting a format. Also, if you include information that frequently changes, you may want to consider a format that allows you to insert newly updated pieces, so you don't have to redo the entire guide too often. Some software programs have great templates that make designing beautiful brochures easy. Consider using a template if you're not naturally artistic. Obviously, updating electronic supplier guides by using a template is easier and less costly.

Step 4: Write an introduction. Your introduction should state what you value in your suppliers. Introduce your theme and tagline here.

Step 5: Compose the main body. Write the details that are relevant to the purpose of the suppliers' guide. Repeat your theme and tagline throughout.

Step 6: State next steps. Tell suppliers what to do next. Should they submit specific materials in a binder, register on a website, or contact someone personally?

Step 7: Review the guide with stakeholders. Get the input of other departments who may need to approve the Suppliers' Guide. Legal may wish to include disclaimers. Marketing may want to ensure proper use of the corporate brand and identity. Leaving these people out of the review process may cause more work or problems later.

Step 8: Publish and distribute the suppliers' guide. For those who plan to post their supplier guide on a website, make sure to inform your supplier community about your electronic document. Send printed guides to all stakeholders.

Step 9: Evaluate. After seeing the Suppliers' Guide in use, evaluate whether it is achieving your purpose. What can be improved in the next revision?

Step 10: Improve the suppliers' guide as needed. In the spirit of continuous improvement, review the content of your guide and make the appropriate modifications routinely.

CLOSING REMARKS

We hope that this chapter has made you realize that a well-executed supply management strategy results in value creation for your organization. Procurement professionals need to clearly understand how their enterprise chooses to compete. This is important for the obvious reason of working off the same *playbook*, and because it forces the supply management operation to see itself as an entity supporting and serving the competitive goals of the enterprise—not merely an operational department.

REFERENCES

1. Porter, Michael. *Competitive Strategy: Techniques for Analyzing Industries and Competitors.* New York, Free Press, 1980.
2. Orr, Deborah. April 24, 2006. "Slave Chocolate." Organic Consumers Association.
3. Lobe, Jim. October 31, 2003. "Send Those Halloween Chocolates Back to Mars." International Labor Rights Forum. Available from http://www .laborrights.org/stop-child-labor/cocoa-campaign/news/11085.
4. Flynn, Dan. September 19, 2009. "Chi-Chi's Hepatitis A Outbreak." *Food Safety News.*
5. "Officials Link Chi-Chi's Hepatitis Outbreak to Green Onions." November 21, 2003. *USA Today.* Available from http://www.usatoday.com/news/ health/2003-11-21-onions-outbreak_x.htm.
6. Raskin, Martin. April 25, 2000. "Criminal Enforcement in the Aviation Industry." National Transportation Safety Board (NTSB).

3
CHAPTER

PROCUREMENT TALENT MANAGEMENT: ENSURING THAT YOU HAVE THE RIGHT PLAYERS ON YOUR TEAM

Whether you have been newly appointed to a procurement leadership role or are a long-time leader poised to embark on a performance improvement initiative, it is essential to formally and quickly learn about the capabilities of the players on your team. There may or may not be existing internal documents that can help accelerate your learning faster than NASCAR Cup Series drivers accelerate their racing vehicles.

Usually, when a sports coach gets hired, he or she knows a little bit about his or her new team: who the players are and their strengths; which superstars can carry the team; and where the players statistically rank for their position. There are plenty of resources to research prior to taking the leadership job.

Unfortunately, when you are a new procurement leader, you don't have the luxury of public statistics about a team that you inherit. Yet, like the new sports coach, you are expected to get the team to perform well, right out of the gate.

So, in short order, you have to execute a talent management strategy. There are five facets to the procurement talent management cycle. Note that we used the word *cycle*. This means that these five facets need to be continuously repeated. Notice also that we used the word *facets* rather than *steps*. That's because these facets are not to be addressed in sequential order—they may all need to be addressed simultaneously. The five facets of the procurement talent management cycle are:

- A. Assess
- B. Retain
- C. Develop
- D. Recruit
- E. Unify

Figure 3.1 illustrates the procurement talent management cycle and its five facets, which are discussed in the following sections.

Figure 3.1   The five facets of the procurement talent management cycle

PROCUREMENT TALENT MANAGEMENT FACET A: ASSESS

Have you ever watched *Rudolph, the Red-Nosed Reindeer*—the beloved animated children's TV movie that is aired every year around the holiday season in December? If so, do you recall the part where the characters Rudolph, Yukon Cornelius, and Hermie end up in the place where there is a cowboy riding an ostrich, a toy train with square wheels, and, of course, the Charlie-in-the-box? They were all residents of the Island of Misfit Toys, a destination for toys that no one wanted.

What does this excerpt from an animated children's TV movie have to do with procurement? You're probably expecting a clever answer and we are happy to oblige! You see, many procurement departments have been staffed in the same manner as the Island of Misfit Toys; when an employee did not perform well elsewhere in the organization and management didn't have the heart to fire him or her, that employee was sent to work in the procurement department. As a result, some poor performers ended up in procurement!

Hence, procurement departments became a home for the organization's *misfits*. This practice was bred from the old-fashioned thinking that the role of procurement is unimportant, and that not much can be messed up there.

Well, thankfully, times have changed and procurement has become recognized as a true profession. Now, procurement is a place for educated people who want careers, not just jobs. As opposed to being in backrooms, procurement professionals are now in boardrooms making meaningful contributions and positively impacting the bottom-line profitability of their organizations.

However, some misfits do remain in procurement departments. These are the people who don't approach their work as strategic, produce measurable results, or have the positive attitude necessary for success. Thus, leaders of procurement departments who want to transform procurement in their organizations need to have a strategy to deal with the misfits. There are two options for the existing misfits.

The first option is to give the misfits the benefit of the doubt and give them the opportunity to come on board with the strategic direction of the procurement department. This can be done through external training, accompanied by mentoring by the leader or one of the more talented members of the team. This first option is the best one. If you can make leaps forward in procurement without having to lay off anyone, that's great. You end up looking like a great leader, your employees are happy that they get to keep their jobs and perform well, and there's no risk of potential legal action.

If you find misfit resistance or that they still don't meet the goals expected, then you have to resort to the second option: cutting them from the team. Headcount is precious and limited. For the sake of the profitability of the organization and procurement's reputation within it, you cannot afford to have one seat in a procurement department filled by a misfit.

You also need a strategy for dealing with management when they are trying to dump misfits into procurement (yes, it still happens in some places). Quite simply, just say, "No." Procurement is *not* the Island of Misfit Toys.

Now that you've addressed misfit situations, you can evaluate the rest of your team. If you are like most procurement leaders, you are only partially satisfied with the results your team is producing and, therefore, feel that you don't have a full complement of world-class procurement professionals on your team. You are expected to deliver bigger and better results, but you worry that the skill levels possessed by your team may limit your ability to achieve your goals.

Do you find that you only have one or two team members who can handle your most challenging projects? Or do you find that you are spending too much of your time helping your team members with situations that you desperately wish they could handle themselves? Would you love to upgrade the capabilities of your procurement team, but don't know where to start?

Procurement departments can be centers of excellence. They can be comprised of people who apply their skills to deliver measurable bottom-line impact to the organization. They can be departments where the leader actually has the time to do what he or she is paid to do—lead.

If your procurement department is not quite there yet, you are not alone. It is easy to get stuck in a rut unless you have a step-by-step plan for identifying opportunities for improvement, and then act upon those opportunities. But it hasn't been easy to find an easy plan to implement—until now!

There are five easy steps for assessing the skills of your procurement team. Follow each of these steps carefully to develop a plan for how you are going to improve those skills.

Step 1: Document the Department's Goals

Yes, we know. You already have your goals documented. So why are we including this as a step? Simple. Any effort to develop a team's skills should be aligned with the goals of the department and, ultimately, with the goals of your organization. That sounds like common sense, but we've seen a lot of companies spend their limited training dollars on seminars, workshops, and the like that are not really relevant to what the department is trying to accomplish.

By *beginning with the end in mind,* you can increase the probability that all actions that you take will move you in the direction of achieving your goals. So, let us guess that some of your goals probably look like this:

- Achieve net cost savings of $x
- Improve supplier delivery performance to x percent from y percent
- Decrease quality defects to x percent from y percent
- Increase internal customer satisfaction rating to x from y

With your team's input, establish a timeline for each goal. From time to time, review the goals and adjust the timeline if necessary.

Have those documented goals visible—or at least accessible—to you and your team as you walk through the remaining steps of this process. Never forget the ultimate reason for skills development: to enhance the company's ability to achieve its goals.

Step 2: Determine the Skill Dimensions Required

A *skill dimension,* also called a competency, is one particular facet of the profession in which specialized skills are required.

Examples of skill dimensions in procurement include:

- Procurement fundamentals
- Analysis and spreadsheets
- Contract law
- Project management
- Procurement best practices
- Sourcing
- Negotiation
- Leadership
- International business
- Financial acumen
- Supplier relationship management

Now, back to the goals. Each goal will likely require a high level of skill in one or more skill dimensions. Different members of your team will likely have strengths in *different* skill dimensions. Thus, you need to determine (a) which team members contribute to which goals and (b) in which skill dimensions those team members will need to be strong in order to maximize their contributions to the organization.

For example, if one of your department's goals is to achieve $10,000,000 in cost savings, the individuals who are accountable for contributing to that goal will likely need high levels of skill in sourcing and negotiation. If another of your department's goals is to support the launch of a new product, the individuals who are accountable for contributing to that goal will likely need high levels of skill in project management. Consequently, with your goals in mind, answer the question: "Who needs what skills?"

In some organizations, the aspiration may be to have uniform skill levels in all skill dimensions across all positions, which gives you the flexibility to move team members among various roles, and mitigates the risk that can arise when the incumbent becomes unavailable (e.g., due to resignation, illness, vacation, etc.). However, if that is too lofty of an aspiration, the remaining steps of this process will help you to identify and prioritize the specific skill dimensions requiring improvement for each team member.

Step 3: Determine How to Assess Skill Levels

Now that you know the skill dimensions in which each of your team members should be strong, the tricky part is determining what skill levels each team member actually possesses in each skill dimension. There are three common methods for doing so: self-assessment, assessment by manager, and assessment by a third party.

Method A—Self-assessment

One commonly used approach is to have each team member complete a self-assessment. While this can get the job done quickly, it is not likely to be accurate.

First, self-assessment is inherently subjective. Any skills assessment should be able to challenge a skill level claim with the questions "according to whom?" and "compared to what standard?" The answers to these questions for this method would be "according to the individual" and "compared to that individual's opinion," respectively. Not the strongest benchmarks.

Second, there is a risk that a self-assessment might be completed defensively. Individuals may feel that the reason for the assessment is to identify candidates to be downsized, or to award promotions or raises. Therefore, individuals may rate their skills higher than they truly are in order to avoid punitive measures or to achieve rewards. Attitudes of individuals in these situations may be characterized by statements such as, "If I don't recognize my skills, how can I expect others to recognize them?" and "If they knew my real skill levels, they wouldn't be asking me to do this self-assessment, so why be modest?"

Method B—Manager assessment

Another approach is to either: (1) begin with a self-assessment and validate it with a manager's review and update of that assessment, or (2) to simply have the manager assess each staff member's skill levels independently. Of course, this approach is also subjective and *inside the box*. An internal assessment does not compare skills with best-in-class procurement professionals—it compares them with internal expectations, which often can drift to one of two extremes: (1) the current team has inadequate skills, or (2) the current team has been here a long time, and the team members know their jobs inside and out.

Method C—Third-party assessment

Another approach is to have the skills assessment performed by a third party. A third-party assessment can provide the most objective data. You may be surprised that, depending on the provider, you can have a procurement skills assessment performed at little to no cost with minimal effort.

Regardless of the method chosen, you need to have an idea of at least two tiers of skill level in each skill dimension: acceptable and unacceptable. A graduated measurement with data between these two tiers is better, but you must at least know the demarcation point between acceptable and unacceptable.

Step 4: Determine the Skill Gaps

In Step 3, you decided how to assess the skill levels of your team. In Step 4, you execute the process of assessment that you selected in the previous step. This process will conclude with measurements of—or at least opinions about—the skill levels of each employee across several skill dimensions. For each individual, you should now know:

- In which skill dimensions the individual has an acceptable level of skill
- In which skill dimensions the individual has an unacceptable level of skill

The skill dimensions where individuals had *unacceptable* skill levels are considered your *skill gaps*.

Step 5: Develop a Skills Development Roadmap

Once you know what the skill gaps are, it is necessary to prioritize how you will address them through training and professional development. There are five common methods for deciding upon the order in which skill gaps are addressed. In all methods, usually only the individuals whose skills levels were rated as unacceptable in a certain skill dimension would be required to participate in professional development for that skill dimension.

The five common methods of prioritizing professional development are:

- Prioritization by complexity
- Prioritization by individual weaknesses
- Prioritization by departmental weaknesses

- Subjective prioritization
- Hybrid prioritization

The prioritization of professional development is the heart of your skills development roadmap. A skills development roadmap is simply a document listing the timeline for the training that each team member will receive over the course of a certain period.

PROCUREMENT TALENT MANAGEMENT FACET B: RETAIN

After doing an assessment, you know what types of players you have on your team. At this point, many leaders focus on recruiting and then developing their teams, leaving retention as an afterthought. We think that this is a mistake and that waiting to address retention may actually lead you to do more recruiting!

In the book *Good to Great: Why Some Companies Make the Leap . . . and Others Don't*,[1] author Jim Collins talks about, "getting the right people on the bus," then, "getting the right people in the right seats." However, we'd like to dedicate this section to *"keeping* the right people on the bus."

We've seen so many organizations lose talented procurement professionals in the past few years. What is disturbing is that these organizations often lose the replacements of those people quickly as well.

Organizations often seek employees who are interested and able to deliver continuous improvement to the organization. What these organizations fail to realize is that a professional who is interested in delivering continuous improvement to his or her employer is also interested in achieving continuous improvement in a procurement career. Consequently, after two productive years at a job—after they've accomplished some nice things to add to their resumes—procurement professionals know they are more valuable, and they want to move up.

In large companies like Walmart or ExxonMobil, this is not that big of a challenge. Their procurement departments have hundreds of positions. Higher-level openings aren't that uncommon. But what about midsized companies (i.e., those with $100M to $1B in annual revenue)? It is more challenging because the procurement manager may report to the CFO. Is it likely that a procurement manager will make the jump to CFO? Probably not. Thus, a go-getter in procurement leaves the company after only a few years, and the mid-sized company is recruiting a new procurement manager every two years. Continuity is always interrupted, and the potential for world-class procurement is never realized. What should you do?

Well, there are a few things for a midsized company in this situation to consider. If it is important to have a procurement agent or manager remain in the position for the long term, do not hire a young hotshot who just saved a major car manufacturing company a billion dollars. That person won't be happy for very long in a midsized company with no upward mobility. You need to hire the *right* person, not necessarily the *best* person. A career development plan can help you figure out what *right* means in accordance with the scope of the position, and also help you prepare employees to be the *right* person for future roles as well.

Career Development Plans

Ideally, you will have a career development plan starting from junior buyer all the way up to VP of procurement. Make it foreseeable for someone to move up the ranks or rotate to another function. Rotating talented procurement employees to another function requires a career development plan at the company level with the full buy-in and cooperation of the leaders of various departments.

Leading-edge companies rotate talented employees from one function to the other. As a result, their procurement organization does not just recruit highly skilled procurement professionals but, more importantly, they rotate in individuals with science, engineering, and marketing and sales backgrounds. As an example, Soheila, who has a strong science background, was given the opportunity to take rotational positions with increasing responsibilities during her tenure at a global corporation. Ultimately, a rotation of increasing responsibilities landed her in a strategic procurement leading role.

If you have a career development plan in place, hire people who have the potential to move up or rotate out. If you hire people with limited potential, you won't want to promote or rotate them later.

Once you document your career development plan, do not change it without careful consideration. If it requires three years of experience for someone to be promoted to a supervisor's role, one of your talented employees gets those three years of experience, and then you change it so that four years of experience is required, what is that talented employee going to do? That's right—go somewhere else before that additional year expires.

Education as a Retention Tool

It is your organization's responsibility to train your workforce to be world-class performers. If you have an open management position and feel that none of your buyers is qualified for promotion, it is *your fault* for failing to develop them. Talented people won't stay in your organization for long if they keep getting passed up for promotions.

Nothing is more damaging to morale (and therefore, to productivity) than hiring from the outside when you could have promoted from within or brought in a talented individual from another department within your organization. People need to feel valued. If they don't feel valued by your organization, they probably will go to an employer who does value them.

Reward employees for their educational achievements. Accomplishments like earning a certification from Next Level Purchasing (CPOS, formerly SPSM), Institute for Supply Management (CPSM), the Association for Supply Chain Management (CSCP), or any other accredited organization can make a procurement professional more valuable in the marketplace. If you don't reward them, they are probably thinking about how much more job satisfaction or money they can get elsewhere.

PROCUREMENT TALENT MANAGEMENT FACET C: DEVELOP

Having completed an assessment, you know *who needs what skills*. So, it is time to identify the training that can help you increase the skill levels in the skill dimensions where there are skill gaps.

Training and Certification

Today, there are a lot of options for training, and this book could not attempt to describe every possible course from every provider. But we can group the types of available training into three categories:

- Public seminars
- On-site training
- Online training

Another consideration when selecting training is the concept of certification. Some training can lead to certification, as well. You will need to decide whether or not pursuing certification for your team members should be a part of your plan.

Beyond the skills gained in the training required for certification, team certification can have other benefits, including:

- Being able to demonstrate value to management and your stakeholders by achieving a third-party standard for excellence in the profession
- Raising the morale of team members who can get personal recognition for their new skills and achievements

As with any sourcing decision, selecting the provider of your training is critical. Just because two organizations may offer training on a topic with a similar name does not mean that the quality of the training they provide will be equal. Ways of evaluating a training provider include:

- Reviewing customer testimonials
- Reviewing relevant trade publication articles
- Reviewing any free sample educational material

- Interviewing the management and/or instructors of the provider
- Determining differences in the value-added services that are only offered by select providers, such as retention tools, instructor access, management reports, and the like

Supplementing Training Programs

While training is a formal and effective way of improving the skill levels of your team, there are other tactics you can, and should, employ to supplement training, such as:

- **Share relevant trade journal articles, newsletters, podcasts, and blog posts with your team**—These types of media can help your team understand what is going on in the world. They will get to see how other organizations are going about achieving success in procurement. They will be exposed to great ideas and will eventually be able to separate real-world ideas from theory.
- **Coach your team**—You are the expert. Your team will only appear *unwise* if you think that they don't know what you know. So, impart your knowledge and your experience, don't withhold it. You will have a stronger team for it.
- **Employ shadowing**—When one of your experts is working on a challenging project, think about having one of your more junior employees assist on the project. No, it is not the most efficient use of resources, especially if you have a busy department, but it will pay long-term dividends when you have a more experienced team and less dependency on one specialist.
- **Rotate job responsibility within your team**—One of the richest assignments in Charles' career was when he and three coworkers were in a two-year program in which they switched positions every six months. Even though they were in the same company and the same procurement department, each position taught each person something new about procurement and the organization. Job rotation can give your team new skills and reinforce those procurement principles that have cross-category applicability.
- **Lunch and Learn meetings**—Since time is precious, you may need to be creative with organizing group meetings. In the United States, once-a-month or quarterly, informal *Lunch and Learn* meetings, where progress updates, new tools, or innovative ideas are shared, have gained popularity. You will be pleasantly surprised by the results that you can get from informal sessions conducted during lunch time. During these sessions, your team members or guests from other departments can conduct mini-seminars on different topics. After a year, your team is exposed to a variety of topics ranging from using Excel spreadsheets for analyzing complex data (e.g., pivot tables), to continuous improvement tools and advanced negotiation techniques.

PROCUREMENT TALENT MANAGEMENT FACET D: RECRUIT

Generally speaking, getting approval to hire new people is not easy—far from it. There are a variety of ways to involve new people in procurement tasks: by offering internships, increasing headcount, or developing the profile of the right candidate.

Internships

A creative way of recruiting much needed resources without adding headcount is to hire interns. By working with the business schools of the universities in your area, you can hire (at no cost/credit only or at minimal cost) intelligent and hard-working interns to take away the burden of tactical work from your strategic sourcing team members. During our tenure at different organizations, we implemented this practice with great success. The students benefited from the internship opportunity and gained real-life work experience, preparing them for future employment. Our staff members were pleased since they had more time to devote to strategic projects. University administrators and professors also welcomed our partnership for developing the future workforce.

Increase Headcount

Of course, if your department's workload is growing, as part of your business plan you should make an appeal to senior management for a proportionate increase in permanent staff so that you can maintain the quality of your strategic work. But you better be prepared when you do make that request.

As alluded to earlier, senior management usually does not approve staff increases easily. The practice of adding headcount is often scrutinized by them and Human Resources.

Among other things, they want to know:

- What have you done to improve the productivity and efficiency of your department?
- What non-value-added things have you stopped doing?
- What time and project management tools and techniques have you implemented?
- What are the current and historical measurements of output-per-person, and precisely how much additional work has been added to your team's plate over time?

Senior management needs to separate chronic complainers from savvy business people who have truly exhausted all alternatives. Thus, demonstrating the alternatives that you have already tried (and the measurable improvements you've made) can give you a better chance at having an appropriately staffed procurement department.

A pool of candidates who should be considered for new positions is existing employees. But getting promoted is not something that should happen just because an employee has been on board for the requisite amount of time. That person needs to qualify for the position and have the skills necessary to succeed in it. That is why the *develop* facet of the talent management cycle is so important.

If existing staff is not qualified for an open, more challenging, internal procurement position, it is the management team's fault for failing to develop them. After all, if you have employees who have been with the organization, know the processes, products, and services, and are in tune with the organizational culture, finding an appropriate candidate in-house should be easy.

Not only does having opportunities for professional development and mobility give you a better pool of internal candidates for new positions, it also makes the recruiting process easier for those times when circumstances require that you bring someone in from the outside. Then, you have created an environment that will appeal to the movers-and-shakers and talented individuals from other functions in your organization.

Developing the Profile of the Right Candidate

With the knowledge that the best candidates may not be the right candidates, you need to develop a profile of the *right* candidate. In terms of characteristics of the *right* candidate, consider the skill dimensions previously discussed under *Procurement Talent Management Facet A: Assess*. But, in addition to procurement-specific skills, there are other characteristics that are valuable, too. These characteristics include general problem-solving capabilities and industry-specific expertise. Some thought leaders have even debated the value of general problem-solving capabilities versus industry-specific expertise, saying that general problem-solving skills should take priority over industry-specific expertise.

It is necessary and not unreasonable to expect any good candidate to have both general problem-solving skills and industry-specific expertise when recruiting for more strategic procurement jobs. Plus, in our experience, we have seen real-world regret for filling a strategic position with people who exhibit excellent raw intelligence, but have no closely-related experience, instead of people with industry-specific expertise.

As individuals who have spent significant parts of their careers recruiting procurement professionals, we know the importance of hiring someone who can *hit the ground running*. Yes, we agree that some procurement skills can be taught and learned rather quickly. But what about more complex capabilities like understanding how to execute hedging strategies for fuel purchasing, or leading a team responsible for multiple and diverse categories?

These skills are not as easy to teach. Waiting two years for an individual with a high degree of intelligence and good soft skills, but no direct procurement experience, to learn the *ins and outs* is not a luxury that a lot of procurement leaders have. Today's management wants results now!

Accordingly, managers have to recruit people with both general problem-solving skills and raw intelligence, as well as industry-specific expertise, in addition to sound project management skills and high levels of procurement-specific skills. If there has to be a tie-breaker, a candidate's track record of succeeding in, as well as enjoying, a particular industry or category can tip the scales in that candidate's favor.

PROCUREMENT TALENT MANAGEMENT FACET E: UNIFY

Consider the capabilities needed to play basketball. Players need to be able to throw, catch, shoot, block shots, and dribble a basketball. But if you put a group of people who have never played basketball before onto a court and tell them to throw, catch, shoot, block, and dribble, would you have a basketball game? No! What would you have? Chaos!

You need to provide *players* with the objective and the rules of the game, along with a rigorous schedule for practicing. Likewise, you need to provide your procurement team with objectives and rules, unify them with a common focus, and give them the opportunity to practice.

Procedures are important. The problem with most procedures manuals, however, is that they are quite voluminous, and most people don't read them cover to cover. In addition to providing each procurement employee with a procedures manual, we recommend providing them with something shorter, yet quite powerful, to keep the team unified and focused. Whether that is a printed mission statement, a code of conduct, or some other document, a tangible representation of what the team is trying to accomplish can only help when it comes to getting the team to strive towards a common goal.

We like to recommend using a certain, fun list of unifying statements that we've developed. It is called The Procurement Professional's 10 Commandments.

The Procurement Professional's 10 Commandments

1. Thou shalt always make decisions in the best interest of thy employer. Good procurement professionals avoid any real, and even perceived, conflicts of interest.
2. Thou shalt always involve thy internal customers throughout the procurement process. Good procurement professionals never act alone.
3. Thou shalt never make price the only criterion in a procurement decision. Good procurement professionals take quality, delivery, and other criteria into consideration also.

4. Thou shalt measure thy performance and communicate thy performance to management. Good procurement professionals know and show their value.
5. Thou shalt treat suppliers fairly. Good procurement professionals don't attempt to take advantage of suppliers' mistakes nor trick them into accepting unfavorable terms.
6. Thou shalt embrace change and new technologies rather than resist them.
7. Thou shalt negotiate with the understanding that there may someday need to be a close relationship with the supplier across the table.
8. Thou shalt realize that it is a global economy and never make assumptions that thou knowest every supplier available.
9. Thou shalt acknowledge that thy manager's job is to develop and implement a strategy for the department and, therefore, thou shalt challenge thyself to solve problems independently rather than involve thy manager in tactical crises that can reasonably be resolved at the buyer level.
10. Thou shalt commit to continuous improvement of thy skills, never letting a year go by without learning new practices used by other procurement professionals.
11. Thou shalt always exceed expectations, consistently delivering more than anticipated. That is why there is an 11th Commandment amongst the 10 Commandments. Good procurement professionals will also fulfill obligations sooner than expected.

After you've made it through all five facets of the procurement talent management cycle, you are still not done! You must continually repeat the procurement talent management cycle in order to stay on top of the ever-changing aspect of leading a procurement team—managing talent.

MEASURING TALENT MANAGEMENT SUCCESS

After you have improved your team's skill levels through professional development, it is important to measure and sustain those skill levels, both for the individuals and the team. Measuring and documenting improvement is important as the management of some organizations may take a position such as, "I authorized a big training budget for you. What did I get for my investment?"

Here are some ideas for measuring the skill improvements in a way that can be communicated to management.

Performance Metrics

How does your team's performance, after skills development, compare to its performance in the period just prior to skills development? While perhaps not 100 percent of any improvements could be attributed to training, it is likely to have played a major role in any procurement transformation, and should be noted.

Observations

As a leader, you work with your team day in and day out. You can observe things that do not necessarily show up *in the numbers*. What difference do you notice in your team members? More confidence? Speaking the same language? Better morale? More professionalism? More respect from internal customers?

If you have made good decisions along the way, the improvements to your team should be apparent. It is then critical to sustain those improvements. We recommend repeating any skills assessment that you have done, annually or semiannually. It provides a way of measuring the improvement of your team's skills. Plus, reassessments can actually help sustain those skills.

If an individual knows that they will be *tested* and that there is a certain expectation for the results, they are more likely to take the training seriously and study. Will their studying for this reassessment *cheat* the test results? Absolutely not.

Studying for a reassessment will help them refresh their memory of some things that they learned but, perhaps due to their roles, could not put into practice right away. What is important is not just that they learn new skills during training, but that they retain those skills in their toolbox for a lifetime. Brushing up can only help!

Finally, it is a given that the individuals on the team will change over the years. You can't afford to have every departure of a trained professional push you backwards. So, as new employees enter your procurement department, it is advisable to assess their skills, identify any gaps, and close those gaps sooner, rather than later.

CLOSING REMARKS

Effectively managing talent is not something that a procurement department does by accident. It is a deliberate undertaking that can be advantageous to the department, each of the individuals within the department, and the entire organization. If your team members feel valued and on a career path where they will personally grow and benefit, productivity tends to increase and they are far less likely to seek employment elsewhere.

We hope that this chapter has helped you to realize the fact that your team can benefit from developing and retaining each player. Similarly, players can benefit from a leader who encourages and develops them to meet their aspirations. A well-planned and executed talent management process is vital to achieving the goals of your team, the individuals, and the organization.

REFERENCE

1. Collins, Jim. *Good to Great: Why Some Companies Make the Leap . . . and Others Don't*. New York, HarperBusiness, 2001.

4

CHAPTER

SOCIAL RESPONSIBILITY IN PROCUREMENT: THE NEW RULES FOR A MORE RESPONSIBLE GAME

While most sports have penalties or violations that are unique to the sport (such as offsides in American football, tackling from behind in soccer, slashing in hockey, double dribble in basketball), there is one infraction that is common to several sports: unsportsmanlike conduct. There is a certain higher standard of professional behavior that is expected of athletes and sports teams. Likewise, there is a certain higher standard of professional behavior that is expected of procurement professionals and organizations. That higher standard of behavior is called *social responsibility*.

Organizations have realized that they are responsible not only to shareholders but also to the community, environment, and human beings in general. Social responsibility is an institutionalized commitment to these constituencies. Socially responsible organizations utilize hiring practices that promote diversity, implement environmentally friendly processes, refuse to make use of child labor, and engage in other initiatives to maintain a high standard of ethical behavior. Procurement organizations have begun to mandate that suppliers follow social responsibility rules, either to support the purchaser's standards or to satisfy the requirements of the purchaser's customers.

Because procurement is a decision-making department, it has the opportunity to positively contribute to an organization's social responsibility initiatives. In this chapter, you'll learn about the various ways that procurement can become more socially responsible in its practices. We will start with basic ethics, then move to sustainable procurement, animal rights, supplier diversity and inclusion, and other aspects of social responsibility.

ETHICS

While social responsibility has been encompassing more and more aspects of business, it starts with ethical behavior.

Buying from Relatives or Your Own Company

Let's begin with a couple of common ethics questions: "Is it okay to be a supplier to the company I work for?" and "Is it okay to grant business to my relatives?" It can be ethical for you or your relative to be a supplier of your own organization if:

- Someone else makes the purchase decision
- The decision is made objectively, giving no favorable treatment to your organization or your relatives' organization
- You do not access, or try to access, confidential information about other suppliers that is not available to all competitors

With that said, it probably isn't the best idea to be a supplier to your own organization or your organization's competitors, or to grant business to your relatives. Totally ethical practices are those where there is no real or perceived conflict of interest. While you may avoid a real conflict of interest, it is likely that others will *perceive* that something unethical is happening. That is an unhealthy situation for an organization, its employees, and its management.

Accepting Gifts from Suppliers

Another common question is: "Is it ethical to accept gifts from suppliers?" The answer may depend on cultural and other considerations.

Cultural Considerations

Accepting gifts is a tricky situation, depending on where in the world you are doing business. In some countries, based on those cultures, giving gifts and accepting them among the companies who do business with each other is a way of life.

As an example, we would like to mention *guanxi*, which is a Chinese word translated as *relationship* or *network*. It is the social infrastructure that successful people in China erect around themselves to *get things done*.

But why is guanxi important? Introductions are very important in China. An individual needs to know someone who can introduce him or her to the right person. In China, everyone has guanxi. It is a way of life to pay visits to, have meals with, and give gifts to people with whom you want to build a relationship and do business.

However, this can be a dilemma for U.S. companies who want to do business with China and have a different policy. Our recommendation to you is that you need to learn about the culture and business practices of other countries before you do business with them. In addition, raise awareness and educate potential suppliers of your company's policies and practices.

In the United States, a conservative approach, where you leave no opportunity for the perception of conflict of interest, is advisable. Putting in a policy where you prohibit all gifts, or gifts that exceed a threshold of value (e.g., $25), can be easy in some organizations. However, in other organizations or industries, it can be a real challenge. Healthcare is one of those industries.

Internal Pressures

We all have politically powerful people in our organizations. These people will often try to exert their power so that they can keep their favorite suppliers, no matter what the cost is or how blatantly the supplier is taking advantage of that relationship. Whether their *victims* realize it or not, those suppliers use gifts or *freebies* to psychologically win over people over time, and firmly entrench themselves in budgets for years.

When evaluating your spend and where it should be directed, sometimes you can persuade people to participate in objective, multi-criteria decision making. Other times, you can't.

From what we've observed, medical doctors are perhaps the most difficult group of people to collaborate with on business decision making.

Some internal customers have big egos that make them say to themselves, "I'm the world's leading doctor/aerospace engineer/whatever, and there is no way that I'll let procurement agents tell me what suppliers to choose!"

In addition, internal customers in each industry will have their trump card—their argument that is designed to be impenetrable—that helps them keep their favorite suppliers. For example, in healthcare, that trump card can be found in the form of statements like, "It is unreasonable for you to propose that we sacrifice patient care to save a few pennies! These are people's lives we're talking about here. And do you think you know better than I about how to treat a patient?" How can you argue with that?

The step that the University of Pittsburgh Medical Center (UPMC), a leading healthcare organization with 92,000 employees, took in a highly publicized effort to curb supplier gifts was to get the highest levels of executive support to limit gifts.[1] We see executive support as the only way to implement ethical policy changes in a highly political organization.

Government Scandals

While private organizations are affected by ethical scrutiny, they probably are not under the same high-powered ethical microscope that government organizations are. The media simply love to expose government ethical scandals.

Being from Pittsburgh, we can't help but think back to a scandal involving our former mayor. Years ago, a huge photo of Pittsburgh Mayor Luke Ravenstahl consumed about 80 percent of the above-the-fold space on the front page of an edition of the *Pittsburgh Post-Gazette*. It accompanied an article[2] that described the scandal in which Ravenstahl was embroiled. His transgression? Golfing with city suppliers.

Yes, Ravenstahl accepted two days of golf in the Mario Lemieux Celebrity Invitational from UPMC and the Pittsburgh Penguins, valued at $9,000 (the article wasn't clear if that was $9k per day or total). Because the city does business with each organization, and each organization depends on the city for various approvals, Ravenstahl's acceptance was viewed as a potentially big ethical violation.

Ravenstahl's defense? The city's ethics code which, according to the article, says that, "[charitable] outings are exempted from a code limit stating city officials may only accept admission to cultural or athletic events valued at $250 or less per year, or worth $100 from a single person or organization." The Lemieux Invitational does indeed benefit a charity. But Ravenstahl's *it's-within-limits* defense didn't satisfy all of his critics.

A point we made earlier in this chapter is worth repeating: you should avoid any *real or perceived* conflicts of interest. Even if certain activities with suppliers may not bias your decision making, others may have the perception that they do, which can be just as harmful to your internal influence as a real conflict of interest.

That perception certainly made Ravenstahl sweat over the course of a few days as he appeared before the city's ethics committee.

Being invited to play golf, going to a sporting event, or having lunch is not uncommon for a procurement professional. So, whether you run the risk of going before your company's equivalent of the ethics committee or whether you'll merely have internal customers grumbling behind your back, it is always best to scrutinize your interactions with suppliers. Be aware that how much time you spend, who pays, and how much fun you have can affect how you are perceived in your organization. We emphasize that you need to pay close attention to your company's policy when it comes to accepting or giving gifts, or going to lunch or events with your suppliers.

It should be noted that perception in procurement is more important than ever. Think about the consequences before you accept an invitation from a supplier. Even if the *rules* say it's okay.

Unfortunately, Ravenstahl was involved in another uncomfortable situation months later. The following spring, the Pittsburgh Penguins secured an appearance in the Stanley Cup finals. Well, when this matchup was determined, Ravenstahl attempted to obtain free tickets to watch a game or two in the opponent's city. Unlike the time when he accepted $9,000 in golf from city suppliers, he asked for an official legal opinion from the city on whether or not he could accept those tickets.

This raised some ire and some publicity. The local news broadcast a segment where a member of the Pittsburgh City Council revealed Ravenstahl's six-figure salary. The council member said he makes half of that and pays for his hockey tickets out of his own pocket, and the mayor should do the same.

We wholeheartedly agree. When it comes to ethics—in politics as well as in procurement—if you feel that you have to ask whether something is ethical, *don't do it*! It reminds us of a saying used in a driver's education class: "When in doubt, don't!"

In addition, make one of Soheila's favorite mottos your motto: "Do the right thing because it is the right thing to do!" Because even if something is *technically within ethical guidelines*, your opponents will still have the opportunity to find fault with you and question your integrity.

In true spirit, ethics is not about being within guidelines; it is about demonstrating integrity above and beyond what is expected. This principle applies whether you are the mayor of a big city or a junior buyer.

Oh, but golfing with suppliers doesn't just get scrutiny when it is the mayor of a big city who is involved, and investigations don't always end with just a slap on the proverbial wrist in the form of negative public relations, either.

Consider the case of David Safavian, a top U.S. government procurement executive, who was convicted of crimes related to breaches of government procurement ethics.[3] It appears that the charges stemmed from Mr. Safavian accepting an invitation from a lobbyist to go golfing in Scotland. Then, Mr. Safavian lied about the lobbyist's business dealings with the government. As a result, Mr. Safavian was sentenced to 18 months in prison. It's hard to imagine the golf trip being worth that punishment, isn't it?

What's interesting is that, according to *Supply Management* magazine, Safavian had asked a government ethics officer for permission to go on the trip. If you were Safavian, wouldn't feeling compelled to ask an ethics officer for permission maybe give you a clue that perhaps something was not quite appropriate about accepting this trip? Doesn't it make you feel like there was some doubt in Safavian's mind that accepting the trip was ethical?

"When in doubt, don't."

Any time we teach ethics in procurement courses, we always say that if you have to think about whether something is ethical or not, just play it safe and decline. The safer you play it, the less risk you expose yourself to.

Not everyone will be in a position where they could end up serving jail time for a breach of procurement ethics. But every procurement professional should use the same amount of care as if that possibility existed.

Fairness to Suppliers

Ethics boundaries aren't limited to being too friendly with suppliers. There are ethical guidelines that are meant to keep you from being *unfair* to suppliers, too.

If you are like most procurement professionals, you are under pressure to generate significant cost savings. Unfortunately, the pressure to boost the bottom line compels some less-skilled procurement professionals to cross the ethical line. They use questionable techniques. Soheila recalls an example of crossing the ethical line by a purchasing manager when she conducted a procurement opportunity assessment for a client. One of the site purchasing managers of the client's company, whom she met during the discovery phase of the engagement, proudly bragged about how he shared the pricing information of the incumbent supplier for a key production material with a local supplier, and how he was able to get better pricing than what was negotiated by the corporate folks with the incumbent. Obviously, not only had this manager crossed the ethical line, but his actions were on the borderline of being illegal in the United States. In addition, it is important to indicate that this manager's action and *maverick buy* had an adverse impact on many negotiated terms and conditions of the corporate contract, spend management, volume rebates, and supplier performance and relationship management, to name a few.

Ethical and Unethical Profiles

It is noteworthy to share our view of five common ethics-related profiles of procurement negotiators. Observe your everyday business behavior to see if any of these profiles could possibly apply to you:

- **The Liar**—will tell any number of lies to a supplier to persuade that supplier to improve its terms. An example of a lie could be telling a supplier that another supplier has a price that is 10 percent lower when such a statement isn't true. *Unethical!*
- **The Exaggerator**—might not tell an outright lie, but his or her words and behavior may be designed to trick a supplier into thinking that a larger quantity or longer term contract is to be expected. The Exaggerator's intent is to get a better price and not follow through with implied quantity or term commitments. *Unethical!*
- **The Open Book**—will give a supplier information about competitors' proposals in order to persuade a supplier to offer a better deal. Of course, the competing suppliers expect their proposals to be kept confidential. *Unethical!*
- **The Cheap Date**—will accept meals, entertainment, or gifts at the supplier's expense, despite the fact that he or she is engaged in a negotiation situation with the supplier. Even if such acceptance does not actually influence the Cheap Date's decision making, it creates the perception within the Cheap Date's organization of being bought. *Unethical!*
- **The Professional**—considers ethics when negotiating. He or she knows the characteristics of the other four profiles, and consciously avoids that type of behavior. The Professional does a great job of negotiating, too!

There are many effective ethical negotiation techniques available. You should never have to resort to the practices of the Liar, Exaggerator, Open Book, or Cheap Date to get the results you want. For practice at thinking through an ethically challenging situation, see the procurement ethics exercise "No Such Thing as a Free Ticket!" in Exhibit B in the back of this book.

Now that we've covered some ethical matters, we can move into the broader aspects of social responsibility.

SOCIAL RESPONSIBILITY

Because procurement is responsible for many decisions that affect society and the environment, you have a key role in helping spread social responsibility. Not only can you make your organization more socially responsible, but you can also compel other organizations (i.e., your suppliers) to be more socially responsible.

Socially Responsible Request for Proposal (RFP) Questions

You can increase global social responsibility by including social responsibility among the other criteria used in selecting suppliers. Here are 12 questions you can include in RFP templates to probe suppliers' commitments to social responsibility:

1. How does your organization support the communities in which it operates?
2. How does your organization encourage suppliers to support those communities?
3. How much money does your organization spend annually with socially diverse suppliers?
4. How does your organization promote diversity in its own employment practices?
5. How does your organization encourage its suppliers to have a diverse workforce and supplier base?
6. What does your organization do to make its operations more environmentally friendly?
7. How does your organization encourage its suppliers to be more environmentally friendly?
8. How does your organization monitor compliance with its ethics policy?
9. How does your organization ensure that human rights are valued in its operations?
10. How does your organization ensure that its suppliers value human rights?
11. How does your organization ensure maximum safety in its working conditions?
12. How does your organization ensure that its suppliers have safe working conditions?

Suppliers who positively respond, or not, will get the message that social responsibility is important to your organization.

Supplier Code of Conduct

Today more than ever, the public judges a business by the companies with which it spends its money. Such judgments are usually negative in nature. Laws and customs vary from country to country, and standards of *ethics* and social norms may also vary in different business environments. Nevertheless, for decades, there has been a growing public awareness regarding social responsibility around the world and it only appears to be getting stronger as time goes on.

If this seems new, consider the breadth of these high-profile examples of public reactions to social irresponsibility in business. In the late-twentieth century, TV celebrity Kathie Lee Gifford was accused of being responsible for the sweatshop labor management activities in the Far East, where clothes were made for her Kathie Lee line and sold at Walmart.[4] In the early 2000s, actress Pam Anderson rallied supporters to boycott the KFC food chain, claiming that KFC used suppliers that abused animals.[5] In 2020, a group of investment firms and shareholders asked Nike, FedEx, and PepsiCo to terminate their sponsorships with the NFL team then known as the Washington Redskins because of the racist implications of the team name.[6] Subsequently, FedEx threatened to remove its signage from the team's stadium, for which it purchased naming rights, because it didn't want its brand to be associated with a racial controversy.[7] The team eventually capitulated under this cascade of pressure and temporarily renamed itself the *Washington Football Team* before later adopting its permanent new name, the *Washington Commanders*.

All of this means that your work choosing suppliers and directing your organization's money to them is under more scrutiny and can have a bigger impact on your organization than ever. An organization's perception by the public is now often heavily influenced by the reputations of the customers and suppliers with whom it chooses to do business. Smart procurement professionals know this. One of the outcomes of this awareness is a document that has become widely used across many industries: the supplier code of conduct.

A simple Internet search will link you to many supplier codes of conduct from top companies such as Google, Whirlpool, Mastercard, The Hershey Company, Airbus, and countless other organizations in a variety of industries, both manufacturing and service. Is there a reason for you not to use a supplier code of conduct?

If you want to quickly prepare a supplier code of conduct, let us save you a little time with some suggestions. While an infinite number of items can be addressed in a supplier code of conduct, here are the 14 most commonly addressed points:

1. All employment must be freely chosen (i.e., your suppliers must have true employees and not slaves or victims of human trafficking)

2. All employees must be at or above a specified age
3. All employees must work less than a specified number of hours per week
4. The supplier must comply with wage laws
5. All employees must be treated humanely and with dignity, free of harassment
6. The supplier may not be discriminatory in its employment decisions and practices
7. The supplier's facility must meet safety standards and otherwise actively promote worker health and safety
8. The supplier must have a plan for emergencies
9. The supplier must allow employees freedom of association and the right to collective bargaining
10. The supplier must comply with all applicable environmental laws and customer-driven environmental rules such as obtaining permits, monitoring and reducing pollution, and avoiding the preventable use of hazardous materials
11. The supplier must abide by the customer's ethics policy, including nonparticipation in activities like gift giving, back-door selling, etc.
12. The supplier must have a governance/management system in place to ensure compliance with all laws as well as the supplier code of conduct
13. The supplier must notify its employees of the applicable supplier code of conduct
14. The supplier's compliance with the supplier code of conduct is subject to audit

Some other things that you can address in your supplier code of conduct include:

- The supplier must require its suppliers to abide by a supplier code of conduct acceptable to your organization
- The supplier must comply with ethical guidelines regarding treatment of animals
- The supplier must not place advertisements in media where violence, sexual harassment, racial intolerance, homophobia, transphobia, or profanity is promoted
- The supplier must have a written plan for pollution reduction
- The supplier must have a supplier diversity program in place, or have a plan for starting a supplier diversity program

SUSTAINABLE PROCUREMENT

When the first edition of this book was published in 2012, *green business* and *green procurement* were popular buzz phrases. Those terms described an effort to do business in a more environmentally friendly manner.

However, *going green* was environmentally responsible business in an embry-onic stage. It often was manifested in adopting a paperless approach to communi-cations. And, let's face it, that came across as more of a tactic for companies to save money rather than doing something wonderful for our planet. Since then, organi-zations have matured in their approaches to being environmentally responsible.

What Is Sustainability and Why Is It Important?

The mind-set of environmental responsibility has changed to one of trying to pre-serve the Earth and its resources for future generations—to *sustain* the wonderful gift of the Earth as long as possible. After all, if the Earth is destroyed, that's not exactly great for business, you know? So today, that focus on keeping the planet healthy for the future is at the heart of what is now referred to as *sustainable busi-ness* and *sustainable procurement*.

The more serious nature of the sustainability movement compared to the green movement is apparent in many ways. One of the ways is that more and more companies are adding another office to their *C-suites*. That office is for the Chief Sustainability Officer—a C-level executive responsible for ensuring that the orga-nization keeps environmental sustainability as a top priority alongside profit. Of particular interest to the procurement world, we are seeing executives who have dual titles: Chief Sustainability Officer *and* Chief Procurement Officer. This fact underscores both the importance of procurement and the massive amount of in-fluence that procurement and supply chain work have on sustainability.

Sustainability involves looking at the factors that threaten the continuity of the world we have today. One of the most often-addressed threats—though certainly not the only threat—in the practice of sustainable business is climate change.

What Is Climate Change?

Climate change has been called "the greatest existential threat of our time."[8] That's quite a statement. Increasingly, behavior in the business world is reflecting a seri-ous recognition of that threat as well as actions to slow or solve climate change.

Now, we know you didn't buy a procurement book to become a science expert. But, it's fun to point out that Soheila does have a Ph.D. in chemistry. Also, in her career, she did use chlorofluorocarbons (CFCs) in formulating rigid foams for in-sulation in the wall of refrigerators and freezers in the 1980s, and admits that ban-ning the use of these blowing agents that destroy the earth's protective ozone layer was not a high priority, at that time. Nevertheless, in the late 1980s, efforts began to reduce the use of CFCs by replacing them with water as a blowing agent.[9]

All that aside, not every procurement professional needs Soheila's level of edu-cation and experience in science. However, it is important to at least understand a little bit about the Earth's circumstances so that you understand how your procurement decisions can make those circumstances better or worse.

While acting to destroy the ozone layer, CFCs also act to trap heat in the lower atmosphere, causing the earth to warm and climate and weather to change. In addition, the Earth's temperature is regulated by the presence of greenhouse gases in the atmosphere which trap the sun's heat. Greenhouse gases include carbon dioxide (CO_2), methane, and others. Human activities add to the greenhouse gases in the atmosphere, which results in an increasing amount of the sun's heat being trapped. Thus, *global warming* occurs.[10] Global warming is just one component of climate change, which also includes changes in precipitation, wind patterns, and other aspects of weather.[11]

The human activities that emit greenhouse gases—particularly carbon—include transportation, electric power generation, and industrial processes. These activities began happening with the dawn of the Industrial Revolution in the late eighteenth century. Record-keeping of global temperatures started around 1880.

Climate experts warn that an excessive increase in the average global temperature will cause more severe weather, more frequent and costly weather disasters, dirtier air, more health consequences, higher wildlife extinction rates, and flood threats to entire island nations and the world's largest cities.[12] One of the international efforts to reign in the rise of the average global temperature is the Paris Agreement—a legally binding international treaty on climate change that was adopted by 191 countries in December 2015. The goal of the Paris Agreement is to keep the rise in the global average temperature less than 2 degrees Celsius higher than the pre-industrial global average temperature, and preferably no more than 1.5 degrees Celsius higher. A primary approach to achieving this goal is for the countries to achieve *net zero carbon emissions* by 2050.

Net zero carbon emissions means that a country—or organization—has achieved a status where the amount of carbon it adds to the atmosphere is no greater than the amount of carbon it removes from the atmosphere. We already talked about how carbon is added to the atmosphere, but carbon can also be removed from the atmosphere through activities such as planting new forests, restoring old forests, implementing technologies that suck CO_2 out of the air, or preventing it from leaving industrial smokestacks. So, achieving net zero carbon emissions—also called being *carbon neutral*—is a combination of cutting emissions and removing CO_2.[13]

All of the attention on greenhouse gas emissions has resulted in the adoption of *carbon footprint* as a de facto standard measurement for an organization's environmental responsibility. Calculating an organization's carbon footprint involves quantifying an organization's greenhouse gas emissions by examining facility energy usage, business travel methods and mileage, shipping methods, and—most important to anyone reading this book—its supply chain! The unit of measure used for carbon footprint is tons of CO_2 emitted per year. Just like golf, the lower the score, the better. So, organizations seek to reduce their carbon footprints.

How Is Climate Change Influencing Business and Procurement?

With countries signing on to the Paris Agreement, they are now turning their attention to the businesses and industries that are responsible for the greenhouse gas emissions within their borders. You can bet that a litany of regulations will be drafted and imposed on businesses and industries as we approach 2050. However, organizations aren't just waiting for their governments to impose regulations on them. More than ever, businesses are truly interested in environmental responsibility and are being proactive.

In fact, over 100 companies including Verizon, PepsiCo, Best Buy, Microsoft, and more have signed onto *The Climate Pledge*. The Climate Pledge, cofounded by Amazon, is a voluntary commitment by companies to achieve net zero carbon emissions by 2040—10 years earlier than prescribed by the Paris Agreement.[14] As such, corporate leaders are demanding the use of sustainable business processes throughout their organizations. And, with that, procurement and supply chain management departments are getting most of the attention for driving improvement.

Why? Well, according to McKinsey, the typical consumer company's supply chain accounts for more than 80% of its greenhouse gas emissions and, according to the United States' Environmental Protection Agency, some organizations' supply chains account for more than 90% of their greenhouse gas emissions.[15,16] This means that the responsibility for achieving compliance with the Paris Agreement, keeping commitments to The Climate Pledge, and achieving business sustainability will fall largely on procurement.

Never in history has procurement been more important. And, when you think about all of the climate-change-driven disasters that could happen if carbon neutrality isn't achieved, procurement actually has the capability of saving the world!

Wow!

What Else Does Sustainable Procurement Address?

As if the push toward carbon neutrality wasn't enough of a challenge, sustainable procurement addresses many more aspects of environmental responsibility. Here are a few:

- **Deforestation**—According to *Live Science*, deforestation is "the permanent removal of trees to make room for something besides forest." Deforestation can be done to make way for agriculture—both to plant things to later be harvested and to provide grazing room for animals that will be used for industry or to acquire valuable timber for use in wood products. One particular example of an industry that contributes to deforestation is the $66 billion palm oil industry. Palm oil is found in half of all supermarket items, including food and health and beauty products. Tropical forests are leveled and local peatlands are destroyed in order to grow more palm trees, which has a harmful impact on the ecosystem. The negative effects of deforestation include destruction of animals' homes, degradation of water quality, droughts, a reduction of CO_2 capture, and more.[17]

- **Pollution**—Factories, such as those potentially operated by your suppliers, are notorious for burning coal and fossil fuels, using toxic chemicals, releasing gas and liquid waste into the environment, and improperly disposing of radioactive material. These activities can contaminate drinking water, release unwanted toxins into the air, reduce the quality of soil, and pose health hazards to humans and animals.
- **Energy Conservation**—Much of the energy used today comes from sources such as petroleum, natural gas, coal, and nuclear energy. These sources are called *nonrenewable* because, once they're gone, they're gone. So, to be sustainable, our world must conserve these resources by using less of them for energy production. This involves being more efficient with the use of these resources as well as switching to renewable energy sources such as solar energy, wind energy, and hydropower.[18]
- **Water Conservation**—Water is obviously important to sustain human life. It's important because humans need to consume it directly. It's also important because humans consume agricultural products that depend on water. Droughts could threaten both the direct availability of water as well as the availability of water to the agricultural industry that feeds us all. Therefore, water conservation has become a high environmental priority, including among those managing supply chains. Leading companies are working to drive water stewardship throughout their value chains.[19,20]

By addressing these matters with suppliers and possibly building strict requirements for supplier behavior, procurement is well-positioned to minimize these serious environmental problems.

Broad Sustainable Procurement Strategies and Tactics

So, now that we know what issues sustainable procurement addresses, what specifically do procurement professionals do to make their supply chains more environmentally responsible? A few strategies and tactics follow.

Developing KPI's

Knowing what you want to accomplish and how close you are to accomplishing it requires measurement in the form of key performance indicators (KPIs). Which KPIs should be used in a sustainable procurement initiative?

"That's a classic question—the answer is not that straightforward," according to Thomas Udesen, Chief Procurement Officer for Bayer AG, headquartered in Germany, and the cofounder of the Sustainable Procurement Pledge. "It depends a bit on where you are on your evolution." He sees at least three stages in sustainable procurement performance measurement (see Figure 4.1).

"Maybe, initially, you focus on more activity-based KPIs," Udesen says. "How much coverage do you have in terms of your code of conduct, your assessment, your audits?" For the second stage, "you move into impact," he explains. "Do you start seeing an improvement of performance? Do you close your open corrective actions quickly?" An example of a performance-based KPI would be percentage of natural resources procured from sustainable sources. At the most strategic level is where Udesen says an organization can begin "tracking your carbon footprint, your impact in terms of water use, et cetera." This stage may require segmenting greenhouse gas emission KPIs by category, such as CO_2 footprint of supplier delivery logistics, CO_2 footprint of purchased electricity, CO_2 footprint of business travel, and so on.[21]

Getting Teamwork from Your Supply Base

It should be clear by now that, to have a truly sustainable business, you need suppliers who are equally committed to sustainability. This may mean sourcing for new suppliers. It may mean working with existing suppliers. It may mean working with

STRATEGY-BASED KPIs
🍃 Supply chain carbon footprint
🍃 Supply chain water footprint

PERFORMANCE-BASED KPIs
🍃 Percentage of natural resources procured from sustainable sources
🍃 Average time to close corrective actions

ACTIVITY-BASED KPIs
🍃 Percentage of suppliers who have accepted sustainability code of conduct
🍃 Percentage of suppliers who have had sustainability assessment

Time ⟶

Figure 4.1   Sustainable procurement KPI's throughout an organization's evolution

fewer suppliers. Most likely, it will require a combination of approaches to the supply base. Regardless of the approach, "the direction should be made crystal clear," according to Udesen. "We need to tell them, 'We are going this way and you are invited. In fact, we will work with you to make you capable of coming with us. But, if you choose a way that is not aligned with our responsible behaviors, that means we're out of here.' It's not a nice-to-have, it's a qualifier."

Using Third-Party Supplier Ratings and Assessments

When seeking new suppliers, it can be a time-saver to access third-party supplier sustainability ratings. In the past, onboarding a supplier in the hopes of becoming more environmentally responsible involved guesswork and a leap of faith. Fortunately, the available ratings and assessments can provide you with the data you need to better gauge a supplier's ability to positively contribute to your sustainable procurement initiative. It's like having a referee to make sure your potential suppliers can play within your boundaries.

Requesting Suppliers to Set Science-Based Climate Goals

A big part of sustainable procurement is demanding more environmentally friendly practices of your suppliers. But, when you're just getting started, it can be awkward being an environmental novice telling your suppliers how to change their businesses. So, some procurement teams begin by requesting that their suppliers set science-based climate goals. At a minimum, your suppliers should be familiar with the climate-impacting business principles discussed in this chapter. They, then, might be in the best position to prescribe the contributions that they can make. Their initial goals and performance can serve as a baseline on which performance can be improved each successive year.

Seeking Supplier Feedback and Input

Your organization is likely not your suppliers' only customer, and, your organization may not be their most advanced customer in terms of sustainability. Suppliers have the unique opportunity to observe how their customers make environmentally responsible enhancements, including the ways in which they work with them. So, it can be very beneficial to ask your suppliers—either informally or through a more formal survey—how their other customers improve their environmental responsibility, how your organization compares, and how your organization can change the way it works with them to better serve the planet.

Reporting

Because so much of an organization's environmental impact occurs in its supply chain, the procurement team will be looked to for measuring and reporting what is happening in the supply chain. Supply chain sustainability efforts are "another reason for the stakeholders in the organization and the board members to look to the procurement organization for direction, data, and leadership," says Jack Freeman, Principal of Peakspan Capital. Freeman expects sustainability reporting to have a prominent role in the required reporting of publicly held companies. "The board members and the CEO of, say, a Fortune 500 company want to make the carbon neutral claim. But, they need the help of the procurement team," he says. "I'm excited by the importance this set of trends is placing on the procurement department and the role technology will play in helping procurement in serving up those insights to the board."

Cost Implications of Sustainable Procurement

So, how do you account for a sustainable preference when you are sourcing? Two common methods are weighted average scorecarding and total cost of ownership analysis. Deciding between the two often depends on the market. If the market is one where sustainable alternatives actually save costs over the life cycle of the purchased product or equipment, then total cost of ownership analysis is the proper method. Adobe Systems was one of the first companies to gain significant publicity for demonstrating that energy efficiency investments produced a noteworthy return on investment while also being more environmentally friendly.[22]

However, some sustainable alternatives have higher prices without a cost-saving benefit associated with them. You pay a premium for the comfort of knowing that you did something environmentally responsible. In these cases, you should use weighted average scorecarding.

When using weighted average scorecarding, you need to decide how much weight should be given to environmental responsibility. Should it be five percent? Ten percent? Twelve percent? More? Less?

Even with total cost of ownership analysis, you can apply similar logic to determine how much of a premium your company is willing to pay for a more sustainable alternative. One study[23] showed that nearly half of the respondents were willing to pay more for a more sustainable alternative, so it is important to know your organization's philosophy.

Top management should be involved in these decisions. It really is a decision that is based on the values of the company. There are many conflicting studies that state whether or not consumers or businesses are willing to pay a green premium (a *greenium*?) indicating that it is important to continually monitor top management's support for sustainability initiatives as priorities change over time.

Animal-Friendly Procurement

While in the first decade of the twenty-first century much of the focus of sustainability initiatives was on paper reduction, other aspects of environmental protection found their way under the *green* umbrella. For example, the front page of *USA Today* (February 5, 2008) featured the results of a survey that asked American kids if they could change one thing about the world, what would it be? The number one answer was "save environment/protect animals," with 44 percent of the responses.

All these years later, those *kids* are in the workforce, making business decisions. So, in the eyes of our now-current and emerging corporate leaders, protecting animals is a part of saving the environment or the sustainability movement that has done nothing but grow in the past two decades.

The remaining responses? The results are as follows and also illustrated in Figure 4.2:

> End wars/terrorism—21%
> Cure disease/cancer/AIDS—14%
> Feed the hungry—11%
> End racism/prejudice—4%

% of Respondents

■ Save environment/protect animals ■ End wars/terrorism
■ Cure disease/cancer/AIDS ■ Feed the hungry
■ End racism/prejudice ▨ Other

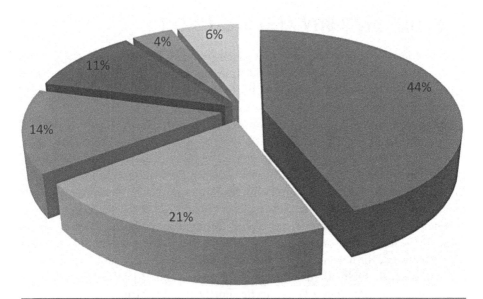

Figure 4.2   What kids want to change about the world (Source: *USA Today*)

Unfortunately, protecting animals is a topic that's been sorely missing from nearly every set of socially responsible procurement guidelines that we've seen. So, consider this section as one that breaks new ground and gives you a glimpse into the future of socially responsible procurement by addressing that missing topic.

Now, it's easy to assume that animal welfare doesn't affect your buying. But if you analyzed a list of the products that your organization buys, you might be surprised to learn that your organization purchases products that adversely affect animals. These products may include seemingly innocuous items such as laptop bags, furniture, and cleaning products. Some laptop bags are made from leather that was produced from cattle skin. Some furniture may be made from wood that became available by illegal logging or deforestation, which destroys the homes of animals. And some cleaning products may have been tested on animals.

We expect that this aspect of socially responsible procurement will escalate soon for many reasons. One is that the media has become more interested in exposing animal cruelty scandals. Another is that today's youth increasingly factor animal rights into their consumer choices. A third is that some organizations clearly label cruelty-free products as such, whether it's a manufacturer placing a statement directly on the product's packaging or a retailer including a badge on its website to identify cruelty-free products, as Target does.

The increased exposure of animal cruelty is resulting in pressure on executives to eliminate the atrocities that corporate spend supports. That pressure will prompt edicts to adopt animal-friendly procurement practices.

SUPPLIER DIVERSITY AND INCLUSION

In case you have started thinking that social responsibility is all about *things* that we may never come in contact with—like the ozone layer—think again! We're now going to cover how human beings are the focus of elements of socially responsible procurement, too.

Again, we can look to the sports world for a parallel. In the National Football League (NFL) in the United States, there is something called the *Rooney Rule*, which was originally implemented in 2002. The initial incarnation of the Rooney Rule—named after Pittsburgh Steelers' co-owner Dan Rooney, who pushed the NFL to adopt the policy—required NFL teams to interview at least one minority candidate when they were interviewing for a vacant head coach position.

The Rooney Rule did not require NFL teams to hire a certain percentage of minority head coaches, only to give minority candidates the opportunity to interview for the vacant head coach positions. In 2007, the Steelers franchise followed this rule and eventually hired its first African-American head coach, Mike Tomlin. According to the *Pittsburgh Post-Gazette* shortly after his hiring, Mr. Tomlin "acknowledged that the so-called Rooney Rule may have helped him get noticed, but not to get the job."[24] Tomlin continued to coach the team without a losing season over a decade later and led the team to two Super Bowl appearances, winning one of them and becoming the youngest head coach in NFL history to both coach in and win a Super Bowl.[25]

In 2020, the NFL expanded the Rooney Rule to require clubs to interview at least two external minority candidates for head coaching openings, at least one minority candidate for coordinator jobs, at least one external minority candidate for senior football operations and general manager jobs, and minorities and/or female applicants for senior-level executive positions.[26] And, though not part of the Rooney Rule, the American football world hit additional diversity and inclusion milestones when Sarah Fuller became the first woman to play during a regular season game in one of college football's Power 5 conferences when she kicked off for Vanderbilt University in 2020 and when Sarah Thomas became the first woman to referee a Super Bowl in 2021.[27,28]

Now, American football hasn't exactly been the best historical model for diversity and inclusion, but, if American football can evolve, certainly the business world can do much better. Accordingly, the procurement profession plays a vitally important role in helping organizations become more diverse and inclusive in their business dealings.

Definition and Categories of Diverse Suppliers

While there is no uniform rule that applies to every procurement department throughout the world, in the United States, many organizations have developed their own version of the Rooney Rule in the form of supplier diversity and inclusion programs. Supplier diversity and inclusion programs—sometimes called supplier diversity programs or supplier inclusion programs—are generally designed to encourage the use of suppliers meeting certain ownership criteria and, in some cases, to *set aside* a percentage of a procurement award for only suppliers meeting such criteria. These suppliers are sometimes called *diverse suppliers, small disadvantaged businesses*, or *disadvantaged businesses*. The simplest supplier diversity and inclusion programs may sum up all of the applicable suppliers as small disadvantaged businesses, whereas the most comprehensive programs may recognize a half dozen or more categories of diverse suppliers. Supplier diversity programs, in many cases, have the apparent mission of making up for inequities in cultural treatment that members of certain ethnic demographics have received, not received, or have been subject to.

A definition of a small disadvantaged business that reflects many organizations' philosophies toward supplier diversity can be found on techtarget.com, where a *small disadvantaged business* is defined as a *small business that is at least 51 percent owned by one or more individuals who are both socially and economically disadvantaged.*[29] This definition is pretty nonspecific, though. After all, what is a *small business*? How do we know if someone is *socially or economically disadvantaged*?

Well, the organization that provides the benchmarks for these types of designations is the U.S. Small Business Administration (SBA). The SBA is the U.S. Federal Government's arm that sets goals with other federal departments and agencies to award contracts to small businesses, including many categories of diverse suppliers.[30] Those categories of diverse suppliers that are recognized by the SBA often serve as a guide for private sector businesses' supplier diversity programs as well.

Getting back to the idea of a small business being owned by someone who is socially and economically disadvantaged, you may think that the definition of a small business is simpler than the definition of a socially or economically disadvantaged individual. But, that's actually the opposite. So, let's tackle the concept of socially and economically disadvantaged individuals first.

Per the SBA, socially disadvantaged individuals are people who have been subjected to "ethnic prejudice or cultural bias within American society" because of their membership in the following specified groups: Black Americans, Hispanic Americans, Native Americans, Asian Pacific Americans, and Subcontinent Asian Americans. Okay, that takes care of the social aspect of socially and economically disadvantaged.

"Economically disadvantaged" individuals are "socially disadvantaged individuals whose ability to compete in the free enterprise system has been impaired due to diminished capital and credit opportunities as compared to others in the same or similar business who are not socially disadvantaged."[31] This is clarified somewhat by thresholds for net worth and total assets, which were maximums of $750,000 of net worth, $350,000 of adjusted gross income, and $6 million of total assets (prior to subtracting liabilities) at the time of this writing.[32]

In most cases where ownership of a diverse supplier is discussed, you will see phrases such as "owned and controlled," "owned and operated," "owned and managed," or a hybrid of these such as "owned, controlled and operated." While some organizations publish distinct definitions for each of these terms, they all similarly describe owners who are active contributors to their businesses. Basically, this is to ensure that the owners are not just absentee, potentially rich, investor-type owners who seek to buy up businesses in order to benefit from programs designed to benefit disadvantaged entrepreneurs. For the sake of simplicity, we will use the phrase "owned and controlled" in this chapter.

Now, we can get to the *small business* part. The SBA's definition of small business actually depends on the industry. Depending on the industry, the threshold for being a small business will depend on either annual revenue or employee count.

In some industries where annual revenue is the determinant of supplier size, small businesses can be those businesses with less than $1 million in annual revenue. In other industries, businesses can generate as much as $41.5 million in annual revenue and still be considered a small business. In industries where employee count determines whether or not a company qualifies as a small business, that maximum number of employees ranges from 100 to 1,500.[33]

Common Public Sector Diverse Supplier Categories

The SBA divides up this universe of small businesses into five categories of diverse suppliers. These five categories are defined in the following list. For readers in the U.S. public sector, these categories may represent all of the diverse supplier categories that your organization may recognize (we'll get to the more inclusive private sector categories later in the next section):

- **Socially and Economically Disadvantaged Small Business**—This is a business that meets the criteria for being a small business and is at least 51% owned and controlled by an individual or individuals who are socially and economically disadvantaged as previously defined. These businesses are also referred to as *small disadvantaged businesses* or *8(a) suppliers* after the SBA's *8(a) Business Development Program* which is geared to assist socially and economically disadvantaged small businesses.
- **Women-Owned Small Business**—This is a business that meets the criteria for being a small business and is at least 51% owned and controlled by a woman or women.
- **Service-Disabled Veteran-Owned Small Business**—This is a business that meets the criteria for being a small business and is at least 51% owned and controlled by an individual or individuals who qualify as service-disabled veterans. A *veteran* is defined as a person who served on active duty with the Army, Air Force, Navy, Marine Corps, or Coast Guard for any length of time and who was discharged or released under conditions other than dishonorable.[34] A service-disabled veteran is a veteran who has a disability that was incurred or aggravated in the line of duty in the active service in the United States Armed Forces.[35] Lest there be any confusion over what disabilities may qualify, Title 38 of the U.S. Code of Federal Regulations provides descriptions and ratings of over 100 conditions.[36]
- **HUBZone Small Business**—The U.S. Federal Government seeks to help businesses in what they call *historically underutilized business zones*, or HUBZones for short. The SBA has a nationwide map of HUBZones. Small businesses that have their principal offices in HUBZones are recognized as diverse suppliers if at least 35% of their employees live in a HUBZone and the business is owned and controlled by one or more U.S. citizens, a Community Development Corporation, an agricultural cooperative, an Alaska Native corporation, a Native Hawaiian organization, or an Indian tribe.[37]

- **Small Business**—This category serves as both a parent category that encompasses all previously listed categories as well as a catch-all category that accommodates all suppliers who meet the size criteria to be considered a small business, but don't qualify as any of the more specific types of small businesses.

Please note that all of these SBA diversity supplier designations apply only to small businesses. The U.S. Federal government has goals for these five categories. In total, it seeks to award 23% of prime contracts to small businesses, of which it aims to award the following percentages to the following small business subcategories:[38]

- 5% of prime contracts and subcontracts for small disadvantaged businesses
- 5% of prime contracts and subcontracts for women-owned small businesses
- 3% of prime contracts and subcontracts for service-disabled veteran-owned small businesses
- 3% of prime contracts and subcontracts for HUBZone small businesses

Common Private Sector Diverse Supplier Categories

Naturally, as with most things, the private sector does things a little differently than the government in terms of supplier diversity and inclusion. Surprise, surprise!

There are two main differences between government and private sector supplier diversity and inclusion programs. First, private sector supplier diversity and inclusion programs tend to include more diverse supplier categories than the five aforementioned ones that are recognized by the SBA. Second, private sector organizations don't always require a supplier to be a *small business* to qualify as a diverse supplier.

So, for our definitions of these categories of diverse suppliers, *percent owned* can mean the total percent of ownership split between certain owners of a privately held company or the percent of total percent of stock shares owned by certain owners of a publicly traded company. It may seem like a *splitting hairs* type of detail, but it's worth mentioning. Some organizations recognize the possibility that a person who *owns* a business and a person who *controls* a business may be two different people, but actually may have the same demographic characteristics and, therefore, should qualify as a diverse supplier.

Say, for instance, one service-disabled veteran owns a business but does not control it. However, the owner hired a service-disabled veteran as the CEO to manage or control the business. Some organizations may not recognize that business as a service-disabled veteran-owned business because the owner does not actively participate in the daily operation of the company. However, other organizations may recognize this company as a service-disabled veteran-owned small business because the company is indeed 51% or more *owned and controlled* by a service-disabled veteran or veterans. It's a seemingly unusual situation. But, one that you could face with some of the diverse supplier categories we discuss, so it's good to be prepared.

An organization that we feel has a great supplier diversity and inclusion program to use as an example is United Parcel Service (UPS). UPS has always seemed to be ahead of the pack in terms of supplier diversity. One shining example came from 2008. That year, UPS shocked the procurement world when they introduced a new category of diverse suppliers: Lesbian, Gay, Bisexual, and/or Transgender-Owned Business Enterprise.

While this category was unique at the time, it is a category that is a veritable industry standard in supplier diversity and inclusion programs today. Let's take a look at supplier diversity and inclusion categories at UPS since their categories and definitions are very common among leading procurement teams and would serve as a good starting point if you were to construct your own supplier diversity and inclusion program.[39]

- **Small Business**—While some organizations like UPS use SBA size criteria to determine whether a supplier is a small business or not, others use more simplified criteria that apply to the entire supply base, like 100 or fewer employees or $1 million or less in annual revenue, regardless of industry. Unless your organization needs to report its supplier diversity spend to a government agency, customer, or other third party, you may have freedom in determining your own size thresholds.
- **Minority-Owned Business Enterprise**—The UPS definition of a *minority individual* means someone who is a member of the Asian, Black, Hispanic, or Native American racial/ethnic groups—pretty much the same groups recognized by the SBA. While a large number of organizations recognize identical racial/ethnic groups, a small number of organizations recognize other groups such as Native Alaskans, Aleuts, and Asian Indian Americans.[40] A minority-owned business enterprise is a business that is at least 51 percent owned and controlled by one or more minority individuals.
- **Woman-Owned Business Enterprise**—A business that is at least 51 percent owned and controlled by one or more women.
- **LGBT-Owned Business Enterprise**—A business enterprise that is at least 51 percent owned and controlled by one or more self-identified lesbian, gay, bisexual, and/or transgender (LGBT) persons.
- **Veteran-Owned Business Enterprise**—While the SBA's veteran-related diverse supplier category required the associated veteran to have a disability, many organizations simply require a veteran status, without regard to whether such veterans are disabled. Therefore, this type of business is one that is at least 51 percent owned and controlled by one or more veterans.
- **Service-Disabled Veteran-Owned Business Enterprise**—A business that is at least 51 percent owned and controlled by one or more service-disabled veterans.

- **Disability-Owned Business Enterprise**—One of the more recently added categories of diverse suppliers involves companies that are owned by individuals with disabilities. The UPS supplier diversity program defines a disability as a "physical and/or mental impairment that substantially limits one or more major life activities." A disability-owned business enterprise is a business that is at least 51 percent owned and controlled by one or more persons with a disability.
- **HUBZone Small Business**—This is one category where private sector organizations often simply recognize the SBA's definition without modification.

While the U.S. Federal government publicly publishes its goals for awards to diverse suppliers, the private sector often keeps its supplier diversity goals *private*. So, it can be difficult to set appropriate supplier diversity goals for your organization. Where do you start if you have no history of your spend with diverse suppliers? Perhaps you can apply the principles from the Rooney Rule into your procurement.

It might be that, for purchases that exceed a certain dollar threshold, at least one diversity supplier must be given the opportunity to bid. Not necessarily that a certain percentage of business be set aside for diversity suppliers, just that they be given a fair chance on a level playing field. Once you have a baseline for how much you've spent with diverse suppliers in a year, it's much easier to set goals for subsequent years.

Reasons for Supplier Diversity and Inclusion

If you're not sure of the reasons that some nongovernment organizations voluntarily implement supplier diversity, here are the four primary reasons:

1. **Their organizations have a diverse customer base**—By showing support for the demographic groups of its customers, an organization hopes to strengthen its appeal to them.
2. **Their organizations serve customers that support supplier diversity and inclusion**—Companies that are committed to supplier diversity and inclusion don't just select diverse suppliers. They require their suppliers to support supplier diversity and inclusion. And, for companies in the business-to-consumer space, consumers are increasingly demanding that their sources of products and services support diversity and inclusion. A Piper Sandler survey found that Generation Z—the group of people born between 1996 and 2011—care more about social justice compared with former generations, and that racial equity is their number one social issue.[41]
3. **The government may require it**—When an organization accepts a grant or contract from the government, that organization may be required to subcontract a portion of the award to diverse suppliers.

4. **Their organizations want to demonstrate social responsibility**—Many organizations voluntarily utilize a diverse supplier base because the leadership feels that it is the right thing to do for society and the community.

Ten Supplier Diversity and Inclusion Challenges

Though supplier diversity and inclusion programs have penetrated most major corporations' procurement strategies, starting and running a supplier diversity and inclusion program has its challenges.

We share these challenges not to discourage you from pursuing supplier diversity and inclusion. We share them to ensure that you are prepared to succeed amid the potentially unexpected complexities of these types of programs. Supplier diversity and inclusion has risen dramatically in terms of importance and gotten C-level executive attention. Hopefully, this chapter in general, and these challenges, in particular, will help inspire decision makers to ensure that supplier diversity and inclusion teams are staffed with an appropriate amount of quality talent.

The following paragraphs explain ten of the common challenges of supplier diversity and inclusion programs.

Challenge 1: Deciding what types of suppliers will be considered diverse suppliers

While this may not seem complicated, it is actually important to think through the options at the very beginning. Not recognizing one supplier group as diverse suppliers while recognizing others can cause problems later. Recognizing diverse supplier groups later can negatively impact your year-over-year comparison of metrics.

Challenge 2: Tracking the use of diverse suppliers

There's an old business saying, "What gets measured gets done." To ensure and prove the actual use of diverse suppliers, you need an easy way to determine how much your organization is spending with them. There is a lot of *behind-the-scenes* work required in order to make this happen, including:

- Setting up fields in your procurement system to accommodate a supplier diversity classification
- Identifying diverse suppliers in your system and updating their profiles with the appropriate diversity classification
- Revising your supplier registration process so that the appropriate diversity classification is applied to new suppliers entered in the system
- Having your information systems specialists create custom reports based on the entries in the supplier diversity classification fields

Challenge 3: Finding qualified diverse suppliers

There are many resources for purchasing professionals to use when finding diverse suppliers, including the National Minority Supplier Diversity Council and its local affiliates, the U.S. Small Business Administration, and local government offices.

Challenge 4: Verifying that a business is truly a diverse supplier

Some organizations set aside a certain amount of business for diverse suppliers. Supplier diversity experts work to identify *pass-throughs* and *fronts*, which are businesses that represent themselves as diverse suppliers to win *set aside business* and then outsource it to nondiverse suppliers. This has led to the need to prove that a business is truly a diversity supplier. Some organizations certify suppliers' diversity status. Examples of these organizations include National Minority Supplier Development Council, Women's Business Enterprise National Council, National LGBT Chamber of Commerce, and Disability:IN, to name a few.

Challenge 5: Setting supplier diversity goals

Many purchasers feel that setting supplier diversity spend goals conflicts with their primary goals, such as reducing costs and securing the most reliable supply. After all, how can you strive to spend a certain amount of money with a certain type of supplier when there is no guarantee that those suppliers will be competitive in terms of price and/or reliability? But savings, delivery, and supplier diversity goals don't have to conflict. Having multiple types of goals motivates procurement teams to work diligently at finding highly qualified diverse suppliers and maximizing the number of bidding opportunities granted to diverse suppliers.

Challenge 6: Understanding the risks of supplier diversity programs

With supplier diversity getting executive-level attention, there is always the risk that decision makers will get overzealous and make supplier selections based primarily on the fact that a supplier is a diverse supplier at the sacrifice of cost, quality, delivery, or service. Procurement professionals must maintain common sense and an objective set of criteria in making all supplier selections.

Challenge 7: Sustaining supplier diversity momentum

According to the SBA, a third of businesses fail within their first two years, and only about half survive beyond five years.[42] Because diverse suppliers are often new and small in size, they are more susceptible to failure than larger, established businesses. Some organizations actively invest in developing their diverse suppliers through training and setting up alliances with other suppliers.

Challenge 8: Lack of support from internal customers

In our careers, we experienced situations where we had the support of our top-level management while internal customers were against the idea of selecting a minority supplier due to their own misconceptions. To overcome this challenge, we provided training to our internal customers. Once we were able to raise awareness and involve the internal customers in the RFP and supplier selection process, they became believers. These internal customers realized that we were not just blindly handing business to diverse suppliers—we were selecting qualified suppliers who just so happened to fit into a diversity category.

Challenge 9: Avoiding double counting diversity supplier spend

Let's say one of your suppliers is a small business with only 12 employees. The supplier's principal office is located in a HUBZone. That supplier is owned by a Native American. That owner is also female. And bisexual. And disabled. You spent $600,000 with that supplier last year. You are asked for a report on how much money your organization spent in each of its supplier diversity categories. Depending on how your supplier profile is set up in your procurement system, it is possible that—based on your spend with this one supplier alone—your report would show $600,000 spent with small businesses, $600,000 spent with HUBZone small businesses, $600,000 spent with minority-owned business enterprises, $600,000 spent with women-owned business enterprises, $600,000 spent with LGBT-owned business enterprises, and $600,000 spent with disability-owned business enterprises. That sounds like you spent $3.6 million when you only spent $600,000.

For various reasons, some organizations prefer not to limit a supplier to just one diversity category. Others think that evenly splitting spend among multiple categories is inappropriate. Others may or may not want to invest in technology that can create reports that can leave double-counted spend in each category, but omit redundant entries when calculating the total supplier diversity spend amount.

There's not one obvious, globally appropriate solution to this challenge. So, it is important to understand how your existing technology works and what stakeholders' preferences are for how double-counted spend should be handled.

Challenge 10: Keeping up with changes

As you'll read in the next section, a highly publicized event or flashpoint can suddenly make supplier diversity and inclusion a much higher corporate priority. Managing a supplier diversity and inclusion program requires agility. You may have to provide new types of executive-requested reports, add new categories of diverse suppliers, and/or increase diverse supplier spending, all at the drop of the proverbial hat. A supplier diversity and inclusion program is not a set-it-and-forget-it type of initiative. It is something that has to evolve over time, with the supplier diversity and inclusion team always learning emerging best practices and keeping a finger on the pulse of cultural changes in the world.

Cultural Impact on Corporate Demand for Supplier Diversity and Inclusion

Throughout recent years, there have been many cultural movements that have woken up the world—including business leaders—to the fact that inequality continues to be pervasive in the world and that oppressed population segments will fight harder than ever to achieve equality. One of these movements was that which led to the U.S. Supreme Court declaring same-sex marriage legal in all 50 states. Another was the #MeToo movement, which shocked people into an awareness of how women were mistreated in society, including in business.

While these movements are likely to have had some influence on supplier diversity and inclusion, few movements like the one we saw in 2020 had as massive an impact.

On May 25, 2020, George Floyd, an unarmed Black man, was killed by a Minneapolis, Minnesota police officer, who had pressed his knee on the neck of Floyd for approximately nine minutes. The cell phone camera footage of this event spread quickly on international television and social media and outraged many throughout the world. Extremely large protests under the mantra of "Black Lives Matter" occurred in major, as well as small, cities throughout the United States and even the rest of the world.[43]

This movement became more than a mourning of the death of one man—it became a rallying cry to end racial inequality. The message was heard loud and clear by businesses, many of whom immediately acted to make changes, including procurement changes that promised increased spending with Black-owned businesses. Within a few months, websites, search engines and apps had all seen surges in searches for Black-owned businesses.[44] Here are some examples of supplier diversity and inclusion initiatives that arose in the wake of Floyd's death.

Sephora, a large cosmetics retailer, pledged to devote at least 15 percent of its shelf space to products from Black-owned businesses. In a New York Times article, Sephora's chief merchandising officer was quoted as saying that this pledge "starts with a long-term plan diversifying our supply chain."[45]

Coca-Cola announced plans to "step up spending with Black-owned enterprises across its supply chain by at least $500 million" over five years. That pledge is more than double the Black-owned spend rate at the time of the announcement.[46]

Target committed to spend $2 billion with Black-owned businesses over a five-year period. This new spending was not only on its products for resale, but—as pointed out in a company press release—also on indirect spend categories, specifically naming marketing agencies, construction companies, and facilities maintenance.[47] In demonstrating its recognition of its diverse customer base and its customers' own support for social responsibility, the retail juggernaut also implemented a badge on its website to help its customers identify products that are procured from Black-owned brands and brands with Black founders.[48]

All of these initiatives were major news items for the companies. It had historically been rare for procurement initiatives to be the subject of major news stories, but times have changed. Culture has manifested changes in many aspects of life and business, including procurement.

A Vision for More Impactful Supplier Diversity and Inclusion in the Future

While it's likely that some organizations may push their supplier diversity and inclusion programs mainly to score public relations points, we believe that many supplier diversity and inclusion programs are created out of true good-hearted intentions—to support groups that may not have historically been treated fairly in business and still may not be getting equal treatment today. With that in mind, we think that a closer look at supplier diversity and inclusion as it is today reveals that a change in how supplier diversity and inclusion is framed could actually lead to a lot more social benefit.

Here's what we mean . . .

Let's say that your organization tracks—and tries to increase—its spend with women-owned businesses. That indicates that your organization wants to help women. But, let's say that one of its women-owned suppliers is 100% owned by one woman. Then, let's say that supplier's employees are all men. How many women is your organization helping by doing business with that supplier? One.

But, let's say that, in selecting the woman-owned supplier, your organization chose not to do business with a supplier who failed to fit into any of your supplier diversity and inclusion categories because of the demographics of its owner. However, that supplier's employee base of 100 workers consists of 65% women and it ensures that women's pay is equal to men's pay for similar jobs with similar levels of experience. Would doing business with that supplier actually be helping more women? You bet it would! Interesting, huh?

Supplier diversity and inclusion to this point has focused solely on the demographics of the suppliers' owners and not their employees. Naturally, there are more employees than owners in a supply chain. That means there are many members of disadvantaged groups that procurement organizations can help, if only they sought to identify where those people worked. Are you starting to see how supplier diversity and inclusion could have a much larger social impact if we weren't myopically focusing on who owns the businesses from whom we procure goods and services?

What would it take to start driving additional criteria for deciding who qualifies as a diverse supplier? At least these things:

- Suppliers who are willing and able to track and share employee demographics
- RFP questions
- Technology-supported employee base analysis
- Third-party verification
- Periodic supplier employee demographic updates
- Audits

Companies today tout the amount of money they spend with diverse suppliers. Imagine them also bragging in the future about how many equally paid women or minorities or disabled veterans they have in their supply chain.

Proliferating this new way of thinking about diversity and inclusion in the supply chain is not something that can happen overnight. But we feel strongly that these ideas represent a very logical evolution of supplier diversity and inclusion. Getting a change like this to take hold will require leadership by example. As we've shared earlier in this chapter, organizations that have made bold moves in supplier diversity and inclusion were later followed by others, eventually causing their pioneering approaches to become industry standard.

All it takes is one influential leader to get the ball rolling. Who will it be?

CLOSING REMARKS

Today's procurement professionals need to focus on managing, monitoring, and improving the ethical, social, and environmental policies and practices of their organization as well as their suppliers. The reality is that fundamental changes are occurring in the world economy that are forcing nearly every company to reassess their practices and relationships with suppliers in the local and global supply chain.

The content of this chapter was designed to provide insights about how procurement professionals, their team members, and their suppliers are obligated to a higher standard of ethical and socially responsible behavior. We also provided some tips and techniques to raise awareness and to help readers to expand and improve their social responsibility practices.

REFERENCES

1. Fahy, Joe. November 12, 2007. "UPMC Tightening Policy on Drug-maker Relationships." *Pittsburgh Post Gazette*. Available from http://www.post-gazette.com/pg/07234/811154-53.stm.

2. Rotstein, Gary. August 22, 2007. "Mayor Defends His Golf Outing." *Pittsburgh Post-Gazette.* Available from http://www.post-gazette.com/pg/07234/811154-53.stm.

3. Snell, Paul. July 6, 2006. "Top U.S. Government Purchaser Guilty of 'Lying.'" *Supplymanagement.com.* Available from http://www.supply management.com/news/2006/top-us-government-purchaser-guilty-of -lying/.

4. National Labor Committee. "Children Found Sewing Clothing for Walmart, Hanes & Other U.S. & European Companies." Harvard Law School. Available from http://www.law.harvard.edu/programs/lwp/NLC _childlabor.html.

5. Bhatnagar, Parija. October 21, 2003. "Pamela Anderson Takes on KFC." *Money.cnn.* Available from http://money.cnn.com/2003/10/17/news/ companies/pamela_kfc/index.htm.

6. Russel, Chris. July 2, 2020. "Nike, FedEx and PepsiCo Challenged to Divorce Redskins." *Sports Illustrated.* Available from https://www.si.com/ nfl/washingtonfootball/news/nike-fedex-and-pepsico-challenged -to-divorce-redskins.

7. Clarke, Liz. July 10, 2020. "In Private Letter to Redskins, FedEx Said It Will Remove Signage if Name Isn't Changed." *The Washington Post.* Available from https://www.washingtonpost.com/sports/2020/07/10/private -letter-redskins-fedex-said-it-will-remove-signage-if-name-isnt-changed/.

8. "Five Reasons Climate Change is the Greatest Existential Threat of Our Time." October 5, 2018. *The Elders.* Available from https://theelders.org/ news/five-reasons-climate-change-greatest-existential-threat-our-time.

9. Choe, K.H. et.al. May 15, 2004. "Properties of Rigid Polyurethane Foams with Blowing Agents and Catalysts." *Polymer Journal.* Available from https://www.nature.com/articles/pj200451.pdf?origin=ppub.

10. Osmanski, Stephanie. March 30, 2020. "How Do Carbon Emissions Affect the Environment." *Greenmatters.* Available from https://www.green matters.com/p/how-do-carbon-emissions-affect-environment.

11. "What Is the Difference Between Global Warming and Climate Change?" *United States Geological Survey.* Available from https://www.usgs.gov/ faqs/what-difference-between-global-warming-and-climate-change-1?qt -news_science_products=0#qt-news_science_products.

12. Denchak, Melissa. March 15, 2016. "Are the Effects of Global Warming Really that Bad?" *Natural Resources Defense Council.* Available from https:// www.nrdc.org/stories/are-effects-global-warming-really-bad.

13. "Climate Solutions." *Union of Concerned Scientists.* Available from https:// www.ucsusa.org/climate/solutions.

14. "The Climate Pledge: Quick Overview." *The Climate Pledge*.
15. Bové, Anne-Titia and Steven Swartz. November 11, 2016. "Starting at the Source: Sustainability in Supply Chains." *McKinsey & Company*. Available from https://www.mckinsey.com/business-functions/sustainability/our-insights/starting-at-the-source-sustainability-in-supply-chains.
16. "Supply Chain Guidance: Information for Organizations Interested in Reducing Their Supply Chain Omissions." *United States Environmental Protection Agency*. Available from https://www.epa.gov/climateleadership/supply-chain-guidance.
17. Derouin, Sarah. November 6, 2019. "Deforestation: Facts, Causes & Effects." *Live Science*. Available from https://www.livescience.com/27692-deforestation.html.
18. "What Is Energy?" May 7, 2021. *U.S. Energy Information Administration*. Available from https://www.eia.gov/energyexplained/what-is-energy/sources-of-energy.php.
19. Kammeyer, Cora. February 15, 2018. "Water Stewardship in Supply Chains: The Missing Piece?" *CEO Water Mandate*. Available from https://ceowatermandate.org/posts/water-stewardship-supply-chains-missing-piece/.
20. "Why Conserve Water If It's Renewable?" January 13, 2019. *Get Green Now*. Available from https://get-green-now.com/why-conserve-water-if-its-renewable-all-about-the-water-cycle/.
21. Potter, Pauline. "Starting Your Sustainable Procurement Journey: Establishing KPIs." *Efficio*.
22. Nachtigal, Jeff. October 19, 2006. "It's Easy and Cheap Being Green." *Money.cnn*. Available from http://money.cnn.com/magazines/fortune/fortune_archive/2006/10/16/8390307/index.htm.
23. Rackspace Green Survey. June 30, 2008. "Fewer Willing to Pay Premium for Green." Available from http://www.environmentalleader.com/2008/06/30/fewer-willing-to-pay-premium-for-green/.
24. Dyer, Ervin and Robert Dvorchak. January 23, 2007. "Black Leaders Hailing Steelers' Pick of Tomlin." *Pittsburgh Post-Gazette*. Available from http://www.post-gazette.com/pg/07023/755981-66.stm.
25. "Mike Tomlin Biography." *Pittsburgh Steelers*. Available from https://www.steelers.com/team/coaches-roster/mike-tomlin.
26. Patra, Kevin. May 18, 2020. "NFL Instituting Changes to Rooney Rule." *National Football League*. Available from https://www.nfl.com/news/nfl-instituting-changes-to-rooney-rule.
27. Brassil, Gillian R. November 28, 2020. "Sarah Fuller, with a Kickoff, Is the First Woman to Play Football in a Power 5 Game." *The New York Times*. Available from https://www.nytimes.com/2020/11/28/sports/sarah-fuller-woman-kicker-vanderbilt.html.

28. Novak, Analisa. February 10, 2021. "Sarah Thomas on 'Falling in Love' with Officiating Football and Being First Woman to Referee a Super Bowl." *CBS News.* Available from https://www.cbsnews.com/news/sarah-thomas-nfl-super-bowl-history/.
29. http://searchitchannel.techtarget.com/definition/Small-Disadvantaged-Business.
30. https://www.sba.gov/about-sba/organization.
31. "8(a) Business Development (BD) Program Suitability Tool Statements." *U.S. Small Business Administration.* Available from https://web.sba.gov/sbtn/sbat/8aAssessmentTool.html.
32. "8(a) Business Development Program." *U.S. Small Business Administration.* Available from https://www.sba.gov/federal-contracting/contracting-assistance-programs/8a-business-development-program#section-header-2.
33. "Table of Small Business Size Standards Matched to North American Industry Classification System Codes." *U.S. Small Business Administration.* Available from https://www.sba.gov/sites/default/files/2019-08/SBA%20Table%20of%20Size%20Standards_Effective%20Aug%2019%2C%202019_Rev.pdf.
34. "The Veteran First Verification Program." *U.S. Department of Veteran Affairs.* Available from https://www.va.gov/OSDBU/docs/preparing-for-verification.pdf.
35. "Office of Government Contracting & Business Development | Resources." January 12, 2005. *U.S. Small Business Administration.* Available from https://www.sba.gov/offices/headquarters/ogc_and_bd/resources/5526.
36. "Title 38, Chapter I, Part 4." *Electronic Code of Federal Regulations.* Available from https://www.ecfr.gov/cgi-bin/text-idx?rgn=div5;node=38:1.0.1.1.5#se38.1.4_129.
37. "HUBZone Program." *U.S. Small Business Administration.* Available from https://www.sba.gov/federal-contracting/contracting-assistance-programs/hubzone-program#section-header-5.
38. "Agency Contracting Goals." *U.S. Small Business Administration.* Available from https://www.sba.gov/partners/contracting-officials/small-business-procurement.
39. "Categories and Certifications." *UPS.* Available from https://www.ups.com/us/en/about/supplier-diversity/categories-and-certifications.page.
40. "Supplier Inclusion." *Walmart.* Available from https://corporate.walmart.com/suppliers/supplier-inclusion.

41. "Piper Sandler Completes 41st Semi-Annual Generation Z Survey of 7,000 U.S. Teens." April 7, 2021. *Piper Sandler.* Available from https://www.pipersandler.com/3col.aspx?id=130&releaseid=19011&title=Piper+Sandler+Completes+41st+Semi-Annual+Generation+Z+Survey+of+7%2c000+U.S.+Teens.

42. "Do Economic or Industry Factors Affect Business Survival?" June 2012. SBA Office of Advocacy Small Business Facts. Available from https://www.sba.gov/sites/default/files/Business-Survival.pdf.

43. Forliti, Amy. March 4, 2021. "Prosecutors: Officer Was on Floyd's Neck for About 9 Minutes." *Associated Press.* Available from https://apnews.com/article/trials-derek-chauvin-minneapolis-racial-injustice-060f6e9e8b7079505a1b096a68311c2b.

44. Miller, Kaitlin. August 9, 2020. "Black-Owned Businesses See Wave of Support but Still Face Barriers, According to Survey." *The Active Times.* Available from https://www.theactivetimes.com/black-owned-businesses-black-business-month.

45. Maheshwari, Sapna. June 10, 2020. "Sephora Signs '15 Percent Pledge' to Carry More Black-Owned Brands." *The New York Times.* Available from https://www.nytimes.com/2020/06/10/business/sephora-black-owned-brands.html.

46. "Coca-Cola Commits $500 Million in Additional Spending with Black-Owned Suppliers." October 20, 2020. *The Coca-Cola Company.* Available from https://www.coca-colacompany.com/news/coca-cola-accelerates-commitment-to-black-owned-businesses.

47. "Target Commits to Spending More Than $2 Billion with Black-Owned Businesses by 2025." April 7, 2021. *Target News Release.* Available from https://corporate.target.com/press/releases/2021/04/Target-Commits-to-Spending-More-Than-2-Billion-wit.

48. Hall, Chelsea. July 16, 2020. "Target Just Made It Easier to Support Black-Owned Brands Online." *Marie Claire.* Available from https://www.marieclaire.com/beauty/a33338661/target-black-owned-business-badge/.

5
CHAPTER

GETTING CHEAP SHOTS OUT OF THE GAME: PREVENTING AND MANAGING BACK-DOOR SELLING

In sports, there are rules. Those rules are designed to ensure that the truly best team wins. If everyone follows the rules, the proper result occurs when the game is over.

However, we all know that the rules are bent in almost every game—some more than others. And, the most vicious violations of the rules come in the form of *cheap shots*: when a player breaks a rule without a referee seeing it, hurts his or her opponent, and changes the competitive balance of the game from that point forward.

Rules and cheap shots are part of procurement, too. One *rule* is that all qualifying purchases must be made only after a strategic sourcing process is conducted. One type of cheap shot is back-door selling: something that salespeople do to subvert procurement rules, get information and/or commitment from unsuspecting stakeholders, and influence the buying organization to award an order without conducting strategic sourcing.

A recent situation inflamed the authors' passion for this subject and inspired this chapter. The year prior to our writing this edition, Soheila was invited to join the Board of a nonprofit organization as it began its new fiscal year. The first meeting of the fiscal year started with current and new members, including Soheila, introducing themselves, their professional background, hobbies, and interests. When it came time for a Board member who used to hold a high-level position in sales to introduce himself, he indicated how much he enjoyed sales. He went on self-proclaiming how successful he was in his role and proudly indicated, with a grin on his face, that he usually went straight to the stakeholders or end users, bypassing procurement. Funny or not; it felt like a cheap shot to Soheila!

This fellow Board member's claim reminds us of one of the exploitation tactics, *back-door selling*, that some sales forces employ to undermine procurement's leverage during negotiations and the sourcing process. Back-door selling practices, aggregated over all purchases, can have a significant negative impact on both cost reduction efforts and the bottom-line profitability of an organization. Unfortunately, many employees within various organizations have little or no idea that they are involved in back-door selling conversations and prenegotiation sessions.

WHAT IS BACK-DOOR SELLING?

Back-door selling is an attempt to entice end users and stakeholders to purchase goods or services without competitive bidding. It occurs when sales personnel deliberately bypass the procurement department to obtain information they would otherwise not expect to receive. Information is power, and controlling the information flow is critical in gaining and maintaining power in negotiations. Essentially, sales personnel use the back-door approach in order to obtain information that competitors do not have and gather sensitive information about the customer's organization. Purposefully, sales personnel target stakeholders at all levels to build relationships designed to undermine procurement's efforts to maintain a level playing field for suppliers. This selling technique uses well-crafted and innocent-sounding questions tailored toward key and important people within a company. Line managers, HR personnel, information systems staff, engineers, scientists, warehouse workers, and others can fall prey to the perceived innocently asked questions by suppliers. In the sales community, these stakeholders have been labeled *Chumpions* (a hybrid of *champions* and *chumps*).[1] Once the seller has built a relationship with key stakeholders and gained their trust, procurement's role becomes much more difficult during the formal negotiations. Even more devastating, many sales personnel pursue senior-level management relationships that can be used to control the pace and outcome of negotiations through decisions made by individuals not within procurement or the formal negotiating team.

WHY BACK-DOOR SELLING?

Sales employees deploy back-door selling techniques for several reasons:

- To obtain valuable information from stakeholders or end users within an organization that can be later used to strengthen their sales position
- To close deals before they can be negotiated
- To direct the buying organization to a single- or sole-source strategy
- To bring division between procurement and technical people (the *divide-and-conquer* approach)
- To create fear of change among end users—they try to convince the end users that if they make a change, they may experience delays or have to deal with inferior products or services

BACK-DOOR SELLING QUESTIONS

The phrase "the early bird gets the worm" applies very well to sales. The sooner that a salesperson can start a relationship and gather information from a prospective client, the more likely they feel they are to get a deal. Having certain information early can help a sales organization plan its strategy in a way that discourages prospective clients from selecting—or even considering—other suppliers. Here are some questions that a salesperson engaging in back-door selling will ask stakeholders as early as they can in order to have an advantage over their competition:

- Are you able to select a supplier based on best fit, or do you have to get multiple bids?
- (If the customer states they have to get multiple bids) What other suppliers might be asked to respond to a request for proposal (RFP)?
- What is your budget?
- Do you need help with writing specifications?
- If your resources are limited, our technical people or engineers will be available to help with drawings—would that be helpful?
- How does our product compare to the competition?
- How does the quality of our product compare to the others?
- What aspects do you like most regarding your present supplier?
- When do you need this product or service?
- When is your deadline for making a supplier decision?
- Does procurement have veto power, or does your department or another division make the decision?
- What other departments (e.g., IT, HR, or Engineering) will be signing off on this agreement?
- Is our pricing in the ballpark?
- What have you been offered in terms of services?
- What payment terms are others offering?
- Who are the end users?
- Is a site visit or a plant tour possible?

Sales personnel deliberately and skillfully ask these questions directly to the end users or to the person who makes the final decision. Often and intentionally, they bypass the procurement function to obtain information they would otherwise not expect to receive in order to influence the buying process and improve their negotiating position. Exhibit C provides an example of a back-door selling conversation between a salesperson and an end user.

It is very possible that internal users are not aware of back-door selling tactics. They are trying to be helpful and are innocently answering questions. It is important for your end users to question whether or not they actually need to provide answers to salespersons' questions. Or whether, by answering them, they might be doing more harm than good.

HOW TO RESPOND TO BACK-DOOR SELLING QUESTIONS

While back-door selling efforts are often directed at unsuspecting nonprocurement employees, new procurement professionals can also be caught off guard if not properly prepared. Procurement professionals and stakeholders should be trained to recognize back-door selling questions and the fact that there is no need to answer these questions in many cases. The following paragraph contains some tips on how to respond to back-door selling questions.

When faced with certain questions, one should stress the fact that it is against company policy to share proprietary and confidential information with suppliers. In addition, sales representatives should be told when their questions are not relevant. When appropriate, they should be told that it is unethical for your organization to share information about the incumbent supplier with others. Remind them that they need to focus on their organization's capabilities and offerings and on providing you with their most aggressively competitive proposal. Turn the table on them by asking your own questions. Your questions should mainly be focused on their expertise, product performance, company's stability, customers, and best practices. Ask about new technologies and innovative processes and approaches they have offered to other customers. Find out what novel practices other customers of theirs have implemented that your organization has not adopted yet, and how they may be able to help so that you can achieve similar results. When the buying organization takes the lead in the conversation, it will discourage salespeople from back-door selling.

IS BACK-DOOR SELLING LEGAL?

Back-door buying and selling is an unethical means to skip the bidding process and can result in a veritable *under-the-table agreement* that works against the best interest of the buying organization. Due to various country laws and cultural differences, back-door selling tactics are perceived and treated differently. However, in some cases in the United States—particularly involving doing business with government agencies—back-door selling could end up being considered illegal if the deal that gets cut undermines the competitive factor that brings about the best price, the best quality, and the best service.

HOW DO YOU DETECT BACK-DOOR SELLING?

When a salesperson is more interested in learning about competitors and their offerings as opposed to focusing the conversation on their own capabilities, that should be a signal that they are trained in back-door selling tactics. Another signal is when the seller seeks a meeting with stakeholders without the knowledge of procurement professionals. When you see a supplier's representative in your facility without your prior knowledge of their visit, their presence should alarm you to the fact that they are searching for information or seeking to influence a noncompetitively bid deal. Controlling the unannounced visits of sales personnel is considerably more difficult in schools, colleges, and hospitals than it is in an industry with reception lobbies where visitors cannot get past that area without clearance.

Another possible scenario is when you see the sales representative (e.g., from a telecom supplier) having lunch with employees from your IT department at a nearby restaurant. Obviously, you know what is happening at this so-called quick lunch meeting. Back-door selling questions are being asked and valuable company information is, perhaps innocently, being shared.

The most dreaded scenario is when an end user hands you a contract and wants you to finalize it. That indicates meetings have occurred and agreements have been made without procurement department involvement. It is obvious that selling has already taken place and what the end user is looking for is a quick, rubber-stamped approval.

CAN YOU NEGOTIATE AFTER BACK-DOOR SELLING?

Negotiating with a supplier who believes he has already won your company's business is one of the toughest situations you will encounter. To combat back-door selling, applying the following techniques will help shift control of the negotiation back in your favor:

- **Use Benchmark Data for Improving Your Negotiation Position**—If your company has purchased the same item(s) in the past, use last price paid, your average historical cost, or other data to justify your demands for a lower overall cost of the deal. Where available, use benchmark cost data published by periodicals and industry trade groups, or recent quotes from other suppliers. Also, using the Producer Price Index[2] in conjunction with historical price information, even if it is dated, can help you to determine if the supplier is charging you a competitive price.
- **Involve End Users in the Negotiation Process**—Meet with the end users and advise them that their involvement with the supplier has weakened your negotiation position. If their action has resulted in a supplier violating

your organization's policy, they need to know that the supplier may be banned from doing business with your organization. When appropriate, it is important for them to realize that their order may be in jeopardy. Once stakeholders understand the issues, let them know that you will take the lead during the negotiations while they need to be present and supportive. This can be the most appropriate and fastest way to address the problem. They need to be reminded that suppliers' negotiating strength stems from their relationship with end users. Including them in the negotiation sessions reduces supplier leverage.

- **Seek Added-Value Services**—In addition to seeking a price reduction, skillful procurement professionals look for improving other aspects of doing business with a supplier. Asking for an improved and extended warranty, technical training for end users at no cost, and dedicated personnel for six months or more to take care of administrative work due to the changeover to a new supplier are some of the examples of positively impacting total cost of ownership for your organization. By negotiating extended payment terms or an early payment discount, you will be able to improve your organization's cash flow. Extending discounts to employees for personal purchases (e.g., office supplies, computers, cell phones, etc.) can be an added value to your employees, making your organization one of the *best places to work*. Depending on how deep the back-door selling went before you got involved, it may not be possible for you to negotiate a much lower price—especially if the supplier has been given by stakeholders an indication of a high degree of certainty of getting the deal and you are under a difficult deadline. But, by exploring various ideas, you still stand a good chance of bringing additional value to your organization and, at the same time, becoming a hero in the eyes of your organization's employees. Be creative!
- **Use the *Carrot-and-Stick* Motivation Tactic**—Remind the supplier that improving the terms of their contract and providing additional cost reductions will help them with extended or future contracts. This will be the *carrot* dangling in front of them for a positive outcome. Conversely, remind them that bypassing procurement and an unwillingness to provide added benefits can jeopardize future business with your company. This will be the *stick*, and a negative consequence for making a deal with an end user without the knowledge of procurement.

HOW TO PREVENT BACK-DOOR SELLING

If your organization's procurement department has not been radically overhauled during the past 15 years, then chances are that a large portion of your supply base has been exploiting your organization's weaknesses for years. Without the preventive measures and skills to tackle suppliers' back-door selling tactics, they will continue taking advantage of you.

So, how can procurement executives and professionals avert the damaging effects of back-door selling? Here are some tips for proactively stopping the leakage of vital information:

- **Secure support from the executive team**—It is essential that your senior management understands the ramifications of back-door selling and is supportive of putting an end to this unethical practice. Proactively reach out to your senior management and raise awareness.

- **Include prohibition of back-door selling in your supplier code of conduct and your procurement policies**—Hopefully, your company has developed and documented procurement policies. Back-door selling needs to be defined and included in those policies as well as your supplier code of conduct. Furthermore, procurement policies should be tied into your corporate ethics policy. A sample procurement ethics policy that is simple and effective can be found in Exhibit D in the back of this book.

- **Educate and train stakeholders (prevent *chumpions*)**—Often stakeholders and requisitioners don't realize that by answering suppliers' questions they are weakening their organization's negotiating position. Every conversation with a supplier, no matter how innocent or *technical* it might appear, is part of the negotiation process. Having routine meetings, at least biannually, with your stakeholders to discuss various topics, including back-door selling and its harm to the bottom-line profitability of your organization, should be one of your goals.

- **Raise awareness**—In addition to routinely meeting with end users, utilize other avenues such as publishing newsletters and short articles on your company intranet site for raising awareness and education.

- **Speaking with one voice**—*Speaking with one voice* means ensuring that suppliers receive a consistent message about which information is available and unavailable from anyone in the organization, whether it is an end user, a procurement professional or even the CEO. Promoting speaking with one voice across your organization will send a strong message to your suppliers. It will start from the top and continue all the way down to the administrative and support staff.

- **Optimize your sourcing process**—Implement a clear cross-functional sourcing process with well-defined roles and responsibilities for each team member. There should be a designated contact person from your sourcing team who receives any and all questions from the suppliers. Your stakeholders and requisitioners should know who this person is and direct suppliers' questions to him or her.

- **Communicate**—Your procurement ethics and back-door selling policy should be shared with the supplier community. The consequences of back-door selling need to be communicated clearly. The following paragraph is an example of a communique that can be included in the RFP or in communications with your incumbent supplier.

> *Suppliers are asked to direct all inquiries through the corporate sourcing groups and to avoid using any* back-door selling *techniques through other organizations (e.g., Engineering, HR, Information Systems, Manufacturing, etc.). Back-door selling can result in disqualification from award scenarios or elimination from our supplier base.*

Well-seasoned sales employees have been trained to skillfully bypass procurement, get past gatekeepers to C-level executives, and go straight to end users. As a procurement professional, it is your responsibility to educate, train, and obtain buy-in from everyone in the organization to discourage and stop suppliers from back-door selling. You don't put procurement policies and rules in place just to complicate things. Employees at all levels need to understand that your goal is to get the most value for the organization's money, and that efforts like competitive bidding requirements and being fair and ethical to all suppliers are designed to make achieving that goal more likely. When employees realize that cutting back-door deals damage their organization's competitive position and negatively impacts the bottom line, it will become easier to obtain their cooperation. Proactively preventing and addressing back-door selling will be much more effective financially and will create less aggravation for procurement professionals.

CLOSING REMARKS

If you successfully prevent back-door selling, you can play the procurement game by the rules and do what you're supposed to do: *conduct strategic sourcing!*

REFERENCES

1. Shanto, Tibor. July 5, 2008. "Selling to Procurement." *TiborShanto.com.* Available from https://www.tiborshanto.com/selling-to-procurement/.
2. "Producer Price Index." *U.S. Bureau of Labor Statistics.* Available from https://www.bls.gov/news.release/ppi.toc.htm.

6

CHAPTER

STRATEGIC SOURCING FOR MORE EFFECTIVE PROCUREMENT: MARCHING TOWARD THE GOAL LINE

Cost savings is the most common procurement goal, and strategic sourcing is arguably the most comprehensive method for achieving savings. Just as the American football field has the 50, 40, 30, 20, and 10 yard lines for a runner to cover on the way to the end zone, strategic sourcing has a similar step-by-step path toward the goal. In this chapter we will cover the basics of strategic sourcing.

WHAT STRATEGIC SOURCING IS

Strategic sourcing is generally defined as a rigorous process of identifying the *right* supplier. Not necessarily the *cheapest* or *highest quality* supplier, but the supplier that offers the greatest overall net benefit to the organization, all things considered.

Because strategic sourcing typically culminates in a contract with a term of at least three to five years, and sometimes longer, strategic sourcing should be perceived as the first step in a long-term relationship. By consummating this relationship in the form of a contract with a supplier, strategic sourcing aims to reduce the cost of doing business. A reduced cost of doing business includes not just a lower price, but also other efficiencies that will positively impact the organization's bottom line.

REASONS FOR ADOPTING STRATEGIC SOURCING

Companies generally like strategic sourcing for three reasons:

1. Strategic sourcing is based on repeatable best practices. Instead of each department trying to figure out how to go about conducting competitive

bidding for its own categories, strategic sourcing is a formalized process with a defined sequence of steps that have taken into consideration the most effective methods of competitive bidding. This maximizes both the efficiency and the effectiveness of the sourcing process.

2. Strategic sourcing is led by experts in the sourcing process. There are many challenges to strategic sourcing. Many mistakes can be made if the process is managed by someone without deep experience. When the strategic sourcing process is led by someone who has experienced all of the veritable land mines of sourcing, the quality of the results is much better.

3. Most important, strategic sourcing has proven to be effective at reducing costs. Cost reductions of 20 percent or more in a category of goods or services are common.

OVERVIEW OF THE STRATEGIC SOURCING PROCESS

The strategic sourcing concept was promoted early on by the Harvard Business School.[1] At that time, consulting firms packaged the concept as a seven-phase process. Shortly after, variations of the same phases evolved in different consulting firms. Regardless of which version, the *strategic sourcing process* is a collaborative and organized process that promotes cross-functional teams for unified decision making with the guidance and leadership of executive level (C-level) supply chain or procurement. A four-phase practical approach to the strategic sourcing process is highlighted in Figure 6.1 and described in the following paragraphs.

Phase 1: Organize Sourcing Team

The first phase of the process starts with a diagnostic of the company's overall spending, the broad defining and profiling of the various spend categories that comprise that spending, and the selection of a particular spend category for strategic sourcing. At a high level, there should be a good understanding of the spend and usage level at all operating units and locations; existing supplier relationships; and costs associated with logistics, quality, environmental effects, and other factors. This type of knowledge will be helpful for deciding on a category and selecting team members for sourcing that category. Later in this chapter we will discuss indicators of the appropriateness of strategic sourcing for various categories and suggestions for sourcing multiple categories in a logical sequence.

Let's consider an example of a procurement organization that selects for strategic sourcing the category of laboratory equipment and supplies. Once this category has been selected, a sourcing team will be recruited. Later in this chapter we will focus on who should be on the team and the value each member brings to the team.

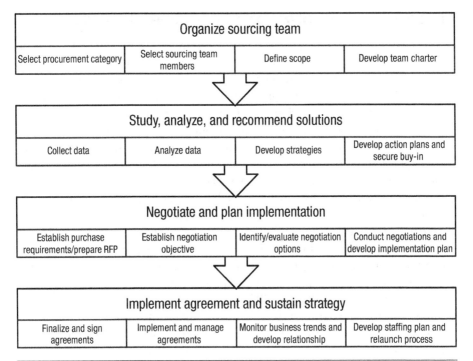

Figure 6.1   Four-phase practical approach to the strategic sourcing process

The focus of other steps in the first phase is on defining the scope and developing a team charter. Referring back to the example of laboratory equipment and supplies, the sourcing team may, as part of its scope, decide to focus on addressing supplies first and then going after laboratory equipment second if there are no common suppliers between the two subcategories. It may decide that all resulting contracts should apply to all of the company's worldwide locations. It may decide that the scope should encompass 100% of products and services purchased in those categories. Or, it may decide to focus more narrowly. The important points of scope development are that the team knows precisely what is going to be included in the strategic process and what is not, and that the decisions were arrived at logically and with the team's consensus.

Once the scope is agreed upon, the team should develop a written charter, comprised of the sourcing project's overall objectives, scope, resources, risks, and constraints. A charter is often the document that formalizes management's authorization of a sourcing project. The charter holds the team—including leadership—accountable to all of the same principles. It highlights roles and responsibilities in a clear and measurable way. It defines operations including communication, ways to adapt to change, securing stakeholders' buy-in, and addressing roadblocks.

Phase 2: Study, Analyze, and Recommend Solutions

In this phase, team members focus on gathering more specific internal and external information and data. Internal critical data include current pricing paid by the organization, incumbent suppliers, volume, specifications, technical support, quality, delivery, and service requirements throughout the organization, including all operating units and various locations. External data, such as market intelligence, are obtained to provide information about prices in the broader market, plus information on available suppliers and their offerings and capabilities. In addition, other supply market research involves determining whether the market is a global, regional, national, or a local market. External data, such as information about new technologies, best practices, environmental awareness, social responsibility, and regulatory trends, should also be gathered in this phase.

A detailed spend analysis of the selected spend category or categories should be done, not just to allow the sourcing team to have an expert level of knowledge about the organization's buying patterns, but also to enable the sourcing team to present the size of potential business to suppliers who will be participating in the bid process. Having reliable data will assist the team in creating a competitive environment in the supplier marketplace. It will demonstrate the *size of the prize* that can be won to motivate potential suppliers, and it communicates the seriousness of the outcome of the strategic sourcing initiative to the incumbent supplier.

A word of caution is to avoid spending months and months on data gathering and analysis when doing so appears to offer diminishing returns. In other words, we recommend staying away from over-analyzing or *analysis paralysis*! Once the sourcing team has gathered ample information and has conducted a thorough analysis, it should move on to developing sourcing strategies based on their findings. Those strategies relate to how proposals will be requested and evaluated, the role of negotiation in the process, and more of the techniques we cover later in this book.

Another important step in this phase is developing action plans as to who is going to do what, and by when. Frequently communicating with end users and stakeholders is essential. By sharing the team's findings with stakeholders, soliciting their ideas at this early stage, and securing their buy-in, team members will avoid rework and headaches down the road.

Phase 3: Negotiate and Plan Implementation

In this phase, team members prepare a request for proposal (RFP), analyze responses, and narrow down the number of potential suppliers for negotiation. How to prepare robust RFPs and how to avoid poorly written documents will be thoroughly discussed in Chapter 7. The next steps in this phase are devoted to establishing negotiation objectives, evaluating different options, and preparing for win-win negotiation outcomes. Since effectively negotiating is a core competency of procurement and supply management professionals, we have dedicated Chapters 8 and 9 to that topic.

Phase 4: Implement Agreement and Sustain Strategy

Once negotiations are complete, commercial and legal terms are finalized, and a contract is executed, the focus turns to transitioning to the new supplier, or transitioning to a new business relationship with a retained incumbent. When introducing a new supplier with advanced technology or modern processes, we recommend a testing period or a *pilot program* with a couple of operational units or sites. This provides an opportunity to involve stakeholders or end users and to address problems while increasing the success of implementation and ramp-up at the organization level. The pilot program should not only involve the purchased product or service, but also the administrative, operational, logistical, systems, quality, environmental, and regulatory requirements that are important to the buying organization or the customer.

Once the sourcing team's strategy has been successfully implemented with the help of end users and stakeholders, it is essential to continuously benchmark— monitoring business trends and changes in the supply market. Monitoring supplier key performance metrics and receiving timely updates regarding new products, new technologies, and general market knowledge can enable the sourcing team to continuously improve processes, practices, and the bottom-line profitability of their organization.

Because strategic sourcing is an ongoing process and not a project or a one-time event, the sourcing team members' subsequent step is focusing their efforts and attention on the next subset of spend within the category, if applicable. Going back to the example of laboratory equipment and supplies, after completing the implementation of a strategy for laboratory supplies, the team needs to focus on using the same principles of the four phases of the strategic sourcing process for optimizing the procurement practices and processes of laboratory equipment buys.

COMPOSITION OF A SOURCING TEAM

The size and composition of a sourcing team will vary from company to company, and from procurement category to procurement category within the same company. However, these five roles are typically included in each sourcing team: procurement specialist, technical specialist or subject matter expert (SME), financial analyst, end user, and executive overseer/sponsor. We will list the characteristics of each of these roles in the following sections.

Procurement Specialist

The procurement specialist is typically the leader of the sourcing team and is a specialist in the sourcing process, as he or she has usually conducted many sourcing initiatives over his or her career.

The procurement specialist drives criteria for supplier selection, making sure that the team knows what combination of characteristics would make the *right* supplier. The procurement specialist is keenly focused on the goals of process. A procurement specialist's performance is usually judged on the team's performance *vis-à-vis* their goals (e.g., cost savings).

One characteristic of the procurement specialist, which some find peculiar, is that he or she may have just finished sourcing an unrelated category. Today, the procurement specialist may be starting a sourcing initiative as a member of fleet management services sourcing team. Last week, they may have just finished a sourcing initiative for telecommunications equipment. Several months ago, that same procurement specialist may have wrapped up a sourcing initiative for enterprise-wide office furniture. So, while the procurement specialist is an expert in the sourcing process, he or she is a generalist in the technical aspects of each category who is serving on various cross-functional strategic sourcing teams.

Technical Specialist or Subject Matter Expert

The technical specialist or SME is the person in the organization who knows the product or service best and is usually responsible for writing the specifications for that particular product or service. The technical specialist or SME can have a variety of titles such as engineer, fleet manager, director of telecommunications, and such.

Financial Analyst

The financial analyst calculates the bottom-line impact of the options available to the sourcing team to ensure that the savings estimates are credible and that the profitability of the company will be maximized. The role of the financial analyst becomes more important in complex purchases, such as those involving payments over time that must be converted to present value, lease-versus-buy decisions, or where other financial factors, like depreciation rates, must be considered.

End User

The end user is the person who works most closely with the purchased product or service. The end user can have a variety of roles, from a salesperson who drives a company car, to the janitor who uses the trash bags purchased by the organization.

All end users want a problem-free, day-to-day experience where the purchased product or service allows them to do their job in the most hassle-free manner.

Executive Overseers/Sponsors

For large, enterprise-wide contracts, establishing a formal or informal executive oversight committee that consists of high-ranking executives from key business units is highly recommended, with one executive taking the lead in interfacing with the sourcing team. The executive overseer/sponsor will not be doing sourcing work. His or her role is to be briefed throughout the process. More important, the sponsor will remove organizational barriers and set high-level strategic direction for the sourcing teams.

The executive overseer will be keenly interested in ensuring that there is transparency in the sourcing process. Former procurement critics among the oversight committee will likely be delighted to learn that the sourcing process is being conducted fairly and with the broader interests of the organization in mind.

STRATEGIC SOURCING DECISION MAKING

While the decision maker varies from company to company, most often the ultimate decision maker is the vice president of procurement or the vice president of supply chain. While these executives are not actually a part of the sourcing team itself, they are well aware of the work of the team and consider the sourcing team's recommendations in making final decisions.

HOW STRATEGIC SOURCING IS IMPLEMENTED

Every procurement organization should have a long-term plan for its strategic sourcing work. We suggest a three-stage strategic sourcing plan.

Stage 1: *The Easy Wins*

When launching a new process, starting with little risk and gradually accepting more risk is wise. So, begin your strategic sourcing initiative with a category where success is easier to achieve.

Office, shop, and janitorial supplies are often the first *easy wins* pursued. These types of items are considered indirect materials because they are not incorporated into the product or service that the organization sells to its customers. Why pursue these types of categories first? Well, in these industries, there are many good suppliers who compete very hard against each other. In many cases, any major supplier can perform, and the price wars you might incite can produce nice savings.

Demonstrating that good performance and sizable savings can be achieved through strategic sourcing is vital. When a strategic sourcing initiative is announced, your internal customers aren't exactly celebrating by throwing confetti and hugging each other in the hallways—they are skeptical. Good results in Stage 1 will help your cause.

Stage 2: *Wheelhouse Categories*

Even the greatest home run hitters in baseball hit plenty of singles, ground outs, and fly outs. Why? Because of the pitches they get. Some pitches are inside, outside, low, high, etc. But when they get a pitch in their preferred part of the strike zone— their *wheelhouse*—they often can send that pitch 450 feet over the outfield wall! They've encountered a pitch with that certain placement before and they know exactly what to do in order to leverage their physical and mental strength to get the optimal result.

In terms of procurement, an organization's *wheelhouse categories* can be thought of as the purchased products and services that are close to the core of what the organization is in business to do. So, after the strategic sourcing concept is proven in Stage 1, organizations tend to address their wheelhouse categories. In manufacturing, the wheelhouse categories include raw materials and subcontracted services. These are also referred to as *direct materials and services* because they are incorporated directly into the product or service that the organization is selling to its customers.

Wheelhouse categories are where big money is spent and where big money can be saved. But there is also more risk, so you must perfect strategic sourcing before you tackle your organization's core competency.

Stage 3: *Nontraditional Categories*

After a purchasing department gets through Stage 2, and saves the company a significant amount of money, does the staff just sit back and revel in their success? Of course not! They now seek other opportunities to use sourcing to save money.

Stage 3 involves addressing categories that have been traditionally managed outside of procurement. Some examples of these areas include health benefits, advertising, travel, contingent labor, and fleet services. Identifying these areas and learning to work with your new internal customers is a challenge all to itself.

A well-planned strategic sourcing initiative for a particular procurement category consists of a well-defined implementation plan. Through this plan, the role of team members, stakeholders, and the supplier team is well-defined and communicated.

DETERMINING STRATEGIC SOURCING PRIORITIES

The category selection criteria for addressing a *nontraditional category* are slightly different than the criteria used for the other stages, so we can save the nontraditional category for later and focus mainly on how to prioritize categories within the *easy wins* and *wheelhouse category* stages.

So, how do you determine which categories are the priorities for strategic sourcing? The quick answer to this question is *spend analysis*. Simplified, spend analysis is the systematic review of historical purchase data. The output of a spend analysis is a summary of purchases by a range of variables such as category, supplier, and/or business unit.

The primary reason for conducting a spend analysis is to identify opportunities for cost savings. When you look at the output of a spend analysis, there are at least four indicators that point toward opportunities for cost savings. They are described in the following sections.

Indicator 1: A Large Amount of Spend in Categories with No Contract

Today's educated procurement professionals can apply best practices (e.g., strategic sourcing) so that their companies minimize cost. However, when best practices have not been utilized in a category, or purchase decisions are left up to nonprocurement professionals, there is a likelihood that the company is overpaying for goods and services. Identifying areas where procurement should be more involved in getting contracts for those categories is a sound strategy for cost savings.

Indicator 2: A Significant Purchase Price Variance

Purchase price variance (PPV) is the difference between the average price paid and a standard cost. Standard cost is an accounting term that estimates the amount of money, on average, it would cost to make/perform or buy a product or service. A standard cost can be based on thorough research of materials costs, labor costs, and overhead rates; previously paid prices; or other data considered.

A large PPV indicates one of two things: either your standard cost is not valid or you are paying too much. In the latter case, you should consider taking some type of action, such as sourcing or negotiation, to ensure that you are paying a fair price.

Indicator 3: An Unusually Large Number of Suppliers

Procurement 101: the more you buy from a single supplier, the better discount you will qualify for. If you are buying from too many suppliers, you are not leveraging your volume or maximizing your discounts. Seeing a large number of suppliers in a category can tip you off that supplier consolidation can deliver savings to your organization through price reduction and through the more advanced benefits of an optimized supply base.

Indicator 4: Rising Prices over Time

If you're paying more to a supplier year after year, you simply need to pay more attention to the purchases in that category. With no one *minding the store*, price creep can easily set in. During inflationary times, we frequently get questions on how to deal with industry-wide price increases due to buying in an inflationary market.

Our view is that procurement should always challenge price hikes through sourcing and/or negotiation, except when doing so will increase the risk to the continuity of supply. Also, procurement professionals need to have good forecasting skills to estimate where prices are going.

If increases are expected to continue, locking in a long-term deal at today's prices is a good idea. However, if the procurement professional feels that prices are peaking, the last thing one would want to do is lock in a long-term deal at today's price. When prices peak and subsequently decline, the strategy of only committing to a quantity required in the near future (also called *hand-to-mouth buying*) works best until the prices bottom out, at which time a long-term deal makes sense.

TARGETING NONTRADITIONAL CATEGORIES

There are generally five characteristics of a nontraditional category, each of which indicates that the category is ripe for strategic sourcing:

1. **The spend is significant**—Whenever a lot of money is spent in a category of goods or services, there is likely an opportunity to save through strategic sourcing. In most companies, a spend of over $1 million (US) is considered significant.

2. **Annual price increases are the norm**—While many individuals accept annual price increases as *normal inflation*, procurement departments like to contain costs, if not consistently reduce them year-over-year. Observing years of unchallenged price increases is a *red flag* that money can be saved through strategic sourcing.

3. **Existing supplier was selected by a nonprocurement professional**— Once again, a core aspect of strategic sourcing is that it utilizes best practices developed over years of experience. If the existing supplier was selected by someone without the consultation of a procurement professional, there is a likelihood that procurement best practices were not

followed and, therefore, there is *money on the table* (i.e., the potential for a better deal to be made).

4. **Professional negotiator not involved**—Experience in negotiation is critical to minimizing costs. However, for many purchases in nontraditional categories, the negotiation of the agreement is handled by someone who negotiates infrequently. For example, health care benefit packages had been commonly negotiated by a senior-level representative of human resources. Because this person's job does not typically involve supplier negotiations, they generally have less than optimum proficiency with negotiation. Because a procurement department is staffed with a team of individuals who negotiate, sometimes daily, procurement professionals can often get better results.

5. **Perception that a *relationship* influenced supplier selection**—Today's procurement professionals are educated as to proper ethics with regard to supplier relationships. This knowledge of ethics often does not filter down through an entire organization. So, while many procurement professionals feel that accepting gifts, lunches, sporting tickets, golf invitations, and the like creates a real or perceived conflict of interest, the nontraditional area decision makers often accept these *perks*, not realizing that they may impair their ability to make unbiased decisions that are solely in the best interests of the employer. Therefore, the procurement department may choose to intervene in these situations to apply a degree of objectivity to the supplier selection process.

MEASURING STRATEGIC SOURCING SUCCESS

In business, one of the most important statistics is net income. Simplified, net income is the numerical difference between sales and expenses. By reducing expenses, strategic sourcing increases net income.

While reducing the price of goods or services is an important way of improving net income, it is not the only way. Selecting a supplier with improved performance can reduce the cost of poor performance, which includes costs that are incurred when the company's resources must be used to deal with the effects of things like late supplier deliveries, poor supplier quality, and unacceptable service.

Therefore, strategic sourcing success is not always measured by cost savings. It can be measured by the value of solving a costly supply problem. It can be measured by the value of improving performance in the supply chain. It can even be measured by revenue growth where procurement decisions positively impact the organization's ability to produce more goods, perform more services, develop an advantage over competitors, or influence a shift in customer behavior.

STRATEGIC SOURCING SURPRISES FOR SUBJECT MATTER EXPERTS

One thing that procurement specialists insist on is that specifications support a level playing field, where they are written so that no supplier is unfairly disadvantaged by the requirements. Procurement specialists also watch that there is no *over-specification*, where the organization is asking for more than it actually needs (e.g., specifying penthouse suites for the travel accommodations of the company's service technicians when a junior suite—or even a standard hotel room—would be more prudent, appropriate, and in-line with industry standards).

Procurement specialists also encourage standardization. Through the basic laws of economies of scale, the more one buys of one particular item, the lower the unit price. Therefore, if an organization buys a quantity of 100 of each of three different variations of an item, it will pay lower unit prices than if it purchased a quantity of 50 of six different variations. As such, procurement specialists will encourage technical specialists or SMEs to employ as much standardization as is practical when developing the specifications.

STRATEGIC SOURCING SURPRISES FOR SUPPLIERS

Because procurement specialists work in various industries rather than just one, they identify cross-industry best practices and often introduce those best practices to new industries. This manifests itself in the form of requirements that are new to the suppliers in less progressive industries. These suppliers often resist these new requirements using the mantra, "We don't do that in our industry!" Procurement specialists generally don't care, and proceed. That's how industries evolve. So, what are some of these requirements? They include:

- Signing bonuses
- Training at no cost
- More buyer-friendly payment terms
- Tiered volume rebates
- Delivery, quality, and service guarantees where, if the supplier fails, they have to pay liquidated damages to the buying organization

PROPOSAL EVALUATION METHODS

Though proposal evaluation processes vary from organization to organization, there is usually a two-step process involved. First, the sourcing team will identify any proposals that do not conform to the requirements set forth in the RFP. Many times, the suppliers submitting nonconforming proposals will be disqualified from further consideration. Examples of nonconformances may include refusal to offer a signing bonus and unsolicited substitutions.

All conforming proposals are then compared, and one of the following supplier selection methods is used to determine the successful bidder:

- Low bid
- Total cost of ownership analysis
- Weighted scorecard

PITFALLS OF STRATEGIC SOURCING

Often, the members of a sourcing team do not operate in harmony. Procurement specialists tend to perceive that technical specialists and end users have a narrow view of the process, and are more concerned with changes related to their work and relationships with incumbent suppliers than the profitability and success of the organization overall. However, this can often be the lack of top-level management's support or the fault of procurement departments and their personnel who fail to educate others about the process and apply good change management principles to their work.

When there is a lack of harmony among the sourcing team members, ethical issues often arise. Technical specialists may meet with suppliers against the wishes of the sourcing team and the potential for the disclosure of confidential information (i.e., content of competing suppliers' proposals) is increased. Where there is such a breach of confidence, it is common for a participant to be removed from the team.

World-class procurement organizations, however, provide training for their strategic sourcing team members before they start the sourcing process. During training sessions, the importance of working together and *speaking with one voice* is stressed. Team members become familiar with different phases of the strategic sourcing process and often their sponsor highlights the consequences of undermining the work of the team. Team members are held accountable for their actions and the results of their work. It should also be noted that in these organizations, team members are recognized and financially rewarded when they finalize their work and deliver significant cost reductions.

CHANGE MANAGEMENT FOR SUBJECT MATTER EXPERTS

When asked for advice to give to SMEs who are being introduced to strategic sourcing, we have several points for you to consider.

First, have an open mind. Have you ever heard of the phrase, "I'd rather deal with the devil I know, than the devil I don't?" This is like saying, "Yes, I know we have problems with this supplier. But if we get another supplier, it may be worse!" That is the wrong attitude to have. In business today, companies need to focus on continuous improvement.

Second, speak in the language of the sourcing team. Talk about supplier performance in measurable events. Quantify the impact of those events, and use dollars (or whatever currency your organization uses). For example, instead of saying, "You have no idea what a headache it is for me when a supplier delivers late," say, "When a supplier delivers late, we have to acquire a substitute at a cost of $300. Plus, the process to implement the back-up plan costs us three hours of productivity at $40 per hour." Regardless of the currency, *money talk* always gets attention.

Finally, talk about the *big picture*, not inconvenience to you. Things that everyone in the company should relate to are:

- Profitability
- Costs saved
- Costs incurred
- The effect on your company's customers
- Productivity

THE FUTURE OF STRATEGIC SOURCING

How will strategic sourcing change in the future? We are going to separate a response to this question into two categories: (1) sourcing initiatives that only affect a single internal customer group within a company and (2) enterprise-wide sourcing initiatives. First, let's talk about sourcing initiatives that only affect one internal customer group. As pointed out earlier, sourcing initiatives usually address three stages in a certain order: the easy wins, wheelhouse categories, and nontraditional categories. Because most large companies have gotten through the first two stages, we'll talk about Stage 3: nontraditional categories. These areas of spend are categories that have been traditionally managed outside of procurement. Some examples of these areas include health benefits, advertising, travel, and fleet services.

Sourcing Maturity Model for Nontraditional Categories

We foresee major changes in how nontraditional categories will be handled in the future. Specifically, we see a migration across a sourcing maturity model, meaning that sourcing of the categories will be handled differently and will require different skills. The four steps of the model are illustrated in Figure 6.2 and described in the following list.

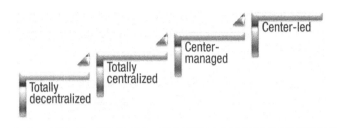

Figure 6.2   Strategic sourcing maturity model

- **Totally decentralized**—The sourcing process and decisions are handled entirely within the internal customer group (customer) and procurement is not involved at all. The work distribution is: customer = 100 percent, procurement = 0 percent.
- **Totally centralized**—The sourcing process is executed by procurement with the internal customer group represented on a sourcing team. These internal customer group representatives usually have the opportunity to participate in the decisions, but procurement usually has ownership of the decision-making process. The work distribution is: customer = 10 percent, procurement = 90 percent.
- **Center-managed**—Procurement will manage the process, still doing a lot of the work, but delegating some responsibilities to the internal customer group. The work distribution is: customer = 25 percent, procurement = 75 percent.
- **Center-led**—Procurement is responsible for leading strategic sourcing efforts, negotiating, and executing company-wide contracts. The internal customer group will handle most of the sourcing execution work using templates, processes, and technologies provided by procurement. There will be a few checkpoints for procurement to step in and review progress, provide guidance, and perform some specialized duties. The work distribution is: customer = 50 percent, procurement = 50 percent.

Different skills are required at each step of this sourcing maturity model.

Skills for Future Nontraditional Category Strategic Sourcing

In a totally centralized situation, procurement must have strong sourcing skills (including skills in procurement negotiation). They do the lion's share of the work. But they also must have good relationship-building skills as their entry into the category will not be well-received!

A prerequisite to moving to the next step of the maturity model is mastering— absolutely *mastering*—sourcing skills. Before any sourcing work is delegated, the delegator must have sourcing down perfectly. Procurement must be like Mr. Miyagi in the classic movie *The Karate Kid* by preparing the internal customer group for every possible situation, so that the reaction is perfectly executed and automatic. Wax on, wax off.

In the center-managed step, procurement must be very skilled at project management. Now, instead of executing the sourcing strategy, they are utilizing resources to accomplish the goal. During this stage, procurement must also utilize best practices in process improvement and process quality control skills. The next step requires even more delegation, so it is important that they have the ability to identify efficiency opportunities, variables, and ways to keep the process under control, not unlike what is done when implementing Lean Six Sigma.

By the time that the organization has reached the center-led step, the prior sourcing initiatives should have built up quite a sourcing competency within the organization. Traditional sourcing techniques are unlikely to add significantly to the bottom line. So, procurement will migrate to being a source of business intelligence for incremental impact. This can involve a variety of skills such as:

- Knowing where to find additional suppliers in previously untapped parts of the world
- Identifying alternative materials and processes to take cost out of the purchased product or service
- Understanding economic and geopolitical situations to identify opportunities for global source development, not just source selection
- Knowing the cost drivers and how to reduce the associated costs through advanced sourcing techniques
- Identifying opportunities to address social responsibility concerns

However, all of these new skill requirements do not mean that the procurement professional should ignore traditional skills. These are, and will continue to be, valuable. For example, while an eSourcing solution will certainly eliminate the need for some negotiations, some of the more involved sourcing projects will necessitate the need for personal negotiation. Of course, we would always feel comfortable having our negotiator be someone who is seasoned in the art of negotiation, rather than someone who hasn't negotiated since three years ago when the contract was last renewed.

There is a danger in progressing down the maturity model. If progression is done too fast, a company could jeopardize its competitive position for years. It is absolutely key that the procurement team masters the sourcing skills before moving from the totally centralized step. There is always a desire for speed and progress, but we believe that the *quality* of the sourcing process must be the priority. Quality is contingent upon having the skills for success in these areas already:

- Procurement fundamentals
- Analysis and spreadsheets

- Contract law
- Project management
- Procurement best practices
- Sourcing
- Negotiation
- Leadership
- International business
- Financial acumen
- Supplier relationship management

Now let's talk about the future changes we expect to see in enterprise-wide sourcing initiatives.

Strategic Sourcing Simulations

Strategic sourcing has shown signs of maturity. Best practices have been implemented and stabilized at the Fortune 100 companies. The rest of the procurement world has been catching up.

As indicated, today's strategic sourcing decisions are made by senior procurement or supply chain management executives based on the recommendations of strategic sourcing teams. The more complex strategic sourcing decisions usually involve a total cost of ownership (TCO) analysis or, at least, a multiple-selection-criteria analysis using a weighted average supplier scorecard. It is not uncommon for this analysis to be done within the context of an eSourcing solution.

Thus, project management and analysis and spreadsheet skills are indispensable skills for successful sourcing today.

Both TCO and supplier scorecard analysis methods take into consideration the differences in cost, quality, delivery, and service of the competing suppliers. They work well to position today's strategic sourcing on somewhat of a plateau. We also believe that the sourcing world is ready to go to the next level. In the not-too-distant future, we will look back at today's supplier selection methodology and consider it archaic.

The purpose of putting together a TCO analysis or a weighted average supplier scorecard is to give some acknowledgment of the potential impact of differences in suppliers on the buying organization. Anyone who has ever negotiated selection criteria or relative weights with an internal customer or commodity team knows that each team member's own personal speculation of the results greatly impacts the internal negotiation.

In the future, we foresee speculative *bickering* to be replaced by the widespread watching of artificial intelligence-driven simulations of various scenarios associated with the various supplier selection opportunities. The sourcing team will see the risks and the impact on the buying organization if those risks come to fruition. These simulations will be delivered through technologies that factor in all of the variables associated with a supplier selection: supply chain logistics, material availability, supplier financial health, competition in the marketplace, and such. The simulations will show the impact and probabilities of potential scenarios for almost every situation imaginable, large or small, such as:

- Materials getting caught in a customs delay
- A supplier having a major quality issue
- A supplier declaring bankruptcy
- Chronic billing errors
- Erratic lead times
- Weather-related natural disasters
- Every situation you can imagine

The newer simulations will give the entire sourcing team a more comprehensive, tangible understanding of the factors that should influence the decision.

So, does that mean procurement professionals will need fewer skills in the future? Not at all! The implication for procurement professionals is that they have to be *smarter* than the simulators. Look, you could have a computer choose your suppliers for you and just quit your job, but, in jobs where levels of uncertainty are high, a human has to make the decisions.

To be *smarter* than the simulation means understanding what factors the simulation considers and then knowing how to evaluate those factors to arrive at the optimal decision. What new and different *additional* skills will simulations require of procurement professionals? Here are a few:

- Skills in quantitative analysis, with an understanding of statistical probabilities, decision trees, and the like
- Knowledge of macro- and microeconomics
- The analytical ability to quantify the total cost and value of the supplier relationship, not just the TCO of a product
- Skills in developing creative risk-mitigation strategies for risks that artificial intelligence can predict

Before the world gets to this new plateau of sourcing, there is still a lot of *current-style* sourcing to be done with a comprehensive blend of skills that are in demand today for the successful execution of a sourcing strategy.

ESTABLISHING STRATEGIC SOURCING RULES AND PARAMETERS

So far, we hope that this chapter has given you a good overview of what strategic sourcing is all about. Now, let's move on to some rules and parameters that should govern a sourcing process. One rule is to consider whether strategic sourcing alternatives like leasing and/or target pricing may be beneficial. Let's talk about each of those.

Leasing versus Buying

You probably buy a variety of items. If you are like most procurement professionals, you rarely consider whether or not you should lease the items rather than buy them. *Purchasing* is the function of paying for the ownership of an item, whereas *leasing* is the function of paying for the right to use an item for a finite period of time.

Leasing is not an option for many items, particularly consumables like maintenance, repair, and operating supplies. However, it can be a viable alternative when acquiring expensive assets such as vehicles, office equipment, and shop-floor machinery. When do you know if you should compare leasing versus buying options? Here are a few situations that may favor leasing:

- When there is a high likelihood that the asset will be obsolete before it is fully depreciated from an accounting standpoint.
- When the current year capital budget is not large enough to support the purchase of the asset.
- When the time period for using the asset is shorter than the asset's useful life and your organization does not want the burden of reselling the asset.
- When purchasing the asset would require extensive record keeping and asset management and your organization does not have sufficient record keeping or asset management resources.
- When your organization needs to demonstrate a stronger financial position to its customers, prospects, potential and current investors, creditors, and others. Unlike leasing, financing a purchase shows debt on the balance sheet. Too much debt is unattractive to the aforementioned constituencies.

If the acquisition meets one of these criteria, your organization can accept restrictions on how the asset can be used, and the present value of total lease costs is not substantially higher than the present value of total purchase costs, leasing may be the better alternative. You owe it to your organization to consider the option. We highly recommend that you work with your counterparts in the treasury and accounting departments to decide between buying or leasing options.

Target Pricing

Based on the recommendations of the financial experts in your company, if you choose to buy rather than lease, you can accept proposals from suppliers to determine prices or you can use target pricing. Target pricing has both supporters and opponents among procurement experts. With target pricing, it is neither right nor wrong to provide target pricing to suppliers, you just need to do so in the right context. Target pricing works well when:

- You are buying a custom product that is manufactured to your specifications
- The material costs and labor hours can be clearly identified
- The primary materials are not commonly subject to volatile commodity pricing fluctuations
- The buying organization understands the costs
- Labor represents a significant enough portion of total cost so that the buyer can factor in aggressive productivity improvements in the target price

Let us elaborate on the last two points. In many cases, procurement professionals purchase a variety of items, but can't be technical experts in every category. Those procurement professionals need to get quotes from suppliers to know what their price will be. In these cases, target pricing should not be used.

When procurement professionals have expertise in a category, they know what the costs will be prior to getting quotes. So, they can set a target price for their suppliers rather than the supplier telling them what the price will be.

Of course, procurement professionals want a low price. The key to getting one is factoring in labor productivity improvements for the supplier. Let's look at some numbers. Assume that material costs $400 per unit, labor hours required per unit are eight, labor typically costs $50 per hour, overhead in the industry is typically 10 percent of material and labor, and profit is typically 10 percent of material and labor. Doing the math, the price would be $960. The supplier sees this as $880 cost, $80 profit.

You want the supplier to take advantage of the learning curve—the more you do something, the faster you'll do it. So, assuming that by the end of production, you expect the supplier's labor hours to decrease to six hours per unit. Starting at eight hours and ending at six hours will give you an average of seven hours of labor per unit. If you base labor costs on seven hours instead of eight, the price will be $900.

With a target price of $900, you will likely get pushback from suppliers claiming that there is barely any profit since their costs are $880. There is a reason that target pricing is controversial: suppliers think that it is about setting prices so that they can't make a profit. But when you communicate that (a) you expect productivity improvements from your supplier; (b) their profit margin still represents 10 percent of materials and labor (or whatever is typical for the industry); and (c) if they beat the productivity targets, they increase their profit margin, then target pricing is perceived as much more reasonable. So, use target pricing in the right context. Otherwise (e.g., for a volatile commodity), it will fail and fuel the controversy.

OVERCOMING INTERNAL CUSTOMER RESISTANCE

As you read in the last section, managing supplier expectations is important. But those aren't the only expectations you have to manage when you implement strategic sourcing. Consider this statement from an internal customer: "You can sign a contract with whomever you want. But our division won't use your supplier!"

Have you ever heard this type of statement? Many procurement leaders have. Their work is a struggle. As a reaction to resistance, many procurement leaders seek ways to force business units to support their supplier selections, but the best practice for reducing maverick spending is proactively preventing resistance.

Involving Stakeholders

How do you prevent resistance to strategic sourcing initiatives? You have to involve your stakeholders, and their involvement can't be superficial—they must have input into key decisions throughout the sourcing process.

To implement this best practice, plan on having stakeholders participate in discussions during which each of the following 10 questions are answered within the sourcing process:

1. What are our specifications?
2. What are our supplier performance requirements?
3. What suppliers are we going to invite to bid?
4. How are suppliers differentiated, and what is the measurable value of the differences between them?
5. What criteria are we going to use to evaluate proposals and suppliers?
6. What are the relative weightings of those criteria?
7. What hidden and tangential costs might we face that could distort our TCO calculation?
8. What costs of poor performance might we incur?
9. Who makes the final supplier selection decision?
10. What is the process for dealing with poor performance from the selected supplier?

Stakeholder suggestions may not always match the final decisions. These decisions will require collaborative internal negotiation. However, using this best practice will help you avoid hearing the claim of, "We did not know procurement was working on this category," or the threat of, "We will not use that supplier."

Using Psychology

If you are not sure whether involving stakeholders in developing the answers to the preceding 10 questions will work, then think for a moment about psychology. Think of a decision that you made that was later criticized. How did you feel about that criticism? In most cases, people feel defensive when their decisions are criticized.

Even if they agree that the outcome did not turn out well, they are more likely to try to justify and defend a decision rather than just say, "You're right. I have no idea what I was thinking. I made a bad decision." This is human. So, what does this have to do with stakeholder resistance to strategic sourcing initiatives? Plenty.

Involving your stakeholders in answering those 10 questions will help them feel ownership of the outcome. In addition to soliciting answers to those questions, best-in-class procurement organizations invite their stakeholders to become members of different sourcing teams. By involving stakeholders in the sourcing process, they become your best resources for implementing new contracts or solutions. Instead of the strategic sourcing process being *your* initiative that you impose on them, they will feel as if it is *their* initiative, so, they will put more effort into making it work.

They don't want to fail. If *their* decisions are criticized, they will follow the typical human pattern and try to defend them.

The bottom line is that you will know that you've successfully integrated stakeholders into the process when they stop referring to things like *your supplier* or *your project*, and start using ownership terms like *our supplier* and *our project*.

IT IS NOT ALL ABOUT PRICE

One internal customer perception that you will have to battle is their feeling that procurement work is *all about price*. Actually, this is a perception in the supplier community, too.

We recently had the enriching opportunity of speaking to a group of sales professionals. We asked them to tell us about the experiences they've had with procurement groups that have frustrated them the most. We got some interesting responses!

One phrase that was repeated often was, "It's all about price!" These sellers felt that many procurement professionals do not seek the supplier that will best serve their organization, but instead always seek the cheapest supplier. We assured them that this was not the case in most progressive procurement departments. However, that is not to say that their perspective did not have merit—it does.

We summed up why they had the experiences that they had in this statement: "It all comes down to what can be quantified in financial terms. When price is the only thing that appears to be quantifiable then, yes, it does all come down to price. However, when paying a higher price can yield a quantifiable return (e.g., minimizations of other costs), a well-trained procurement professional will make the decision that has the most favorable net impact on the bottom line."

There are many other aspects of doing business that affect the bottom line. Are you considering them? If not, consider evaluating how these costs differ among competing suppliers of a product or service:

- The cost of acquisition, which always includes the price and may include the *cost of a purchase order*, as described in Chapter 14

- The cost of using that product or service
- The cost of supporting that product or service
- The cost of maintaining that product or service
- The cost of disposing of that product or service
- The cost of poor performance
- The cost of logistics

Based on our experience, typically, the cost of acquisition is 25–40% of total cost. The other costs represent the remaining 60–75% of costs associated with acquiring that product or service.

We've mentioned TCO a few times in this book so far, but had not yet told you how to calculate it—this is a good spot to do so. In order to calculate TCO, add the extended price (i.e., price multiplied by quantity) to the sum of the foregoing costs minus the salvage value, quantifiable value-added services (e.g., extended warranty at no additional cost), and rebates as shown in Figure 6.3. When comparing offerings from two or more suppliers, you'll need to perform separate TCO calculations for each supplier.

As you have learned throughout this chapter, there are a lot of interested parties who want to make sure that your supplier selection is done correctly—and we didn't even mention management! This brings us back to a topic that we discussed

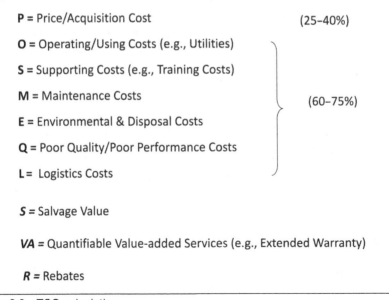

Total Cost of Ownership = P + (O+S+M+E+Q+L) – *S* – *VA* – *R*

P = Price/Acquisition Cost   (25–40%)

O = Operating/Using Costs (e.g., Utilities)

S = Supporting Costs (e.g., Training Costs)

M = Maintenance Costs   (60–75%)

E = Environmental & Disposal Costs

Q = Poor Quality/Poor Performance Costs

L = Logistics Costs

S = Salvage Value

VA = Quantifiable Value-added Services (e.g., Extended Warranty)

R = Rebates

Figure 6.3 TCO calculation

earlier, but can't be discussed enough—how ethics is of utmost importance in procurement.

ELEVEN SIGNS OF ETHICAL COMPETITIVE BIDDING

You need to evaluate whether your strategic sourcing process is completely ethical and if it isn't, fix it. You can conduct this evaluation by referring to the following *11 Signs of Ethical Competitive Bidding*, which you should refer to every time you solicit bids on anything:

1. Your specifications are not based upon a single supplier's capabilities.
2. You determine objective supplier selection criteria before you issue a solicitation.
3. You share the selection criteria with all bidders.
4. You set a time frame to respond that is reasonable for all capable bidders.
5. You do not accept lunches, gifts, or any other contribution from any competing supplier, as such acceptance could appear to influence your decision.
6. You answer all suppliers' questions at the same time with the same words using an email or letter with each supplier seeing all questions asked by other suppliers (but not the identity of the suppliers who asked the questions).
7. If you offer an extension of the bidding deadline to one supplier, you offer the same extension to all suppliers at the same time.
8. You refuse to give information about other suppliers' bids, including the price or percentage differential between one bidder and the lowest bidder.
9. You do not give one supplier an opportunity to negotiate without giving all more favorably ranked or lower priced suppliers an equal opportunity.
10. No member of the group who is evaluating bids is employed by, holds any position with, serves as a director of, has a financial interest in, or has a personal relationship with any bidder.
11. You stick to the rules that you set forth in your solicitation. For example, if you say no late bids will be accepted, don't accept any late bids under any circumstances.

When you are working on or leading a sourcing team, it is important to share these guidelines with all of your sourcing teammates.

CLOSING REMARKS

As more companies continue to face the challenges of today's world economy, procurement professionals continually look for effective and innovative means to reduce costs and positively impact their organizations' bottom line. Many have attempted to adopt the strategic sourcing process with the hope of delivering significant cost reductions. But what makes one sourcing initiative successful and another a disappointment?

As highlighted in this chapter, strategic sourcing is a proven best practice and a systemic process focused on getting maximum advantage of cost, process, quality, and technology by leveraging the company's buying power. It is an organized and a collaborative approach to reducing cost while maintaining or improving service and quality. In order for the strategic sourcing process to be successful, procurement professionals and their top-level management need to have a holistic approach and avoid attempting shortcuts. If you follow what we have outlined in this chapter, you will have meaningful results of which you and your team members can be proud.

REFERENCE

1. Venkatesan, Ravi. December 1992. "Strategic Sourcing: To Make or Not To Make." *Harvard Business Review*. Available from http://hbr.org/1992/11/strategic-sourcing-to-make-or-not-to-make/ar/1.

7

CHAPTER

COMPARING AND QUALIFYING SUPPLIERS: SEPARATING THE WINNERS FROM THE LOSERS

In the United States, many sports have drafts during which they select players from colleges or minor leagues. This process for the owners, coaches, and general managers is based on asking themselves, "What is the ideal type of player for our organization? How many of those types of players do we need?"

When you are ready to begin a strategic sourcing process for your first spend category—or any subsequent category, for that matter—you need to contemplate the ideal types and number of suppliers in order to have the highest probability of a mutually beneficial supplier relationship.

CONTEMPLATING THE IDEAL TYPES AND NUMBER OF SUPPLIERS

You may have heard some procurement experts say, "The key to superior supplier performance is measuring supplier performance." Let us unequivocally say that this statement is a myth.

Yes, it's true that measuring supplier performance is critical for improving supplier performance. However, the most important element in achieving superior supplier performance is sourcing and selecting the right supplier in the first place.

Predicting Supplier Performance

There is no foolproof way of selecting a supplier whose performance will never disappoint you. However, there are three questions you can ask about a supplier that will help you better predict that supplier's future performance:

1. Is this category the supplier's core competency? Some suppliers do only one thing and do it well. Others do a multitude of things, but specialize in one. That area of specialization is called a *core competency*.

As examples, an office products supplier may also provide printing services, and a computer manufacturer may also make printers, but you need to identify what the supplier's core competency is. If you purchase products or services outside of a supplier's core competency, the risk of poor performance is greater. It is impossible to overemphasize the topic of supplier core competency. In all of our years in procurement, we have seen many problems arise because of buying a category from a supplier where that category is not the supplier's core competency. When you have a good supplier, your natural instinct tells you to funnel as much business as possible to that supplier. But just because a supplier is good in one category does not guarantee that supplier's success in other categories. That is so important, let us say it again: *just because a supplier is good in one category does not guarantee that supplier's success in other categories.* They may be an *A* player in Category 1, but a *C* player in Category 2. Your organization deserves better than *C* players.

These are all mantras that you may hear from top management: *Reduce the number of suppliers. Leverage our spend. Partner with suppliers.* They are all good initiatives when applied correctly. Your job is to make sure that they are not applied incorrectly. As a procurement professional, your job is to educate others in your organization about the little nuances. Awarding noncore business to a supplier is one of those nuances that can be the difference between success and failure.

Now, having said that, we also believe in supplier development, which is working with suppliers to develop new capabilities. However, supplier development needs to be applied appropriately.

If there is a supply base with several highly capable and competitive suppliers, then we do not feel that you will get much return on your investment by developing a supplier in that marketplace. Only in those situations where there aren't many capable suppliers, or you need strategic categories custom manufactured, or you can further a supplier diversity and inclusion initiative, does supplier development give you a gain that justifies the effort.

2. Does the supplier have experience with requirements like mine? Find out if the supplier has provided products or services of similar specifications, with similar lead times, to similarly sized customers in similar industries. The more similar the supplier's successful experience is to your requirements, the more likely that the supplier will perform well for you.

3. How will my contract impact the supplier's capacity? Some procurement professionals will research the answers to Questions 1 and 2. Those are important questions, but there is still a significant probability that the supplier will fail unless you confirm the supplier's capacity. Capacity represents the available people, equipment, and/or facility space required to fulfill your orders. Just because a supplier is successful with a customer similar to your organization does not mean that they have the resources to duplicate that success simultaneously. For critical contracts, you need the supplier to thoroughly explain how they are going to allocate people, equipment, and facility space to your orders. Are those resources in use today? Will they be freed up by a project coming to completion? Will the supplier have to add resources? If not, how challenging will it be for the supplier to squeeze your requirements into the current resources' capacity? As an added measure, it is best to arrange for a site visit to find answers to these questions before granting a contract to a new supplier.

Question 3 may make you think that selecting the biggest supplier with the most available capacity is the right decision. That is not necessarily so.

Supplier Size Matters

You need a supplier who will stay in business on a long-term basis. You need a supplier whose capabilities are scalable, so that your delivery, service, or quality will not suffer if your volume increases. But you also need a supplier who values your business. When you are unhappy with the supplier or you need special assistance, you need your supplier to put forth extraordinary effort towards satisfying you.

Selecting a supplier of the *right* size—relative to your spend with them—can meet all of these needs. Generally, if your business represents less than 1 percent of a supplier's annual sales, you won't be extremely valuable to them. So, you may not get the service or attention you may need at critical moments.

Conversely, if your business represents over 15 percent of a supplier's annual sales, that supplier may be too dependent on you. Decreases in your volume could force them to lay off portions of their workforce or adversely impact their business in other ways. That would negatively impact your ability to satisfy your requirements when regular demand patterns are restored. In addition, volume spikes could clog the supplier's operations.

When comparing suppliers' proposals, note the percentage of each supplier's sales that would be comprised by your business. Assign one of three designations to your evaluation sheet to represent that percentage:

a. < 1 percent
b. 1–15 percent
c. > 15 percent

If the highest-ranking supplier is assigned either less than 1 percent or greater than 15 percent, reconsider how the supplier's size may negatively affect the performance you get out of that supplier during your relationship.

Supplier size may or may not change your decision, but it is something to consider. Personalize this process by thinking about your own attentive and inattentive suppliers. Calculate the percentage of their sales that is comprised by your spend. Then, adjust the percentage thresholds (1 percent and 15 percent) to reflect the correlation between supplier size and attentiveness in your experience.

In business, both large and small suppliers have their place. Just like on American football teams, large players and small players have their place. An offensive lineman may weigh 350 pounds and be the best at his position. A wide receiver may weigh 185 pounds and be the best at his position. They are both great football players. But you wouldn't want one doing the other player's job! The 185-pounder wouldn't be able to block blitzing 280-pound linebackers, and the 350-pounder wouldn't be able to outrun cornerbacks for a touchdown. All these skilled players are of different weights, and all contribute to the team's victory or defeat. Wrestling is another sport where a range of competitors are matched and then paired off in various weight categories to find the very best competitor at that specific weight. Here again, a single team can win as a team if enough of its various weight members are the most skilled within their weight categories.

This principle applies to suppliers—you want the right supplier in the right situation. So, let's talk about some better ways to manage suppliers of varying sizes.

Evaluating Big Suppliers

Several years ago, we prepared a series of case studies covering real-life experiences, challenges, and successes with suppliers. From those studies, we developed guidelines for considering supplier size in sourcing and supplier management decisions.

Big suppliers have advantages as well as unique supply risks. Resolving problems with a big supplier can be tough: finding someone with control over an issue is not easy, and having that person's first priority be promptly addressing the issue of one small customer like you can be even harder. Sadly, you often discover this after you're already committed to the supplier.

But you can predict the likelihood of such problems. For a strategic buy or major project, take these actions *before* taking the risk of committing to a big supplier:

- **Require a single point of contact (SPoC)**—When you request a proposal, always require suppliers to designate a SPoC, who will be responsible for addressing situations requiring interaction beyond typical day-to-day business. In addition, make sure the designated SPoC remains with your account through the life of the contract. Initially, to impress the potential customer, some suppliers designate a seasoned employee, and then they replace him or her with a less experienced employee once they seal the deal and gain the new business.
- **Interview the SPoC**—A SPoC's aptitude can reduce or fuel supply risk. Before committing to a supplier, assess the SPoC's communication skills, knowledge of various aspects of the supplier's business, and relationships

with key contacts in each area. If the SPoC seems weak in such areas, there is heightened supply risk.

- **Require an escalation plan**—As good as the SPoC may be, some purchases are just too risky and critical to wait for the SPoC to respond. So, require the supplier to provide in its proposal an escalation plan with the names and contact details of people to call if you do not get a response within a certain time frame. This plan should start with the SPoC and end with the CEO or equivalent top executive, with an appropriate number of levels in between.
- **Test the escalation plan**—Before committing, call the people in the supplier's escalation plan. Do they answer their phones? If not, leave messages requesting responses by a certain time. If they don't answer phones nor return calls, there is heightened supply risk.

While every procurement project will have some risk, these actions can help you assess the risk of selecting a big supplier and guide a proper selection.

Evaluating Small Suppliers

Now that you know there are risks associated with doing business with big suppliers, it is time to talk about doing business with small suppliers. Small suppliers have certain advantages such as fewer channels to go through to get responses and sometimes even lower cost due to less overhead. But you also need to understand that small suppliers can cause big problems when they perform poorly. Four precautions we recommend taking with a new, small supplier are:

- **Investigate the supplier's history**—We are shocked when buyers don't even do a quick Internet search on suppliers for small orders. That is inviting trouble. Beyond search engines, the Better Business Bureau (BBB) in the United States, Canada, and Mexico offers a valuable, free Internet-based service for consumers and corporate buyers to investigate supplier histories. "[The BBB can] help by collecting and reporting information on over 6.5 million businesses to help prospective buyers make informed decisions," said Warren King, President of the BBB of Western Pennsylvania. By visiting its website at www.bbb.org, you can learn if a supplier has had any reviews and/or complaints filed against it and, if so, whether they typically resolve them. It is a great way to identify a problem supplier before experiencing any problems yourself.

  We recommend that you use the BBB—or a similar resource if you work outside of the United States—to report and resolve disputes with suppliers. Doing so creates a *social history* of supplier problems, so that all buyers can benefit from others' experiences and fewer mistakes will be made.
- **Evaluate the supplier's capacity**—With small suppliers, especially one-person firms, you have to worry whether they will have too much work

to respond to you. Interview the supplier and find out their other commitments, both in progress and in the pipeline. Make them demonstrate their available capacity.

When doing business, you need fast supplier response. Before ordering, call the supplier a few times to test if the response time is adequate for *real* situations.

- **Check supplier references**—As part of the sourcing process, ask for two to three references from the supplier and give the references a call. Although they will most likely give you the names of the customers who are happy with them, during the conversation you will find out *lessons learned*, which may be helpful as you begin your relationship with the new supplier.

- **Do not pay 100 percent up front**—When capacity fills, a supplier must prioritize the customers that it will serve on time. If you're concerned about a new, small supplier's capacity filling, it is best to pay in multiple payments rather than up front, even if you will pay a bit more overall. Having to earn a payment is a strong incentive for a supplier to deliver high-priority performance.

Dual Source versus Single Source

Leasing or buying? Target pricing or no target pricing? Core competency or secondary business? Large supplier or small supplier? You might be asking, "What more presourcing decisions could there possibly be?" Well, there is one more! That decision revolves around the dual-source (managed competition) versus single-source choice.

To *dual source* means to split the business and use two preferred suppliers to provide the same product or service. To *single source*, means to use just one preferred supplier, despite there being multiple capable suppliers available.

Many procurement professionals decide to single or dual source prior to issuing a request for proposal (RFP) or tender based on certain assumptions. Common assumptions are that there is a lower cost with single sourcing due to leveraging your volume, but less risk with dual sourcing due to having a qualified supplier up and running if the other fails to perform.

Those assumptions may be right sometimes but, as a professional, you should make decisions on facts, not assumptions. To acquire facts, request three prices from your suppliers: (a) for 100 percent of your business, (b) for 70 percent of your business, and (c) for 30 percent of your business.

Upon bid receipt, compute the cost of doing business with the two qualified suppliers who bid the lowest for the 70 percent and 30 percent chunks of your business. Compare that cost with the lowest qualified single source bid. Is there a cost difference between the single and dual source options? If so, does the lower risk justify the premium?

How do you do this comparison? To do this comparison, you have to identify the total cost of all possible combinations. For example, if you had three suppliers bidding, your possible combinations would be:

- 100% to Supplier A
- 100% to Supplier B
- 100% to Supplier C
- 70% to Supplier A + 30% to Supplier B
- 70% to Supplier A + 30% to Supplier C
- 70% to Supplier B + 30% to Supplier A
- 70% to Supplier B + 30% to Supplier C
- 70% to Supplier C + 30% to Supplier A
- 70% to Supplier C + 30% to Supplier B

See Table 7.1 for a tabular representation of these options.

Table 7.1   Single versus dual sourcing scenarios

	Supplier A	Supplier B	Supplier C
Scenario 1	100%	0%	0%
Scenario 2	0%	100%	0%
Scenario 3	0%	0%	100%
Scenario 4	70%	30%	0%
Scenario 5	70%	0%	30%
Scenario 6	30%	70%	0%
Scenario 7	0%	70%	30%
Scenario 8	30%	0%	70%
Scenario 9	0%	30%	70%

The more bidders you have, the more combinations. The bottom line is to make sure you have identified all of the combinations and computed total costs for each combination. If your number of suppliers and/or distribution percentages gets bigger or more complicated, then it may be time to consider investing in sourcing optimization software, as discussed in Chapter 13.

Be aware of these caveats when tackling a dual source versus single source decision:

- Executives may resist paying a premium for goods and services. If they need to be sold on the concept, compare it to buying insurance—expending funds to protect your company from the unexpected.
- A dual source situation can have disadvantages beyond just a higher cost. Consider any potential problems from inconsistencies in quality or the extra work involved in managing two suppliers.

- For simplicity, we used price as the only decision criterion in the previous discussion. Complex supplier decisions should be made on a total cost of ownership basis, considering quality, delivery, service, and other variables.
- Keep in mind that, just because you contract with a single source, it doesn't mean that a noncontracted supplier will not be available if you need one.
- Why might one of the dual source suppliers fail? Could any reason cause both of those suppliers to fail at the same time? If so, dual sourcing may either (a) not truly reduce your risk and/or (b) work well only if you choose suppliers with materially different traits.

Being in the profession for many years, we have seen preferences for dual sourcing versus single sourcing go back and forth like a pendulum. In one of our college purchasing classes years ago, dual sourcing was introduced as a *Japanese purchasing technique* that was made to seem new and cutting edge. The constant post-award competition would keep the primary supplier on its toes and the *carrot* or hope of becoming the primary supplier (and doubling its business) would keep the secondary supplier working hard.

Then, in the late 1990s, all the talk was about doing business with a single source to leverage volume for lower cost and *partnering* with your suppliers. After Hurricane Katrina in 2005, everyone suddenly had a greater appreciation for the dual source approach. Organizations that reacted to that learning event by institutionalizing dual sourcing—particularly those that had a domestic alternative source for every critical international source—were rewarded in 2020 when the COVID-19 pandemic impacted virtually all business, but especially international business.

As we collaborated on this chapter, the dual source versus single source argument reminded Charles of a war story from years ago. We'll use *Alternate Company* as the supplier name to keep it anonymous.

Charles was working on a procurement project that represented perhaps the biggest service procurement in the history of a particular industry. He had an intense meeting at the headquarter's boardroom with the VP of Purchasing, his manager, and himself—his title was *Purchasing Representative* at the time (kind of a senior buyer).

The VP and Charles felt strongly that, due to the amount of supplier capacity that was going to be chewed up, dual sourcing sounded smart. His manager disagreed. The VP and Charles said that with two suppliers, there would be less risk. The manager became impassioned, and said, "If something went wrong, I'm sure Alternate Company would be there for us in a heartbeat!" That shut them up. She was right. So, they single sourced, and they never had to get Alternate Company to bail them out of a jam.

So, what do we recommend as far as dual sourcing versus single sourcing? We recommend evaluating each major procurement on a case-by-case basis, and then deciding what is best for that particular situation. We think it is absolutely foolish when we see dual sourcing or single sourcing—or any other rubber-stamped approach to selecting suppliers—being adopted as the *trend du jour*.

Buying from Sister Companies

Speaking of rubber-stamped approaches for selecting suppliers, one of our education/consulting clients recently sent a very interesting question to us. She asked how to handle buying products and services from *sister companies* (i.e., companies who are owned by the same parent company that owns your company). This is a great question, and one for which there is no definite answer, only opinions.

Our opinion is that you should treat your *sister* companies just like any other suppliers if dealing with low-risk categories. Where service, delivery, and quality are substantially equivalent among suppliers, you should not pay a premium to use a sister company. Your business unit's president or general manager (GM) is responsible for the profit and loss of your business unit, and doing sister companies a *favor* by purchasing from them at a premium may actually hurt the performance of your business unit's president or GM.

This topic might be worth a conversation with the president/GM to make sure you're making the right assumptions.

For high-risk categories, it's another story. Many of us have been in situations where we need a critical product or service immediately, and we can't get through to a C-level supplier decision maker to get above-and-beyond treatment. So, for high-risk categories, it may make sense to pay a premium to use a sister company because, theoretically, it would be easier to escalate requests for above-and-beyond treatment to the highest levels of decision makers.

Notice the use of the word *theoretically*. Investigate the truth of an assumption before making any critical decisions.

WRITING THE REQUEST FOR PROPOSAL

If this chapter seems like a lot to think about prior to requesting proposals, it is. The good news is that you've learned to think about these things at a time when you have the ability to apply best practices to ensure an effective result. Many procurement professionals only think of these things when it's too late—or not at all!

But it has come to the point where the excitement of a sourcing process starts—the issuance of an RFP. There are effective RFPs, and there are RFPs that leave a lot to be desired.

Critical Ingredients for an Effective RFP

A poorly written RFP can result in consequences such as proposals that are too dissimilar to fairly compare, supplier performance that fails to meet expectations, or additional fees that surprise you later. Therefore, it is important to ensure that your RFP does not omit any details. Here are the critical ingredients for an effective RFP:

- Overview of the intended purchase
- Specifications/statement of work
- Indication of whether or not deviations from the technical specifications will be considered
- Estimated quantity to be purchased
- Terms and conditions
- Selection criteria
- Summary of supplier information required
- Deadline for proposal submission and timeline for completing the RFP process
- Method of proposal submission (e.g., email, postal mail, eSourcing system, etc.)
- Response form

Some organizations like to include a disclaimer so that they don't risk being legally bound by anything stated in the RFP. Your disclaimer may address these points:

- The RFP is not an offer or a contract
- Proposals become your organization's property
- Bidders will not be compensated or reimbursed for costs incurred in preparing proposals
- Your organization is not obligated to contract for any of the products/services described in the RFP
- Your organization reserves the rights to:
  - ▫ Accept or reject any or all proposals
  - ▫ Waive any anomalies in proposals
  - ▫ Negotiate with any or all bidders
  - ▫ Modify or cancel the RFP

For most straightforward purchases, it is often advisable to minimize the variables that you have to evaluate. This means to specify certain terms rather than to ask the supplier to propose terms. So, in some cases, instead of asking suppliers for their lead times or delivery/performance dates, you specify when you need the goods to be delivered or services performed. Instead of asking suppliers to propose payment terms, you specify what payment terms their proposal should be based on.

The same approach can be applied to shipping terms, warranty terms, and more, in some situations.

Seven Common and Costly RFP Mistakes

So far, we have highlighted how to write effective RFPs in order to select the best supplier who can meet your organization's requirements and expectations. On the other hand, faultily-written RFPs with costly mistakes will fail and reflect poorly on you. Even committing just one of these mistakes could negatively affect the outcomes of your procurement efforts, costing your company both time and money. To be a valued player on your procurement team, make sure to avoid the following mistakes when preparing RFPs:

- **Mistake #1: Asking too many questions**—Some RFPs require suppliers to answer question after question, many of them not even relevant to the purchase. It is very likely that some suppliers get frustrated before getting to the end of such an RFP, thinking you will never even read their responses. Many will leave it sitting unfinished in the recycling bin. The goal of the RFP is to give yourself an adequate number of supplier options, not scare the best suppliers away. Think of what questions you really *need* to ask in the RFP and which you can ask later—because you can always ask later.
- **Mistake #2: Requiring too many variables**—An RFP asking for quotes for every variable under the sun is an RFP that is nearly impossible to complete honestly. Too many variables also make it hard to summarize and compare bids once they are received.
- **Mistake #3: Requesting too many pricing options**—This mistake is similar to requiring too many variables. Prices will fluctuate, and the best you can ask for is an honest estimate based on past experiences, market trends, and current market conditions. Asking for price points for every possible situation will drive your suppliers to madness (and unresponsiveness).
- **Mistake #4: Omitting key information**—If your RFP omits key information, you will find your team members getting multiple phone calls and emails from suppliers asking the same questions. If only you had included the essential information, you would not be wasting time responding to the same questions over and over.
- **Mistake #5: Carelessly using RFP templates**—Rather than creating an RFP, you used a template with the goal of saving time. If you failed to modify an RFP template to your situation, some parts of the RFP may simply not make sense and you may receive fewer supplier responses. This can result in insufficient competition, higher costs, and suboptimal supplier performance.

- **Mistake #6: Carelessly cutting and pasting RFP language**—Dr. Frankenstein created his monster out of various, random parts that were lying around. And it didn't turn out well! Most RFPs that are created that way don't turn out well, either, mostly because the author uses what he or she has and doesn't rewrite the various sections to unify them. Cutting and pasting previously-used RFP sections can save time, but sometimes you need to massage the contents to make them all work in one seamless document. The quality of the RFP that you send to the bidders dictates the quality of the responses that you will receive. You get what you give!
- **Mistake #7: Forgetting about the people**—As much as the RFP process is about experience, pricing, and ideas, it is also about forging relationships between the buying and selling organizations that bring energy, productivity, creativity, and prosperity to both parties. If the RFP process allows zero opportunity to assess the human side of things, then it is doomed to be less productive with corresponding results.

Set Your RFP Writing Standards High

RFPs are among the most important documents that you compose. When writing RFPs, do the necessary preparatory work to think through the strategic sourcing process and resulting supplier performance from beginning to end. Make it your aim to avoid leaving out any details that will cause consequences later. Hold yourself to high standards to make sure that your RFP exudes professionalism and represents the type of quality for which your organization desires to be known.

How many times have you issued an RFP that indicated the dates by which you would begin negotiations, execute the contract, begin receiving the goods/services, as such, and you failed to meet those dates? It happens all the time, unfortunately. Yet everyone in procurement expects suppliers to never miss a deadline. Even though the consequences for failing to meet RFP dates are minimal, you know in your heart that failing to meet the dates is symptomatic of too little research, poor planning and/or inefficient processes.

CREATING A STANDARDIZED RESPONSE FORM

In the typical sourcing process, one task that is often unnecessarily time consuming is summarizing proposals so that they are in an easily comparable format. This task is made difficult by the fact that all bidders' proposals look different, may have fine print hidden in four-inch, densely packed binders, and do not make it equally clear what is included in or excluded from their pricing.

Efficiency in Analysis

Including a standardized response form (e.g., in Excel format) in your RFP can help make the summarization task easier for you. Responses should be sent to you electronically to further simplify the summarization and data analysis tasks. If you are not sure what elements comprise the pricing, you can send out a request for information (RFI) in advance of launching the RFP.

The RFI should contain this requirement: *In some industries, it is common to quote pricing as a series of separately priced line items. Please submit a list of all of the typical price components that contribute to your total price. For example, hardware, software, implementation services, training, and maintenance.*

Considering the bidders' responses will enable you to create a single page RFP response form that summarizes all of the cost information that you need to review. Always include a field for *Other Costs* with a requirement that such costs be explained. In Chapter 9, you will learn another reason why it is important to have costs broken down into components on the response form.

Identifying Hidden Fees

By including a well-developed response form in your RFP, which is distributed electronically, you will be able to quickly analyze supplier responses (electronically forwarded to you) without scouring dozens of pages of fine print and worrying that you'll learn too late that the low bidder was not actually the low bidder because of a detail that you missed. And, you just may be able to adhere to the dates that you specify in your RFP. Hidden fees abound, so you have to work hard specifically to flush them out. What situations may prompt your suppliers to invoice you for an amount different from what they proposed?

A few years ago, both corporate buyers and consumers alike found themselves in fights over *fuel surcharges* that raised the prices they had been paying for on-site services. A rapid, nationwide rise in gasoline prices had service providers resorting to what some may consider *dirty tricks* in protecting their profits by adding fees to their invoices that were not previously disclosed.

While state governments reacted with laws against such fees, legislating against hidden fees has been like playing Whack-A-Mole: as soon as a law seems to address one type of sneaky fee, another is created. The communications, travel, and financial industries all have various line items that comprise their total price. It is imperative to know all possible components of the prices you will pay from all suppliers before completing any analysis to compare and select a supplier.

Consumers and businesses base purchase decisions on the price information at hand. Finding out later that you chose the wrong store or supplier because it charges hidden fees is an unfair situation.

One of our biggest frustrations in the early part of our purchasing careers was dealing with those *over-and-above charges* that somehow never were mentioned in a response to an RFP, but seemed to show up in an invoice as if they were quite expected and common. We learned to minimize these occurrences through RFP language, negotiation questions, and contracts.

In one crazy situation, when Charles was buying aircraft component maintenance outsourcing services, there was an unbelievable amount of discussion between him and a prospective supplier over the contractual definition of *severe damage*. Basically, if a component qualified as having *severe damage*, the supplier had the right to charge more than its contractually agreed fixed cost for the repair to that component. Well, obviously, Charles' company wanted the frequency of a severe damage diagnosis to be rare. The supplier wanted it to be applicable on seemingly every occasion.

They decided to do a pilot program with the supplier, which effectively exposed the differences in opinion on what *severe damage* was. They ended up actually choosing another supplier after it became clear that the first supplier had its eyes on frequent *over-and-above charges*. The contractual relationship with the second supplier went great; perfect quality, 100-percent on-time delivery, and no over-and-above charges.

In a similar situation, Soheila discovered that one of her clients was paying setup charges each time they had a printing job with their existing supplier. By reviewing the contract, it became evident that setup charges were a hidden cost that had not been negotiated or mentioned in the contract. With Soheila's facilitation, her client was able to renegotiate and eliminate this hidden cost.

We are glad that, in many circumstances, governments are coming to the aid of consumers to protect them from over-and-above charges or hidden costs. But for procurement professionals—you are on your own to a certain extent. You have to be smart about really capturing total cost when you get proposals from suppliers. A *No Fuel Surcharge* or similar clause in your RFP templates and contract templates may not be a bad idea.

ANALYZING PROPOSALS

As if identifying *true* supplier pricing isn't difficult enough, it can get even more complex when price is just one factor being evaluated for supplier selection. When there are multiple criteria for supplier selection, procurement professionals often rely on supplier scorecards as a guide.

Supplier scorecards include scores for all of the supplier selection criteria (e.g., cost and value, quality and safety, delivery, etc.) that the sourcing team has decided to apply to a particular procurement. Typically, each criterion is scored on a scale of 0 to 100, with 0 being the worst rating and 100 being the best. This rating is called a *raw score*. Suppliers' scores for each criterion are based on predetermined point award schemes.

For example, one criterion may be *delivery* with a maximum of 100 points. The sourcing team may award 100 points if the supplier's lead time is one week or less, 50 points if the supplier's lead time is between one and two weeks, and 0 points if the supplier's lead time is two weeks or more.

As you learned in Chapter 2 in the discussion of the *Hierarchy of Constraints and Criteria*, in most sourcing situations, the importance of each supplier selection criterion is not equal. Therefore, scores must be *weighted* or given different degrees of significance when calculating suppliers' total scores. Applying different *weights* to scores is referred to as using weighted average scoring. In *weighted average scoring*, each criterion is ranked in terms of importance and assigned a percentage such that, when all percentages are added together, they equal 100 percent. The more important criteria are assigned higher percentages and the less important are assigned lower percentages. The raw scores are multiplied by the applicable percentage or weight to obtain a weighted score for each category. The weighted scores are added together to obtain a total score which, by virtue of using 100 as the maximum score for each criterion and 100 percent as the sum of all weights, will have a maximum value of 100.

Criteria like *delivery* require a little bit of qualitative input. Getting delivery in two weeks rather than one may be acceptable and, thus, double the lead time does not necessarily mean *twice as bad*. But cost is a different story. A price of $2 will always be half of, and twice as attractive as, a $4 price. So, the scoring for *cost and value should be handled in a scientific manner.*

We've seen many procurement professionals struggle to figure out a scientific way to score prices for comparison. So, while in his role as president of Next Level Purchasing, Charles introduced to the procurement community a supplier scorecard price comparison formula that he dubbed the *Dominick Formula*, for ease of recall.

The Dominick Formula is built on this principle: the penalty to a supplier's pricing score should be proportionate to the degree that its price varies from the lowest qualified bid (LQB). So, if a supplier's price is 25 percent higher than the LQB, its pricing score should be 25 percent lower than the pricing score of the supplier who submitted the LQB. If the supplier's price is 40 percent higher, its pricing score should be 40 percent lower. Here is the Dominick Formula:

$$PS = MP \times (1 - ((SP\text{-}LQB)/LQB))$$

where,

PS = Pricing score
MP = Maximum points
SP = Supplier's price
LQB = Lowest qualified bid

We've set up a supplier scorecard spreadsheet for you to download from the Web Added Value resource center at the J. Ross Publishing website (www.jrosspub.com/wav), so you can easily use the Dominick Formula in your own work.

As highlighted earlier, in addition to pricing, there are other criteria that need to be taken into consideration when evaluating potential suppliers. As a result, we've developed a simple *Supplier RFP Scorecard* to objectively rate each supplier's capabilities and responses to RFP questions. See Exhibit E for a template of the Supplier RFP Scorecard and Exhibit F for instructions on how to use it.

MITIGATING RISK IN SOURCING DECISIONS

When some people think of sports, they think of gambling. No sooner does a sports season start before the oddsmakers indicate which teams are most likely to win the championship. The Tampa Bay Buccaneers were given 12:1 odds to win Super Bowl LV at the beginning of the 2020 NFL season.[1] Better odds were given to several other teams, but, with the brilliant execution of star personnel—such as iconic quarterback Tom Brady—the Bucs became the Super Bowl champs that year.

Just like some sports teams look better or worse *on paper* than others, suppliers may or may not be as good as they look on paper. That's why a proposal alone isn't enough to make a supplier selection.

When contemplating the purchase of a new product or service or doing business with a new supplier, you face risk. Many bad things could happen, including:

- The product or service could be of unacceptable quality
- The supplier could fail to perform
- The supplier may go out of business

There are consequences if these things happen. Your organization may fall behind on its schedule, or it could lose money and customers. Your reputation as an excellent procurement professional could be tarnished.

As an agent of your organization, you must take steps to protect it from this risk. Here are three simple tips for managing risk when dealing with a new product, service, or supplier. These tips can apply to any procurement: critical, noncritical, direct materials and/or services, and indirect materials and/or services.

1. **Get a sample before making a long-term commitment**—If you're buying a product, ask for a low- or no-cost returnable sample of the product so that your organization may assess its quality. If you're buying a service, have the service performed on a one-time basis or over a period of time (e.g., 60 days) for the same reason. There is no better proof that a product or service will suit your organization's needs.

2. **Ask for a money-back guarantee**—You shouldn't lose money if you are not satisfied. Ask for a money-back guarantee. If the supplier declines, you're probably better off not doing business with that supplier. After all, why should you have confidence in the supplier's product or service when the supplier doesn't? If the supplier offers the guarantee, the load on your shoulders is much lighter.

3. **Conduct a supplier quality audit**—For the most important procurements, ensuring acceptable supplier quality is essential. During your visit, probe the financial health of the organization, find out about the supplier's capacity, and focus on their quality initiatives. A supplier quality audit is more than just walking onto a supplier's shop floor and looking around.

The specific aspects of suppliers' operations that you should evaluate when doing a supplier quality audit are discussed in the next section.

SUPPLIER QUALITY AUDITS

You should leave a supplier quality audit with a greater understanding of at least the following items:

- **Quality methodologies**—Many quality methodologies are used today, including Total Quality Management, Six Sigma, and Lean Six Sigma. Ask about which methodology the supplier employs and how it is used.
- **Lot determinations**—The American Society for Quality, a well-respected association for quality professionals, defines a lot as *a defined quantity of product accumulated under conditions considered uniform for sampling purposes.*[2] In quality recalls, good suppliers know exactly which lots were affected by the nonconforming material, ingredient, or whatever. Thus, it is important to learn how the supplier tracks lots.
- **Tools**—How is the supplier monitoring its quality? One common tool being used is statistical process control (SPC) charts (see Figure 7.1). SPC identifies an acceptable range of quality measurements and then graphs actual measurements, both between upper and lower limits of acceptability and outside those limits. Ask the supplier to show you how quality tools are used to monitor quality.
- **Improvements**—Suppliers often use numbers to gauge their quality performance. Ask the supplier for a few years of reports with these metrics. Are the metrics getting better, worse, more static, or more erratic?
- **Team empowerment**—Experts agree that quality improves when line workers are empowered to watch for defects. Can the supplier's employees tell you what they do when a defect is discovered?

- **Sampling arrangements**—In mass production, not every unit made is inspected. How does the supplier choose the size and composition of inspected samples?
- **Inspection process**—How does the supplier inspect items before shipment? Is this inspection method similar to the way your company evaluates conformance?

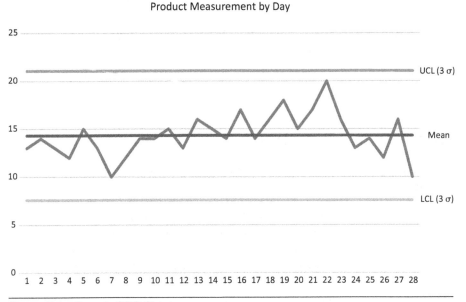

Figure 7.1   Sample SPC Chart

THE NEGOTIATION BEFORE THE NEGOTIATION

In the process of evaluating which suppliers you want to consider doing business with, suppliers will invariably try to move the process toward a commitment from you. They will likely ask you a series of questions to help them ascertain the certainty of getting your business. If you're not careful, what you say at this stage of the process can impede your ability to maximize your negotiation performance later. We call this the *negotiation before the negotiation.*

Fortunately, there are some common questions that suppliers use to get information that they hope to use to their advantage. Prepare for these supplier questions to stay in control of the negotiation:

- **Question 1: "Are you going to negotiate or just accept the lowest bid?"**— Suppliers ask this prior to sending proposals so they know whether to offer their true best deal or a *padded* price to be negotiated lower later. Question 1 is tricky; you naturally want suppliers to offer their best deal, yet stating an intent to negotiate will keep you from getting the best deal right away. However, saying you won't negotiate, but later negotiating is dishonest and unethical. So, respond with something like, "It depends. We reserve the right to negotiate. But if it is clear that we've been offered the best possible deal, we may accept that proposal without negotiating. I encourage you to submit your most competitive offer to maximize your chances of being considered."

- **Question 2: "Are you the decision maker?"**—Suppliers hate negotiating with someone who doesn't make the final decision. They fear that their selling points will be lost and their work wasted. Therefore, they often circumvent the procurement process by avoiding the buyer or the strategic sourcing team and contacting an executive directly. This sales practice is unfair to the buyer and the team, unfair to other suppliers, and can result in decisions that are not fully informed. As such, you should preempt this sales behavior and definitely not reward it. A good response to Question 2 is something like, "We make decisions as a team. However, I'm your point of contact. All discussions about this project must be coordinated through me."

- **Questions 3 and 4: "How does my proposal look?" and "If I improve this aspect of my proposal, do we have a deal?"**—Suppliers often ask Question 3 before you select the successful bidder. A buyer's usual response cites one unacceptable aspect of the supplier's proposal such as, "Your price is too high," which invites Question 4. If you answer Question 4 before completing your proposal review, it can put you in an uncomfortable position. Saying *no* creates several negative impressions: that you aren't the decision maker, that you've unethically preselected the successful bidder, and that you're bluffing about an acceptable proposal aspect. Such impressions can diminish the supplier's respect, which you need in order to be persuasive. So don't provide feedback on a supplier's proposal, thus only allowing Question 4 to be asked when you're ready to negotiate. Simply answer Question 3 with a response such as, "Our proposal review process is not yet complete, so I can't fairly answer your question."

Three regulation periods and overtime shootouts are both aspects of hockey. But they are vastly different and involve different skills and different styles of play. Thus, they must be prepared for separately.

We see both strategic sourcing and negotiation to be important aspects of procurement. But they are vastly different, and involve different skills and approaches. So, we treat them as discrete functions and have separated them into individual chapters of this book.

You, too, should endeavor to keep negotiations from prematurely sneaking into the sourcing process, despite your suppliers' valiant efforts to question you until they get a commitment. To achieve your best results, you need to ensure that you prepare adequately.

In the next chapter, we will cover negotiations and the preparation that you should do prior to them.

CLOSING REMARKS

Selecting the right supplier requires some time up front as you do your homework, determine your needs, ask the right questions, and sift through the possibilities. But choosing the wrong supplier is guaranteed to take up even more time, more money, and cause an endless array of aggravation and frustration. Your choice will depend on a wide range of factors such as value for money, quality, reliability, and service. How you weigh the importance of these different factors will depend on your organization's priorities and strategy.

Throughout this chapter, we provided techniques and approaches that will hopefully guide you toward the right choices. They should help you to decide what you need in a supplier, identify potential suppliers, and separate the winners from the losers.

REFERENCES

1. Rome, Anthony. "Super Bowl Futures Odds, 9/4/2020: Chiefs Remain Favorites, then Ravens." *The Spread*. Available at https://www.thespread .com/nfl-articles/090420-super-bowl-futures-odds-9-4-2020-chiefs -remain-favorites-then-ravens.
2. "Quality Glossary—L." *ASQ*. Available from https://asq.org/quality -resources/quality-glossary/l.

8

CHAPTER

NEGOTIATING WITH SUPPLIERS: JOCKEYING FOR POSITION

What is the most exciting part of a horse race? Right—the final moments when the horses are jockeying for position. Usually, there are a few horses that separate themselves from the pack and are striving to be ahead as they cross the finish line.

This is very much like procurement. After issuing your request for proposal (RFP) and qualifying the potential suppliers, you usually have a short list of suppliers to choose from, all who are eager to be the *winner*. At this point, perhaps, the most exciting part of procurement begins—the negotiation process!

DECIDING UPON SUPPLIERS WITH WHOM TO NEGOTIATE

The first decision to make at this point is with which suppliers to negotiate. We often get questions about the ethics of negotiating with a select number of bidders—or even just one—after receiving proposals. Should all bidders be given the opportunity to negotiate? Well, the following describes an approach that we usually take.

We create and continuously maintain a ranking of best bidders at the post-proposal stage of the sourcing process. The ranking is usually based on a number of criteria, not just lowest price (see Exhibit E: Supplier RFP Scorecard). And, our personal rule is to not give a negotiating opportunity to a supplier without giving the same opportunity to all *higher* ranked bidders.

So, if you have seven bidders and want to negotiate with the bidder who has the third-best rank, the bidders ranked first and second should also be given the opportunity to *sharpen their pencils*. We don't worry about the lower-ranked bidders unless we think that they also have a legitimate chance at actually earning the business. Usually, at that point, we've already ruled them out.

Now, if we negotiated with the third-best bidder and, as a result, got *the best deal* and never gave bidders ranked first and second an equal opportunity to revise their proposals, that situation would reek of poor ethical judgment. In addition, if given the opportunity, the other bidders may have also revised their proposals to be even more beneficial to the organization.

One thing about this approach is how it might be abused by the suppliers whom you frequently engage in sourcing processes. If they know from experience that they don't have to put their best proposal forward because they will have the opportunity to negotiate later, you may find your sourcing process becoming more complex, lengthy, and less efficient than it needs to be.

You also have to do a self-evaluation, and ask yourself, "Why am I negotiating with someone other than the top two bidders?" In some cases, it may be due to internal political pressure to keep the incumbent.

Using the competitive bidding process to simply lower the incumbent's price without a realistic chance of actually switching suppliers is unethical. So, you need to employ some change management to shape the culture of your organization while also keeping the process fair.

STRUCTURING THE ULTIMATE CONTRACT

After identifying the suppliers with whom you are going to negotiate, the preparation phase of the negotiation begins. As you plan on how to approach the negotiation, you will want to end up with the *Ultimate Contract*, an agreement representing the best offer in the market for all terms: price, warranty, delivery, payment terms, and such. What often happens is that one supplier offers the best price, a different one offers the best warranty, a third offers the best lead time, and so on, but rarely does one supplier offer the best in all categories.

You should never approach a negotiation feeling that you have to sacrifice a good deal on one term for a good deal on another. Use the following process for planning the Ultimate Contract negotiations:

1. **Summarize RFP responses**—Use eSourcing software or create a spreadsheet to compile and compare a list of each major term and each supplier's offer.
2. **Identify the best deal for each term**—Table 8.1 illustrates an example RFP response summary with the best deal for each term in bold font.
3. **Create the Ultimate Contract in tangible form**—Create a single page with the best offer for each term as if a single supplier offered all of those terms. In some cases, you may reasonably believe that you can get an even better result than the best proposed term. In such a case, you can substitute those terms, which we refer to as most desirable outcomes. That is what

the Ultimate Contract will look like. This sheet will represent your goals for negotiating.

4. **Decide what you can sacrifice if you must**—Sometimes, it's not possible to get the Ultimate Contract. So, you must prioritize the terms you *need*, and the ones you simply *want*. For example, can you accept a shorter warranty if you get an even better price? Can you forgo the liquidated-damages clause as long as you get the desired payment terms? We are not suggesting approaching the negotiation in a softer way—always strive for the best— but that you should simply know what the most important terms are.

5. **Put yourself in a confident, ethical mind-set**—Because at least one supplier has offered you the deal you are asking for, related to each individual term, you can feel confident that the market can bear your demands. Therefore, approach the most attractive bidder with your demands. Just be careful not to cross the ethical line. Do not disclose that you are requesting a certain term because a specific competing supplier has proposed it. But if a supplier suggests that your demand for a certain term is unreasonable, let that supplier know that you have proof that it is reasonable.

Table 8.1   Example RFP response summary

	Supplier A	Supplier B	Supplier C
Unit price	$143	**$139**	$144
Payment terms	**60 days**	30 days	45 days
Warranty	1 year	1 year	**2 years**
Lead time	**10 days**	15 days	15 days
Took exceptions to contract terms?	Yes	**No**	Yes

Here's a real-life story from a procurement professional's past that drives home the point that suppliers do hold back on some terms when submitting their proposals. We changed the name of the procurement professional to Jeff to protect the not-so-innocent. The company that Jeff worked for was buying signage like crazy. His internal customer's approach to determining demand was ultra-nonstrategic. If Jeff had known then what he knows now, things would have been very different.

Anyway, there were some specialty-type sign items that the organization was buying. Not every sign manufacturer had the capability to produce the type of precision-cut lettering they were looking for. When the internal customer determined the sign needs for one location, they were wanted *now*! That meant no waiting to determine what else could be packaged into a deal to have more leverage and get a better price.

This also was a high-profile project with Chairman of the Board involvement so, as a new buyer, Jeff wasn't going to push back. Instead, he went out to bid for a certain type of sign, selected a supplier, and a couple of weeks later, would go out to bid for a different type of sign, again. The company found itself primarily using two suppliers who met the quality requirements, were competitively priced, and so on.

In this one solicitation for signage, a supplier (Supplier A) offered a slightly better price, but the lead time was two weeks longer than that of another supplier (Supplier B). So, Jeff decided to pay a small premium to get a better lead time. Knowing the jobs that the organization had in Supplier A's shop didn't give Jeff any reason to question their lead time.

In the debriefing, Jeff told Supplier A that they didn't win the award because their lead time was eight weeks instead of six weeks (what Supplier B proposed). The supplier ranted and raved that they could have done the job in six weeks.

In Jeff's mind, he said, "Well, if you could have done it in six weeks, why didn't you say that! Doesn't it make sense to put your best foot forward? Duh!" But the supplier shouldn't take all of the blame in cases like this.

With a quick phone call to each supplier to see how flexible their important variables were, Jeff could have saved his organization a few dollars—much more than they would have spent paying Jeff for the few minutes he spent *negotiating*.

The moral of the story is that a procurement professional should never assume that any variable is inflexible. Ask for improvement on all of them. That's one of the keys to negotiating the Ultimate Contract. It is best to ask for anything that is on your most desirable outcome list, you may be pleasantly surprised by the answers you get. You never know until you ask!

We recommend that you have a preplanned course of action in the event that an agreement cannot be reached. In the book *Getting to Yes*, Roger Fisher and Bill Ury highlight the fact that one of the most important aspects of preparing for negotiations is the development of the company's *best alternative to a negotiated agreement* (BATNA).[1] Your BATNA may be a decision to *make* versus *buy*, work with an alternate source, incorporate a substitute, deal with a manufacturer as opposed to a distributor, or take another alternative.

STRUCTURING PAYMENTS

As you structure what a deal should look like, you should consider how to keep your organization important to the successful supplier. When you're an *important customer* to a supplier, your needs get immediate attention. You don't have to be a huge company to be an important customer. Being a large customer doesn't hurt, but there are other ways to become and stay important to your suppliers. Let's explore one approach.

In contracts involving multiple payments, a supplier wants as much money as possible up front. This may lead them to desert you toward the end of the contract when their revenue from you is small, and their revenue from new customers is large. It is better for you to have an arrangement where less money is paid in the beginning of a relationship and more is paid in the end.

Table 8.2 illustrates an example of a typical initial proposal from a software supplier for a three-year contract. Of course, you're going to negotiate this offer, right? A revision that is left up to the supplier may reduce the licensing and implementation fees by 20 percent and reduce the annual maintenance fee to $20,000, resulting in a total cost of $312,000 and a savings of $183,000, as illustrated in Table 8.3. That's a nice savings, but the arrangement makes you less important as time goes on. A better way to restructure the pricing and achieve the same savings is illustrated in Table 8.4.

Table 8.2   Example initial proposal

Cost component	Amount	Payment due
Licensing fee	$165,000	Upon signing
Implementation fee	$150,000	After implementation
Maintenance fee	$60,000	@ start of 1st year
Maintenance fee	$60,000	@ start of 2nd year
Maintenance fee	$60,000	@ start of 3rd year
TOTAL	**$495,000**	

Table 8.3   Example negotiated proposal with suboptimal payment structure

Cost component	Amount	Payment due
Licensing fee	$132,000	Upon signing
Implementation fee	$120,000	After implementation
Maintenance fee	$20,000	@ start of 1st year
Maintenance fee	$20,000	@ start of 2nd year
Maintenance fee	$20,000	@ start of 3rd year
TOTAL	**$312,000**	

Table 8.4   Example negotiated proposal with improved payment structure

Cost component	Amount	Payment due
Licensing fee	$72,000	Upon signing
Implementation fee	$60,000	After implementation
Maintenance fee	$60,000	@ start of 1st year
Maintenance fee	$60,000	@ start of 2nd year
Maintenance fee	$60,000	@ start of 3rd year
TOTAL	**$312,000**	

By distributing costs toward the end of the contract, the supplier has a financial interest in being responsive late in your relationship. Other ways of staying important include using option years, termination provisions, and liquidated damages clauses in your contracts. So, when you're negotiating a long-term deal with a supplier, consider how you are going to remain important to your supplier throughout the entire contract.

SITUATIONS THAT AFFECT THE BALANCE OF POWER

Thus far in your preparation, you have decided what you want out of a negotiation. But deciding what you want, and actually getting what you want, are often two different things. Your ability to get what you want is determined partially by your negotiation acumen, and partially by the *balance of power* between you and your supplier. We will work on your negotiation acumen later in this chapter. For now, let's probe the balance of power idea.

How many of us *armchair quarterbacks* watch an American football game and say, "They should have run the ball more!" or "They should have exploited their passing attack!" When we say such things, what we don't take into account is that the other team is using a defensive scheme that influences the play calling. Similarly, the supplier's tactics must influence our *play calling* in the context of a negotiation.

The balance of power should shape your approach to negotiating. That balance of power is sometimes affected by some common situations (see Figures 8.1 and 8.2). The following sections describe some situations that will impact the balance of power.

Essential factors that tip the scales in favor of the **"Buyer"**

• Executive (C-level) support
• Stakeholders' buy-in
• Multiple sources
• Stable pricing
• No urgency
• Low switching costs
• Plenty of substitutes
• Buying "Goods" vs. "Services"
• Commodity buys
• Few buyers
• You are a major buyer
• Your organization's global recognition (brand name)

Figure 8.1   Essential factors that tip the scales in favor of the buyer

Essential factors that tip the scales in favor of the **"Seller"**

- Lack of executive (C-level) support
- Stakeholders on supplier side
- Few sources
- Volatile pricing
- Urgent need
- High switching costs
- No close substitutes
- Buying "Services"
- Custom orders
- Many buyers
- You are not a major buyer
- Your organization lacks global recognition

Figure 8.2   Essential factors that tip the scales in favor of the seller

Goods versus Services

When buying goods, you can generally take a more tenacious approach to negotiation. With services, negotiating can be trickier, particularly when you are negotiating with the person who will ultimately be providing the services such as a consultant, accountant, graphic designer, or similar professional. These individuals tend to take pride in the work they perform and view your attempts at negotiating a better price as a devaluation of their work. They may respond by providing services demonstrating that *you get what you pay for* instead of giving you their best efforts. So, take a firm, but diplomatic, approach when negotiating with service providers. We recommend that, in these situations, you turn the focus of negotiation from price reductions to creative ways of securing added value for your company. You may be able to get some training opportunities at no fee or improved payment terms to positively impact your organization's working capital.

Custom Orders versus Mass Production

When you place a second order for mass-produced goods, you probably won't be able to negotiate a much better price than the price that you negotiated for your first order. However, with custom-made goods, you do have a little leverage. On the first order, the supplier probably built 100 percent of its nonrecurring costs (e.g., process design, set up, production instructions, etc.) into the fee you paid. If you end up placing an unplanned second order, the supplier has already recouped its nonrecurring costs and, thus, your unit price should be lower than it was on your first order.

Technically Committed versus Technically Uncommitted

Let's face it, when other people in your organization have worked with a supplier to determine the technical specifications for what they are going to buy, and only one supplier can comply with them, there is little leverage that you have in negotiation. So, when other people interact with potential suppliers, your negotiation power depends not so much on how you communicate with the supplier, but more so on how you prepare or educate your internal team. Everyone responsible for the technical decisions should be advised of these things:

- No one should share a supplier or specification selection with suppliers until a purchase order is issued
- The uncertainty a supplier has about getting the business will translate into more price flexibility and improved total cost of ownership (TCO)
- Your approach is not necessarily designed to choose the lowest-cost supplier, but rather to ensure the lowest possible cost for the preferred specifications, backed up by compliant supplier performance

THE IMPORTANCE OF NEGOTIATION PREPARATION

Once you have assessed the buyer/seller power balance, it is time to actually prepare for the negotiation. Benjamin Franklin[2] said, "By failing to prepare, you are preparing to fail." This statement should be the motto of every negotiator!

The most general level of negotiation preparation is putting yourself in either a *win-win* or *win-lose* mind-set. A common analogy used in negotiation is that of dividing a pie between two parties; the more pie one party gets, the less pie is left for the other. The concept of a win-lose negotiation means that one party's gain is the other party's loss. In a win-lose procurement negotiation, a more favorable price for the buyer generally means a less favorable profit margin for the seller.

The concept of a win-win negotiation is not one that has one party seeking gain through the loss of the other party. It is one where both parties collaborate so that they can find ways for both to benefit more than they would if they simply fought over opposite positions. Experts call this *expanding the pie* in contrast to *dividing the pie*. In a procurement negotiation example, *expanding the pie* might mean finding a way to obtain a more favorable price for the buyer while also finding a way to obtain a more favorable profit margin for the supplier (e.g., adjusting batch sizes to support the most efficient production process). The point of a win-win negotiation is for both parties to benefit more by collaborating rather than competing.

Win-win negotiations are often preferred because it allows organizations to start doing business in a friendly, productive—rather than an adversarial—manner.

HOW A SKILLED NEGOTIATOR PREPARES

Colleagues want each other to succeed. Enemies hate to see others succeed and will try to prevent such success. Most probably, you have read some examples about being an enemy in negotiations, or what win-lose negotiations are like. But what is a win-win negotiation like?

We will cover win-win negotiating techniques in an upcoming section that covers tactics. For now, we're going to keep concentrating on preparation. The following eight sections discuss the characteristics of the way that a skilled negotiator prepares.

The Skilled Negotiator Knows What a Product or Service Should Cost

For decades in the procurement profession, it was accepted that negotiation was the process for determining how much a product or service should cost. But, think about that for a moment. If procurement professionals went into a negotiation with no idea what a *good deal* was, how would they know if they ended up with one?

This practice gave all the power to sellers. Sellers had all of the information and buyers could only hope that they could strike a nerve of emotion in a way that persuaded a seller to relent on price and terms. While emotion can and does play a role in successful negotiation today, it is helpful if you have more than just one arrow in your quiver. One of those additional arrows is logic. And, if you know what a product or service should cost, you can use the associated logic to persuade a supplier to be flexible.

So, today, procurement professionals use *should-cost models* to estimate the final prices they will pay for important goods and services. A should-cost model is a documented calculation of an estimated price. It factors in carefully researched estimates of material costs, labor costs, overhead costs, and profit margins that would apply to the manufacture of the item or the performance of a service.

When creating a should-cost model, you are essentially behaving as if you were an estimator or cost accountant for a supplier of the product or service. Should-cost models are especially important when buying a custom item that hasn't been made before and doubly important when only one supplier can produce an item or perform a service.

Should-cost models can be valuable negotiation tools, either as something you keep private from your supplier for your own guidance or, under the right circumstances, something that you share with your supplier during the negotiation process. Therefore, accuracy is key. A supplier may be happy to discount your should-cost model as inaccurate as they are likely to have put a lot of work, experience, and expertise into estimating their costs. You need to aim to be as smart as—or smarter than—the supplier about the supplier's own business. You can even enlist the help of someone from your organization's Finance team to play devil's advocate and stress test your should-cost model.

However, having a supplier challenge your should-cost model isn't the worst thing that can happen. By challenging your should-cost model, the supplier may correct you with more accurate information that they may not have shared otherwise. You can even say something like, "Well, if my numbers are wrong, what do you say the right numbers are?"

So, should-cost models can help you develop a negotiation target to shoot for as well as help you uncover information that you can use later in the negotiation.

The Skilled Negotiator Knows Their Counterpart

Procurement professionals often fail in negotiations due to being caught off guard by the experience and/or aggressiveness of the supplier's negotiator. So, always learn about your counterpart before you begin negotiations. Insist on a phone conversation prior to the negotiation. You can tell the supplier that the purpose of the call is to shore up logistical details such as time, location, and length of your meeting. And do shore them up! But also find out more about your counterpart through *small talk*. How long has she been selling the product or service? Is he an aggressive personality? Then, adjust your tactics for that type of counterpart.

The Skilled Negotiator Knows Their Worst Enemy

If we were to ask you who your worst enemy is in the context of a negotiation, we'd bet there's a high likelihood that you would respond that it is your supplier counterpart. That is, the salesperson on the supplier's team who is trying to get the highest price for the product or service that he or she is trying to sell to you. And in some cases, you'd be right.

In other cases, we would say that you're close, but not quite right. Why is that? Well, in our opinion the procurement negotiator's worst enemy is the set of assumptions that the procurement professional makes in the context of the negotiation. Let us explain by giving a real-life story.

This story is about a buyer responsible for buying signage for his company. Let's call this buyer *Chuck* to protect the not-so-innocent. In one of his first signage buys, Chuck was buying signage with a baseline price of $100,000. Chuck negotiated with the top-rated supplier and was able to persuade that supplier to reduce his price by 20 percent. Chuck felt pretty good about this so he went into his boss's office and said, "Boss, I think we're ready to sign the contract with this supplier. I was just able to negotiate a 20 percent price decrease." Chuck expected his boss to be pretty happy about that, but the boss turned to Chuck and said, "Is that as low as they will go?" So, Chuck said, "Well, yeah." The boss said, "How do you know?" Chuck sheepishly said, "Well, that's the price we ended up at when we concluded the negotiation." Then the boss said, "Well, how do you know that they wouldn't be willing to go even lower if you continued with the negotiation?" Chuck looked like a deer trapped in headlights because he didn't have a good answer for his boss. At that point, Chuck realized that the assumption that he was making about the supplier's pricing was limiting his ability to maximize his success in the negotiation.

Unfortunately, these types of assumptions do get in the way of a lot of procurement success. We have many other examples. We've had conversations with distributors who have said, "Well, we don't train our buying teams in negotiation because we don't negotiate with our manufacturers. They set the price and that's the price that all distributors pay." Now, personally having been in a procurement department for a distributor, we know that is not true in all cases. But do you see how powerful that assumption is? That assumption is standing between the distributor and that distributor's ability to improve profits through negotiation. Even if the price isn't flexible, maybe payment terms or some other benefit is.

We've also seen a lot of examples in inflationary times of price increases being just accepted and buyers will say, "Well, commodity market prices are going up, there's nothing I can do about it." Yes, it may be true that commodity prices have gone up, and maybe you won't pay the same price that you did last year. But that doesn't mean you shouldn't try to negotiate and maybe take a little bit of the price increase away just through negotiation. Because of the assumption that commodity markets are going up and price increases are therefore nonnegotiable, procurement professionals, in some cases, are not helping their company's profitability as much as they could.

What we suggest is for you to evaluate your assumptions—your worst enemy—before going into a negotiation. Try to catch yourself making these types of assumptions. When you do, ask yourself, is that assumption correct? Challenge each assumption and see what happens. We guarantee you that, over the course of your career, you will be more successful in some negotiations because of it.

The Skilled Negotiator Understands How Negotiation Styles Will Affect a Negotiation

Have you wondered why some negotiators always seem to get what they want, while others more often tend to come up short? What might make some people better negotiators than others? In addition to the negotiation skills we have covered in this chapter, the answer may be, in part, that people bring different negotiating styles and strategies to the bargaining table, based on their different experiences, personalities, beliefs, and cultural differences about negotiating.

What Is Your Negotiating Style?

Individuals' negotiation styles differ in part due to their different social motives, or preference for certain types of outcomes in interactions with others. In general, there are two approaches to bargaining:[3]

1. Distributive or *win-lose* outcome
2. Integrative/mutual gain or *win-win* outcome

The social motives that drive behavior correspond to five basic negotiating styles (see Figure 8.3):

- **Competing Style**—These negotiators seek to maximize their own outcomes with little regard for their counterparts' outcomes. They are bottom-line driven, over-confident, and have a tendency to impose their own views that, in extreme, can become domineering and aggressive (*win-lose* outcome).
- **Avoiding Style**—These negotiators are passive, prefer to avoid conflict, and pass responsibility onto another party. They fail to show adequate concern,

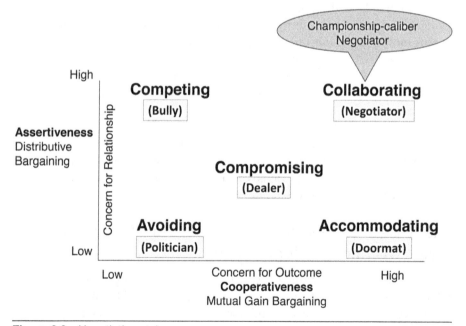

Figure 8.3 Negotiation styles

drag negotiations, withdraw from the situation, and lack making an honest attempt to get a resolution.

- **Collaborating Style**—These negotiators strive to maximize both their own and other parties' outcomes to mutually benefit from the relationship. They use open and honest communication, are open to innovative ideas, and focus on finding creative and new solutions (*win-win* outcome).
- **Accommodating Style**—These negotiators (who are quite rare) put their counterpart's needs and wants above their own. They maintain relationships with the other party, smooth over conflicts, and downplay differences.
- **Compromising Style**—These negotiators aim to find middle ground and frequently engage in give-and-take trade-offs. They often split the difference between parties and accept moderate satisfaction on both parties' needs.

Which Is the Best Negotiating Style?

Is one negotiation style *better* than another? Most research suggests that negotiators with a primarily collaborative style are more successful than hard bargainers at reaching novel solutions that improve everyone's outcomes. Negotiators who lean toward collaboration and cooperation also tend to be more satisfied with the process and their results. In multi-issue negotiations, those who have a collaborating style of negotiation are most likely to *expand the pie* and generate value for both sides.[4]

Collaborators are open to sharing information with their key suppliers, focus on long-term gain, and aim for mutual gain by *creating value* for both parties. They are also skillful at focusing on strategies that can improve their own outcomes by *claiming value* for their organization. Such negotiators are the most-valued players or championship-caliber members of successful negotiating teams.

Does Identifying Your Negotiation Style Matter?

When people with different negotiation styles meet, the results can be unpredictable. By diagnosing your own and your counterpart's negotiation styles, you will be better prepared to negotiate and work together constructively.

Most negotiators have one or two preferred negotiating styles. Do you know your predominant style of negotiating?

It is ideal to be able to choose and apply the most appropriate negotiation style at different stages of negotiations. In fact, skilled negotiators are flexible in switching their negotiating style depending on:

- Their role on the negotiating team
- Strategic or tactical overriding goals
- Different stages of negotiations

- Whether products or services are commodity or specialty
- A counterpart's responses during negotiations

How can you improve your negotiation style to reach better outcomes? Rather than trying to give your negotiation style a complete *makeover*, it is best to focus on strengthening your natural talents and the effective negotiation skills that you have acquired throughout your career. In addition, by observing skilled negotiators and practicing the best elements of other styles, over time, you will become more comfortable and skillful in choosing and adapting various negotiating styles at different stages of negotiations.

The Skilled Negotiator Uses Deep Logic

Logic can be a powerful negotiating tool. But a skilled supplier negotiator will anticipate your logic and shoot it down. For example, let's say you were buying used aircraft parts. You may say to the supplier who bid $3,000 for a part, "I always see these parts selling for $2,000, so your price isn't fair." That might be good logic, but the supplier may say, "But those parts are in *repaired* condition rather than *overhauled* condition, and don't have the same warranty." If you didn't go deep with your logic and consider all possible supplier responses, you likely have no more ammunition for persuasion.

The Skilled Negotiator Controls the Meeting

Salespeople are taught to control meetings. In a negotiation, this disarms you and prevents you from reaching your negotiation goals. Don't let the supplier control the meeting. Either present an agenda or prepare a set of probing questions to lead the conversation. When you've achieved the results you're looking for, give signals that the meeting is over (e.g., stand up and say, "Thank you for your time in meeting with me today," etc.). If you are at an impasse, suggest a break and reconvene for negotiations at a later date. This will allow you to go over your notes and prepare for the next session.

The Skilled Negotiator Knows What the Supplier Will Ask, and How to Answer

At the outset of negotiations, suppliers want to learn if they can earn your business with their current proposals or if they have to improve them. Be prepared for their questions and know how you are going to answer them. What the supplier wants to learn is:

- Do you have the budget to pay the current price?
- How quickly do you need to make a decision?
- Are there other suppliers that you're courting?

Some suppliers may even directly ask you these questions, so be prepared for them. If you have a negotiating team representing your strategic sourcing team, role play and script your responses before getting into the negotiation sessions.

Because each situation will be different, it is impossible to provide the single best answer to each question in every case. But we can tell you how certain responses affect your leverage. We highly recommend that you educate your end users and stakeholders since skilled sales personnel are trained to bypass you and your negotiation team to gather valuable information to strengthen their negotiation position. This practice of *back-door selling* was covered in Chapter 5. Here are things to think about when faced with the aforementioned questions.

Do you have the budget to pay the current price?

This can be a two-edged sword. Saying you have the budget will make the supplier feel less compelled to change his price. Saying you don't have the budget will make the supplier feel that you are not serious about buying and therefore feel that negotiation is pointless. We like to use a standard response like "As a matter of policy, we simply do not discuss budget with suppliers regardless of the situation."

How quickly do you need to make a decision?

The necessity to make a quick decision will make a supplier feel that you might be pressured to accept a higher price. If you need a supplier to perform extraordinarily fast when you do award an order, you don't want to give them the impression that your need is not urgent. But, you don't want them to feel that you're willing to pay whatever they ask to get started today. Tailor your response to your situation. You can always preface your answer with a phrase like, "We have to move quickly, but we also plan to move intelligently."

Are there other suppliers that you're courting?

In response to this question, we always say, "As a matter of policy, we do not discard any options until a deal is signed."

Please note that these questions may be asked directly or the information can be gleaned more subtly. A savvy salesperson will find less intrusive questions to ask to get at the same information. You need to be prepared for such conversations.

The Skilled Negotiator Recognizes the Importance of Timing

Your preparation must not only cover *what* to say, but also *when* to say it. *Timing is everything* is a phrase used in topics from stock market investing, to comedy, to gadget play calling in football. It very appropriately applies to supplier negotiations as well.

Negotiating at the wrong time can harm a supplier relationship and even cost your organization money. There are points in time when it is appropriate to negotiate and points in time when it is not (Figure 8.4). Here are some tips on whether or not to negotiate at those points:

- **Before the proposal**—Imagine yourself in a situation where you are discussing a product or service with a potential supplier prior to getting that supplier's proposal. If pricing comes up, you may be compelled to ask for big discounts. Don't! Why not? Well, if the supplier senses that you are going to push hard for cost cuts, how will the proposal be crafted? That's right—the supplier will inflate the price so that you feel like you *won* the negotiation after wringing a price reduction. In reality, the supplier may have padded the price so much that your final price is more than you would have paid otherwise.
- **Immediately after the agreement**—After concluding supplier negotiations, some procurement professionals ask for something else due to a forgotten issue or wanting to win bigger. Negotiating after a *handshake* can hurt a supplier relationship. A supplier who negotiates in good faith only to have an agreement reopened immediately will likely be on guard against you. This supplier may not treat you like a partner and may even behave opportunistically in the future. There are plenty of good supplier negotiation techniques to use prior to the handshake. You don't need to resort to bad faith to get the results you want.
- **Prior to contract expiration**—The months prior to a contract's expiration represent an excellent negotiation time. An incumbent supplier doesn't want to lose the business he or she has worked so hard to secure. Extending the contract would save time and money in a supplier's sales process. You can often negotiate excellent concessions if you dangle the prospect of extending the contract without going out to bid. But the key is *timing*. Doing this well in advance of the expiration creates the perception that you have

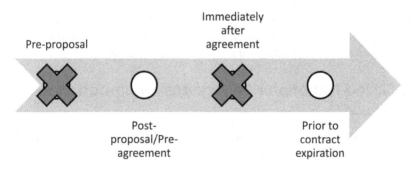

Figure 8.4 Appropriate times to negotiate

options, and suppliers are often happy to cut good deals to become your only option.

INCREASING YOUR NEGOTIATION CONFIDENCE

The foregoing aspects of negotiation preparation are important. However, a skilled sales negotiator can disarm you, even if you're only missing one ingredient: your confidence.

Power persuades, and confidence translates into power. Can you learn to be more confident? Absolutely! Here are five specific things to do to be more confident in negotiations:

1. **Visualize**—Early in preparing to negotiate, take time to visualize a successful end result. Picture yourself shaking hands with your supplier and smiling. Imagine how you'll feel when you've secured a great deal for your organization. Most tangible results start with a thought that is later brought to reality. If you can't think it, you will have a harder time achieving it. So, visualize, and feel the power!

2. **Rehearse**—Before going into any negotiations, you and the members of your negotiating team need to rehearse different scenarios and questions. Having up-front agreements and *speaking with one voice* will provide the necessary confidence that you and your team members need for a successful negotiation outcome.

3. **Affirm**—Say this out loud to yourself throughout your preparations: "I am a confident negotiator." The last time you are by yourself prior to commencing a negotiation, say it to yourself again. The negotiation power that your supplier will sense about you stems from outward evidence that you believe in yourself. Affirmations strengthen your belief in yourself.

4. **Use confident language**—Suppliers who are trained in negotiation look for signs of weakness in you through your behavior and the words that you use. Try to never appear subservient or in doubt. For example, saying, "Your brochure said that technical support is included with every purchase, but your proposal said that support is available for an extra charge. So, I guess that you can't include support for free, right?" is weak. Don't expect to change a supplier's mind about the deal with words like that. Say, "Your brochure said that technical support is included with every purchase, but your proposal said that support is available for an extra charge. Let's fix that." This sends the signal that you are confident and in control, and that you have power. The opening minutes of a negotiation are a particularly critical time for using confident language. Avoid using words such as *like, prefer, look for,* and *target.* Replace them with words like *need,*

must have, and *it is essential* when you open the negotiations. Not only are these words stronger, more important, they show your confidence and the criticality of your priorities.

5. **Self-assess**—During a negotiation break, ask yourself, "Was I confident? Did not appearing confident hurt me? What can I do to appear more confident?" In addition to showing that you are confident, you must be knowledgeable and have done thorough research about the products or services that you are going to purchase. Remember that *knowledge is power*!

SUPPLIERS' PSYCHOLOGICAL WARFARE

Now that you are prepared to negotiate, we can turn our focus to things that will happen during the actual negotiation process. First, let's look at how suppliers may try to shift the aforementioned balance of power in their favor through some psychological techniques.

Sellers use psychology-based negotiation techniques to dissuade you from asking for better terms. If you are aware of these techniques, you can resist being influenced by them and you'll always remember to ask for the discount, price reduction, and/or value-added services you are seeking. Those techniques include:

- **The preemptive strike**—Sensing an imminent price discussion, a seller may say something like "We don't play games with our pricing. We give a price and, if you like it, we'll do business. If not, we'll wish you luck with someone else."
- **The self-proclaimed good deal**—The *power of suggestion* is a real phenomenon in psychology. By telling you that you are getting a good deal, the seller hopes that you agree and don't challenge the pricing. Of course, just because a seller says a price is a good deal, that doesn't make it one.
- **The final detail**—Sellers often refrain from talking price until they have covered all the details and benefits of their offering. They hope that you or your internal customers will be *sold* on doing business with them before considering price.
- **The red-tape-wrapped price**—Salespeople are rarely the final decision makers for price improvements. Usually, prices are decided upon by their management. When salespeople sense that you're rushed, they'll make getting price approvals seem like a time-consuming, bureaucratic task.

THE SUPPLIER'S *BACK POCKET*

Ken Knudsen, the CEO of sales coaching firm Eagle Rock Enterprises, was interviewed by Charles about suppliers' thoughts when negotiating with procurement managers on an episode of the Next Level Purchasing Association Podcast.[5] Through the course of this conversation, we identified several negotiating principles for procurement managers.

From the supplier's side, "The key to negotiation is that you have to start with a pretty wide spread," Knudsen shares. "If my goal is to sell something for $20 a case and I open at $20, we don't have negotiating room. Most sales professionals have something in their *back pocket.*"

So, what can compel a salesperson to offer the better deal in her *back pocket?* The goal of many salespeople is to earn more and work less. That goal is best accomplished by working with customers who exhibit long-term relationship potential.

BODY LANGUAGE IN NEGOTIATION

That doesn't mean that your only necessary negotiating tactic is to promise a long-term relationship. Salespeople are trained to identify whether a procurement negotiator is serious or bluffing.

Before negotiating, they consider the states of the procurement professional's company and the industry. While negotiating, they evaluate the body language of the procurement professional. Certain actions may signal a misleading representation, such as:

- Keeping the hand over the mouth
- Scratching the nose
- Failing to make eye contact

There are really two lessons to be learned with regard to body language:

- You must be aware of your mannerisms, as they may be being interpreted by the salesperson
- You should also observe the salesperson's body language

"One of the things that I coach clients on is that you should always take someone into the sales call with you because they're observing while you're trying to present," explains Knudsen. "Most purchasing managers try to (negotiate) one-on-one or one-on-two, and therefore, fail to be as effective at observing the supplier's body language."

To Knudsen, an indicator that the procurement professional is interested in a long-term relationship is the manner in which the procurement professional communicates. We pointed out that procurement professionals often open a sales call or a negotiating session with a phrase like "You have five minutes, what do you got?" Knudsen identified that as one of many *red flags* that positions the procurement professional as a *short timer* and compels the salesperson to withhold better deals.

LEARNING THE SUPPLIER'S INTERESTS

Knudsen acknowledges that one of the salesperson's objectives is to get her procurement counterpart to talk, but he also says, "Most purchasing managers should try to get the salesperson to talk more." By learning about a salesperson's interests, you can uncover opportunities for good deals that the supplier is withholding for potential long-term relationships or *reference accounts*. Sometimes, salespeople are sent into a meeting with the instructions: "Price is not an issue. Get the account." But you may risk never discovering that if you don't foster an open dialogue.

In the summer of 2008, the sports world had an example of how strong someone's interests are in terms of shaping their decisions in negotiations. Hockey fans in Pittsburgh were shocked to hear that a star in the Pittsburgh Penguins' playoff run, Marian Hossa, signed with the Detroit Red Wings. What's the shocking part? It was a *one-year* deal!

Most players in their prime, like Hossa was at the time, try to get the longest-term deal possible in addition to the most money. According to an article in the *Pittsburgh Tribune Review*,[6] the Penguins then offered Hossa a five-year deal, then a six-year deal, then a seven-year deal—all for similar money, all to no avail.

This is a classic case of a negotiation failing because one party's true interests weren't addressed. Hossa's interests are best summed up by his quote in the aforementioned article: "I want to have the best chance to win the Stanley Cup. I feel like Detroit is the team."

We're not saying that the Penguins failed to address these interests verbally; we don't know what else went on during negotiations. Perhaps Hossa had his mind made up about Detroit and didn't feel bullish on the Penguins' immediate future. But we wonder if the Penguins stressed in the negotiation their commitment to winning by having Sidney Crosby and Evgeni Malkin, arguably two of the three best players in the league and not yet in their primes, each signed to long-term deals as a way of persuading Hossa to stay.

Detroit knew Hossa's interests. So, they got him for a lower price and terms more favorable to them. Hossa's agent probably pushed for a longer-term deal and more money. But we bet that Detroit knew they had what Hossa wanted, held their ground, and ended up with a pretty good deal. So, uncovering and appealing to your counterpart's interests in procurement, in sports, or in life, is important.

The ironic ending to this story is that the Penguins defeated Hossa and the Red Wings in a rematch in 2009 to win the Stanley Cup. Hossa subsequently left Detroit as a free agent, and signed with the Chicago Blackhawks, where he finally won his first Stanley Cup in 2010.

So, what are your suppliers' interests? Do you just assume they want the highest price from you and that's it? You don't have to guess. In casual conversation with prospective suppliers, you can ask them questions such as:

- What benefit would there be to landing our account?
- Beyond just the money, what would it mean to your organization to add us as a customer?
- Why is acquiring us as a customer important to you?

The answers can be interesting and enlightening. You may learn that your suppliers' interests are different than you expected!

DECIDING WHAT INFORMATION TO SHARE

After reading this chapter so far, there is a chance that you might think that disclosing information to your supplier could put you in a disadvantage in a negotiation and, in some cases, it might. But there are other cases where open communication can pay big dividends, too.

Procurement professionals are often reluctant to share information, and Knudsen sees that as a barrier to their success in negotiating. He says that the sharing of information is often important for a salesperson to be able to go back to her management for approval to offer a better deal.

We agree, but also feel that you need to be proficient at distinguishing good-intentioned salespeople from unscrupulous ones who are just seeking a negotiating advantage. No single rule applies to the sharing of information in a negotiating situation. You have to make the decision that is right for the specific circumstances.

More open communication may make some procurement professionals nervous since some feel that developing a relationship plays to the salesperson's advantage and to the procurement professional's disadvantage. That does not have to be the case. By communicating openly, you can learn the objectives of both the salesperson and the supplier, and how a win-win result can be achieved. A relationship-building demeanor has many times influenced Knudsen to believe in a higher probability of a long-term relationship, which gave him the *ammunition* to go back to his boss, or his boss' boss, or the company, in order to help his company.

USE TODAY TACTICS

As you can tell, we think preparation is extremely important for a successful negotiation. Some people tend to think that the quickest thinkers are the best negotiators. But, good planning reduces the need to be so quick on your feet—you anticipate what to say and when to say it—which makes you appear to be a quick thinker when really you're just a great preparer. Deciding on your tactics is part of preparing for a negotiation and more than something you do on the spur of the moment or in the heat of the negotiation battle. Most people want to jump straight to negotiating tactics. But preparation should come first.

Now that we've covered preparation, we can talk about tactics. Again, tactic selection is really part of preparation itself. Negotiating tactics don't have to be complex to be effective. Some are simpler than others. We have three tactics that we call *Use Today Tactics* because they really are so simple that you can use them today without much practice:

1. Don't Use All of Your Ammunition at Once

There may be several logical reasons for a supplier to reduce his price: ordering early, being eligible for a multiple-product-purchase discount, and the like. Suppliers may often try to convince you that their first price reduction is a great deal that you should accept. If you used all of your reasons for getting a price reduction at once, the supplier has more power to defend his price, and you have run out of reasons for getting a lower price. Instead, follow these steps:

- Know the reasons for requesting a price reduction
- Decide the sequence to introduce those reasons
- Ask for a price reduction based on one reason
- Thank the supplier after getting it
- Ask for a better price for another reason, and repeat

2. Ask About the Supplier's Questions

During a negotiation, the supplier will ask you questions. For example, when trying to decide how much to reduce his price, the supplier may ask, "When did you want delivery to take place?" It would be easy to say, "In two weeks," and leave it at that. We would respond by saying, "We originally wanted delivery in two weeks, but does our delivery time frame make a difference in our pricing?" If the answer was, "Yes," we would follow up with, "What delivery date will qualify us for the best deal?"

3. Listen to the Suppliers' Dialogue

We never endorse *spying*—such as listening to or recording someone's conversations against their wishes. But we feel that cell phone calls made in your presence while negotiating without a privacy request are fair game for listening.

In such conversations, you can pick up clues about the factors the boss is considering in revising his offer. For example, let's say you overhear the salesperson say, "No. They'll be paying 100 percent upon completion instead of a down payment." From this, you can tell that payment terms affect your pricing. Then, you can say, "I overheard you mention payment terms. How might altering our payment terms help us get a lower price?" This tactic often uncovers otherwise hidden savings opportunities.

Yes, paying attention for clues in your counterpart's words can help you be a more successful negotiator, and so can looking for clues in your own words.

WORDSMITHING

One of our education and consulting clients recently wrote to us with a request: "Normally we have been using the word *best* for price negotiations with suppliers as in 'Your price is too high, please quote your best price.' But, sometimes we use *better*. Kindly advise which is the suitable word for price negotiations, which, as I understand that, is *better*."

Actually, when you are leading a procurement negotiation, you should use the word *lowest* rather than *better* or *best* when discussing price. Think about it. The *best* price in the mind of the supplier will not likely be the *best* price in your mind, right? If a supplier says, "We gave you our best price," that may be true because the best price for them is the highest price. If the supplier is convincing, you may believe that they've given you their lowest price.

But the best price for you is the lowest price. So, ask for the *lowest* price, not the *best* price. Once again, we stress the fact that although your focus in this particular conversation is price reduction, you should not lose sight of achieving the lowest TCO for a product or service. In addition to the price of a product or service, consider all of the other costs (e.g., transportation, warranty, maintenance, setup charges, training, insurance, etc.) before making the final decision.

These tactics can be successfully applied in most situations. However, not all other tactics are equally effective. Some tactics will work in some situations, but not in others.

TACTICS THAT CAN BACKFIRE

One of the reasons that negotiation is one of the most exciting business processes is that there is never 100 percent certainty. The following sections discuss three examples of negotiation tactics that have proven to be very effective, yet still can fail if not applied in appropriate situations.

The Crying-Poor Tactic

The crying-poor tactic is used by publicly held companies whose poor financial performance is well known, and by small companies and nonprofit organizations with small budgets. Buyers from these companies will stress to the supplier their financial state (e.g., "You know we don't have a lot of money, so we need lower pricing.").

This negotiation tactic can indeed be effective. However, it can also raise suspicion in your supplier that can have a negative effect on the deal. The supplier may be wary that they won't be paid on time or at all. The supplier may worry that your company won't be around to fulfill its contractual commitments, and, as a result, the supplier may withhold its best deal.

The Saving-the-Toughest-Issue-for-Last Tactic

Deciding the order in which the various issues will be discussed with your supplier is critical. Some negotiators like to save the toughest issue for last.

Saving the toughest issue for last does work well in certain situations. It allows you and your supplier to agree on easier issues, thus building a rapport and spirit of cooperating for mutual success. It also helps you assess your supplier's negotiation style, strengths, and weaknesses while preparing to negotiate the big issues.

However, if there is a deadline for your negotiation, saving the most difficult issue for last can be disastrous. You could have little time left to finish the negotiation and feel pressured to concede to a less-than-optimal deal.

So, while deadlines can work for you in a negotiation, they can also work against you. Evaluate the deadlines: When are they? Who imposed them? Are they negotiable? If the deadline was imposed by an internal customer or management and is not negotiable, address the most difficult issues sooner, rather than later.

The Get-It-from-Someone-Else Tactic

The fear of losing a deal to a competitor can get a supplier to the lowest price very quickly. Saying, "If you can't lower your price, that's okay—we'll buy it from someone else," can work in certain competitive situations.

However, not all markets are so competitive that you can, indeed, buy the same exact item from any supplier and get equivalent quality, delivery, and service. Suppliers in these less-competitive markets know this. If you attempt to use the get-it-from-someone-else tactic on them, they will realize that you have less knowledge of the marketplace, which will make them feel like they have more leverage in the negotiation, and they will be less likely to concede.

This brings us to a sales negotiating tactic that can be adapted for procurement negotiation. When negotiating, suppliers may mention how they are different than their competitors and, therefore, better for you. They often base their difference on common problems that procurement professionals encounter with other suppliers.

In sales, that technique is called *differentiation*. You can use a variation of this technique when negotiating with suppliers. We call it *reverse differentiation*.

REVERSE DIFFERENTIATION

In using the reverse differentiation negotiation technique, you identify common problems that suppliers have with other customers. Then, when negotiations are at an impasse, you appeal to their emotions by showing how working with your company isn't as painful as working with some of their other customers.

The key is that your point(s) of differentiation must be true. If your organization has one or more of the following characteristics, you will be different than most of your suppliers' customers and can use these characteristics to *sell* your supplier on the benefit of giving you a better deal in order to earn your business. Positive points of differentiation in your organization may include:

- **Quick decision making**—Some organizations take weeks or months to make a procurement decision, have it approved, and place an order. If your company moves on its decisions quickly, stating how you can help your suppliers have shorter sales cycles can persuade them to offer better deals when negotiating.
- **Prompt paying**—Some organizations take 45 days, 60 days, or longer to pay their invoices, which is costly to their suppliers. If your organization pays promptly, you can use that fact to your advantage when negotiating.
- **Evangelistic**—Supplier marketing is more effective when their materials contain customer testimonials. Unfortunately, many companies do not permit their staff to offer testimonials. If your organization willingly provides testimonials, you can demonstrate that your value as a customer is higher and that the supplier would benefit from giving you a better deal.
- **Low maintenance**—Some customers whittle away at supplier profits by demanding more attention than other customers in the form of requesting special procedures, customizations, or other unique attention. If you aren't a *high maintenance customer*, you can mention this when negotiating to give the supplier assurance that a thinner profit margin won't be eaten away by forcing the supplier to respond to special requests.

Earlier in the chapter, we talked about a win-win negotiation being the preferred approach to modern negotiation. Using the reverse differentiation negotiation tactic is a great first step toward becoming an effective win-win negotiator, or expanding the pie, if you will.

If you're just getting started as a negotiator, expanding the pie is a quantum leap. Using the reverse differentiation negotiation tactic is a great intermediate step between being an adversarial negotiator and a seasoned expand-the-pie negotiator. It inspires you to *sell* the supplier on the benefits of working with you rather than beating the supplier up and stating the consequences of not agreeing to your every desire.

If you are not quite prepared for expanding the pie, using the reverse differentiation negotiation tactic can really help you become more of a collaborative negotiator.

WHEN SUPPLIERS REQUEST CONCESSIONS

In procurement negotiation literature, much attention is focused on the buyer getting concessions from a supplier who is simply defending a proposal. In the real world, suppliers try to get concessions from buyers during negotiations as well. For example, a supplier may ask you to have all of your organizations' requisitioners place orders through their website, to take deliveries only on certain days of the week, or to allow the supplier to automatically extract payment from your organization's bank account rather than invoicing you. These approaches may deviate from the approaches that your organization is comfortable with. Yet, if you negotiate properly, you can use these concession requests to your advantage. Here are three approaches that you can use to avoid giving up too much.

1. **Just say no**—If a supplier asks for a more favorable term in a contract, a higher price, or any other concession, start out by simply saying, "No." No justification is required. You would be surprised how many suppliers will just drop the issue then and there, and not ask you again.
2. **Introduce consequences**—If a supplier asks for a concession, test how important the concession is to the supplier by tactfully introducing consequences. For example, you could indicate that agreeing to a shorter warranty period would require the approval of management, technical staff, and others, and that such approvals would result in a long delay of formalizing the deal. If the delay in securing your business (the consequence) is unattractive to the supplier, the request for the concession may be dropped.
3. **Trade**—If a supplier wants one term of an agreement changed to its benefit, and you absolutely cannot convince the supplier to drop their request, try to only concede on the condition that you receive a concession of equal or greater value. For example, if a supplier cannot complete a service within 30 days as originally sought, attempt to obtain a more favorable fee structure to compensate for the concession that you have to give.

By using the approaches we've introduced, you will likely be asking your supplier for a large number of improvements in its proposal. You want to aim high, but you also want to maintain your place in the win-win negotiation mode.

THE ROLE OF INTERPERSONAL SKILLS IN NEGOTIATION

Win-win negotiations are characterized by the fact that both parties feel like they ended up with a good deal. To achieve optimal results in a win-win negotiation, the parties must view the negotiation as a collaboration of colleagues rather than a clash of enemies.

How do you create a collaborative, win-win atmosphere? It starts with having good interpersonal skills. Here are three things you should plan to do in your negotiations, as well as other interpersonal situations:

1. **Listen to your counterpart**—Each party in a negotiation has ideas. Each party wants those ideas heard. Grant your counterpart the courtesy of your attention. Doing so will earn you return attention and create a collaborative atmosphere. Interrupting your counterpart will create an enemy that will feel satisfaction if you fail.

2. **Acknowledge your counterpart's ideas**—Negotiators take pride in the ideas that they bring to the table. To discredit those ideas will hurt your counterpart's pride and, again, create a situation where your counterpart would love it if you fail. Instead of saying, "That's a bad idea," say, "That's an interesting idea, but it may not work in our situation. I would be open to exploring variations of it, though."

3. **Mention mutual success when needed**—If your counterpart becomes hostile, remind him or her that you are seeking a win-win solution. Phrases like, "We just have to work together to reach an agreement that works for both of us," or, "I agree that this must be a win-win situation for us to work together," can be effective when used respectfully. Most people would feel guilty for playing win-lose in a win-win scenario, so reminding your counterpart that you both need to feel good about the outcome can stabilize a tense situation. Win-win requires skill, but not necessarily sacrifice.

POWER NEGOTIATION MADE EASY

Win-win negotiations work great when both parties are committed to the concept. However, just like the *back nine*—the last half of a round of golf—introduces some new challenges, the late stages of a negotiation often involve new challenges such as an increase in supplier resistance. Therefore, should you transition into a *tougher* negotiator at these times?

Many procurement professionals sometimes feel that their negotiation styles aren't *tough* enough. They feel that they could deliver better results with a more powerful negotiation style. But there is a misconception that *tough* negotiation requires an intimidating personality or superior on-your-toes thinking. This is not necessarily true. You can use the following firm techniques—and stay in win-win mode—to create the anxiety necessary to persuade a supplier to concede to your requests without being the villain:

1. **Set deadlines**—Even though many negotiation books advise you to avoid deadlines, they can be very advantageous if used correctly. Having an absolute time by which your supplier must have its best and final offer on the

table or risk losing the business will accelerate your receipt of the best deal. This principle is one of the reasons that the reverse auctions that we will discuss in Chapter 13 are so effective.

2. **Introduce next step prerequisites**—Suppliers will gladly haggle over less significant issues like packaging requirements, on-time delivery criteria, etc., to delay discussing the *big* things like price. By telling your supplier that you will not discuss peripheral issues until there is a satisfactory improvement on the significant negotiation points, you will get your supplier to his or her bottom line more quickly.

3. **Use cooling-off periods**—Some negotiations can drag on for months with little or no progress. This is usually because the supplier feels that you are *sold* and that you will no longer be able to delay acquiring the product or service. If you want to regain your leverage, tell your supplier that you are going to suspend contact with the supplier for seven days while you reassess the situation and your alternatives. Suppliers hate to be out of touch. A break from negotiations may persuade the supplier to reevaluate the importance of your business. In best-case scenarios, just the threat of a cooling-off period will get your supplier motivated to move from its position.

Use common sense when considering these techniques. They work best when you have alternatives to doing business with your negotiation counterpart, and may not work well in all situations.

THE EASIEST—AND OFTEN MOST EFFECTIVE— NEGOTIATION QUESTION YOU CAN ASK

In this chapter we have given you many tactics to use in your negotiations. For some of you, it may feel overwhelming. It may feel that if you don't master every little detail we've written about, your negotiation is doomed to fail. You may feel that you are not a natural negotiator and you'll never be good enough to win big at negotiation. Let us tell you right now, that is not true. Sometimes, all you need is one simple tactic to get good results.

In this last section of this chapter we will teach you a negotiation question so simple, yet so effective, that you will wonder if it's too simple. Spoiler alert: it's not!

First, let's talk generally about the best type of questions to use in a negotiation. There are closed-ended questions and open-ended questions. Closed-ended questions can be answered with a simple *yes* or *no*. Open-ended questions require some type of explanation.

Closed-ended questions are not preferred for negotiation. Imagine asking a supplier, "Can you lower your price?" It would be so easy for the supplier to simply say, "No." There's nothing to explain. You essentially asked for a one-word answer, where that one word can only be one of two possible choices. And, even if that one word is a lie, you got the type of answer that is appropriate for the question.

Just like we encouraged you to prepare for your negotiations, your supplier counterparts are encouraged to prepare to negotiate with you, too! Saying, "No" when asked to lower their price is something they can do easily, with or without preparation. That type of question won't catch a good supplier negotiator off guard and won't lead them to disclose details that you can use for persuasion.

Open-ended questions require more than a yes or no answer. Here are examples of open-ended questions:

- "What's the lowest price you offer to any of your customers for this item?"
- "What are all of the material, labor, and overhead costs factored into your price?"
- "Why is your price so much higher than I expected?"

More probing questions like these can start a helpful conversation. The supplier may be open about some things that you can dig deeper into and work into your negotiation.

Of course, we know that some purchases are of smaller value and less criticality. And, you won't have an extra hour—let alone days—to prepare for them. That's why so many procurement amateurs default to questions like "Can you lower your price?" But, there's a question that's just as easy to ask, and it's a question that has gotten us a surprising amount of price reductions and cost savings throughout the years.

When you first read the question, you may think we're crazy to say it works so well. But it has for us and we bet that it will work for you, too, in straightforward, transactional situations where it's most appropriate.

What is that question? It is, "How flexible is your price?"

What? That's it? A simple question like that makes a difference? As legendary Olympic and WWE wrestler Kurt Angle used to say, "It's true. It's damn true."

Responses to this question have ranged from an uncomfortable, "Ah, geez, I don't have much wiggle room here . . . Maybe we could trim two- to three-hundred dollars off," to a quick, "I'm authorized to offer a 10% discount." It seems to get results more often than not.

So, if you only have time to ask one negotiation question, ask "How flexible is your price?" And—regardless of how simple it seems to you in your very professional role—don't modify it.

Once, we were teaching a negotiation workshop, and we taught the "How flexible is your price?" question. Then, we did a role play where each attendee was a buyer and one of us was a seller. We were shocked. More than 50% of the attendees asked a modified version of the question—sometimes, even as a closed-ended question—which we easily were able to deflect in our role as sell-side negotiators. It's a five-word question: How. Flexible. Is. Your. Price? Use this question *as-is* and see what happens. We think you'll be pleased with the results!

CLOSING REMARKS

Despite the raw talent possessed by sports teams today, you would not expect them to show up to their opponents' stadiums without preparation. They study their opponents in advance, predict how their opponents will play, devise strategies for how to approach each game, and practice their own plays.

Likewise, you should not enter into a negotiation relying solely on negotiation experience. You still need to predict how your counterpart will negotiate, devise strategies for how you want to approach the negotiation, and practice your techniques. With adequate preparation, you can more effectively execute the techniques you have selected. And while win-win is the ultimate goal, you want to make sure that you win what you set out to win. Good preparation will lead to a good plan. Good execution of that plan will lead to winning results.

REFERENCES

1. Fisher, Roger and William Ury. *Getting to Yes: Negotiating Agreement Without Giving In.* 2nd ed. New York, Penguin, 1991.
2. Benjamin Franklin quotes. *BrainyQuote.* Available from http://www.brainyquote.com/quotes/quotes/b/benjaminfr138217.html.
3. "Identify Your Negotiation Style: Advanced Negotiation Strategies and Concepts." March 15, 2021. *Harvard Law School Program on Negotiation Daily Blog.* Available from https://www.pon.harvard.edu/daily/negotiation-skills-daily/identify-your-negotiating-style/.
4. "Business Negotiations: How to Improve Your Reputation at the Bargaining Table." February 15, 2021. *Harvard Law School Program on Negotiation Daily Blog.* Available from https://www.pon.harvard.edu/daily/business-negotiations/let-your-reputation-precede-you/.
5. "Supplier Secrets for Negotiating with Purchasing." August 8, 2006. *Next Level Purchasing Association Podcast.* Available from https://podcasts.apple.com/us/podcast/suppliers-secrets-for-negotiating-with-purchasing/id267161044?i=1000020063072.
6. Rossi, Rob. July 3, 2008. "Hossa spurns Penguins, signs with Red Wings." *Pittsburgh Tribune Review.* Available from https://archive.triblive.com/news/hossa-spurns-penguins-signs-with-red-wings/#:~:text=Marian%20Hossa%20spent%20much%20of%20his%20four-plus%20months,the%20defending%20Stanley%20Cup%20champion%20Detroit%20Red%20Wings.

9

CHAPTER

NEGOTIATING IN SPECIALIZED SITUATIONS: ADAPTING YOUR GAME PLAN FOR DIFFERENT CONDITIONS

In the previous chapter we discussed negotiation approaches and tactics that can apply to any negotiation. However, there are some specialized situations where specific negotiation approaches and tactics are required. Just like a golfing guide that tells you when to use a driver, when to use a putter, and when to use a pitching wedge, this chapter will focus on several specific negotiation situations and will help you to decide which negotiation tactics to use in each situation.

NEGOTIATING WITH SUPPLIERS OVER POLICIES

Don't you hate to hear a supplier say "But our policy states . . . ?" That statement usually means that you'll hear bad news, followed by a claim from the supplier that nothing can be done about it.

But you usually can do something. Negotiating with the supplier's firm, non-empowered customer service rep is not a likely solution, so ask for the email address of someone empowered to waive policies; then email them, stating:

- What you want
- Why you want it
- What you were told about the policy
- Why you disagree with the policy (use logic)
- Your personal experience with policies
- That humans can waive policies (use emotion)
- A call to action

Here is an example, in the form of a letter, which you can adapt to your own situation.

March 1, 20XX

Dear Difficult Company:

I would like you to reconsider my request to return item #12345 from my order #67890 for a refund. This item does not work as the manual describes.

I was told that your policy states that widgets are not returnable. However, I do not consider this item to be a widget. Both your website and the manufacturer call it an external USB interface, not a widget, which is generally a small chip-board installed inside a computer. I know what your policy states. But even if you disagree with my notion that your policy does not apply to this item, I believe that you can and should grant my request.

In my procurement department, we have policies. But human beings can waive policies. And if one of my internal customers justifiably felt that the enforcement of a policy would be unreasonable, I would waive it.

I trust that the management of Difficult Company, Inc., shares this customer-centric view of how exceptions to policies can be granted by intelligent, caring business leaders.

Please reply with the instructions for arranging my refund.

Thank you.

This may seem like a very specific example that challenges a return policy, but you should be able to change just a few words and have it apply to nearly any policy dispute.

NEGOTIATING PRICE INCREASES

January is a common time for supplier price increases. At that time of year, procurement professionals are trying, perhaps unsuccessfully, to negotiate those price increases away.

How do you negotiate price increases? Better yet, when should you begin preparing to negotiate price increases? The answer to that second question may surprise you. You should have begun preparing to negotiate a price increase when you originally obtained the current price. Before we elaborate, consider a typical supplier justification, such as, "We must raise your price by 28 percent because aluminum costs went up 28 percent last year." That point is tough to argue if you're not prepared. So, when first obtaining responses to your request for proposal (RFP) or quotes for high-annual-spend products or services, ask for suppliers' cost breakdowns.

A cost breakdown will indicate the percentage of the total cost that is comprised by each major material, other materials, labor, overhead, and profit. For example, a cost breakdown may look like Table 9.1.

Table 9.1 Example cost breakdown with percentages

Cost component	Cost as % of total cost
Wood	20%
Aluminum	7%
Other materials	3%
Labor	45%
Overhead	13%
Profit	12%

If a supplier proposes a price increase, and tries to use a justification based on an increase in a component of the supplier's cost, you can say something like, "Aluminum increased by 28 percent, but aluminum only comprises 7 percent of your price. Considering nothing else, your price should only go up by 2 percent."

Should you stop negotiating there? Absolutely not! You can argue that productivity gains should have reduced labor costs enough to offset the small materials price increase. Maybe you can even convince the supplier that productivity gains more than offset the materials price hike, and that your price should go down!

NEGOTIATING FOR A COST BREAKDOWN

Successfully negotiating in the situation that we just described requires that you have a cost breakdown. However, you may find that getting the cost breakdown you need for negotiations can be a negotiation in itself! The key is to get a cost breakdown when you first obtain pricing from a supplier. Suppliers can be hesitant to share such information, but are usually more willing when they are competing for your business through negotiations or during the RFP process.

When we suggest getting a cost breakdown to procurement professionals, they sometimes cite a single or sole source situation with an incumbent supplier being the reason that they can't get the breakdown. A single source situation is where you have a choice of multiple suppliers, but voluntarily contract with only one. A sole source situation is where there is only one supplier capable of providing you with the product or service as desired. We have done a lot of negotiating for cost breakdowns in our careers with a lot of success, so we know that it is possible.

While it is true that the more certainty the supplier has of retaining your business, the less interested they will be in giving you a cost breakdown, it is a huge mistake to fail to ask for a cost breakdown simply because you *think* that the supplier will resist. Ask anyway. If you don't ask, you won't get.

If the supplier resists, which suppliers have done to us in the past, we have always appealed to them in an emotional style of negotiation to get the results we've wanted, saying:

- "We're spending $XXXX with you each year. Why do you feel that we do not deserve to know what we are paying for?"
- "By withholding this information, I am kind of getting the feeling that your management is trying to hide something. What's the big secret?"
- "We have been doing business with you for a long time and consider you a strategic partner. In a true partnership, there has to be transparency and openness, and I'm not feeling that right now. How much of a partner do you consider us?"

Even after saying these things, you may encounter resistance. There's the ever-famous "that is proprietary information and we are not allowed to share" and other questionable reasons. There are two different strategies for securing the breakdown if you've heard this excuse for refusing to share cost data: *escalating information exchange* and *promoting mutual cost reduction.*

Escalating Information Exchange

Quoting "proprietary information" is evidence that you are hearing an answer from the wrong person during negotiations. The "we are not allowed to share" response reminds us of the common situation in the section *Negotiating with Suppliers over Policies.*

Every organization that has a policy has an individual who can waive that policy. You, or someone in your organization, needs to speak with that person because the supplier representative you are speaking with is too apprehensive or unable to present your case to that person on your behalf.

The attempt at moving negotiations to another person can get challenging because business etiquette may require that if the supplier is going to escalate the request, you should too. That means it may take executive-to-executive communication (i.e., your president talks to their president). Obviously, you don't want to run up the chain of command unless the potential profit improvement would be significant (at least several thousand dollars). Your president or VP may even be asked to sign a confidentiality agreement if the supplier is persuaded to share the breakdown.

The bottom line is that the greater the opportunity for savings, the harder you should push—adding executive firepower, if necessary.

Promoting Mutual Cost Reduction

Psychologically, you have to consider the reason why the supplier is so reluctant to give you the cost breakdown. Basically, when the breakdown is requested, the supplier is likely to assume that you are going to use the information against the supplier.

If you find fault with their breakdown or conclude that their profit margin is too high, you are going to push them for better pricing. Giving you the breakdown will be a strictly losing proposition. From their point of view, they can see no benefit of giving you the breakdown. However, if the savings opportunity is significant, you may present your request as an opportunity to pursue a savings-sharing project. By getting the breakdown, your technical team responsible for specifying the technical requirements, can review the breakdown to identify cost drivers, and then consider respecifying the product in terms of material used, standard items that could be substituted, or other cost saving changes. And, if your team finds that they can take cost out, both your organization and the supplier can share equally in the financial benefits.

Let's use an example based on the previous cost breakdown, assuming that the unit price of the item is $100 (see Table 9.2). What if your technical team found that they could eliminate aluminum and replace it with plastic at half the cost ($3.50 per unit), without sacrificing quality?

Table 9.2 Example prenegotiation cost breakdown

Cost component	Cost in USD
Wood	$20.00
Aluminum	$7.00
Other materials	$3.00
Labor	$45.00
Overhead	$13.00
Profit	$12.00
TOTAL	$100.00

That change would result in a reduction of the total costs of $3.50. Splitting the savings would mean that half of that price reduction would go to the supplier's profit and half would go to a reduction in your price. The new cost breakdown would look like Table 9.3.

Table 9.3 Example postnegotiation cost breakdown

Cost component	Cost in USD
Wood	$20.00
Plastic	$3.50
Other materials	$3.00
Labor	$45.00
Overhead	$13.00
Profit	$13.75
TOTAL	$98.25

If you buy 100,000 units a year, that change would save you $175,000 and give the supplier an extra $175,000 in profit per year—a true win-win.

Now, you have to be realistic about using these advanced negotiation strategies. The payback has to be there if you're going to involve top management or your technical team. Since each supplier and each sole source situation is different, there are no guarantees.

Recall that for these advanced strategies to work, as stated previously, the key is to get that cost breakdown when you first obtain pricing from a supplier. Suppliers can be hesitant to share such information at times, but are usually more willing when they are competing for your business.

After a supplier has your business, you are less likely to get the cost breakdown. While you can't change the past, you can avoid having to struggle to get cost breakdowns in the future by always requesting them while the supplier is still bidding for your business.

NEGOTIATING TIME AND MATERIALS CONTRACTS

You probably prefer fixed-price service contracts, right? In those types of contracts, if the service requires more time or material than planned, the supplier's profit is reduced, not yours. Sometimes, a supplier will refuse such risk and insist on using a time and materials contract.

In a time and materials contract, you pay the supplier for the number of hours actually required to perform the service. So, the supplier has no incentive to minimize the number of hours expended on the service. The less efficient the supplier is, the more money it makes!

Buyers often feel that using a time and materials contract is like issuing a blank check, but it doesn't have to be. You can negotiate these items to control final pricing:

- **Labor rate**—Suppliers not quoting fixed prices may charge *list price* for labor. If you are a big company or sourcing a big project, do not pay list price. Negotiate a lower labor rate to reduce your total cost.
- **Maximum number of labor hours**—Experienced suppliers should be able to estimate the hours needed for a job. Negotiate a cap on the number of hours where, if the supplier exceeds that number of hours, you don't pay for the overage. This avoids the *less-efficiency-equals-more-money* issue of time and materials contracts.
- **Markup on materials**—When billing for a time and materials contract, the supplier usually calculates the materials cost by adding a markup (usually 15–35 percent) onto the prices it paid. If a supplier paid $1,000 for materials, it will bill you about $1,200. We have had success getting suppliers to only charge what they paid for materials, with no markup.

- **Not-to-exceed total**—The next best thing to a fixed-price contract is a time and materials contract with a not-to-exceed (NTE) amount. Under this arrangement, the supplier can charge you for its labor and materials up to a certain maximum. If the time and materials costs exceed that maximum, the supplier charges you the NTE amount and assumes the excessive costs. This offers incentive for the supplier to work efficiently, and helps you provide a good estimate for your internal customer's budget.
- **Incentive plan**—To entice a supplier to complete your project earlier than the expected deadline, provide them with an incentive plan that can bring value to both organizations.

NEGOTIATING FORCE MAJEURE CLAUSES

Once again, we would like to refer to Hurricane Katrina. That natural disaster produced a watershed moment in procurement in many ways, with many important procurement lessons learned that should not be forgotten.

In the months after Hurricane Katrina, it was difficult to walk into a manufacturing procurement manager's offices without noticing the stacks of envelopes in their inboxes. What was in the envelopes, you ask? Letters from suppliers claiming that the recent U.S. hurricanes have caused them to declare force majeure and that shipments will be substantially delayed.

Up until that point in our careers, we had never seen this volume of force majeure claims. Thus, it was an appropriate time to revisit how force majeure clauses should be negotiated and written. Today, force majeure clauses are generally much stronger than they were in the pre-Katrina days. However, we continue to come across weak force majeure clauses from time to time. So, it's wise not to assume that yours is strong enough.

Plus, single events can forever alter how acceptable your force majeure clause is and will be in the future. A force majeure clause from 2005 that adequately addressed the supply chain challenges in the wake of Hurricane Katrina still may not have been well suited to address the supply chain challenges of the COVID-19 pandemic 15 years later. Look at your force majeure clause through a lens that reflects what is happening—and could happen—in today's world as well as tomorrow's.

In the past, force majeure was an easy term with which to agree. The thinking was, "Sure, Mr. Supplier, if you get hit with once-in-a-blue-moon disasters like hurricanes or terrorist attacks, you can delay shipments." But suddenly, force majeure events are becoming more common. Procurement professionals who took force majeure lightly started struggling to maintain continuity of supply. So, when negotiating a force majeure clause, address these three things:

1. **Will you get to waive any obligation of exclusivity to your supplier in the event of force majeure?** Sure, you may still have to accept delivery and pay for the quantity you ordered. But if your management decides that it is worth it to buy an additional quantity from another supplier during the time your contracted supplier is recovering, you should have the legal right to do so.

2. **Will you get *most favored customer* treatment after your supplier has recovered?** Large companies often negotiate a guarantee that they will get the best pricing out of all its supplier's customers, but getting scarce materials first in the event of force majeure is perhaps a higher priority.

3. **Can your supplier provide you with a written contingency plan for each event that the supplier wants to be defined as force majeure?** Insist on specificity like the quantities of materials, tooling, people, and other resources that will need to be redirected to another facility along with the process of redirecting them.

USING A CONTRACT TEMPLATE

If a supplier signs your contract, that supplier is legally bound to the obligations within that contract, right? Before you answer, let's talk about adhesion contracts.

An *adhesion contract*, defined in *Jones v. Dressel*, 623 P.2d 370, 374 (Colo. 1981), is a contract "drafted unilaterally by a business enterprise and enforced upon an unwilling and often unknowing public for services that cannot readily be obtained elsewhere. An adhesion contract is generally not bargained for but is imposed . . . on a take-it-or-leave-it basis."[1]

Adhesion contracts are like those you accept when you park your car and receive the claim check, which purports to waive your rights. Preprinted forms with small print—you've undoubtedly seen many of them.

Courts have interpreted and enforced adhesion contracts differently from ordinary contracts.[2] Adhesion contracts have been found to contain terms that almost outrageously limit the obligations and liability of the party authoring the contract. They have also been known to combine those one-sided protections with unreasonably oppressive terms that would not be reasonably expected by the weaker party to the contract.[3] Contracts and clauses within a contract found to be unconscionable are not enforceable. Contracts that are very one-sided are often considered unconscionable.

Today's procurement professionals regularly use contract templates with their suppliers. Sometimes, the templates of larger companies, who are financially stronger than some of their suppliers, often share the characteristics of one-sided adhesion contracts common to those used between large companies and consumers.

So, could your contract template be unenforceable? "Forms and templates should always be used cautiously," states Ernest Gabbard, former Executive Director of Corporate Strategic Sourcing for Allegheny Technologies (ATI), who is also an attorney. "It is always best to negotiate and reach agreement on the critical and the controversial clauses, to ensure that all elements of the contract are appropriately established and enforceable."

Of course, no part of this book is intended to offer legal advice. Laws differ between states and countries. Always consult an attorney when dealing with contractual matters.

NEGOTIATING WITH A SUPPLIER IN ANOTHER COUNTRY

The key to establishing a successful relationship with a supplier in another country is to learn and adapt to the culture of the supplier's country. Cultural research can be a big job. Where do you begin?

With a particular country in mind, answer these 20 questions to discover a lot of what is necessary for a positive international relationship:

1. Should I address my counterpart by his/her first name or in some other manner?
2. How should I greet my counterpart (e.g., shake hands, bow, etc.)?
3. What is important about the way business cards are exchanged?
4. Should I give a gift or expect to receive a gift from my counterpart?
5. How close should I stand to my counterpart?
6. Should I expect physical contact from my counterpart (e.g., a hand on the shoulder)?
7. What comes first: establishing a relationship or working on business matters?
8. Should we discuss political or personal matters?
9. Which common clichés or idioms are not globally understood?
10. Are there any common hand gestures in my country that my counterpart may consider offensive?
11. Is sharing an entertainment experience important to my counterpart?
12. What time should meals start and end?
13. Is it acceptable to discuss business during meals?
14. What laws will govern our transactions?
15. How quickly can I expect my counterpart to make a decision?
16. Is being on time for a meeting or negotiations important for my counterpart?

17. How might currency differences have an impact on the negotiated prices?
18. How are minorities or female negotiators perceived in other countries?
19. What are the potential risk exposures in dealing with overseas suppliers?
20. How are social and environmental responsibilities handled in my counterpart's country?

NEGOTIATING BY PHONE, VIDEO CONFERENCING, AND TEXT

Negotiating remotely has similarities and differences with negotiating in person. Therefore, there are some special rules that you must apply when negotiating by phone, video conferencing, or text. These six rules may sound simple, but don't dismiss them. Little things can make a big difference in your negotiation success.

- **Rule 1: Don't shortchange your preparation**—Yes, negotiating remotely is different than negotiating in person, but you must prepare just the same. Know, in advance, what your target terms are, what you will say to persuade your supplier to agree to those terms, and how much you are willing to concede. You must also be prepared for the questions your supplier counterpart may ask you. Whether you stumble in your speech in person or stumble on the phone, you always weaken your negotiating position when you stumble. So be prepared!
- **Rule 2: Prepare an agenda**—Having an agenda will keep you and your supplier focused. We recommend that you prepare the agenda and manage the conversation and the time devoted to each topic.
- **Rule 3: Always initiate the call**—Negotiating successfully requires focus. If you are caught off-guard by a supplier calling you, your focus will not be as strong. If you pick up a ringing phone and there is a supplier representative on the other end and she wants to discuss terms, ask to call her back in five minutes. Use that time to review what you prepared and then call the supplier. Initiating the call gives you more control.
- **Rule 4: Turn off your nonessential screens**—In today's connected world, we expect ourselves to multitask. That's great, but not during a negotiation. Checking texts, email, or—gasp!—social media during a negotiation will dull your focus and could result in your failure to object to terms that the supplier is introducing. Eliminate the risk of such a distraction. Turn off your computer screen if you're negotiating by phone. If you're using your office phone or negotiating via video conference on your computer, turn your smart phone off. Don't try multitasking in other windows while negotiating on a video conference. Simply put, use one device when negotiating

remotely and don't let nonessential screens distract you. Your texts, emails, notifications, and cat memes will be waiting for you when the call is over.

- **Rule 5: Reserve negotiations-by-text for the most simple things**—Texting is such a popular form of communication because it's fast, portable, and part of what we do so often during a typical day. So, naturally, we are going to gravitate toward texting as a form of communication for many purposes, including negotiation. However, for most negotiations that a procurement professional is involved in, texting is not going to be a one-stop-shop for your bargaining communication because of its inherent disadvantages: not well-suited for long messages, ease of making typos, and difficult to file for corporate purposes. That doesn't mean it should be avoided completely. It's just best to be saved for things like answering or asking yes-or-no questions; confirming agreement on a previously discussed topic; or proposing something numeric, like the number of years of warranty coverage (though we recommend employing very careful proofreading—remember, there's a big difference between "Yes, we can accept a 2-year warranty" and "Yes, we can accept a 3-year warranty.").

- **Rule 6: Promptly transcribe your notes**—In-person negotiation discussions are easier to remember because you remember what you see, hear, and write. In phone negotiations, you have one less sense for your memory to depend upon. As you negotiate by phone or video conference, you probably scribble down notes about your conversation. They will make sense to you when you read them only until the next day because so much will have happened since you wrote those notes, you will have forgotten what your abbreviations and partial sentences were supposed to mean.

Type up your notes immediately after your remote negotiation so that you can have a clear recollection of the negotiation outcome later. We also recommend that you email or otherwise send the notes from your conversation to your supplier for confirmation and mutual agreement. When the agreed-upon terms are in writing, they are more official.

NEGOTIATION AS A RELATIONSHIP PREDICTOR

Traditionally, the purpose of negotiation was simple: use persuasion techniques and leverage to get the best deal for your organization. Up until now, we have focused on using negotiation simply to get the best deal.

There is no doubt that getting a good deal is vitally important and that negotiation is a key way to get a good deal. But, in today's procurement environment, negotiation is more than a game to determine a winner. A prominent characteristic of today's procurement environment is the focus on developing healthy supplier relationships for competitive advantage.

When do these healthy relationships start? Do they start after doing business for 10 years, after collaboration on a joint project, or after the first supplier performance review? No. Buyer-supplier relationships start at the negotiation table. The side-by-side collaboration inherent in negotiation enables you to observe several things about a supplier. These observations can help you decide whether the supplier is an appropriate long-term partner.

The following list contains some questions that can help you determine how well a supplier will integrate into your organization:

- Is the supplier interested in my organization's long-term success?
- Is the supplier able to make decisions quickly or is there a *behind-closed-doors* decision process?
- Is the supplier flexible or does the supplier insist on doing business according to his own business model?

Asking these types of questions can help you predict how the relationship will work after the first purchase order is issued. You may see some promising signs. You may see some warning signals. Whatever the signs, don't ignore them.

Believe it or not, the supplier may observe some signs about you. The supplier may perceive you as having the potential of being a *high maintenance customer* and pad its pricing accordingly. As you can see, negotiation has now taken on a new role. So, view your next negotiation as the first step in a long-term relationship. It will help you select a supplier that is best for the future of your organization.

While many procurement professionals are beginning to view negotiation as a way to gauge suppliers' interest in partnering, not all of them understand that you have to present yourself as a partner, as well, in the context of win-win negotiation. In fact, the chief procurement officer of a large telecommunications company once told *Supply Management Magazine*[4] in an interview about partnering with suppliers, "You have to see it in the way that people respond to your pushes, challenges, and demands."

WHY ASKING FOR SUPPLIERS' ADVICE ISN'T AS DUMB AS IT SOUNDS

We believe that you can often gauge a supplier's interest in partnership during that first negotiation, many times without *pushes, challenges, and demands*. When working with a new supplier and talking through decisions that need to be made, we like to ask the question, "What would you decide, or do, if you were me?"

Of course, we usually know at that time what decision we would make or what action we would take, but we love to see how the supplier responds. Suppliers are rarely prepared for this question, so their responses are usually revealing and unscripted.

If the supplier responds in a way that recommends a decision that is clearly and heavily skewed toward their best interests and does not consider your best interests, you know that you are not speaking with someone who is committed to a partnership.

In most negotiation cases, showing how smart you are gives you leverage. However, using a question like this and *playing dumb* once in a while can really expose you to the inner workings of a supplier's mind.

A selfish response does not necessarily mean that we will walk away from that supplier. But we will know whether we are entering into a transactional relationship or a partnership. Keep in mind that not every supplier relationship warrants a partnership.

IMPROVING NEGOTIATION SKILLS

We hope that you have learned a lot about negotiating in these last two chapters. But we hope that we aren't disappointing you by saying that reading these chapters once will not guarantee that you will be a great negotiator for the rest of your career.

Negotiation is a skill that must be kept sharp continuously to maximize success. Five important strategies for maintaining your negotiation skills include:

1. **Engage**—Negotiation is a dynamic, interactive process. The best way to improve is to actually negotiate. When you do, you should assess how well you met the targets that you set before negotiating. Evaluate what you did well and document any lessons learned.
2. **Observe**—Watching others negotiate can enlighten you to techniques and approaches that you may not have thought of on your own. If the option is open, ask a negotiation-savvy coworker if you can sit in on his or her next negotiation session.
3. **Network**—Ask other procurement professionals from different industries what works well for them. Filter this advice through common sense, though, as someone claiming to be a good negotiator may actually be a poor one. Try out some of their best suggestions and see what works for you.
4. **Read**—There is no shortage of negotiation books available. Read customer or professional book reviews before deciding which one to buy. Chances are that you will uncover a technique or two from a good book.

5. **Take classes**—Formal training in negotiation and being included in situations involving negotiation may not only help you improve your negotiation performance, but it also looks great on a resume.

CLOSING REMARKS

Baseball, soccer, football, hockey, and basketball are all sports. However, just because a person is a good player in one sport does not mean that they will be a good player in another sport. The same is true with negotiation; someone who has negotiated in one part of his or her life may not be an effective negotiator in a corporate procurement environment.

There are many negotiation situations that are unique to corporate procurement, for example, negotiating for a cost breakdown, negotiating the terms of a time and materials contract, and negotiating as a means of determining supplier compatibility. Without learning the finer points of procurement negotiation situations, a good, but general negotiator can turn out to be below average. Being prepared for the myriad of situations that procurement professionals commonly face can be the difference between you dictating the flow of the game and you simply reacting to the flow of the game.

REFERENCES

1. http://www.openjurist.org/797/f2d/845/mullan-v-quickie-aircraft-corporation.
2. Abdulaziz, Sam K. August 1, 2002. "Adhesion Contracts Get Sticky." *Reeves Journal.*
3. Kagan, Julia. February 24, 2021. "Adhesion Contract." *Investopedia.* Available from https://www.investopedia.com/terms/a/adhesion-contract.asp.
4. NLPA Blog. July 24, 2008. "Gauging a Supplier's Commitment to Partnership." [Blog]. Available from https://www.certitrek.com/nlpa/blog/gauging-a-suppliers-commitment-to-partnership/.

10

CHAPTER

IMPLEMENTING AGREEMENTS AND MANAGING SUPPLIER RELATIONSHIPS: FROM THE WHITEBOARD TO THE FIELD

Completing all of the work involved in sourcing, negotiating, and ultimately deciding upon the best supplier for a procurement project is like a sports coach writing up the game plan on a chalkboard. That game plan looks good in the locker room in the same way that your procurement project looks good in the conference room.

But are sports games won in the locker room? No, they are won on the field. The success of your new supplier agreement implementation is dependent on the execution as well as the planning. This chapter will focus on how to have a plan that looks good on paper and is successful in the real world.

WHEN IS THE NEGOTIATION OVER?

One of the many famous quotes of legendary baseball manager Yogi Berra is, "It ain't over 'til it's over." So, when is a negotiation over?

Well, you should be ready to move from the negotiation phase into the agreement implementation phase when you have all of the required terms agreed upon and both sides are ready to commit the agreement to writing. Those required terms may be different from purchase to purchase. But, we've included a contract review checklist in Exhibit G to help guide you to identifying when a negotiation is *over*.

MAKING SUPPLIER SELECTION RECOMMENDATIONS

Often, the members and the leader of a sourcing team are not the final decision makers when it comes to supplier selection for a large purchase or contract. In some cases, you and the members of your sourcing team need to present a recommendation to management or the sponsor of your strategic sourcing team for approval.

Before negotiations even begin, you should assess how *hands-on* the approver, who is one of your stakeholders, will want to be with the supplier selection. Will the approver want ultimate authority over the decision and be willing to veto your recommendation for his or her preferred course of action? Or, will the approver essentially delegate the decision, but require a well-thought-out and formal recommendation?

If the approver is likely to demand ultimate authority and there is a substantial risk of veto, then you should involve the approver early and often throughout the sourcing and negotiation processes to ensure that you don't waste months going down a fruitless path. However, if the approver just wants to make sure that you've been diligent in your decision making, then you need to carefully prepare that formal recommendation and sell it to him or her.

How will you be able to sell your recommendation? A key to making your recommendation effective is the use of a strong executive summary. An *executive summary* is a one- or two-page document that addresses the most significant aspects of your recommendation, omitting all trivial matters. It should quickly give the decision maker confidence in your recommendation.

What sections should your executive summary include? Consider these:

- A table listing high-level points, such as what is being bought for whom, from whom.
- A description and analysis of the advantages that led you to select the recommended supplier. These include financial, performance, technical, and compatibility advantages, or combinations of various advantages.
- A list including the total cost and independent benchmark costs. Decision makers need to feel like they are not overspending. Benchmarks such as competitive bids, historical prices, internal estimates, or published prices can offer the assurance of fair value.
- A description of how you qualified the supplier, proving its ability to meet your organization's needs.
- An overview of key contractual terms. The most significant terms in most contracts include: term, pricing, delivery, warranty, remedies for failure to perform, termination rights, and service and support.

If the purchase itself must be justified, you will need to describe how spending money on the purchase will result in more money being saved or earned. Remember, try to keep the summary to a maximum of two pages. Details can be attached, but a busy executive needs to get key information *at a glance*.

Once your recommendation is approved, you can notify the successful supplier and get started in implementing the agreement. Because most of this chapter focuses on integrating the new supplier into your organization and building a long-term, mutually beneficial relationship, this is a good time to discuss how you should communicate your decision to the unsuccessful bidders.

DEBRIEFING UNSUCCESSFUL BIDDERS

The procurement function plays an important role in developing an organization's image. Procurement, together with sales, is responsible for most of an organization's contacts with the business community.

The manner in which the sourcing process is managed is probably the most significant factor in shaping how the supply base views the organization. To preserve your organization's positive image, you should treat the sourcing process with care. One facet of the process that is of particular significance is the debriefing procedure.

Debriefing is simply the act of meeting with an unsuccessful bidder to explain why their bid was not deemed to be the most attractive. Debriefing is a fragile process. You want to be as helpful as possible to the unsuccessful bidder, but you also must maintain the confidentiality of other suppliers' information. Here are a few guidelines for conducting debriefings:

- **State your debriefing goals in writing, both internally and to the bidder**—Goals may include: identifying weaknesses in the bidder's proposal, demonstrating that the bidder was treated fairly, promoting good relations within the business community, answering the bidder's questions, and obtaining feedback from the bidder.
- **Provide helpful information to the bidder**—Helpful information includes: strengths of the bidder's proposal, weaknesses of the bidder's proposal, and the reasons for not accepting the bidder's proposal.
- **Protect confidential information**—This type of information includes the names of other bidders, the ranking of other bidders, and the specifics of the other bidders' proposals (such as price or the total value or percentage difference between the winning proposal and the bidder's proposal).

Well-done debriefings can reinforce a positive reputation for your organization. By following and expanding upon these guidelines, you can help your organization secure an identity of fairness, integrity, and professionalism. In addition, you never know what the future may bring. Today's unsuccessful bidder may be the right supplier for your organization in the future. As a result, you do not want to burn any bridges or damage the reputation of your company so that the supplier community does not respond to your future requests for proposals (RFPs).

With debriefing the unsuccessful bidders out of the way, you can turn your full attention to working with your new supplier for a successful relationship!

THE CONTRACT MANAGEMENT PROCESS

A common term for the process of putting into place all of the arrangements you've negotiated with the successful supplier is *contract management*. A good contract management process ensures that both the buying organization and the supplier fulfill all of the obligations that they agreed to in signing a contract. It also helps the buying organization achieve all of the benefits it expected to when contracting with a supplier.

Not having a good contract management process in place has consequences to the buying organization as well as to the purchaser. If no one is managing the performance of the contract, an organization is likely to fail to meet the goals that it had for the project associated with the contract. Such failures may include delayed timelines, cost overruns, or more consequences.

What is also critical about contract management is the personal impact it can have on the procurement professional. If the procurement professional negotiates a great contract and drops the ball in making sure that its terms and conditions were adhered to, he or she may end up looking for a new job.

We have called the contract management process one of the most underrated aspects of procurement. Here's why: lots of attention gets paid to the processes leading up to the signing of a contract—things like strategic sourcing and negotiation. Those processes get attention because they produce the first statement of how much money will be saved over the contract's term, and that's great.

But the savings numbers that are shared at that point are estimates only. No savings have actually been realized, and they may never be realized. Yet, in many organizations, those same estimates are recorded, the procurement department takes credit for them, and no one verifies if those estimates were accurate.

Today's senior executives can be sticklers for details. If savings are estimated, they want to see exactly how and when they affect the organization's financial statements. Without contract management to ensure that savings are realized, it is likely that the estimates will differ greatly from the actual cost savings. That's when senior executives look for someone to hold accountable.

Starting a contract management process doesn't have to be complicated. You can always begin small and grow. Starting may be as simple as creating a spreadsheet with tasks that must be finished by certain dates. The procurement professional simply monitors those dates and keeps in close contact with the supplier to ensure timely performance.

For major, complex contracts, the procurement professional should also hold regular periodic reviews with suppliers to keep channels of communication open, discuss strategic issues, review accomplishments, and discuss action plans for the areas that need improvement. See Exhibit H for a sample supplier business review meeting agenda.

While it gets executive management upset to learn that estimated savings did not come to fruition, there is actually a hidden constituency that will also be upset about it. Who is that hidden constituency? The losing bidders! Let us share with you an event that shed new light onto this issue. At an Automotive Fleet Leasing Association's Annual Conference where we spoke there were buyers (i.e., fleet managers) and sellers. Mention *strategic sourcing* in a room full of sellers, and one begins to see steam billowing from their ears!

During the question-and-answer session, several sellers stood up and asked questions about the accountability for apparent savings generated through strategic sourcing. They asked questions such as, "After the contract has been signed and the winning bidder has made all of its promises of savings, who goes back and makes sure that all of those savings are achieved?"

These folks implied that they felt that no one ever confirmed that savings estimates were achieved, and that their competitors' empty promises unfairly beat them out. They wanted us to confirm their suspicions.

We have to be honest—sometimes actual savings are tracked, sometimes only the initial estimates. But, the point is clear, contract management is necessary—not to pacify losing suppliers, but to ensure that no savings fall through the cracks. Because if rejected suppliers chafe at the thought of savings estimates being incorrect, imagine how your management feels!

MINIMIZING LEAKAGE

The failure to achieve cost savings potential is called *leakage* and poses a threat to the credibility of procurement professionals and departments. A common form of leakage occurs when a procurement department establishes an enterprise-wide contract, yet many users within the organization still buy from other suppliers. This is referred to as *maverick buying*, as discussed in Chapter 1.

Why does leakage occur? It can occur for a variety of reasons, from lack of knowledge, to resistance to change, to preferences for certain processes. The CEO for procurement consultancy Paladin Associates and former chief procurement officer for GE Capital, Don Hoeppner, has found two reasons to be most common in his experiences: "One is, employees are uninformed on where they should buy. Or, employees simply refuse to follow the rules and continue buying from their old buddy or cousin or golf partner."

The following are four strategies for mitigating leakage:

1. **Involve stakeholders in the sourcing process**—If you want to drive compliance with a new contract and achieve the true savings potential of the contract, your new supplier must not be perceived by your stakeholders as *the procurement department's supplier*. It must be regarded as *our*

supplier—the supplier that the company collectively chose. If the *procurement department's supplier* perception exists, especially if you've ousted a popular incumbent, your stakeholders may exploit the reasons why choosing the supplier was a bad decision. In many companies, stakeholders have the power to either help you achieve your cost savings potential or prevent you from reaching it. So, it is important to work in harmony with them. Give them the opportunity to contribute to the criteria used to evaluate suppliers and their proposals. Invite them to be present when proposals are opened and evaluated. Give them the opportunity to voice concerns before the supplier selection is finalized.

2. **Make compliance the easiest alternative**—People inherently gravitate to the most friction-free way to complete a work task and shy away from approaches that feel unnecessarily difficult. It should never be more convenient for a stakeholder to place an order with the wrong supplier than it is to place one with the right supplier. So, make sure that your processes are structured accordingly. "Larger companies, in most cases, have put in place procure-to-pay systems that tend to reduce leakage," observes Hoeppner. "They make the right way and supplier the easy way for employees to buy . . . and the wrong way and the wrong supplier, the hard way."

3. **Monitor expenditures to identify any leakage**—In American football, when a team has multiple touchdowns scored against it, it can observe that right away. The coaches can identify which opposing plays and/or players the team is having difficulty defending and adjustments can be made right away. The team doesn't wait until the end of the game or the season to figure out what went wrong. So, you need to apply this approach to leakage. Use tools like spend analysis systems and backend procurement card reporting, or obtain spend reports from your accounting department to identify leakage in near real-time. Then, you can identify where the leakage is occurring, learn why it is occurring, and stop it. The longer it takes for you to identify and stop leakage, the more cost savings you will lose, so time is of the essence.

4. **Be as creative as is appropriate for your organizational culture**—Leakage is a human behavior problem. How you solve a human behavior problem will vary depending on your organizational culture. Some cultures will tolerate a tougher approach; other cultures require that you be more delicate and diplomatic. Hoeppner shared an interesting story from his experience: "One archaic way that we did in GE that was quite effective [was] we simply told the organization that if you buy things from a supplier that is not an authorized supplier, when their invoice comes, we're not going to pay it. We'd write the supplier that we shut off and say 'Don't accept any sort of order from our company because, if you ship something, you will not get paid and we are not sending it back. We're simply not going to

pay you.' And that worked. Pretty archaic, but it worked. Today, there are all kinds of controls in systems that you can activate to prevent employees from placing an order with an unapproved or unqualified supplier." What worked for General Electric in 1996 may not work for a smaller organization decades later. So, always decide on your tactics after carefully considering your organizational culture.

THE EVOLUTION OF COST SAVINGS TRACKING

By working for years in the field, we have seen an evolution of procurement-driven cost savings. Cost savings are often recorded when a contract is signed and, as such, are only estimates. The evolution has followed this path:

- Procurement department does not achieve cost savings
- Procurement department implements a contract poised to produce cost savings, management is surprised, but nothing is formally recorded
- Procurement department implements a contract poised to produce cost savings and records cost savings, but definitions of cost savings are not formal or defensible
- Procurement department implements a contract poised to produce cost savings and tries to apply strict standards to the recording thereof
- Procurement department implements a contract poised to produce cost savings, applies strict standards to the recording thereof, and compares estimated cost savings with actual cost savings at the end of a period
- Procurement department implements a contract poised to produce cost savings, applies strict standards to the recording thereof, and tracks the actual-versus-estimated cost savings often throughout the life of the contract
- Procurement department implements a contract poised to produce cost savings, applies strict standards to the recording thereof, tracks the actual-versus-estimated cost savings often throughout the life of the contract, and takes all actions necessary to ensure that actual cost savings equal estimated cost savings

No matter where you are in this evolution right now, when you implement new supplier agreements, strive to meet the criteria for the final step of this path.

MEASURING SUPPLIER PERFORMANCE

Earlier in this chapter, you read about maximizing actual cost savings by working with other departments in your organization to achieve compliance with the contract and to prevent leakage. In sports, that's like managing the other team.

A concept that is inherent in procurement, but foreign in sports, is the concept of managing the other team. Who is the other team? Your suppliers. It is not enough just to have all of your internal *ducks in a row*. You must maintain active and frequent communication with your important suppliers throughout the relationship to ensure that your organization achieves all of the benefits that were anticipated when you had finalized your negotiations with those suppliers. We believe that *what gets measured, gets done!*

A supplier who performs well can help an organization be more efficient, produce higher quality products or services, reduce costs, and increase profits. A supplier who performs poorly will have the opposite effect.

Therefore, it is obvious that measuring and managing supplier performance is one of the most important responsibilities of procurement professionals. Do you have a supplier performance rating program in place? If not, here are five important decisions involved with implementing a supplier performance rating program:

1. **Which suppliers will you rate?** Consider rating those suppliers with whom your organization spends a lot of money, as well as other suppliers who can have a significant impact on your operations, regardless of your spend with them.

2. **What personnel in your organization will participate in the rating process?** In addition to the procurement staff, don't forget to include end users and stakeholders.

3. **What performance measures will you use?** Use metrics that are aligned to the measurements that are used to gauge the success of your organization. How many metrics should you use when evaluating supplier performance? The number that we recommend as a starting point is four. We feel that by using four metrics (e.g., quality, delivery, service, and cost), you can address the most important categories of supplier performance and can create a four-quadrant dashboard.

   If you use less than four metrics, you are probably going to miss an important aspect of supplier performance in the evaluation. If you use many more (around eight or more), you are going to dilute the value of each metric. It will be more difficult for the supplier to understand its overall performance, and the priority of each metric becomes unclear.

4. **How will you collect performance data?** Implementation speed, IT support, budget, and data integrity are among the many factors to consider when selecting among the many popular data collection methods.

5. **How will you use performance data?** Performance data must be used to reward good performance as well as to correct poor performance.

DAILY SUPPLIER PERFORMANCE MONITORING

While the previous section described a strategic approach to measuring supplier performance over a longer period of time and a somewhat large sample size of supplier performance events, it is also critical to ensure that the daily details are monitored as well. You don't want to wait until the end of the year to find out there was a problem you could have fixed months prior.

While solving daily problems may seem tactical and *tactical* has undeservedly become a bad word in parts of the procurement field, let's face it: strategic supplier performance is comprised of many tactical events (good or bad) that add up over time. Nip a problem in the bud and strategic supplier performance will look good.

Perhaps a supplier performance mental exercise will get you thinking . . .

Supplier Performance Mental Exercise: Supply Chain Challenge for a Major Culinary Institute

A supplier was delivering a variety of food items including poultry, seafood, meat, and produce to the customer's culinary kitchen. The delivery trucks were arriving earlier than the customer's requested delivery date. Often, trucks had to wait at the customer's delivery dock for several hours in order to offload the shipment.

1. What supply chain problems could this generate for the customer, the supplier, and the trucking company?
2. How can supplier performance monitoring identify and resolve this problem?

Think through your answers before reading ours.

Okay—are you ready to read ours? Great! And it's actually a good thing if you came up with different answers than we did.

1. **What supply chain problems could this generate for the customer, the supplier, and the trucking company?**

   Problems for Culinary Institute (Customer):
   - Space issues—storage problems
   - Inventory carrying charges
   - Possibility of food spoilage—perishable items

   Problems for Supplier:
   - Not meeting customer's delivery requirements
   - Paying for idle trucks (detention or demurrage charges)
   - Dissatisfied customer

Problems for Trucking Company:
- Scheduling of delivery trucks
- Tying up trucks that could be used for other shipments
- Dissatisfied Culinary Institute and the supplier (customers)

2. **How can supplier performance monitoring identify and resolve this problem?**

Implementing a simple supplier performance monitoring system, where daily problems could be recorded, reviewed, and acted upon, would be helpful. We know that some organizations gladly invest in supply chain technologies and others don't. So, don't be discouraged if you don't have the latest supplier performance monitoring platform available. If necessary, use a basic Excel spreadsheet if that's the best technology available to you. With some method of supplier performance monitoring, the culinary institute's procurement specialist could detect deviations from on-time deliveries much earlier. He or she could then stress the fact that early deliveries were not helpful, but more important, they interrupted their supply chain, they were faced with food spoilage, and their inventory levels and storage were adversely impacted. By having proactive measures to monitor supplier performance, the culinary institute could have reduced overall costs, saved time, and eliminated aggravation for their organization and the important players in their supply chain.

CULTIVATING RELATIONSHIPS AND COLLABORATING

One key to maximizing the positive impact of a supplier relationship is *getting your own house in order.* In other words, if your own systems, processes, and people are not up to par, you can adversely affect the supplier's performance.

Michael Massetti, former Vice President of Global Procurement & Quality for Tekelec, agreed, using a golf analogy on an episode of the Next Level Purchasing Association Podcast,[1] "If you're a 95 or 100 golfer and you get the latest, greatest Nike driver, it's certainly unlikely that your game is going to improve." Merely asking your suppliers to perform well isn't going to guarantee good results.

Massetti knows firsthand about looking internally to solve supplier relationship problems. When he took over a procurement leadership role at a former employer, the company had some concerns about a strategic supplier's delivery performance. Naturally, the tendency of internal customers was to blame the supplier. "When we started looking at the root cause of the problems, we realized that there were things on our side that were contributing to that lack of performance," Massetti says.

"When we really started unpeeling the proverbial onion, we found out that there were some issues with our own forecasting process and how we were managing inventory," Massetti shares. Collaborating with the supplier and making changes internally "allowed us to improve the overall delivery performance remarkably."

Not all suppliers are equally important to your organization, so you should not take the same approach to managing supplier relationships with each of them. For example, you would not redesign a complex internal process to improve a relationship with a low-spend supplier of noncritical items. Massetti suggests basing an approach to relationships on a simple supplier stratification scheme that includes three tiers, such as partners, suppliers, and vendors.

Using this stratification approach, partner relationships would involve the most executive engagement, dedicated resources on both sides, frequent performance evaluations, and time and effort spent to develop the relationship.

TRUE SUPPLIER ALLIANCES

Identifying *special* suppliers, whether you refer to them as *partners* or some other term, is important. For suppliers at your highest level of stratification, you should pursue some form of alliance.

A *supplier alliance* is a special, formalized relationship with a supplier; a relationship reserved for an extremely limited number of suppliers. It is characterized by collaboration that results in mutual successes that are not achievable otherwise.

You may pursue a supplier alliance to realize one or more of the following benefits:

- Assure continuity of supply in a tight market
- Achieve significant reduction in the cost of doing business, of which price is only one component
- Attain a flexible and responsive source of supply when demand changes unexpectedly or dramatically
- Access expertise that will contribute to innovation
- Improve your organization's quality or operations

Deciding on alliance partners involves two variables: (1) difficulty of obtaining supply and (2) importance to your organization's mission. One way to identify candidates for supplier alliances is by calculating *supply* and *importance* scores for each major supplier, as shown in Table 10.1, then multiplying the two scores together for a total score.

Suppliers who have a total score of 9 are excellent candidates for supplier alliances. These suppliers warrant more attention, closer collaboration, and vision sharing for future success.

Table 10.1　Supplier alliance scoring tool

Supply score	Importance score
1 point if there are many sources for the product/service, short lead times, and predictable availability	**1 point** if your organization could fulfill its obligations to its customers without the product/service
2 points if there are few sources, occasional long lead times, and sometimes unpredictable availability	**2 points** if the product/service supports the production of a product or provision of a service, but is not directly incorporated into the final product/service
3 points if there are one or two sources, frequent long lead times, and always unpredictable availability	**3 points** if the product or service is directly incorporated into the final product/service

FOUR COMPONENTS OF GOOD SUPPLIER RELATIONSHIP MANAGEMENT

Now that you know who the suppliers at your highest level of stratification are, you can use these four components of good supplier relationship management:

1. **Supplier performance evaluation**—Ask a supplier's representative how she thinks the supplier is performing and you may hear, "Great!" But what if you think the supplier is performing poorly? Who is right? You can't tell without agreed-upon performance standards. For your strategic suppliers, agree upon what to measure (e.g., percentage of orders delivered by their due date) and what the goal is (e.g., 95 percent on-time deliveries). Discuss and agree on the measurement criteria during the negotiations and contract finalization.

2. **Idea sourcing and value creation**—Better profitability can come from ideas. You can greatly increase the number of good and creative ideas by sourcing ideas from your suppliers rather than just from your company's employees. Some leading organizations have systematic processes in place to collect ideas from suppliers, measure their impact, and reward suppliers for them.

   You can sometimes drive innovation simply by offering your input or feedback to a responsive supplier. Many innovations are the result of a prospective buyer communicating a challenge and compelling a supplier to help them overcome that challenge. Another valuable approach is simply asking the suppliers to share with you about their experiences in working with other companies where they have adopted innovative practices. If the practices are not proprietary, you may humbly—or even shamelessly—adopt those same practices to bring value to your organization.

3. **Supplier development**—It is logical that when you improve the capabilities of your company's workforce, your company will benefit. Based on that premise, your company would benefit by improving the capabilities of suppliers who do work that was once done in house, right? It should, but not all companies are focused enough to follow through to ensure that their suppliers are indeed improving and expanding their capabilities in order to deliver higher value.

   Leading companies engage in supplier development. Supplier development can be loosely defined as the process of working collaboratively with your suppliers to improve or expand their capabilities. An example may be teaching a supplier how to manufacture a type of item that they never manufactured before, for the purposes of giving you the option to buy, rather than make, that item. Over the last several decades, it has become increasingly common for buying organizations to train their suppliers in Six Sigma, Lean, and other quality improvement methodologies.

4. **A joint review of purchase costs**—If you work for a big company, you have a lot of buying power that may be wasted if your smaller suppliers have 100% responsibility for buying all of the goods and services needed to provide their product or service to you. By jointly reviewing costs further down the supply chain, you may find opportunities where you can buy some goods and services your suppliers need at a lower cost, ultimately reducing your overall costs.

Having these types of supplier relationship management processes in place is going beyond where most procurement organizations are today. Getting to the level where all four of these supplier relationship management components are working well is a noble goal. But that is not as far as good supplier relationship management can go. There is yet another level.

EARLY SUPPLIER INVOLVEMENT

The foregoing processes are generally applied after you have been working with a supplier of an existing item, service, or project for some time. Involving suppliers when developing a new product or service can produce even greater benefit.

However, if not done well, early supplier involvement can lead to suppliers taking advantage of customers who lack the future threat of competition to reduce costs and improve performance. We have studied this problem and found companies using these techniques to control early supplier involvement deals:

- **Make cost data sharing mandatory**—For the privilege of their involvement in development, a supplier should be required to break down its quoted price into component costs and profit margin. We mentioned this before so, obviously it's important!

- **Minimize the overhead percentage**—Scrutinize how overhead is calculated. Reidentifying overhead costs as direct costs makes it easier to jointly reduce those costs later. For example, costs associated with scrapped material might be buried in overhead. That should be made its own line item.

- **Understand all assumptions**—There are always assumptions built into a supplier's cost structure. For example, a supplier may base its labor costs on an assumed production rate (e.g., 100 units per hour). Document all of these assumptions and have a technical team member evaluate their accuracy.

- **Agree to the right terms**—Suppliers who overestimated their costs (or intentionally quoted them higher) should not benefit. Pricing in early supplier involvement arrangements should be based on a cost plus fixed fee scheme. Suppliers must agree to share with you accounting records of the work they have completed for your organization, and you should agree on the terms that can change if the volume exceeds your estimates.

- **Audit the supplier's books**—You and your technical team must audit the supplier's records to compare actual costs versus estimated costs, and those assumptions you documented earlier, with actual results. Where costs were lower than estimated or actual performance was better than assumed, a price adjustment is warranted.

- **Continuously evaluate cost reduction opportunities**—Auditing a supplier's books can also involve evaluating ways to reduce costs. But let's face it, there is only so far a supplier can reduce its margin until it is unprofitable to do business with you. However, that doesn't mean that cost reduction discussions should stop.

COST REDUCTION OPPORTUNITIES WITHIN THE SUPPLY CHAIN

Speaking of working with suppliers to identify and remove cost from the supply chain, here are four additional ways you can reduce costs in the supply chain without driving your suppliers out of business:

1. **Eliminate redundancies in the supply chain**—For all supply chain partners who are critical to your operation, create a flow chart of all activities involved in the procurement, setup, production, inspection, storage, and transportation of all materials and components that go into the final product. You will likely find activities that are repeated by different supply chain partners (e.g., outgoing inspection by one supply chain partner

immediately followed by incoming inspection by another). If you can work with your supply chain partners to eliminate such redundancies, you can reduce their costs and, as a result, your price.

2. **Shift tasks to the most efficient supply chain partner**—Sometimes the capabilities of supply chain partners overlap. Let's consider a customer's purchase of engraved plaques. The customer's immediate supplier may do direct marketing, fulfillment, and engraving. That supplier's supplier may do design, manufacturing, and engraving. In this case, who should do the engraving? The most efficient supply chain partner should, assuming that either can meet quality, delivery, and service standards. But this means that you have to question *the way we've always done it* so that you can do it the best way.

3. **Leverage the supply chain's buying power**—Often, the products and services purchased by second-tier suppliers are also purchased by a first-tier supplier. Many times, that first-tier supplier gets a better price than the second-tier suppliers. In cases like these, the first-tier supplier can negotiate to add second-tier suppliers' volume onto its agreements, thereby getting even deeper discounts for itself and reducing total cost throughout the supply chain.

4. **Renegotiate when appropriate**—This practice is common in a declining economic environment where cost reductions are the highest priority. While renegotiating a contract to lower price without enduring the costs of switching suppliers is often a good practice, it is not without its pitfalls. One major cause of conflict is the failure to include a discussion of specifications in the renegotiation process.

RENEGOTIATION AND SPECIFICATIONS

Procurement professionals often assume that what they buy will have the same quality, be delivered in the same time frame, and be supported by the same service despite a lower price.

This is a dangerous assumption. Why? Well, the supplier assumes that because the buyer is so desperate to cut costs, the buyer would be willing to accept a *minor* decrease in quality, delivery, or service. You see where this is going, don't you? The following story is an example of how the failure to discuss specifications during a renegotiation process led to conflict.

A large, not-for-profit organization purchased about $600,000 (US) in copier paper each year from a long-time supplier. The supplier always delivered mill brand paper, which is generally regarded as the highest quality. Seeing that the producer's price index for paper had fallen over several *months, the buyer requested that the supplier reduce its price. After some discussion, the buyer and supplier agreed upon a 23-percent price reduction. A few weeks later, the buyer began receiving calls from disgruntled end users who complained of receiving* inferior *non-mill brand paper. The buyer and supplier discussed this dilemma without a mutually satisfactory result. The buyer later began looking for a new paper supplier and ended up replacing the incumbent.*

Suppliers can get defensive during renegotiations. It's a fact. Discussing your specifications and expectations will prevent suppliers from seeing the renegotiation as an opportunity to cut corners to preserve their profit margins. Therefore, *always* be sure to reiterate, in specific terms, the quality, delivery, and service that you expect your supplier to provide.

SUPPLIERS AS A SOURCE OF IDEAS

Suppliers are uniquely positioned to evaluate your company. They work closely with you and get the opportunity to evaluate how your organization operates. Many suppliers can study your company and try to figure out your financial strength, and they see what your competitors are doing better than you, and in what areas. Gathering this type of information from the perspective of suppliers can be invaluable for improving your organization's performance. This type of supplier input is being seen as more and more important for organizations committed to having a competitive advantage.

Increased solicitation of supplier assessments is only one of many ways that procurement departments will tap into external sources of information in the future. We see procurement in the late 2020s and 2030s being quite different than procurement today. We think companies will realize that procurement is their interface with much of the outside world. You see, within a company, you may have hundreds, thousands, or tens of thousands of employees who represent the potential for ideas to help that company succeed and grow. But then when you look at that company's supply base, you realize that there are tens of thousands, hundreds of thousands, maybe millions of other individuals among current and prospective suppliers who can bring ideas into the company for innovation and improvement. We foresee procurement as being the funnel through which the best ideas can travel into the organization and get implemented so that the company can innovate and develop a more competitive edge in the marketplace. Control, cost savings, and supplier performance will still be important, but the supply base will play an even more strategic role in supporting the direction the company is moving.

Therefore, the bottom line is this: supplier relationships are only increasing in importance.

RESOLVING CONFLICTS WITH SUPPLIERS

While the material in this chapter, to this point, will certainly help you have more successful supplier relationships, some supplier relationships just won't work out as you had planned. These next few sections will focus on what to do when you run into the inevitable problems with suppliers.

When something goes wrong, occasionally it seems like someone in the organization wants to blame the supplier and yell and scream at them. Often, this yelling and screaming occurs before the problem is thoroughly investigated. Of course, many times the problem is not the supplier's fault, but rather the fault of your own organization.

The lesson is clear; do not blame the supplier until you've thoroughly investigated the problem and are absolutely sure that the problem was the fault of the supplier.

REASONS THAT SUPPLIER RELATIONSHIPS FALTER

It has been said many times, "Good supplier performance equals good procurement performance." Therefore, to achieve the good procurement performance to which you aspire, you need to foster positive, productive supplier relationships. When supplier relationships fail, procurement performance suffers. In order to help you avoid negative impacts on procurement performance, let's look at a few reasons why supplier relationships falter:

- **Unclear expectations**—Sometimes the performance that the buyer expects is different than the performance that the supplier understands to be required. As a result, the buyer feels that the supplier is incompetent, and the supplier feels that the buyer is overly demanding. To avoid this situation, clearly define, write down, and discuss your expectations with the supplier. Tell the supplier what constitutes good performance (e.g., 99 percent of shipments delivered on the due date on the purchase orders) as well as what constitutes bad performance (e.g., failure to return calls within four hours).
- **Opportunistic behavior**—There is a certain amount of trust involved in a collaborative buyer-supplier relationship. When one party seeks to take advantage of the other's problems (e.g., a supplier charging a large expediting fee for emergency orders or a buyer negotiating a discount every time there is a minor blemish on a product), trust is broken. The parties will lose their interest in committing themselves toward helping each other succeed. While contributing to the bottom line should always be a priority, be careful not to contribute to it at the expense of a valuable relationship that would facilitate good procurement performance and competitive advantage for years ahead.

- **Poor selection methodology**—While the goal of any supplier performance evaluation program is to achieve perfect performance, *hiccups* happen. When they do, a piece of advice that, if followed, will make you a better procurement professional is to adopt this philosophy: *If it is the supplier's fault, it is really my fault.*

TAKING OWNERSHIP OF SUPPLIER FAILURES

You choose and manage your suppliers, so you need to be responsible for them. It is a pet peeve of ours when companies blame suppliers when the companies fail to fulfill their obligations to customers, as if the companies totally absolve themselves of responsibility. Several years ago, over a mere 10-day span, we had two experiences of observing companies avoiding responsibility that we thought were interesting and/or funny enough to share.

First, we decided to take our families to a Pittsburgh Pirates' baseball game. One of the factors in choosing that day was the Pirates' promotion: a slick-looking Freddy Sanchez jersey for kids 12 and under. When we got to the game, a Pirates' representative handed our kids a cheap-looking Freddy Sanchez T-shirt along with a card that read as follows:

Dear Valued Pirates Fan,

Due to a delay on the part of our vendor, the Freddy Sanchez Replica Jersey that you were to receive today will be mailed to you within six to eight weeks. Simply complete and mail in the promotional rain check card that is attached to this notice and the jersey will be delivered to your doorstep. Please accept this Freddy Sanchez player T-shirt as an additional token of our appreciation.
    We are sorry for the inconvenience this may have caused and thank you for your support of the Pirates.

Note the first line: "Due to a delay on the part of our vendor . . ." This is finger-pointing at its finest (or worst, actually).

A few days later, we were planning on working through lunch. Within walking distance from our meeting place was a convenience store that served surprisingly good pizza, so we decided to go there. We walked up to the counter where the pizza display was, but there was no pizza. We asked if they had pizza and were told that there would be no pizza that day.

So, we think, "Okay, we'll get cheeseburgers instead." There are mustard packets, but no ketchup. We'll ask about that later.

Then we went to the beverage coolers. Not a single bottle of water. Okay, Sprite will work.

Next, we went to check out. We asked about the missing ketchup. The cashier said that they did have ketchup packets, and excused herself to go and find them. She returned, saying that they had no ketchup that day.

We start joking between ourselves about the store having nothing. The cashier interrupted us to say, "We don't have any bags, is that okay?"

At this point, we are laughing hysterically. The manager came out and said, "We don't have anything, but it's not our fault." We asked what he meant, and he replied that the store's supplier, "Hasn't delivered in four weeks. I have their customer service number; do you want to call them?"

We said that was his problem, not ours, but he may want to talk to the people across the street (i.e., us) about getting some training about how to manage their suppliers.

Again, *if it is the supplier's fault, it is really your fault.* Treat your work like that, and your suppliers will perform better. You will be inspired to defend your pride to yourself. Don't take the convenience store's approach in the preceding example when conducting your own supplier management.

That said, sometimes a supplier's performance is simply inexcusable. Many instances of poor supplier performance could have been avoided if a solid supplier qualification methodology was used. Look for ways to make your supplier selection process more reliable in the future. If you are buying critical goods and services based on price alone, it's time to change before a key supplier relationship becomes a casualty.

WHEN SUPPLIER RELATIONSHIPS REACH THE POINT OF NO RETURN

Do a good job of selecting the supplier, then do a good job of measuring supplier performance. Supplier performance evaluation programs help keep suppliers in line because suppliers know that they are being observed, measured, and evaluated.

Most organizations usually only formally evaluate a small percentage of their suppliers. Many use the 80-20 rule to determine which suppliers will be evaluated—the 20 percent of suppliers to whom 80 percent of the spend is directed. Of course, the other 80 percent of suppliers can cause headaches for you, too!

In cases where supplier performance is lacking, it is important for you to know how to handle situations where one of your suppliers is not performing satisfactorily. Obviously, the first step is to try to work out the situation calmly and professionally. Unfortunately, that doesn't always work.

You should know what the second step is. It can be a frustrating and emotional time for you, and you should not necessarily be left to your instincts to decide what to do. Many procurement professionals have lost their tempers trying to resolve situations, and later ended up being embarrassed by how they reacted.

Every procurement department should have a plan for what comes next. Here is a list of things you *can* do to address poor performance by a supplier. Depending on the situation, you will decide what you *should* do, and in what order:

- Speak more aggressively but respectfully to your contact at the supplier
- Contact a member of the management team
- Arrange for an emergency on-site visit at the supplier
- Threaten to switch suppliers
- Switch suppliers
- Use social media to expose the supplier's poor performance
- Seek third-party assistance

In the United States, a third party that can assist you with a supplier dispute is the Better Business Bureau (BBB), previously mentioned in Chapter 7. Specifically, if you have a problem with a supplier that negotiation alone cannot resolve, file a complaint with the BBB.

When consumers have a bad experience with a business, they have many outlets for sharing that information with other consumers, whether it is posting on social media, ranting to their friends, writing a review on a website, blogging or—in extreme cases—organizing a boycott and getting attention from the news media. There are few barriers to a consumer sharing his or her views and, consequently, other consumers benefiting from hearing about those experiences.

Of course, in the business-to-business world, it is very different. Procurement professionals generally do not talk about their bad suppliers with buyers in other companies the same way that consumers do. Procurement professionals do not blog about their bad supplier experiences for fear of embarrassing their companies. So, there is not a perfect way of learning about real-world supplier performance issues.

However, the BBB and similar organizations in other parts of the world offer a way to engage in a type of online, social information sharing. You can look up a prospective supplier on the BBB's site to see whether they have a history of complaints and whether they respond to those complaints. Just one unresolved complaint can result in a supplier seeing its BBB rating drop from an A+ to as low as a C–.[2]

But you won't have that information available unless procurement professionals participate. You can benefit when others share their experiences, so you should *pay it forward* and share your experiences by filing a complaint when appropriate.

Anytime that you have to do business with a new supplier, take a few seconds to view their rating on the BBB's website. The rating could introduce a red flag that saves you from a painful experience.

We are shocked when procurement professionals place orders, regardless of the value, with new suppliers without taking a few seconds to search for historical information about that supplier's performance or checking their references. Remember that small orders can cause big problems. Don't pretend that you're too busy to take the steps necessary to avoid the problems that are lurking. Believe us—if problems occur later, you will spend much more time solving them.

Filing a complaint isn't just for making information available. It essentially gives you more leverage in resolving that complaint; not many suppliers want to have a publicly known unsatisfactory rating, so there is extra incentive for the supplier to work toward a resolution. The BBB will be a third party on your side to help show that you are serious about resolving the dispute.

Who couldn't use a little more leverage now and then? Having said this, you should understand that the possibilities for resolving conflicts are virtually endless. But, you should know in advance what you are going to do and in what order, when a problem arises. Actions that should never be a part of your *escalation* or resolution plan are:

- Using profanity
- Making a personal threat—even in jest
- Losing control of your emotions (raising your voice and sounding out of control can, unfortunately, sometimes work better than being professional, but you should remain in control of yourself, regardless of how you sound)

RECONFIGURING THE SUPPLY BASE

As you can tell by now, we believe in good supplier relationship management. For the long-term success of an organization, you must focus on supplier relationship management with your key suppliers.

You may have noticed that we are also big on holding yourself and your organization accountable for bad supplier performance. You may even be thinking, "Don't the authors ever think that something could truly be the supplier's fault or that a problem could occur without any warning signs?" Yes, we do think that a problem could be a supplier's fault and not yours. The only time those types of problems become your fault is if you fail to pay regular attention to the opportunity to reconfigure the supply base. So, now we will give you the other side of the coin—our contrarian view of supplier relationship management.

The way *supplier relationship management* is used by some people connotes that 100 percent of the health of the relationship is dependent on the buyer. We disagree.

As a result of this perception of supplier relationship management, procurement professionals often waste time developing relationships with substandard suppliers. In these cases, those procurement professionals need to spend time finding a supplier who can perform. Managing a relationship with a more competent supplier is ultimately more productive.

Here are some signs that attempting to manage a supplier relationship may be less desirable than sourcing for a new supplier:

- The supplier calls you often during the sales process, but after you give that supplier an order, you can't get anyone to deliver what was promised or to communicate progress.
- The supplier places your organization on less of a priority than other customers. Look, if they are going to give your organization less responsive service than their other customers, they should charge your organization a *lower priority rate.*
- The supplier responds only when you get tough. When something is not going right with a supplier, we always communicate cordially at first. If that doesn't work, then we get tough but respectful. Unfortunately, especially during a healthy economic time, suppliers are busy and service levels decline. Although it drives us crazy when the only thing that suppliers will respond to is tough talk, you have to do what works. If nice, polite requests don't get the job done, you have to remember your obligation to your organization and choose an appropriate alternative approach.

Don't get us wrong. We do not advocate always being tough, and we don't dismiss the notion that supplier relationship management should be a part of every procurement department's repertoire. But sometimes, it makes sense to source *old-school style* or to rationalize the supply base.

FIVE OPTIONS FOR RATIONALIZING THE SUPPLY BASE

Rationalizing the supply base means utilizing both the *right suppliers* and the *right number of suppliers.* Rationalizing the supply base requires you to categorize your spend and identify current and potential suppliers for each category. After identifying your categories and suppliers, you have five options for the supply base in each category:

1. **Reduce it**—Many think of this as the only rationalization option, but it's not. This option works best when you already have enough qualified suppliers and are sure that no others can offer a cost, quality, or other advantage. You consolidate spend with a subset of currently used suppliers; however, you should be cautious and avoid assuming that you are already using the best suppliers. With the proliferation of global sourcing, there are fewer barriers than you might think to finding the best suppliers across the planet.

2. **Increase it**—Despite common teaching, working with fewer suppliers is not always better. By blindly following the supplier reduction trend, you

might award business in one category to a supplier who performs well in another category. This strategy is flawed when the supplier is not as competent in the second category. In many cases, it is better to have two suppliers who can deliver great performance in two categories than one supplier who performs well in one category, but poorly in the other. When analyzing your categorized spend, find suppliers who appear to serve your organization across categories. Ask if they are truly the best choice in each category and what the measurable advantages are to using them across categories.

3. **Maintain it**—If you've done a good job in selecting suppliers, there is no need to change. Period.

4. **Keep the size, change the mix**—Many organizations set goals as to the number of suppliers they should use and measure success simply by the numbers. But the *quality* of suppliers is more important than the *quantity* of suppliers. Even if you have the right number of suppliers, you may need to replace the poor performers with good performers.

5. **Expand, then reduce**—Sometimes, you are under pressure to reduce the supply base, but the suppliers you are currently using are so inadequate that you just can't imagine depending more heavily on any of them. So, you may have to introduce more suppliers to identify the best ones in the market before you start ousting the poor performers. You also need to make sure you are not trading one problem for another. New suppliers must prove themselves so you add them to the list to allow more choices for a future supplier reduction. There is nothing wrong with this plan. Just communicate it to stakeholders as a two-step approach to good supply base rationalization.

Between us, we have worked for a small manufacturer (200 employees), two large educational institutions (both with more than 5,000 employees), a Fortune 500 airline (44,000 employees), and an internationally renowned pharmaceutical/life sciences company (more than 100,000 employees). We have also worked for a small organization, in terms of number of employees, even though it had a global reach.

Historically, the small organization did very little printing. So, we relied on an office products supplier to handle the organization's printing. The supplier actually brokers the printing, which means they source it, find the best deal, and give us a single point of contact. It used to be too small of a category to warrant us focusing on.

At one point, they stopped doing so well with our growing print requirements. Print jobs had been late and, because the supplier brokered the printing, they had little visibility into the status of our orders. Any expediting requests were filtered and untimely due to the communication disconnect.

The purpose of consolidating spend for us, in this case, was to reduce administrative costs, and this arrangement was beginning to increase them. Seeing our printing requirements grow, we decided to exercise supply base rationalization Option 2, and increase it. We sourced for a new printing supplier and split printing off from our office products supplier.

As a result, instead of getting good office products supplier performance and poor printing supplier performance, we got good performance in both areas. The administration across those two categories was reduced, so we were better able to focus on our organization's mission.

CLOSING REMARKS

Suppliers can help your organization move forward, and unfortunately, they can also prevent your organization from moving forward. Continuously managing supplier relationships and regularly optimizing your supply base can result in more suppliers doing the former, rather than the latter.

REFERENCES

1. "Skillfully Managing Supplier Relationships." March 20, 2008. *Next Level Purchasing Association Podcast.* Available from https://podcasts.apple.com/us/podcast/skillfully-managing-supplier-relationships/id267161044?i=1000025853745.
2. "Overview of Ratings." *Better Business Bureau.* Available from https://www.bbb.org/overview-of-bbb-ratings.

This book has free material available for download from the
Web Added Value™ resource center at *www.jrosspub.com*

11
CHAPTER

SUPPLY CHAIN RESILIENCY AND CONTINGENCY PLANNING: BEING AGILE WHEN THE GAME DOESN'T GO ACCORDING TO PLAN

Have you ever wondered why many sports teams have backup players? For example, American professional football teams have more than 50 players on their rosters while they only need 11 players at a time on the field. The *backup* is a player who stands ready to come into the game if the starter is injured or otherwise can't continue playing due to various reasons. Sports teams select and train backups in order to plan for unforeseen circumstances. In addition to having backups, coaches proactively come up with a contingency plan for their team to increase resiliency and their chances of winning.

Similarly, as the world has dramatically changed in recent years, procurement and supply management professionals need to pay special attention to developing contingency plans for responsive procurement and strategic sourcing processes and practices, as a means to mitigate supply chain shocks and disruptions. A contingency plan is an important part of any initiative to achieve or improve supply chain resiliency.

Focusing on efficiency alone to achieve resiliency does not make for a good strategy. The financial crisis of 2008 and the COVID-19 pandemic in 2020 demonstrated the potentially catastrophic dangers of employing a just-in-time strategy. In fact, these two crises have highlighted the need for a strategy that might better be called *just-in-case*, which puts much more of an emphasis on supply chain resilience. Some experts believe that this change in philosophy will become more important now that the public sector owns so much debt in private firms, with governments around the world having printed and distributed so much money to save failing businesses during the COVID-19 pandemic. So, how can companies most effectively make this switch? "By having procurement to focus on creating resilient multi-relational networks rather than linear supply chains," as cited in an article in the Harvard Business Review.[1]

SUPPLY CHAIN RESILIENCE AND REBALANCING IN GLOBAL VALUE CHAINS

Procurement professionals who had historically been masters in reducing over-all costs and keeping the wheels of production turning faced big challenges as supplier operations were interrupted and market demand fluctuated during the COVID-19 pandemic. During this time, finding ways to reduce costly risks, heading off potential pitfalls, and adjusting resources, while being agile and realizing new opportunities, became the keys to operational success.

Adjusting production and sourcing new suppliers requires new levels of agility. To not only survive but thrive in this new normal, organizations must develop responsive procurement and strategic sourcing processes as a means to mitigate supply chain disruptions. Doing so requires real-time decision making by providing frontline workers and leaders with access to current information. Enhanced visibility of information and data supports operational responsiveness in a rapidly changing market, driving flexible and creative sourcing methods required to optimize productivity and reduce costs.

The new environment has produced a new acronym: VUCA. VUCA stands for *volatility, uncertainty, complexity, and ambiguity*. VUCA is more prominent than ever in procurement and supply chain management. In an article entitled "A 4-step Strategy for Building Procurement in a VUCA World," Paulo de Matos writes, "Supply chain disruptions are nothing new." From global trade disputes to Brexit, volatile exchange rates, fluctuating commodity prices, civil unrest, the global pandemic, and all of the situations that will unexpectedly arise in the future, procurement is required to be more agile and resilient than ever before. These challenges have directly impacted the procurement of raw materials and intermediate goods, which are shipped as a part of the global value chain, and then usually assembled in another country. Within the global value chain, China, India, and Mexico (among other countries) are large producers of components and assemblies, but during the COVID-19 pandemic, "many of these distribution channels were shut down with no notification, and very little time to replace suppliers."[2] Such global disruptions and crises are an inevitable factor of life that require procurement and supply chain professionals to proactively plan for the unknown, stay agile, and seek new strategies to remain resilient.

"Most supply chain leaders recognize that becoming more resilient is a necessity in the current environment," says Geraint John, VP Analyst at Gartner. "However, measures such as alternative factories, dual sourcing, and more generous safety stocks go against the well-versed philosophy of lean supply chains that has prevailed in recent decades. The rebalancing of efficiency and resiliency will not be easy. In most cases, increased resilience comes with additional costs. But the cost of doing nothing can also be significant."[3] As a result, we strongly believe that procurement and supply chain leaders need to pursue major strategies to build greater resilience into their multi-relational networks.

SUPPLY CHAIN RESILIENCY STRATEGIES

In the following sections, we highlight five strategies to proactively build supply chain resilience in the wake of global vulnerabilities.

Adopting Digital and Data Analytics Strategies

During the COVID-19 pandemic and its global lockdowns, many manufacturers began to realize the true potential of digital transformation. They have started adopting a range of technologies, such as analytics, artificial intelligence, the Internet of Things, advanced robotics, and digital platforms. Digitalization can assist strategic sourcing and supply chain teams in becoming more predictive, transactional procurement functions to become more automated, and supplier relationship management efforts to be more proactive. Broad availability and adoption of digital source-to-pay, procure-to-pay, and advanced analytics tools will make procurement more capable of successfully reducing or eliminating future supply chain disruptions.

In addition, digital procurement solutions enable future planning for organizations by providing access to previously unavailable insights in supply chain management and bringing order to massive, but unstructured, data sets. This ultimately drives more complex analysis and better supplier strategies for more efficient operations.

A success story[4] is when Nike used predictive analytics to selectively mark down goods and reduce production early on during the COVID-19 pandemic to minimize impact. The company was also able to reroute products from brick-and-mortar stores to e-commerce sales, driven in part by direct-to-consumer online sales through its own training app. As a result, Nike sustained a smaller drop in sales as compared to its competitors. Nike's ability to reroute components and flex production dynamically across sites kept production going in the wake of a shock. This required robust digital systems as well as the analytics muscle to run scenarios based on different responses.

Achieving End-to-End Supply Chain Visibility

A single platform that can track and trace information, in real time, from early-stage planning based on forecasts through production to final delivery on a global scale is a necessity for procurement accuracy and supply chain visibility and resilience. Most companies are still in the early stages of their efforts to connect the entire value chain for higher visibility with a seamless flow of data. Digital strategies can deliver major benefits to efficiency and transparency that are yet to be fully realized.

Consumer goods giant Procter & Gamble, for example, has a centralized control tower system that provides a company-wide view across geographies and products. It integrates real-time data, from inventory levels to road delays and weather forecasts, for its own plants as well as suppliers and distributors. When a problem occurs, the system can run scenarios to identify the most effective solution.[5]

Creating a comprehensive view of the supply chain through detailed supplier mapping is a critical step to identifying hidden relationships that invite vulnerability. In these days, many large companies don't have a clear view of their suppliers' processes and practices. Working with operations and production teams to review each product's bill of materials can reveal whether critical raw materials are procured from high-risk sources and if they lack ready substitutes. Companies can also work with their first-tier suppliers to obtain information that facilitates transparency, thus increasing supply chain visibility.

In addition, supply chain visibility provides other advantages for today's global businesses, allowing reduced complexity, improved communication throughout the organization, nimbleness, and the ability to keep up with a changing regulatory landscape as well as complex social and environmental responsibilities.

Anticipating and Planning for Uncertainty

A primary role of procurement is ensuring that business operations continue like clockwork no matter how disrupted the business environment is. This involves understanding the current environment as well as foreseeing the potential future environments and preparing for them. The challenge is that all businesses currently operate in an environment where there is the constant pressure of market volatility, complexity, and uncertainty. Going forward, businesses are likely going to be operating in more uncertainty and facing more unexpected crises, placing an extra burden on the procurement and supply chain functions.

Making a direct link between supply and demand, organizations can anticipate and prepare a better supply chain management plan for uncertainty. Data driven approaches are beginning to replace the rigorous process of gathering and interpreting supplier, market, and environmental information. This enables real-time decision making with businesses building artificial intelligence-driven and integrated data systems that are supported by predictive analytics. Insights can then be applied in forward planning on both strategy and performance. By applying various platforms and technologies, procurement teams can now better determine purchasing requirements based upon demand and hedge against the obsolescence and waste of critical raw materials stock, minimize uncertainty, and ultimately improve the organization's cash flow.

Predicting and Mitigating Risks

Most procurement and supply chain management teams, even in the most advanced companies, are ill-equipped to address the wide range of risks they are exposed to, affecting their resiliency. Whether the company is a manufacturer of raw materials or finished goods, or a supplier of logistics services, every aspect of an organization's supply chain is exposed to increasing types and levels of risk. Focusing on building supply chain resilience as part of your risk management strategy allows your organization to transform its view of risk to create value rather than just manage it.

In addition to the procurement vulnerabilities and risks that were discussed in Chapter 2, one of the most serious supply chain risks is a cyberattack that can come from anywhere at any time; can be more destructive than some forms of natural disasters; and can lead to operational, financial, and reputational damages that cannot be recovered or repaired.

There is a chance that your organization is under a cyberattack as you are reading this book! The bad guys only have to get it right once in a while to cause catastrophic disruption. Some of the largest companies in the world have been forced to pay a hefty ransom to attackers (e.g., Colonial Pipeline cyberattack in 2021)[6] to restore technical operations. Other companies have lost intellectual property or customer information and did not find out until the damage was already done. To stay resilient, it is vital to identify and protect the critical information and data of your organization as well as your suppliers and partners who could be unwitting attack victims.

In a recent conversation with Patrick Cozzens, president of Modern Transportation, a leading bulk material logistics organization, he shared their strategies for addressing cyberattacks. "The goal is to build a supply chain that is resilient, can stretch, and can recover from the inevitable disruptions from a whole host of threats, including cyberattacks," he said. To do that, transportation companies must be able to respond and adapt as quickly as possible to known and unknown risks. "Embracing technology is part of that solution," he stressed.

At Modern Transportation, software programs are upgraded frequently. Employees are educated to change their passwords frequently and are reminded to not open suspicious emails or attachments. More important, they perform tests to measure their preparedness by running penetration testing and mock breaches of their information systems. "By taking advantage of advanced technology, educating our suppliers, introducing innovative approaches to addressing our customers' needs, and proactively mitigating risk, we have created an organization that is agile and has thrived while others have struggled during these challenging times," he added. For the entire interview with Cozzens, refer to Chapter 15.

Creating a Culture of Empowerment and Collaboration

Resilience is often identified as one of the factors that helps individuals and teams get ahead—whether it's a team of scientists who collaborate and formulate the breakthrough compound for a life-saving medication after years of failed experimentation and trials; or a basketball player who overcomes a severe injury and a shooting slump to advance his team in a big tournament; or more recently when Simone Biles,[7] the most decorated gymnast of all time, made a choice to safeguard her mental health by withdrawing from the vault routine at the 2020 Tokyo Olympic Games. Few of us work entirely alone, and how our teams persevere and thrive matters just as much as how individually resilient we are. Resilient teams are just as important to businesses as resilient individuals, but while individual resilience is built independently, team resiliency must be carefully cultivated by leadership.

A healthy company culture coupled with strong leadership that prioritizes employee satisfaction through valuing, enabling, engaging, and respecting employees can end up increasing profitability and resiliency, even during and after unforeseen disruptions. The relationship may not be as direct as, for example, reducing production costs, but it's important enough to make you think. In fact, a study conducted by Gallup found that an engaged workforce and behaviors connected with such a workforce can lead to a 21% increase in profitability.[8]

It's not by chance that such organizations have higher employee engagement, high morale and productivity, and lower absenteeism, burnout, and turnover. What are they doing that separates them from organizations that are struggling to motivate employees and retain high performers? We strongly believe that the leadership of these organizations makes employee well-being and empowerment a high priority.

For example, an organization that has been successful in creating a culture of valuing and nurturing employees is Costco.[9] Today, the wholesale giant is the second largest retailer in the world with more than $186 billion projected in sales in 2021.

In 2021, as many restaurants, retailers, and other service industry employers struggled dealing with labor shortages and finding workers to ramp up again after post-pandemic closures, Costco remained resilient and profitable. To attract and retain workers, employers will have to do more in the current climate. Costco seems to have a leg up on this since its culture of valuing, engaging, respecting, and fairly compensating employees, while promoting leadership from within, has been a vital part of the company's success for years.[10]

In addition to a culture that promotes employee well-being, empowerment, and collaboration, leaders—in particular procurement and supply management professionals—need to pay special attention toward cultivating a culture that encourages treating suppliers as partners, especially key suppliers. Building resiliency is all about empowering people—from employees to suppliers and customers. In different sections of this book, we have shared strategies and techniques for collaborating closely with suppliers for higher efficiency, improved bottom-line profitability, and *win-win* outcomes. Later in this chapter, we will discuss how best-in-class organizations work with their suppliers to develop contingency plans in order to stay resilient.

In the months and years ahead, effective and resilient procurement and supply chain management will be all about agility, flexibility, creativity, and finding the perfect balance between *just-in-time* processes and *just-in-case* scenarios, while improving resiliency and reducing risk as much as possible.

CONTINGENCY PLANNING

Obviously, you should have contingency plans for common occurrences, such as a supplier production problem that can bring a single supplier's shipments to a halt. But you also need contingency plans for major, unexpected threats to supply.

In the past two decades, we faced several watershed moments that have fundamentally shaped how procurement contingency planning is done today. The COVID-19 pandemic that began in 2020 delivered the biggest and broadest value chain shock in recent memory. But it is only the latest in a series of disruptions.

Hurricane Katrina in 2005, a Category 5 Atlantic storm, caused $125 billion in damages in New Orleans. In 2011, a combination of a major earthquake, a tsunami, and a nuclear meltdown in Japan shut down factories that produce electronic components for cars, halting assembly lines worldwide. The disaster also knocked out the world's top producer of advanced silicon wafers, on which semiconductor companies rely. Just a few months later, flooding swamped factories in Thailand that produced roughly a quarter of the world's hard drives, leaving the makers of personal computers scrambling. In 2017, Hurricane Harvey, a Category 4 storm, smashed into Texas and Louisiana. It disrupted some of the largest U.S. oil refineries and petrochemical plants, creating shortages of key plastics and resins for a variety of industries. Most recently in 2021, Hurricane Ida, a Category 4 storm, with its landfall in Louisiana and then its remnants with torrential rains in New York and New Jersey brought devastation and caused up to $95 billion in damages.

This is more than just a run of bad luck. Changes in the environment and in the global economy are increasing the frequency and magnitude of shocks and disruptions. Forty weather disasters in 2019 caused damages exceeding $1 billion each—and in recent years, the economic toll caused by extreme events has been escalating.

In the wake of several of the aforementioned natural crises, buyers without contingency plans ended up scrambling for supply and paying outrageous fees. But not all crises follow an annual, seasonal pattern the way that hurricanes do. From natural disasters to war and terrorist strikes, from pandemics to emerging threats that haven't been mentioned on the news yet, there is always a looming procurement crisis. Do not wait for a crisis to arrive to learn that contingency planning is something that you should have done when you read this book.

If a large-scale crisis does occur, supply chains lacking good contingency plans could result in companies being driven out of business. The world has withstood pandemics (e.g., Spanish Influenza in 1918 and COVID-19 in 2020), natural disasters, terrorist attacks, financial system collapses, and even nuclear meltdowns in Russia and Japan, so your company can indeed survive with good plans in place. With less-prepared competitors going out of business, your contingency planning may actually help your organization thrive in the long term.

Mandatory Elements of Contingency Plans

Here are some things to consider in any procurement contingency plan:

- **Establish strong supplier relationships now**—They will mean more than ever. In the event of a crisis that reduces the workforce across all industries, supply of critical items will be tight. Suppliers will have to pick and choose to whom they provide their limited stock. Those buyers with arms-length or adversarial relationships with their suppliers will struggle.
- **Make sure that your suppliers have contingency plans**—For a good example of a methodology for contingency planning for one type of crisis, check out the U.S. Government's Business Pandemic Influenza Planning Checklist.[11] Require your critical suppliers to complete and maintain this type of checklist and provide it to you on a bimonthly basis so that you can assess the strength of your supply chain.
- **Adjust your sourcing strategy**—It is common for purchasers to focus on buying from a single source in order to get the most highly leveraged pricing. In times of crisis, this strategy exposes you to increased risk. You

should have relationships with multiple suppliers, ideally in dispersed geographical areas, in case a supplier's operations are brought to a halt by a region-specific crisis like a natural disaster.

- **Reevaluate inventory levels**—In the event of some types of crises, demand for the goods or services that your organization provides will change. For example, the demand for health care products may rise during a pandemic outbreak. In an economic depression, the demand for luxury items is likely to decrease. Discuss with your top management what kind of strategy you want to have for related changes in your inventory levels. If you believe that demand will rise, don't wait until the crisis hits to decide that you need to purchase more inventory; your suppliers may not have the inventory or the staff to handle the increase in demand when everyone is scrambling for the same items. Conversely, if you expect demand for your company's products or services to decline, you don't want to be stuck with tons of inventory. In that case, you may want to take a lean inventory approach to ensure that your company has the funds to survive a period of decreased demand.

- **Assess the location of your suppliers**—In the past two decades, the increase in global sourcing has resulted in many buyers dealing with suppliers across the globe. Low-cost countries, that is, those countries with relatively low labor and production costs, have been viewed as great places to source for reducing product cost. But certain desirable sourcing locations also have recurrent risks. For example, Haiti experienced two major earthquakes within 11 years: a magnitude 7.0 earthquake in 2010 and a magnitude 7.2 earthquake in 2021, which lead seismologists to say *it's only a matter of time* before Haiti gets hit by another major earthquake.[12] China and the United States have a history of modifying tariffs placed on each other's exports, which has driven unplanned landed cost increases for global sourcing teams.[13] And a military coup in the politically unstable country of Myanmar in 2021 resulted in major apparel companies like Bestseller, H&M, and Primark to cease their sourcing from that country temporarily before ultimately resuming business with suppliers there.[14] We are not saying not to source in Haiti, China, the United States, or Myanmar. We are saying that it is critical to know both the cost savings opportunities and the unique risks of sourcing in every country in which you do business and to know where to shift your sourcing in the event that those risks come to fruition. Beyond just knowing where else to find suppliers if a current country becomes an undesirable location for sourcing, you may want to proactively diversify the location of your suppliers to reduce risk.

- **Revise your force majeure clause**—Make sure that your organization's standard contract templates contain a force majeure clause that specifically addresses some of the more recently discussed types of procurement crises. You need to be protected from being committed to any purchase quantity guarantees if your company is affected by one of these crises.

- **Prioritize department tasks**—Identify critical tasks that must continue to be done in the wake of a crisis and identify less critical tasks that could be eliminated. Document procedures for all critical tasks. You don't know which staff members will miss work due to a local crisis so make sure that all staff members are trained on the critical tasks. For each staff member, identify a backup person, or two, for their work.
- **Establish a Disaster Recovery Plan**—Work closely with other departments, including Information Technology, to plan for unexpected events which may require evacuating your facilities. Your employees should be able to perform their main job responsibilities from remote locations.

CLOSING REMARKS

Practical strategies for making supply chains more transparent and resilient have been widely discussed for years. But they do require making long-term investments. For that reason, only a small group of leading companies were well prepared when the aforementioned supply disruptions hit. Change is brewing! Procurement and supply chain executives are taking steps to make their supply chains more resilient. Resilience is becoming a more prominent element considered alongside efficiency, social diversity, and environmental impact as investors, customers, and consumers assess and judge companies.

As organizations focus on balancing efficiency and resiliency, procurement becomes central to strategy. That's because it is uniquely positioned to orchestrate long-term, value-creating processes and systems that can withstand external disruptions, collaborate with suppliers, and grow dynamically. There's an important factor to consider: when resilience is your priority, *procurement done right* can be your strategy!

REFERENCES

1. Ramirez, Rafael, Ciaran McGinley, and Steve Churchhouse. June 17, 2020. "Why Investing in Procurement Makes Organizations More Resilient," *Harvard Business Review*. Available from https://hbr.org/2020/06/why-investing-in-procurement-makes-organizations-more-resilient.

2. de Matos, Paulo. July 7, 2020. "A 4-Step Strategy for Building Procurement Resilience in a VUCA World." Available from https://www.syspro.com/blog/supply-chain-management-and-erp/a-4-step-strategy-for-building-procurement-resilience-in-a-vuca-world/.

3. Hippold, Sarah. June 23, 2020. "Six Strategies for a More Resilient Supply Chain." Available from https://www.gartner.com/smarterwithgartner/6-strategies-for-a-more-resilient-supply-chain/.

4. Arcieri, Katie. July 9, 2020. "Nike Levels Up Digital Game in Wake of Coronavirus Hit." Available from https://www.spglobal.com/market intelligence/en/news-insights/latest-news-headlines/nike-levels-up-digital-game-in-wake-of-coronavirus-hit-59265634.

5. Cosgrove, Emma. June 3, 2019. "How P&G Created a 'Ready-for-Anything' Supply Chain," *Supply Chain Dive*. Available from https://www.supplychaindive.com/news/pg-ready-for-anything-supply-chain-disaster-response/555945/.

6. Turton, William and Kartikay Mehrotra. June 4, 2021. "Hackers Breached Colonial Pipeline Using Compromised Password." Available from https://www.bloomberg.com/news/articles/2021-06-04/hackers-breached-colonial-pipeline-using-compromised-password.

7. Rhodes, Jonathan. July 29, 2021. "Tokyo 2020: Simone Biles' Withdrawal Is a Sign of Resilience and Strength." Available from https://theconversation.com/tokyo-2020-Simone-Biles-Withdrawal-is-a-sign-of-Resilience-and-Strength-165287.

8. Harter, Jim and Annamarie Mann. April 12, 2017. "The Right Culture: Not Just About Employee Satisfaction." Available from https://www.gallup.com/workplace/236366/Right-Culture-not-Employee-Satisfaction.aspx.

9. Relihan, Tom. May 11, 2018. "How Costco's Obsession with Culture Drove Success." Available from https://mitsloan.mit.edu/ideas-made-to-matter/How-Costcos-Obsession-Culture-Drove-Success.

10. Olya, Gabrielle. July 26, 2021. "Why Costco's Employee Culture May See It Through the Labor Shortages." Available from https://finance.yahoo.com/news/why-costco-employee-culture-may-192919281.html.

11. U.S. Department of Health and Human Services. December 6, 2005. "Business Pandemic Influenza Checklist," v. 3.6. Available from https://www.cdc.gov/flu/pandemic-resources/pdf/businesschecklist.pdf.

12. Woodward, Aylin. August 16, 2021. "It's Only a Matter of Time Before Haiti Experiences Yet Another Major Earthquake, Seismologists Say—Here's Why." Available from *Yahoo!* https://www.yahoo.com/now/only-matter-time-haiti-experiences-000415028.html.

13. Bown, Chad P. March 16, 2021. "US-China Trade War Tariffs: An Up-to-Date Chart." *Peterson Institute for International Economics*. Available from https://www.piie.com/research/piie-charts/us-china-trade-war-tariffs -date-chart.

14. Preuss, Simone. May 28, 2021. "Why Bestseller, H&M and Primark Are Resuming Sourcing in Myanmar." *Fashion United*. Available from https:// fashionunited.uk/news/business/why-bestseller-h-m-and-primark-are -resuming-sourcing-in-myanmar/2021052855732.

12

CHAPTER

MEASURING PROCUREMENT PERFORMANCE: ANALYZING THE SCOREBOARD

Think of playing a pickup game of basketball at the local playground. Then, think of a professional basketball game at Ball Arena in Denver. Both locations have courts, hoops, and foul lines.

There are several differences, though. One major difference is that Ball Arena and other professional basketball arenas have a scoreboard, while the local playground does not. Think of trying to watch a professional basketball game—a game with lots of back-and-forth action—without having a scoreboard at your disposal. It would be frustrating, don't you think? Not very professional, right? That is one difference between professional sports and playground sports. The presence of a scoreboard is vitally important to the pros!

Now, think about your procurement department and the way it *keeps score*. Is it more like Ball Arena or more like a playground? If you don't have a solid way of measuring procurement performance, you don't know how well you are doing or, more important, how you can improve. This chapter will focus on how to measure and communicate procurement performance in a professional way.

BASELINES FOR PERFORMANCE COMPARISON

Imagine a famous, highly paid baseball player walking into a crowded sports bar in his team's hometown and yelling, "Hey everyone, I hit 10 home runs this season!"

How would the crowd react? Would they cheer? Would they boo? Would the patrons nod their heads in a way that says, "Not bad?"

Well, it depends, doesn't it? If the player was a first baseman, the crowd may boo since the primary first basemen for professional teams usually average over 30 home runs per year. If the player was a pitcher, however, the crowd may cheer because home runs among pitchers are relatively rare. If the player was a shortstop, the crowd may or may not cheer. The total is a little low, but shortstops aren't necessarily counted on for their power.

In addition to the player's position, you may also want to know how many games he played or how many at bats he had because, sometimes, a percentage is a more useful metric than a total number. Or, you may want to know how many home runs the player hit the previous season, so you can determine if the player has improved or declined.

To have any performance measurement be useful, you need a point of reference, called a *baseline*. Baselines can come from two sources:

- A published industry benchmark (see Figure 12.1)
- The previous year's performance (see Figure 12.2)

For each of the types of performance measurements we discuss in this chapter, you should seek out one of these types of baselines. If neither is available, that doesn't mean you can't measure performance. It does mean that you should measure the current year's performance so that it becomes the baseline against which next year's performance is compared.

Cost savings is the most traditional metric used to evaluate procurement performance. In fact, for decades, it was the only performance metric that some procurement departments used. That has changed. Now, procurement departments

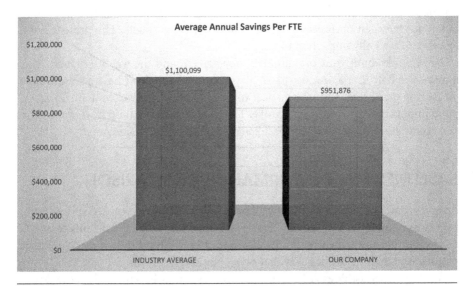

Figure 12.1 Performance versus industry benchmark baseline

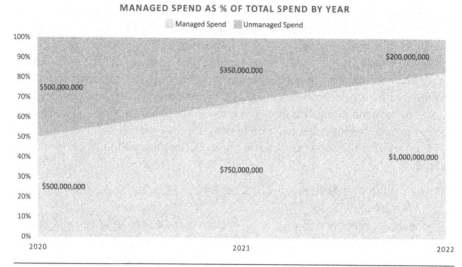

Figure 12.2   Performance versus previous year baseline

take a more comprehensive view of the value that their role adds to the success of their organizations, and they measure multiple things.

We'll begin by discussing some of the non-cost savings performance measurements first. Then, we'll dive deep into cost savings measurement and reporting. Because of the complexities, common misunderstandings, and importance of claiming savings with better accuracy than Stephen Curry's free throws, we dedicate a few extra pages to cost savings measurement and reporting. Please don't interpret this as cost savings being more important than other metrics. Some aspects of procurement performance simply require more explanation.

MEASURING SUPPLY CONTINUITY PERFORMANCE

One can argue that the main job of procurement is simply to get what the organization needs in order to operate. Implicit in this charge is getting what the organization needs *on time*.

In a manufacturing environment, you have production lines running to assemble components into finished products. If one component is not available, a finished product cannot be manufactured. That can create a ripple effect. The production line may have to be shut down. Part of the workforce may need to be paid despite having nothing to do, thereby wasting money. Orders may be late to customers, triggering a disruption to cash flow, lost sales, or even the loss of a customer.

The cause of all of these consequences may have been untimely performance by the supplier of that late component. And supply continuity problems aren't unique to manufacturing—they apply to service industries, too.

We wrote earlier in the book, "Good supplier performance equals good procurement performance." The opposite is true, also: "Bad supplier performance equals bad procurement performance." Therefore, measuring procurement performance means that you must measure supplier performance and base some of your evaluation of procurement performance on how well suppliers perform.

Some metrics that you may use to measure supply continuity performance include:

- On-time supplier deliveries as a percentage of orders (e.g., 97.8% on-time deliveries)
- Average supplier delivery variation from due date, in days (e.g., −0.7 days)
- Average lead time in days (e.g., 13 days)
- Average lead time improvement versus last year, in days (e.g., 1.3 days)

Closely related to managing supply continuity is managing inventory. Because it is such a specialized aspect of procurement, we will discuss inventory management—including measuring inventory management performance—separately in Chapter 14.

MEASURING QUALITY PERFORMANCE

Just like supplier delivery performance becomes something on which procurement performance is measured, so does supplier quality performance.

Examples of quality performance measures include:

- Number of warranty claims
- Warranty claims as a percentage of orders
- Inspection rejections as a percentage of orders
- Number of defective parts per million

MEASURING SOCIAL RESPONSIBILITY PERFORMANCE

In Chapter 4, we wrote extensively about two areas that have increased in importance in procurement over recent decades: sustainable procurement and supplier diversity. If those aspects of procurement are important, performance in those areas should be measured.

We provided some very general key performance indicators in Chapter 4 that were related to sustainable procurement, like the carbon footprint of the supply chain and the percentage of natural resources procured from sustainable sources.

However, in some organizations, it may be important to measure more granular aspects of sustainability depending on what the organization is trying to accomplish. Here are examples of more granular sustainable procurement measurements:

- Percentage of products purchased with recycled content
- Percentage of corporate vehicle fleet comprised of electric vehicles
- Percentage of products purchased with biodegradable packaging
- Deforestation-free mills used as a percentage of total palm oil mills used

We encourage you to adopt or adapt sustainable procurement performance measures that best fit your organization, its culture, and its goals.

Examples of supplier diversity measurements include:

- Percent of spend with diverse suppliers
- Aggregate value of orders placed with diverse suppliers
- Percentage of sourcing projects involving at least one diverse supplier as a bidder

MEASURING SERVICE PERFORMANCE

Service is a big part of what procurement does. After all, procurement buys very little for itself. The overwhelming majority of what procurement buys is for other departments. So, those other departments expect procurement to provide excellent service.

A pure service measurement is *customer rating*. A customer rating score can be obtained periodically (usually annually) by surveying stakeholders and asking them to rate procurement, either overall on a scale of one to five or one to 10, or in specific subcategories of service, which will be calculated into an overall service score.

If you choose to encourage ratings on subcategories of service, you can ask for ratings such as:

- How well does the procurement department succeed in getting goods and services for you on time?
- How satisfied are you in the quality of goods and services acquired for you by the procurement department?
- How would you rate the service of the suppliers selected by the procurement department?
- How would you rate the prices that the procurement department secures for quality goods and services that your department uses?

That is all quantifiable feedback. But, we can't talk about surveying stakeholders without encouraging you to seek qualitative, free-form feedback and suggestions.

Sometimes, the biggest clue for how you can improve is found by simply allowing stakeholders to say whatever is on their minds!

This section describes the measurement of procurement service through the eyes of the stakeholder. However, the measurement of service can also be done by evaluating certain procurement productivity metrics.

MEASURING PROCUREMENT PRODUCTIVITY

Procurement productivity measures how efficiently a procurement department operates. It can relate to the speed at which certain tasks are performed, how much the department can accomplish for each human resource that it has, or even how much return on investment the organization receives from funding the personnel, technology, and other resources that are deployed on procurement activities.

As we mentioned earlier, baselines are extremely important. Comparing performance versus the previous year is essential, as you always want to see improvement. But, benchmarking against industry statistics is key, too. You don't want to get comfortable improving little by little when, in reality, you are way behind your peers in your industry.

Resources like the benchmarking reports presented by CAPS Research offer many procurement productivity statistics to which you can compare your organization. In addition to overall averages, these statistics are also segmented by industry. It's most helpful when you can compare yourself not just to an overall measurement of procurement productivity, but procurement productivity within your specific industry. Remember our example where we said it was important to know a baseball player's position in order to know if his 10 home run performance was good or bad? Well, it's a parallel case with procurement productivity metrics and needing to know the average for someone in your position. Statistics can vary tremendously between a procurement department in, say, the higher education industry and a procurement department in the aerospace industry.

Examples of procurement productivity measurements include:

- Average cycle time of sourcing projects
- Average cycle time of order placement
- Average cost savings per full-time equivalent (FTE) procurement employee
- Contracts executed per year
- Percentage of total spend managed by the procurement department
- Managed spend per procurement FTE
- Ratio of cost savings to procurement operating expenses (i.e., return on investment or ROI)

- Cost savings as a percentage of managed spend
- Procurement operating expenses as a percentage of managed spend
- Procurement operating expenses divided by number of orders
- Average spend per supplier or number of suppliers per million dollars in managed spend

MEASURING AND REPORTING COST SAVINGS PERFORMANCE

Reporting cost savings can be the best way to demonstrate your value to senior management. However, if not done correctly, it can also be the fastest way to lose your credibility.

Cost savings reporting is necessary because saved money is not always apparent when senior managers review the financial health of the organization. This is particularly true in times when the organization is growing, or the overall economy is experiencing inflation. During these times, expenses are rising, and the idea that cost savings are being achieved despite increased outflows of cash may seem contradictory to uninformed senior management. It is up to you to proactively educate management on procurement's positive impact on the bottom line, irrespective of the growth or decline of your organization or of the economy as a whole. Let's begin by looking at how cost savings has been traditionally defined and calculated.

The Traditional Cost Savings Formula

The traditional formula for calculating cost savings is:

$$\text{Savings} = (\text{PYP} - \text{CYP}) \times \text{CYQ}$$

where,

$$\text{PYP} = \text{Previous year's price}$$
$$\text{CYP} = \text{Current year's price}$$
$$\text{CYQ} = \text{Current year's quantity}$$

This is a basic formula that works extremely well when the quantity from one year to the next is equal.

But, what if you negotiated a 5-percent reduction in the price of an item, but you purchased 10 percent more units of that item than you did in the previous year? You would be spending more money than last year, right? Are executives going to agree that money has been saved? Maybe not.

Imagine if cost savings were calculated like this:

$$\text{Savings} = (\text{PYP} \times \text{PYQ}) - (\text{CYP} \times \text{CYQ})$$

where,

PYP = Previous year's price
PYQ = Previous year's quantity
CYP = Current year's price
CYQ = Current year's quantity

After all, this formula more accurately measures the change in spend from year to year. Let's utilize the formula in an example using these numbers:

PYP = $100
PYQ = 10,000
CYP = $95
CYQ = 11,000

With the traditional savings calculation, you would get the result in Example A:

Example A: Traditional Formula

Savings = (PYP − CYP) × CYQ
Savings = ($100 − $95) × 11,000
Savings = $5 × 11,000
Savings = $55,000

But if savings was calculated using the second formula, you would get the result in Example B.

Example B: New Formula

Savings = (PYP × PYQ) − (CYP × CYQ)
Savings = ($100 × 10,000) − ($95 × 11,000)
Savings = $1,000,000 − $1,045,000
Savings = −$45,000

This is a negative number because the expenses increased. So even though you negotiated a lower price, the amount of money your organization spent on the item went up from the previous year to the current year.

Does that mean that your contribution wasn't valued? Of course not—the effort to get a decreased price was honorable. But it does mean that you will have to be more careful when communicating your cost savings to management. There is a need to address some of the challenges that procurement professionals face when factors, such as rising demand, make expenses increase despite the fact that procurement is obtaining lower and lower prices. Next, let's talk about financial performance analysis.

Financial Performance Analysis

It helps to understand how executives think when it comes to the financial performance of your organization. Let's examine one of the tools that executives use in assessing financial performance: the income statement.

An income statement is a document prepared at certain intervals in time (e.g., quarterly, yearly) to document financial changes over that period. Simplified, the three main items recorded on a financial statement are:

- **Sales**—money brought into the organization through selling products or services
- **Expenses**—money the organization spent on goods, services, salaries, and the like
- **Net Income**—difference between sales and expenses

Procurement's primary impact is on expenses, with true cost savings reflected in a reduction of expenses. Executives look at year-over-year change in expenses. If expenses increased, those executives may think that procurement is doing a poor job. But simply having higher expenses does not mean that you are paying more for the goods and services you buy. It may very well be that your cost savings are being offset by other factors that result in higher expenses.

Thus, it is critical to communicate that you are performing well and making a positive financial impact on the organization despite the increasing expenses.

Six Classifications of Procurement Savings Impact

Presenting one big savings number to executives will likely be poorly received in an environment of rising expenses, particularly when most procurement departments accompany that *one big number* with little, if any, supporting detail. Therefore, it is helpful to divide your impact into six classifications, including:

1. True expense reductions
2. Partially offsetting increase in volume with reduction in price
3. Partially offsetting new expenses through negotiation
4. Incurring and reporting price increases
5. Partially offsetting rising prices of volatile commodities
6. Areas outside of procurement's control

Let's examine each of these classifications:

1. True Expense Reduction

When you obtain a lower price for a product or service and your usage of that product or service is the same as the previous year, communicating cost savings is easy. Simply use the traditional savings formula and you're in great shape!

Sometimes you get lower prices and lower demand. While you generally can't take credit for the decrease in demand, you should be aware that expenses decreased for two reasons: you bought less and you paid less for what you did buy. The traditional cost savings formula will calculate the amount that you deserve credit for.

2. Partially Offsetting Increase in Volume with Reduction in Price

Remember Example B, the new formula? Now that you know how senior management evaluates expenses, can you possibly claim cost savings in that type of situation? Yes, you can. The key is not to pretend that the quantity increase is irrelevant. We recommend using the word *offset*. For spend categories where the quantity you buy goes up and the total expense increases despite the fact that you have obtained a lower price, we recommend presenting the additional expenditures due to a rising demand for the category as having been *partially offset* due to a reduction in price.

You might say something like, "Demand for titanium increased by 20 percent. If we paid last year's price, our spend on titanium would have gone from $100,000 to $120,000. However, because we were able to negotiate a 10-percent reduction in price, we were able to offset $12,000 of that increase. Instead, our titanium spend was only $108,000."

Sometimes, price reductions will more than offset a volume increase, in which case, year-to-year expenses will decline. Use these same principles.

The lower-price-but-higher-volume scenario has sparked some controversial behaviors over the years. Sometimes, volume is driven by a related factor. Such is the case with direct materials, which is driven by sales volume of the final product comprised of those materials. Other times, volume is more discretionary. Such is the case with something like employee recognition trinkets.

Problems can arise when volume is discretionary, unit cost reductions are negotiated, and budget holders voluntarily increase volume to exhaust the same budget amount. When this happens, profit is not improved. And, when the reason for the existence of a cost savings program is improving profits, this can feel problematic.

One solution is for budgets to be cut proportional to the cost savings on the same volume. Paladin Associates' CEO Don Hoeppner recalled how his former employer for whom he was the chief procurement officer handled this type of situation. "When we negotiated a new contract, we always went to the finance folks and told them what we did," he recalled. "And they would change the budgets: price adjust them, but not volume adjust them. So, there were still budgets based on the volume you thought you needed at the new price, not the spend you wanted to make."

While that approach can work well—and has worked well—in certain organizational cultures, it's not appropriate for every situation. In one situation, this approach became "a disincentive for the business to engage us early," according to Greg Tennyson, Senior Vice President of Strategy and Procurement at Fairmarkit, talking about an experience he had during his time as Chief Procurement Officer at VSP Global. Stakeholders "got smart to it and said 'If you're going to take the budget away from me, I'm going to engage you late in the process to minimize the amount of the claw back.'"

In response, Tennyson approached his CFO, saying, " 'Let's not claw back the budget. Let's give them the opportunity to repurpose the budget. [Let's] identify the full savings we've been able to capture by engaging early, by partnering with them. But rather than being punitive and doing a claw back, let's partner with them and allow them to repurpose it into other strategic initiatives.' So, it became less about the claw back and more about the best way to repurpose those funds, those savings to bring strategic value back to the organization."

Just because cost savings are repurposed in this manner doesn't mean that they can't count toward procurement performance. They can and should!

Tennyson called this a difficult lesson to learn. But, he also said that the resulting adjustment "allowed us to engage early with the business to identify the opportunity to drive that repurposing of funds toward strategic initiatives." That adjustment reaped dividends in terms of procurement being welcomed by stakeholders and collaborating on future opportunities. "It became more of a success story and it helped us with our trusted advisor journey," he said.

3. Partially Offsetting New Expenses Through Negotiation

By now, you should have a pretty good understanding that senior management looks at consecutive income statements when considering your performance. If you are buying something for the first time (or something that you didn't buy in the previous year), perhaps you are thinking that there is no way you can get senior management to believe that you've contributed to savings through that purchase. After all, any new purchase is just an increase in expenses, right?

Yes, but that doesn't mean that you can't communicate the value that you brought to the purchase. Just like reducing the price of a category that experienced demand growth, you can communicate your impact on new purchases by considering it an offset. In these situations, you may say something like, "We've purchased several products and services this year that we didn't purchase in the past. These products and services included 3D printers, construction services, and artificial intelligence consulting services. These expenses weren't a part of the organization's financial history. Because we engaged the suppliers of these products and services in negotiations, we were able to persuade them to reduce their prices. Had we accepted the lowest bids for these purchases without negotiating, our expenditure on these products and services would have been $200,000. However, we were able to offset 25 percent of that potential expenditure through effective negotiation and our final spend was only $150,000. Therefore, our negotiation efforts on these categories contributed $50,000 to the organization's operating profits."

This type of impact is often referred to as *cost avoidance*. Nothing was *saved* because nothing was previously *spent*, so some managers like to make a distinction in the type of cost impact.

4. Incurring and Reporting Price Increases

Let's imagine a situation where you had $10,000,000 in spend during the prior year: half on services and half on products. This year, you bought the exact same quantities of everything, but prices on all products went up by 10 percent—from $5,000,000 to $5,500,000 in spend. And, your prices on all services went down by 10 percent—from $5,000,000 to $4,500,000 in spend.

How much cost savings would you report? Most procurement departments would report *one big number*, or, $500,000 in savings. But is that a true representation of the impact the procurement department has had?

Quantities didn't change, and spend didn't change. So, where on the income statement is this $500,000?

Quite simply, it isn't there, and your cost savings is really $0. Reporting only the good and not the bad is a recipe for failure. That's why it is important to have all of these classifications, or subsets, that characterize your impact. Price increases should be deducted from your savings.

Getting credit for price decreases, but no blame for price increases, is counter-productive. It rewards you for *not minding the store*. It is only a matter of time before someone to whom you report your savings discovers this.

The main point is to include price increases in your *one big number* that results from combining all of these classifications. The closer you can get your net cost savings to match the change in income statements, the more credibility you will have with management. You just might impress them and get promoted into a position with more financial responsibility, too!

The classifications can work together. The first classification is a 100-percent defensible way to claim cost savings. The second two classifications may be disputed by management at first, but with proper explanation, you should be able to effectively communicate your value. If, in the second and third classifications, you are able to get management to clearly understand how expenses can increase, yet you've positively contributed to the bottom line, that's great. And you may impress them with your honesty if you report price increases, too.

5. Partially Offsetting Rising Prices of Volatile Commodities

If you've got management's respect with the first four classifications, you may be ready to address this challenging classification. In some cases, broader market forces make it nearly impossible for any single procurement professional to reduce costs.

Consider how West Texas Intermediate crude oil prices went from less than $20 per barrel in April 2020 to over $60 per barrel less than a year later. For items and commodities that have petroleum-based products or materials as the biggest cost driver in rapidly inflating markets, buyers are almost defenseless against some price increase. Generally, we absolutely do not advocate claiming cost savings when you negotiate a big price increase and end up with a smaller price increase. A price increase is a price increase, not a cost savings, and therefore should be included in the *price increases* classification. But for some volatile, commodity-type items, you can communicate any cost-related impact that you've made.

Be sure not to lump that impact into one big cost savings number that will not coincide with the change from one year's income statement to the next. For example, you can say, "Due to the massive increase in oil prices, our expenses for petroleum-based products, such as lubricating grease, have gone up significantly this year. Overall, the Producer Price Index reported a 24-percent market price increase in the lubricating grease commodity. Due to negotiation and healthy supplier relationships, we only sustained a 19-percent increase. Therefore, we offset the market price increase by a total of $50,000." Using a chart, like the one shown in Figure 12.3, can help to visually reinforce your positive performance.

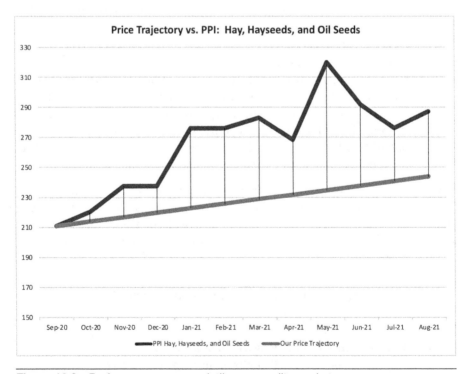

Figure 12.3   Performance versus volatile commodity market

This type of impact is another type of cost avoidance that is treated differently by management. In general, it is best to report cost avoidances separately, so that your actual cost savings become more credible in their eyes.

Let us warn you, though. This isn't an easy sell. It requires that management thoroughly understand market conditions, and that they respect your integrity in cost savings reporting. Use this classification only when you know that it will be understood properly and not viewed as an attempt to artificially pump up cost savings numbers.

One last caveat—do not attempt this classification on categories of purchases that are not related to volatile commodities. While it would be unreasonable for management to expect you to save money on some volatile commodities, trying to mask a price increase on some categories that you should have saved money on will hurt your credibility.

6. Areas Outside of Procurement's Control

Very few procurement departments control every single dollar spent by their organizations. Therefore, it is important to mention the extent of your control when presenting cost savings for a couple of reasons:

- $100,000 in net cost savings to an organization with a $10,000,000 budget may not be impressive to senior management. But when you clarify that you saved $100,000 on just $2,000,000 in spend under your control, your results are more impressive.
- Ideally, you will inspire upper management to think about areas that are not under your control. They may see the results that you produce by managing spend and want the procurement department to be responsible for more categories. In the last 10 years, organizations have shifted responsibility for nontraditional spend areas to their procurement departments. Examples of such spend areas include travel, fleet management, and benefits.

Only when senior management has an understanding of each classification of your impact should you present *one big number*. Prior to any formal presentation, you should have management's agreement on the classifications that they want to be included in or excluded from your reports (don't be surprised if #5 is excluded or combined with #4).

Reporting Cost Savings for Multiyear Deals

Now, let's take cost savings reporting a step farther. Imagine this situation:

- You are responsible for buying a certain item
- Last year, you bought 10,000 units of the item at $100 each

- This year, you've signed a three-year contract with your supplier
- The contract price is $90 per unit of the item
- You will buy 10,000 units of the item in each year of the contract

How much cost savings will you calculate and when will you report the cost savings? Did you say that you would report $300,000 in cost savings when the contract is signed? Management may disagree with you.

As explained, when you report cost savings, management expects to see a reduction in expenses from the previous year to the current year. So, in this scenario, your expenses will not be reduced by $300,000 this year; they will only be reduced by $100,000, which is this year's quantity multiplied by the difference in price.

Then, because there is no price reduction between contract years 1 and 2, senior management usually does not accept cost savings claims in contract year 2, or thereafter. So, the first year of cost savings is all that is recognized by management (as shown in Figure 12.4).

This approach to calculating cost savings concerns many procurement professionals. You may feel that you deserve more credit for achieving a price reduction and locking in that lower price for three years.

That is commendable, but unfortunately, not consistent with the way that executives typically account for cost savings. How can you get credit for cost savings across the entire life of a multiyear contract?

One way is to negotiate a price that declines each year during the contract. For example, instead of starting at the $90 price, you would negotiate the price to be

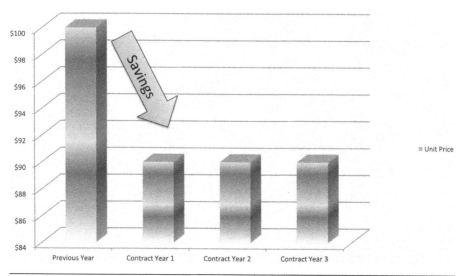

Figure 12.4 Typical savings structure for a multiyear deal

$95 in the first year, $90 in the second year, and $85 in the third. While the contract value is the same to the supplier, you'll get to report savings in each year of the contract, and senior management will recognize three years of year-over-year expense reductions (shown in Figure 12.5).

Like many cost savings topics, what we've shared is best practice among large companies, although certain to be disputed by some people involved in procurement. Therefore, let us add these pieces of advice:

- If your organization is more mature in its cost savings reporting, you report cost savings differently than the way described here, and management accepts that—great! Don't change a thing. The whole point of reporting in the manner described is to gain credibility with senior management.
- If you negotiate a fixed price throughout the multiyear contract, you may not be able to *officially* claim cost savings in all years, but you can still communicate your impact verbally, saying something like, "If we hadn't negotiated a reduction in price, our cost over the next three years would have been $300,000 higher." It may not be official, but it doesn't hurt to show your true impact.

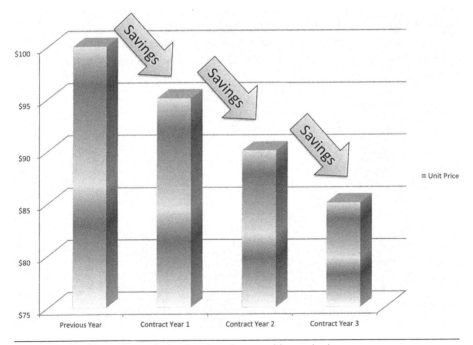

Figure 12.5 Alternate savings structure for a multiyear deal

Recording Cost Savings Data

Now that you know the key philosophies behind what a cost savings is and what it is not, it is time to learn how to record and report cost savings. Cost savings recording does not have to be rocket science. A well-constructed and well-maintained spreadsheet or simple database will do just fine. When you achieve cost savings, there is important data to enter into a cost savings log, such as:

- Date
- Description of product or service
- Baseline price
- Type of baseline or type of savings
- Current price
- Quantity
- Cost savings
- Buyer
- Supplier
- Cost center
- Category or commodity
- Contract duration
- Contract expiration date

Allow us to elaborate on some of these items:

- **Baseline price**—Cost savings is the difference between your current price and a higher price. That higher price is called a baseline.
- **Type of baseline or type of savings**—Baselines may include last year's price, originally proposed price, cost to produce internally, and such. The baseline may determine whether management deems the impact to be cost avoidance or cost savings, and may only be interested in the latter.
- **Cost savings**—This field should be automatically calculated by multiplying the quantity by the difference between the baseline price and the current price.
- **Cost center**—Reporting your cost savings by cost center helps procurement demonstrate the positive impact it made on a specific department's budget.

The best cost savings logs will:

- **Record price increases, too**—Reporting *net* cost savings will better match your reports to financial statements, making your reports more believable.
- **Use a database, not a spreadsheet**—Databases allow you to create separate tables for certain fields and, therefore, select from lists that will ensure the integrity of the data and make it easier to aggregate.

- **Use actual quantities**—While estimated quantities save you the work of having to routinely update the cost savings log, estimated quantities usually vary from actual quantities, which can damage the integrity of your cost savings report if upper management scrutinizes it.

Problems with Cost Savings Reporting

There are certain common pitfalls and problems in many procurement departments' cost savings logs. Evaluate your approach and try to avoid having the following three problems.

Problem 1: Using an Incorrect Baseline

Cost savings are calculated as the quantity to be purchased multiplied by the difference between the price you will pay and a higher baseline price. Make sure that your company's executives agree with the baseline you use. Picking a high but not credible baseline (e.g., the highest bid received) may maximize your cost savings calculation, but hurt your credibility with executives.

Problem 2: Using Poor Quantity Estimates

Because the price you will pay is lower than the baseline price, your cost savings total grows as you purchase more. You may report a certain cost savings value based on quantity estimates. But what if you only end up buying half of that quantity? That's right—your *actual cost savings* will be half of your estimated cost savings. When you estimate your cost savings to executives, they expect the company to realize the cost savings that you estimate. If the cost savings realized is less than your estimate, your credibility could suffer!

At this point, many procurement professionals will say, "I got the quantity estimates from my internal customer. So, it's not my fault if they overestimated and we don't realize the amount of savings we expected to realize!" We disagree.

If you are reporting cost savings estimates, you are (and should be) held accountable for the accuracy of those estimates. Don't try to pass the buck. Executives don't care to hear about other people's roles in why you didn't do a good job. So, when given a quantity estimate by an internal customer, ask questions, such as:

- How *set in stone* are the quantity estimates?
- What are the assumptions that were made in developing the quantity estimates?
- What are all of the circumstances that could cause a deviation from estimated quantities?
- What is the likelihood of each circumstance changing (high, medium, low)?
- Instead of reporting a single number for quantity estimates, if we had to report an extremely certain quantity range, what would the range be?

Problem 3: Failing to Address Budgets

To executives who have not read this book, *cost savings* is likely synonymous with *profit improvement*. When you say that procurement will save $500,000 this year, they expect profits to be that much higher. Let's say that you achieve cost savings of $500,000 for a department within the company. Where does that $500,000 go? Does it free up money that can be spent on other things that were not budgeted? If so, then your *cost savings* is not really a *profit improvement*. The company is still incurring the same amount of expenses. You need to initiate a conversation with senior executives about how cost savings and potential budget adjustments will be treated in your organization. Will your organization's approach be more like the one described earlier in this chapter by Don Hoeppner of Paladin Associates or the one described by Greg Tennyson of Fairmarkit? There is no universally right or wrong answer, only the approach that your organization decides is best for its culture and management style. But, when it comes to setting up your cost savings reporting approach, it's never too early to have that conversation.

Cost Savings Credibility

Once you get professional standards applied to your cost savings log, and you have the sign-off/buy-in of senior management for your cost savings methodology, you are well on your way to demonstrating your value. However, the cost savings log will not be the vehicle you use to communicate your cost savings—it will be too long and have too many details.

You need a clean, concise cost savings report. There are some important principles to keep in mind as you translate the cost savings log into the type of report that management will embrace.

Again, we return to the principle that you can make your cost savings reports more believable if you can understand and reconcile the difference between *cost savings* and *expense reductions*. When you claim cost savings, management expects to see the expenses on its financial statements lower than the previous year. In many cases, the cost savings you report are much different than the change in expenses.

This disparity can hurt your credibility. Managers with a financial background were trained early in their careers to reconcile financial reports, ensuring that differences between numbers from two sources are accounted for. Your cost savings report should reconcile the differences between your cost savings and the actual expense reduction.

Remember, the best way to get your cost savings reports to be accepted and respected by senior management is to try to think like a senior manager. Understand how your impact will affect the organization's income statement. Be sure to account for things like quantity changes and price increases to match your cost savings to the true change in expenses on the income statement.

FINANCIAL TERMS RELATED TO PROCUREMENT

Once you master basic cost savings reporting, you can get into advanced cost savings reporting practices that use terminology that is familiar to management. Here are the definitions of three of the most important terms used by senior management with regard to financial reporting:

- **Earnings per share (EPS)**—Achieving an EPS target is perhaps the most visible goal of the management of a publicly held company. Financial market analysts publicize EPS expectations, and company shareholders evaluate management based on the variation of actual EPS versus expectations. EPS is calculated by dividing the company's profits by the number of shares of stock issued to investors. Procurement can positively contribute to EPS by achieving savings that clearly contribute to profits. Leading procurement departments report savings in EPS. For example, if procurement saved $2 million and the company had 100 million outstanding shares, procurement could say that it contributed $0.02 to the company's EPS.
- **EBITDA**—Executives often pronounce EBITDA as a word. The acronym stands for the accounting phrase *earnings before interest, taxes, depreciation, and amortization*. It is a measure of operational profitability that omits the effect of certain accounting and financial decisions. Because of this, EBITDA emphasizes the impact of operational expenses that procurement can affect. Some procurement departments report cost savings by saying that their actions added a certain amount of money to EBITDA.
- **ROI**—When senior management spends a certain amount of money, they like to see a larger amount of money return to the organization in the form of increased revenue or decreased costs. This concept is called ROI. ROI is often discussed in terms of the amount of time necessary to recoup the expenditure. Most executives like to see ROI in the same fiscal year. Some procurement departments are measured on their ROI. They determine how much it costs the organization to have an internal procurement department (considering salaries, benefits, office space, etc.), and then measure the amount of savings that the procurement department generates, with the goal for the savings to far exceed the cost of staffing and running the department.

DEMONSTRATING THE VALUE OF PROCUREMENT

With this understanding of both cost savings and how management thinks, you can do a better job of selling the value of procurement to senior management if they do not recognize it. Here is a brief, fictional story that represents how procurement leaders at real companies elevated their function within the organization.

ABC Company's owners were unhappy with its recent profits. Every year, ABC's pretax profit was equal to about 10 percent of its sales. This past year, ABC had sales of $100 million and pretax profit of $10 million.

ABC's owners demanded that the president, Charles Aybisi, increase pretax profits to about $15 million or else he would be fired. At first, Aybisi thought that he would have to increase sales by 50 percent to achieve the profit target. He decided to examine the financial breakdown of ABC's operations (shown in Table 12.1).

ABC never paid much attention to its procurement department in terms of financial goals or training. However, Aybisi wondered what would happen if procurement received more emphasis. He mused, "What would the effect on profits be if we looked to procurement to save money on the goods and services we buy?" Then, he drew a new financial breakdown assuming that procurement could save 10 percent on goods and services (shown in Table 12.2).

Aybisi had an enlightening moment—a 10-percent reduction in purchase prices (a realistic goal if using best practices) would produce the same effect as a 50-percent spike in sales! What do you think is easier—reducing purchase prices by 10 percent, or increasing sales by 50 percent? Obviously, reducing purchase prices! By using techniques like strategic sourcing, negotiation, standardization, and value analysis, well-trained procurement departments are likely to contribute to profit improvement like no other department can.

Table 12.1   Financial breakdown prior to procurement savings

Sales	$100,000,000
Purchased goods/services	$50,000,000
Labor/salaries	$30,000,000
Overhead	$10,000,000
EBITDA (10%)	$10,000,000

Table 12.2   Financial breakdown after procurement savings

Sales	$100,000,000
Purchased goods/services	$45,000,000
Labor/salaries	$30,000,000
Overhead	$10,000,000
EBITDA	$15,000,000

MEASURING TOTAL TEAM PERFORMANCE

Doing a good job of recording and reporting cost savings is very critical when measuring procurement performance—but it is more of a starting line, rather than the finish line.

Measuring procurement performance can be tricky. You must compare actual procurement performance with your goals. Even though procurement goals were discussed at the beginning of this book, it is appropriate to revisit the topic now that you know more about recording cost savings and how executives think. The following list describes three mistakes that might be made when setting goals against which procurement performance is measured:

- **Mistake 1: Having cost savings be the lone metric**—One of the most important metrics that a procurement department can share with top management is cost savings. Just because it is one of the most important metrics, does not mean it should be the *only* metric, however. If you only measure procurement performance on cost savings, it could incite buyers to sacrifice quality, on-time delivery, and/or supplier service for lower prices. A cost savings metric should be balanced by measuring these other aspects of procurement performance to produce a clear assessment of the department's impact on total cost and overall company performance.

- **Mistake 2: Not using net cost savings as a metric**—This concept is so important that we are repeating it: *when calculating cost savings, price increases should be deducted from price reductions to produce a* net *cost savings number.* One reason for doing this is that management expects reported cost savings to equal actual profit improvement. Also, consider buyer motivations. By counting only gross cost savings, buyers may be inclined to ignore opportunities to minimize price increases on large spend categories, while focusing their time on less critical categories where price reductions are possible, resulting in an overall lower positive impact on profit.

- **Mistake 3: Not taking markets into account when setting goals**—When some procurement managers set cost savings goals, they look to last year's numbers or another arbitrary figure to determine the targets for the next year. This can set buyers up for failure. In the last few years, there has been cost volatility in many markets. If the procurement department promises year-over-year price reductions in markets where prices are rapidly rising industry-wide, senior management will likely be disappointed when actual performance is compared with those goals. So, give consideration to market conditions when setting departmental and individual buyer goals. That isn't to say that price increases should be readily accepted just because that's the direction of the market, but rather that goals should estimate how much an aggressive effort can offset market price increases.

CLOSING REMARKS

Measuring procurement performance is all about keeping a professional *scoreboard* transparent, easy-to-comprehend, and defensible. When everyone can easily understand the scoreboard, your championship-caliber performance becomes more apparent to all.

13

TECHNOLOGIES AND SERVICES FOR IMPROVING PROCUREMENT PERFORMANCE: THE STICKS, GLOVES, AND BATS OF SUPPLY MANAGEMENT

Most sports require athletes to have some type of equipment: sticks, gloves, bats, shoulder pads, special shoes, and such. Even swimmers must have goggles, and wrestlers must have . . . um . . . athletic supporters. The pieces of equipment serve as tools to help athletes perform better and protect themselves from injury.

There is no shortage of technologies and services to help procurement professionals perform better and protect their organizations from risk. In this chapter we will cover some of the main technologies and services for improving procurement performance.

PROCUREMENT OUTSOURCING

The word *outsourcing* scares a lot of people, conjuring up images of people losing their jobs *en masse*. With that mental image, procurement outsourcing may feel like something to protect yourself against. Actually, if you are a procurement leader, procurement outsourcing can be valuable toward the pursuit of your goals.

Every procurement department has nagging tactical work that has to be done, such as basic research, order management, and the like. When strategic initiatives are falling behind, it can be painful for a procurement leader to deploy human resources on low-value-added tasks. Yet, those tasks must be done.

For the accomplishment of these routine types of tasks, a third-party firm can be engaged. This has an obvious benefit of enabling procurement employees to stay focused on more strategic and long-term tasks. But it also can help push tasks to a lower cost outsourcing provider, thereby more closely matching the value of the work to the cost of the resources doing the work.

Some experts had predicted that traditional, transactional procurement positions would have disappeared in favor of outsourcing by now.[1] They haven't. Although, outsourcing continues to get increasingly serious consideration for assuming some traditional procurement work.

A common view is that all transactional procurement work will be outsourced, leaving strategic work to be done by the highly educated strategic staff that remains in the procurement department. That is already happening, but we do not think that is where the trend matures.

In the early to mid-2000s, as business process outsourcing was really going mainstream, the focus of *business process outsourcing* (BPO) providers was that they would hire people in low-cost countries that could simply work for less money than people in North America or Europe. Their value proposition focused solely around labor cost.

We later observed how BPO providers were gearing up for the next step in the cycle, and saw that procurement BPO providers were investing in two strategies to penetrate the procurement market. The first is more training for their procurement professionals than Fortune 500 companies—the very customers they want to land and keep. The second is coupling a services option with technology.

It is common for procurement BPO providers to enroll their procurement teams in over 40 hours of training per person, per year. Conversely, we see a notable number of Fortune 500 companies enrolling their procurement teams in a mere eight to 16 hours of training per year. According to a survey of over 1,100 procurement professionals, the overall average number of hours of training per procurement professional per year was 19.6 hours.[2] Procurement BPO providers tend to do much more than that, and it's not just tactical training that BPO providers invest in—it's strategic training, too. Procurement BPO providers appear to be building out their capabilities.

In addition, BPO providers are "coupling best-in-class tools [with] managed services, [offering] essentially a BPO model on a platform," explains David Bush, CEO of Simfoni, a procurement technology provider that is expanding its services offering. Bush says that deploying this type of combination is "less expensive than what you can do internally. You don't have the hiring and training and employee type of issues." He also notes that this new BPO model allows procurement organizations to mix and match the services and technologies needed for their specific circumstances. This gives procurement organizations access to various types of expertise and tools, such as "sourcing expertise, buy desk expertise, procure-to-pay (P2P), spend analysis . . . all of these things packaged into one," Bush says. "[Plus], it's a consumption model: you would only pay for as much as you're using. It's the classic pay-as-you-go or 'pay by the drink' [model]."

Basically, it appears that procurement BPO providers not only want to do procurement less expensively than their clients, they want to do it better. We expect to see even more procurement outsourcing, including the outsourcing of roles considered as strategic. Will we ever get to the point where a procurement department that was staffed with 200 people in the early 2020s be reduced to one person whose job it is to manage a procurement BPO provider? That is a stretch to imagine, but the general direction is one in which there are fewer in-house employees, with some of them responsible for managing procurement work done by BPO providers.

GROUP PURCHASING ORGANIZATIONS

A *group purchasing organization* (GPO) is an independent company that aggregates the procurement requirements of its customers, leverages the combined volume to negotiate discounted contracts with suppliers, and makes those contracts available to customers—effectively saving them money on their purchased goods and services. So, instead of each customer's procurement department sourcing for a category of goods or services to establish a favorable contract with a supplier, joining a GPO will give the procurement department access to an existing contract with favorable pricing and terms.

A procurement department will join a GPO primarily for savings. By combining its spend with that of other companies, a procurement department gets the buying power and leverage of a much larger organization.

But using a GPO can also help a procurement department address undermanaged and unmanaged categories. The majority of procurement departments place most of their focus on their strategic categories, like direct materials. Unfortunately, that laser-like focus leaves little time to address less-critical categories, like maintenance, repair, and operations supplies. However, a lot of cost savings can be forgone by ignoring those less-critical categories. Utilizing a GPO and its contracts for less-critical categories can ensure that the available cost savings is reaped without taking valuable and scarce time and resources away from strategic categories in order to source them.

Also, smaller companies that have struggled to get suppliers to correct problems can have more success when their spend is part of a GPO contract. Large GPOs often have large spends and close relationships with many of their suppliers, keeping the incentive on suppliers to perform well, even for smaller GPO clients.

Using a GPO doesn't necessarily mean totally sacrificing control. When sourcing a new category, some GPOs utilize a steering committee consisting of members' procurement specialists to identify and qualify suppliers and vote on the selected supplier.

Like any investment, an investment in a GPO should produce a satisfactory return on that investment. To determine your return on investment (ROI) requires developing a baseline for your current spend and comparing it to the pricing available through the GPO. Your actual savings depends on how well-managed the categories are currently, as well as how effective you are at getting end users to channel their spend through the GPO contracts.

If the savings exceeds the investment, a procurement department can count the net savings toward its goals for the year. And, if the category wasn't going to be addressed due to an already full workload, using a GPO can multiply the success of a procurement department.

The logic of using a GPO is simple: by pooling the spend of several small companies, each company can get the more heavily discounted pricing that a larger company gets. It sounds good in principle. So good, in fact, that many companies may not even challenge that logic by doing analysis. As you may have predicted, our advice is: always do the analysis!

While a GPO may claim that you will save more by engaging with them than you would on your own (which may be true), test the waters. Yes, we know, one of the reasons to go with a GPO is that your organization does not have the time to source on its own, but at least do some checking.

We were reminded of this principle not that long ago when one of our organizations was sourcing health and dental benefits for its team. The organization is a member of a local Chamber of Commerce, and the chamber has a relationship with a company that operates like a GPO for small organizations that source such benefits.

According to that company's website, "[Our] health plans allowed each Chamber to offer its members buying power rivaling the largest companies." Furthermore, the company's brochure touted, "The power of 50,000 businesses negotiating member services, benefits, and health care."

A GPO-like claim, for sure. In other words, we should be able to get better pricing through this company than we can get by sourcing benefits ourselves for only our organization. Well, the analysis proved differently.

We were able to get better rates on health benefits through another provider without joining the GPO-like company. While the company offered a slightly lower monthly *premium* on the dental insurance than the successful bidder, they threw in administrative and billing fees on top of the monthly premium, which resulted in that company being *significantly* more expensive than the provider we worked with on our own—and, we are talking about the same benefits with significantly different costs, depending on the *reseller* you chose.

Of course, the Chamber-related company's additional fees were not obvious in their quote. The heading for the monthly premium column had a superscript that referenced a footnote. That footnote referenced another electronic file that made the buyer do a calculation to figure out the additional fees, so finding the data for the comparison was a little tricky.

The bottom line is: GPOs may or may not be able to get better prices for you when compared to what you can get on your own, so always do a little checking. Sometimes just a few minutes of checking can make a big difference.

We have one more GPO war story to share. In one of the companies that we worked for, a procurement team was having all kinds of problems with the office products supplier, whom we will call XYZ Company. It seemed like the employees of that supplier had a personal vendetta against our company—our employees got terrible service, orders would go unfulfilled, and we had several instances when packages of office supplies arrived in boxes filled with garbage that included dust swept off the floor and loose corn flakes! Needless to say, XYZ Company was replaced with another supplier who was awarded a one-year contract after a swift sourcing process. During the next year, our company was working with the new supplier when management decided that the company should use a GPO for the sourcing of our office supplies. One particular GPO was conducting competitive bidding right around the time that our office supplies contract expired.

For some reason, the procurement group from our company was not involved in the selection of the successful bidder, yet had to go along with the result. Can you guess who the GPO selected as our office products supplier? Yup. XYZ Company!

Although we were not in the office supplies procurement group, as arm-chair quarterbacks, we think that these were the lessons learned:

- When working with a GPO, always choose one that uses performance as a criterion, not just price, in making its selections.
- If possible, always ensure that you have input into the GPO decision. Our company was a Fortune 500 company whose spend comprised a significant portion of the award in this story. There was no reason our company should not have been involved in the decision.

The moral of this war story is *not* that GPOs are bad. Rather, it is to make sure that using a GPO does not mean sacrificing control of your company's destiny. Table 13.1 illustrates a quick list of the advantages and disadvantages of GPOs.

Table 13.1   GPO advantages and disadvantages

GPO advantages	GPO disadvantages
Can give a smaller company "big company pricing"	Can reduce amount of control a procurement department has over its decisions
Can save a lot of sourcing work and produce the same result	Can require an investment that may not be recouped if end users don't use the GPO contract
Can provide an ally to work on complaints that would otherwise be "too small" or "too low of a priority" for some suppliers	Can highlight weaknesses in the procurement department's processes (which can be an advantage if improvements are identified and made)

All in all, our personal opinion is that using a GPO should at least be investigated. If the deal doesn't make sense, then by all means walk away. But, if management ever asks how your pricing is, you'll be able to provide a smart answer and demonstrate that you've investigated some options.

PROCUREMENT CARDS

Blanket orders and procurement cards (P-cards) are two tools that organizations without the procure-to-pay systems that we will discuss shortly can adopt to reduce tactical activities in a procurement department. A blanket order is defined as "a purchase order that outlines an ongoing agreement arranged between an organization and a vendor to deliver goods or services at a predetermined price and on a recurring basis for a specified time period."[3] Once accepted, the supplier will deliver goods against the blanket order on a regularly scheduled basis, upon request, or as specified in the blanket order without the need for the creation of new purchase orders for each delivery. According to the National Association of Purchasing Card Professionals, a P-card is defined as "a type of Commercial Card that allows organizations to take advantage of the existing credit card infrastructure to make business-to-business (B2B) electronic payments for a variety of business expenses (e.g., goods and services)."[4]

Professional procurement staff should rarely *cut POs* for orders under $100 when a supplier and pricing have already been determined by the procurement team. When trying to decide which of these two tools to use, consider speed of implementation, chance of paying for what you did not get, transaction cost savings, and ease of use.

Speed of Implementation

If your organization does not currently have a P-card program in place, it can take some implementation time to research the market, select a provider, strategize a rollout, train users, and such. In contrast, your existing procurement system may already have blanket order functionality, giving you the opportunity to implement blanket orders immediately. If P-cards are your long-term solution across multiple categories, you can always start with blanket orders and migrate to P-cards later.

Chance of Paying for What You Did Not Get

With both P-cards and blanket orders, there is a risk of paying for what you did not receive. It is no secret that the use of stolen credit card numbers is widespread, and P-cards are not exempt from fraudulent transactions. But, if you use a two-way match (PO matches the invoice) instead of a three-way match (PO matches the invoice matches the receiving records), a supplier could invoice you for more line items than they shipped and still be paid. You have to simply determine which of these two methods represents the least risk, as well as which method is easiest to audit.

Transaction Cost Savings

It is widely acknowledged that one of the best benefits of the P-card method is the reduction of administrative costs associated with paying invoices. So, while blanket orders do not provide this type of cost savings compared to having the procurement department place orders, P-cards definitely do.

Ease of Use

Most of your end users should know how to use a credit card to place orders. However, they may struggle with remembering a purchase order number and other relevant details when placing a release against a blanket order. Not a big deal, but something to consider. Because this change affects end users (and may not be popular), you might want to create a team, then invite end users onto the team so that they feel they have control of their destiny, which leads to greater buy-in.

If implementing a P-card program is the path you want to take, you will have a lot of decisions to make. These include:

- Should there be one standard spending limit for all P-card holders; should each card holder have a customized limit; or should there be several spending limit categories?
- What is the standard spending limit per day? Per transaction? Per month?
- What categories should be restricted from purchase by using a P-card?
- Who gets a P-card and what are the criteria used to determine eligibility?
- How many full-time equivalent employees are required to administer the P-card program? (Note: The P-card administrator position is usually staffed by someone who does other things, too. We have seen about 20 to 30 hours per week dedicated to P-card administration in companies with 10,000 or more employees.)
- Should the P-card only be used with contracted suppliers?
- How will you train P-card holders with regard to logging transactions, distributing charges, and security practices?
- What type of transaction information do you need to be made available centrally?

- What type of reports do you need from the P-card service provider (e.g., number of suppliers, spend information in each procurement category, or diverse suppliers)?

Advantages/Pros of P-Card Use

Whether implementing a new P-card program or administering one that has been in place for years, procurement departments need to continually consider these advantages of P-card use:

- P-cards reduce the cycle time of procurement transactions
- P-cards can improve supplier relations as suppliers receive payment within two to five days
- P-cards can provide an avenue for extending payment terms, and thus improve cash flow
- With proper negotiations, P-cards can generate revenue through a rebate program
- P-cards can reduce the number of supplier invoices, which could lead to a reduction in expenses on accounts payable personnel
- With proper controls, P-cards can restrict maverick buying, as well as restrict buying unauthorized categories of goods and services
- Some P-card programs can provide clearer reports of how money is being spent
- P-card programs foster a feeling of empowerment among employees

Disadvantages/Cons of P-Card Use

Consequently, whether implementing a new P-card program or administering one that has been in place for years, procurement departments also need to continually consider these disadvantages of P-card use:

- P-card use could expose the organization to the potential for undetected credit card fraud and identity theft, which can result in lost money
- The work involved in reconciling a P-card statement with a purchase log and distributing charges to the proper accounts can divert resources from value-added work
- P-cards generally do not provide the same level of budget visibility as an enterprise resource planning (ERP) system does
- Multiple ways of placing orders (e.g., P-card, eProcurement, ERP, requisitions, etc.) can confuse requisitioners, who may not know the proper method for each type of purchase
- P-card spend data may not be integrated with other purchase data, resulting in incomplete information when conducting spend analysis

PROCUREMENT TECHNOLOGY

The old adage says: "The only constant is change." Perhaps nowhere else has this been more true than in the evolution of procurement technology.

In the late 1990s, procurement saw a rapid influx of impressive technology solutions. The *dot-com* bust obliterated many of the solution providers and their technologies, but innovation and competition returned a few years later. The late '90s and early aughts were characterized by niche providers offering technology solutions that were specific to certain tasks, like sourcing and order placement. A trend in the late aughts and the early part of the following decade was for providers to start to combine many of those same, specialized capabilities in multipurpose, integrated packages called *platforms*, seeming to signal the end of an era of providers competing on narrow, task-based technologies referred to as *best-of-breed*. However, as of this writing, best-of-breed offerings have re-emerged, giving procurement departments choices whether to pursue comprehensive platforms or one or multiple best-of-breed solutions.

"It used to be that everyone was working their way to being an end-to-end platform: 'I can do everything from front to back, you should only work with me,'" Buyers Meeting Point Managing Director Kelly Barner recalls of long-time procurement technology providers' market positioning. "But now it's changed."

"Best-of-breed is the biggest opportunity that practitioners have, because they can choose small apps instead of massive enterprise platforms," according to Simfoni's David Bush. We provide this history to help you prepare for whatever may be next in procurement technology: the old becoming new again or something completely novel.

The following is a list containing several procurement technologies that are available as best-of-breed solutions as well as part of a platform. We will discuss each individually, with those that have presented particular challenges being explored in greater detail.

- Spend analysis
- P2P
- eSourcing
- Contract life cycle management (CLM)
- Supply chain visibility
- Other Solutions

Spend Analysis

Spend analysis is also referred to as spend analytics and procurement analytics. Spend analysis systems provide procurement professionals with information about spending in a variety of useful ways. Procurement professionals can view spending by category, by supplier, by product or service, and more. Procurement professionals can then use these insights to guide their sourcing strategy, as described in Chapter 6.

Spend analysis is often a logical place to begin a procurement technology journey. "You cannot function as a procurement department without knowing where you're spending, what you're spending [money on], how much you're spending," observes Simfoni's Bush. "That drives every strategic decision moving forward."

P2P

Procure-to-pay systems, also known as P2P or eProcurement systems, bring the ease of a retail shopping experience to corporate procurement. Users browse online catalogs of pre-approved goods and services from contracted suppliers. The requisition to payment process is fully automated. There are many nuances of P2P systems, so we will discuss these in more detail.

Requisition Submission Practices

There are four common practices related to how requisitioners process their requests. Some are so old school that they seem like they would have predated the discus throw as a sport! These practices are listed here, ranked from worst to best:

1. Some companies allow end users to deliver requisitions directly to buyers. In many of these cases, there is no tracking system in place, resulting in the chaos of lost requisitions. Buyers are often interrupted, every request is labeled a *rush order*, and productivity and efficiency are far from optimized. Companies that use this approach often do so to promote internal customer service as a priority over productivity. This ancient practice is found mostly in small, unsophisticated companies, but we mention it in case one of those companies may be yours!

2. Some readers may be surprised that there are companies that still use paper requisitions, but they do. Just search for requisitions on your office supply retailer's website and you'll see that it's true. For companies still using paper requisitions, a common practice is to have them sent to a central location where an administrative employee will distribute them to the buyers. In some situations, the administrative employee will log the requisitions and time stamp them to help track requisitions, as well as to measure cycle time for continuous improvement efforts.

3. When companies do not allow their end users to place orders directly with suppliers, they often have an electronic requisitioning module within their ERP system. The requisitioning module allows for tracking of the status of requisitions and can electronically distribute requisitions to the assigned procurement professionals for placing orders and the subsequent follow-ups.

4. The most sophisticated organizations have P2P systems implemented that feature pre-approved items from contracted suppliers. When requisitioners want an item and their total order is under a certain value, they use the P2P system to place the order directly with the supplier. Procurement staff is not involved in these routine transactions, freeing them up to focus on more strategic procurement work. For larger value transactions, the P2P system distributes requisitions to buyers based on customized criteria (e.g., category, end-user department, or supplier).

When order placement is decentralized, it is wise to consider implementing a P2P system.

Meeting Requirements for Release of Payment

One of our clients recently shared a problem: her company could not get its end users to record receipts in their P2P system. What could she do?

This is a common problem that can arise when an organization moves to a P2P process from a traditional process. In the following paragraphs, we will express our view on how to solve this problem based on observations in the field and on our personal success as practitioners.

The traditional process involves orders being placed by a central buyer and the goods being received by a central warehouse for internal distribution to the end user. Organizations using the traditional structure often use a three-way match to pay suppliers: the purchase order details must match the invoice details, which must match the receiving details (shown in Figure 13.1).

When an organization switches to a P2P-based process, orders are placed directly by end users to suppliers, and the goods are delivered directly to end users. That is fine until it is time to pay suppliers. The purchase order matches the invoice, but many companies struggle to get their end users to record receipts for that third, necessary match. End users are thinking: "Is it really worth a receipt for this $1.99 package of pens?" Without a receipt, the invoice does not get paid. Before you know it, suppliers are refusing to ship because you have not paid them in months!

Some companies fight to get end users to record receipts in the P2P system, and many times, they are unsuccessful. Any time you are dealing with human involvement in a process, there is the opportunity for errors and variation.

So, how have organizations solved this problem? They did away with the three-way match for P2P orders, and a two-way match is becoming more common. If the invoice matches the purchase order, the invoice gets paid. This concept usually sends auditor and accountant types into a panic, fearing that they will be writing checks for things that were never received. But it actually works very well under specific conditions.

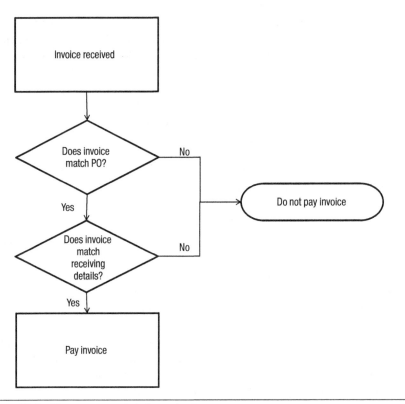

Figure 13.1   Three-way match flow chart

There are certain controls that you must have in place for this to succeed. They include:

- **A monetary threshold when a receipt is required**—For example, you may want to require a formal receipt for orders over a certain amount, such as $2,000. The Pareto Principle may apply here: 20 percent of the orders account for 80 percent of the spend. If so, worry about receiving the significant few orders, not the trivial many.
- **Diligence by end users in ensuring that what they ordered is delivered**— Usually, this is *built in* because the user is ordering goods that they have a need to fill. An unfulfilled need usually keeps their attention, and department budget watchers are usually good at making sure that budget dollars are used appropriately.
- **P2P suppliers must provide summaries of shipments and proofs of delivery for every order, upon request**—You may even want to use their records if you are measuring on-time delivery performance on a periodic basis.

- **Restricted supply base to reduce the risk of fraud**—Concern about fraud is greatly reduced if the end users can only purchase from suppliers selected by a centralized procurement staff, as opposed to allowing end users to *free form* an order to anyone they wish.

Will this approach cause something to be paid for that is never received? It could. But from real-world experience, this is a rare occurrence, and one that can be handled easily between the buying organization and the supplier.

At the end of the day, there are fewer problems with this approach than with the three-way match approach. Fewer resources are used to solve problems, which means a lower cost of doing business for the buying organization.

Be aware, however, that auditors and accountants are tough. How can you convince them to accept this new strategy? Many organizations that implemented P2P systems had also implemented a P-card program years before. They can say to auditors/accountants: "We've actually been doing *no receipt procurement* for years. We don't record receipts for P-card purchases." If compliance with laws, such as the Sarbanes-Oxley Act, is a concern, figure out how P-card purchases earned an exemption from receiving, and apply the same logic to P2P. Combined with the aforementioned controls, that argument is usually sufficient to persuade auditors and accountants.

Dealing with Retail-Type Items

Another P2P challenge is choosing the type of supplier for retail-type items for your P2P system. *Retail-type items* are items that can be purchased at a store (e.g., office and computer supplies). These items can be bought from suppliers with storefronts (retailers) or suppliers who deal strictly with businesses, called B2B sellers.

When enabling a supplier of retail-type items on your P2P system, you may have four choices:

1. Load a static catalog of a retailer
2. Integrate a retailer's website with the P2P system
3. Load a static catalog of a B2B seller
4. Integrate a B2B seller's website with the P2P system

Less internal friction occurs when Option 2 is chosen—integrate a retailer's website with the P2P system. Why? Retailers often run sales with attractive discounts to drive in consumer business. Their websites have updated prices weekly or even more frequently. No other option makes these special discounts available to you as seamlessly.

If a B2B seller is enabled on your P2P system, and a competing retailer runs a sale, your users may be able to get a better deal individually than your organization gets as a whole. So, your users will run to the store instead of using P2P. This undermines the buy-in critical to P2P success.

Should you only enable retailers on your P2P system for retail-type items? Not necessarily. Instead, require any B2B sellers to propose a reliable solution to this potential dilemma before enabling them.

eSourcing

eSourcing allows suppliers to access all request for proposal (RFP) materials online and submit their proposals using online forms. Procurement professionals can view and analyze supplier submissions via a web browser. When a P2P system also includes eSourcing capabilities, it is called a source-to-pay system. The advantages of a source-to-pay system versus separate P2P and eSourcing systems include a single log in, supplier records pulling from the same database, and access to the history between the two functions.

eSourcing has become a broad concept, encompassing all aspects of requesting and receiving supplier quotes and proposals via the web. Today's eSourcing evolved from one of its own components that was the first form of eSourcing—the reverse auction.

Reverse Auctions

You are probably familiar with a *traditional* auction, where one individual, group, or selling organization has a product or service to sell, and a host of buyers compete with each other to buy that product or service. The competitive forces at work ensure that the seller gets the highest price in the market for the offered product or service.

A *reverse auction* is where one buying organization has a requirement to buy a product or service, and a host of sellers compete for the opportunity to sell that product or service to the buying organization. The competitive forces at work ensure that the buyer gets the lowest price in the market for the required product or service. Today's B2B reverse auctions are conducted live, in real time, over the Internet, thereby permitting sellers in different locations to simultaneously attempt to outbid each other. Reverse auctions have generated billions of dollars in savings, and have become embraced by modern procurement professionals across many industries. It should be noted that reverse auctions are not suitable for every spend category. We highly recommend that you do some careful research before conducting a reverse auction.

To combat any lingering misconception, we must reinforce the fact that eSourcing encompasses not just reverse auctions, but also any type of request for information, request for quote, RFP, and the like, in both sealed bid and auction formats.

More advanced eSourcing involves decision optimization based on complex mathematics, which we will cover later in this chapter.

Overcoming Supplier Resistance to eSourcing

Reverse auctions were generally greeted with supplier disdain early on and, still, eSourcing continues to be a challenge in terms of managing supplier relationships. In its early days, suppliers resisted the eSourcing concept. They feared being *beaten up* over price.

Smart buyers *sold* the suppliers on the benefits of participating in eSourcing events. Though the maturation of the market has reduced supplier resistance through the years, you may still encounter supplier hesitancy with eSourcing today, particularly in smaller or less-sophisticated industries. Here are three benefits that you can highlight to persuade suppliers to participate in your eSourcing events:

1. eSourcing gives every supplier equal opportunity to revise their proposals and, therefore, an equal opportunity to earn the buyer's business.
2. In many eSourcing events, certain information submitted by a supplier is seen by all other suppliers. This ensures fairness. The bidding process is transparent and ethical.
3. eSourcing yields precise market intelligence with regard to pricing and terms available in the marketplace.

Communicating these benefits is still a powerful strategy. Many suppliers are now willing, if not eager, to participate in eSourcing events when they become aware of the benefits. But we've also heard sellers say things like, "We've decided not to participate in reverse auctions anymore. We don't want to commoditize ourselves."

So, some suppliers would rather decline an opportunity to earn business than to deviate from their business model. That concerns procurement professionals who realize that, generally, the more competition there is, the lower prices will be.

Common Sense eSourcing Self-Evaluation

Reverse auctions must always be considered carefully. That's because they can work well when used properly; you just have to evaluate the impact on competition.

If you have a significant percentage of suppliers declining to bid because they do not like the format, conducting a reverse auction can effectively *reduce* overall competition, although the competitive forces at work for those suppliers who do participate are still maximized.

Less than successful experiences with reverse auctions can often taint procurement professionals' opinions of the format. However, being too quick to judge the appropriateness of reverse auctions can be a terrible mistake.

Too often, procurement professionals who misuse reverse auctions and get disappointing results may erroneously blame the tool and not the person using the tool. We found a demonstrative example in a *Printing Impressions* article, entitled *The Fading Reverse Auction*, in which a print buyer was quoted as saying, "We only did a reverse auction once, and we'll never do it again."[5]

What was so catastrophic about this print buyer's experience? Apparently, she awarded business to a bidder, who then charged *handsomely* for work that deviated from the specification on which the bidding was based and the buying organization sacrificed *quality and service* for *rock-bottom prices*. Sadly, had this print buyer used some procurement common sense and an eSourcing best practice or two, those problems would not have occurred.

First, it is rudimentary in procurement to know that, if you do any RFP—auctioned or not—you need to do your homework and request pricing for work that goes outside of the specification. A procurement professional should know what the potential *hidden costs* are in that category, and not leave them to chance. The specifications will be the same, whether you request proposals via a reverse auction, email, or postal mail. A well-written contract will clearly delineate when and how much a supplier is permitted to charge for out-of-scope work. Being *nickel-and-dimed* for work above and beyond services on which a supplier has bid can, and does, happen to sloppy procurement departments in offline bidding situations. So, naturally, it can happen to sloppy procurement departments when they use reverse auctions. It is a symptom of inadequate procurement skills, but not an inadequate tool.

Second, we strongly recommend inviting only suppliers to whom you would want to award your business. We are puzzled about why the print buyer would have invited suppliers who have unacceptable quality and service, much less awarded business to one. Think about it: is it the reverse auction format or the skill of the buyer at fault in that situation?

There is one more point we want to make about the print buyer's bad experience. Isn't the *we-tried-that-once-and-it-didn't-work* excuse supposed to be one of the excuses that procurement teams try to fight when working with internal departments? It is one of the worst excuses in business. If something did not work, figure out why, and fix it. That is how you learn and improve.

Fortunately, the *Printing Impressions* article also explored other perspectives. The author conceded that she was "not suggesting that all buying companies are against reverse auctions," noting that 15 percent of the magazine's survey respondents found reverse auctions to be effective, and quoting another print buyer who uses them regularly and finds them to be *useful*.

There definitely are some *key ingredients* necessary for a successful reverse auction. Those key ingredients include having a well-defined commodity, an adequate number of prequalified bidders, and a clear message indicating that business will be awarded at the end of the event so that suppliers know to submit their best and final price by the deadline.

Getting back to *Printing Impressions'* statistics from the article; 15 percent of the surveyed print buyers who used reverse auctions are successful and 85 percent are unsuccessful. That calls to mind the Pareto Principle and sounds pretty typical of success in business. A small number of the buyers account for a large percentage of the success. So, why would the unsuccessful not research the successful 15 percent, learn the secrets to their success, and apply those secrets to eliminate the struggles currently experienced by the majority?

We held off mentioning until now that *The Fading Reverse Auction* article was published way back in 2008. Reverse auctions are still alive and well today!

Reverse auctions are a tool. They are not a replacement for smart buyers. Like any tool, they can be misused by a less-than-fully-educated user.

Integrity in eSourcing

When a procurement tool is controversial among procurement people, you can bet that it will also suffer from a negative perception in the supplier community—and, though it's become the de facto proposal solicitation method in sophisticated industries and big companies, eSourcing still does suffer from that perception to a certain extent in some markets. The supplier resistance requires that procurement professionals make eSourcing events as attractive as possible to suppliers.

Every buyer conducting eSourcing events has the ability to reverse its negative perception. In order for eSourcing to survive and thrive, you need to incorporate the highest levels of integrity in eSourcing processes and apply good procurement practices.

We have been asked, "How can an eSourcing services solution help mitigate a buyer's concern on quality from suppliers they haven't worked with before?" The key to mitigating a procurement professional's concern about ending up with a poor-quality supplier after an eSourcing event is simple—rely on good procurement practice, not just the technology. Use the principles of evaluating, comparing, and selecting suppliers that were highlighted in Chapter 7 to prequalify all bidders, and do not invite a bidder that fails to meet your prequalification standards.

Procurement professionals often make the mistake of not doing offline prequalification because they are so enamored with the online aspect of sourcing. Just because you are using new technology (which we strongly advocate) does not mean that you should abandon more traditional best practices that still apply.

Here are five tips for promoting integrity in eSourcing:

1. Do not display only prices to suppliers when there are other criteria involved in the selection process

2. Do not select a supplier other than the low bidder in a price-only auction, nor a supplier other than the highest scorer in a multivariable eSourcing event

3. Do not determine the supplier you will select in advance of the eSourcing event, thereby *using* the other suppliers simply to drive down the preferred supplier's price

4. Do not negotiate price after the eSourcing event has already determined the lowest price available in the marketplace

5. Do not invite certain suppliers to participate if those suppliers have no chance of winning

If you avoid these mistakes, you will be able to maximize the applicability of the valuable eSourcing process.

Complexities in eSourcing

While discussing eSourcing so far, we have really only discussed basic eSourcing. Some sourcing situations involve more constraints and complexities. *Constraints* are limits on your decisions, for example:

- A requirement that you must select two suppliers (as opposed to one, three, or another number)
- No supplier has the capacity to handle 100 percent of your business
- A requirement that a certain percentage of your award must be placed with diversity suppliers

Examples of complexities may be:

- A large number of line items being bid
- Suppliers offering discounts at different volume levels or in different combinations of line items
- Various delivery locations with differences in the suitability of certain bidders to supply some of them
- A choice of freight lanes at differing costs

When you encounter situations with many constraints and complexities, it becomes challenging to figure out the best supplier for selection. For these types of situations, some procurement departments utilize sourcing optimization technology—a specialized type of eSourcing—to support their decisions.

Optimization Overview

Simply stated, *sourcing optimization* is a technology that applies, "rigorous mathematical techniques to a well-defined sourcing scenario to produce an optimal award allocation," according to Michael Lamoureux, president of ToP KaTS Consulting and editor of the blog, *Sourcing Innovation*. Sourcing optimization helps procurement departments *arrive at the best decision out of all the possible alternatives*.

When there are multiple bidders, multiple constraints, and lots of complexities, there can be a massive number of alternatives and combinations. The more options there are, the higher the probability that you will make a suboptimal decision.

While it is possible to work out some slightly complex bid analyses by hand, there is a significant chance that using sourcing optimization technology can save money and time, and reduce errors. Paladin Associates' Don Hoeppner attests that sourcing optimization has helped several of the consultancy's clients achieve multiple objectives. One such client "wanted to keep some of their suppliers because they were local, but wanted to save a bunch of money," Hoeppner recalled. "We were able to put in various constraints in the system that allowed some of the local suppliers to have part of the business where they had pretty reasonable prices." Ultimately, the client achieved a desirable balance. "The bulk of the business went to larger suppliers that had great prices," he said. "Although we didn't achieve the maximum savings possible, we achieved some pretty nice savings and met the client's desire to support local suppliers."

But sourcing optimization may not be appropriate for every organization or spend category. According to Lamoureux, "You would use [sourcing optimization] to source high-value core commodities, parts, and materials for which there are capacity constraints, associated risks, and multiple potential suppliers."

Because sourcing optimization technology requires a significant investment—Lamoureux estimates a premium of *anywhere from $100,000 per year to a few million dollars* above the cost of a standard eSourcing application—it is typically adopted by larger organizations who are able to achieve a larger ROI due to their spend volume.

Simplified Optimization Example

At this point, you may wonder, "Will I ever need sourcing optimization technology?" Here is a brief test to answer that question. Imagine that you are requesting bids for nuts and bolts in a situation with these characteristics:

- There are three bidders named Alice, Bob, and Carol
- You need 20,000 nuts and bolts (units) at your Atlanta warehouse; 15,000 units at your Boston warehouse; and 25,000 units at your Chicago warehouse
- Alice cannot supply Atlanta, Bob cannot supply Boston, and Carol cannot supply Chicago

- Alice is going to bid $1.10 for a nut and bolt pair, but gives you a 10-cent/unit discount if you buy 20,000 units
- Bob is going to bid $1.05 for a nut and bolt pair, but gives you a 3-cent/unit discount if you buy 10,000 units or a 6-cent/unit discount if you buy 20,000 units
- Carol is going to bid $1.11 for a pairing, but a 9-cent/unit discount if you buy at least 25,000 units
- You are implementing a dual sourcing (managed competition) strategy to mitigate supply risk down the road, and you are going to ensure that any selected supplier is going to get at least 25 percent of the business

Which suppliers would you choose, assuming that delivery, service, and quality were otherwise equal, and price was the only variable?

We suggest working out your answer, and then listening to Charles' interview with Lamoureux for a Next Level Purchasing Association podcast entitled "What Is Supply Chain Optimization?"[6] This will enable you to compare your answer with Lamoureux's. After you realize that the answer is not all that easy to get to, and realize that real-life sourcing situations can be much more complicated, you may be more open to adopting sourcing optimization technology.

Contract Life-Cycle Management

A *contract* can mean a document containing the terms and conditions to which two parties agree. The word can also be used to describe a long-term, formalized relationship between a buying organization and a selling organization, replete with time-bound obligations.

The *contract life cycle* represents all activities from the time that the contract document is first drafted to the time that the contract is no longer in place due to termination or expiration. This includes the activities associated with negotiating and signing the contract document as well as tracking the completion of all obligations of the contractual relationship.

When you think of the term of a contract—some of which last five, ten, or more years—there are a lot of activities that have to happen and a lot of obligations to track. Like most every other procurement challenge, there is technology available to help you manage the contract life cycle.

The contract life cycle begins with the creation of the contract document. That sounds easy enough; but, it is actually far from easy. There are many eyeballs that have to look at a contract before it is ready for a signature. The eyeballs belong to the buyer, procurement management, the buying organization's attorney, and the supplier. This can be messy when handled via the traditional contract creation process.

The Traditional Contract Creation Process

When we think of the traditional contract creation process, we think of a typical desperation play in American football. This desperation play usually comes with mere seconds left in the game when the leading team has just scored and it would take a miracle for the losing team to make a comeback. The leading team kicks off, the kick is received by the losing team, and the losing team makes multiple lateral passes back and forth between teammates to avoid getting tackled and thus ending the game. It's chaos and it rarely works. One of the lateral passes between team-mates gets fumbled or an unprepared recipient gets overwhelmed by the circumstances, dropping to the ground and ending the game. This is how the traditional contract creation process would look to an outsider.

You see, in the traditional contract creation process, a buyer will use a contract template to start the process of documenting the terms and condition of the procurement. That contract template may be one provided by the buying organization, one provided by the seller, or one from another source. That buyer may then *pass* it to the buying organization's attorney or the buyer's manager. Usually, that first *pass* brings up a lot of questions, so the attorney may pass it to the manager or the manager may pass it to the attorney—sometimes multiple times. The contract eventually goes back to the buyer to be forwarded to the supplier. And, if the supplier makes changes instead of accepting the contract as-is, the buyer will get the contract back and the multiplayer passing happens again. Insanely enough, this chaos happens within a context of many buyers passing around many contracts.

Many key pieces of information get lost in this process, such as the order in which contracts are to be reviewed, the priority of the various contracts, who is reviewing what contract at any given time and so forth. That chaos should have been left in the twentieth century, but it still persists today in organizations who have yet to implement CLM technology.

CLM allows procurement departments to guide contracts through several discrete steps, stages, or phases of the contract life cycle. There are many different published variations of what those steps, stages, or phases are, but we like to simplify them into these five phases (see Figure 13.2):

1. Contract Creation
2. Contract Routing
3. Contract Execution
4. Contract Management and Storage
5. Contract Renewal/Expiry

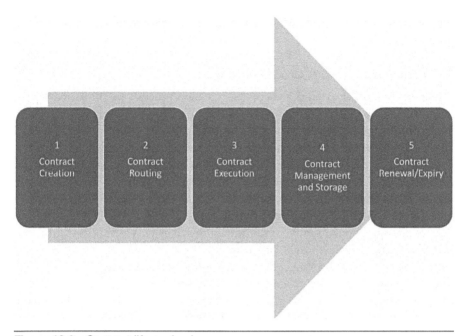

Figure 13.2   Contract life-cycle phases

CLM Phase 1: Contract Creation

A timeless preference for contracting as expressed by attorneys is to have the contract based on their own organization's template as opposed to the other party's template. Attorneys have historically referred to this practice as having contracts *on our paper*. Of course, the other side will prefer to have the contract be *on their paper*. CLM systems create "an opportunity for you to push your contract template to the supplier and manage off your paper versus their paper," according to Fairmarkit's Greg Tennyson. So, the legal and procurement teams will create and prescribe a series of templates to be made available to buyers through the CLM system.

In the contract creation phase, a buyer will know specifically where to find the appropriate template to begin using for a new contract. In cases where multiple templates for multiple situations exist, proper training of the procurement team and labeling of the available templates will guide buyers to the exact template they will need.

As buyers change the template language in the creation of a specific contract—for example, to insert lead times, payment terms, and so on—those changes will be tracked by the CLM system. This makes the work in the second phase much simpler. Let's talk about that second phase now.

CLM Phase 2: Contract Routing

Unlike the desperation football play that we described at the beginning of this section, the contract routing within a CLM system is well-planned and structured instead of random and chaotic. There is a *workflow* setup in the system that determines who gets to review the contract next. When the work at one workflow point is complete, the next user (e.g., manager, attorney, etc.) is notified and can log into the system to work on the contract. All changes continue to be tracked and comments can be inserted to explain changes, ask questions, etc. At all times, it is clear where in the process the contract is and who has responsibility for doing the work to qualify it to move to the next step.

After all changes are made and agreed upon within the buying organization, the contract can move to the next phase.

CLM Phase 3: Contract Execution

Contract execution in the context of CLM technology simply refers to the process of getting the contract signed by the appropriate individuals from the buying and selling organizations. This eSignature capability makes getting the contract to the right person quick and easy, provides instant notifications when signatures are submitted, and are lawful and court admissible.

CLM Phase 4: Contract Management and Storage

In Chapter 10, we discussed how critical the contract management process is. Ensuring that suppliers fulfill all of their contractual obligations on time is mandatory to secure continuous supply and achieve maximum cost savings. CLM systems are valuable tools in helping procurement teams manage time-bound contractual obligations to see that every single one of those obligations is completed.

Especially with long-term contracts, obligations can be forgotten. Misunderstandings of terms and conditions can begin to creep in, especially when knowledge of those terms and conditions is passed down verbally from person to person and not based on a review of the contractual documents to which both parties agreed. That facilitates even more value being extracted from CLM systems.

"Having one source of truth, you can find things as opposed to searching on hard drives [or in a] file cabinet," says Fairmarkit's Tennyson. "And, when you think about the inevitability of an acquisition or divestiture, how do you manage that from a file cabinet, from a hard drive? If it's all in one record, it simplifies doc retrieval, doc review, sharing of documentation, leveraging procurement synergies to drive value back to the organization."

Having *one system of record* can put an end to any misunderstandings very quickly so that the focus of both parties stays on fulfilling the contract.

CLM Phase 5: Contract Renewal/Expiry

The typical contract has a finite term. It has a date when the contract either expires or renews automatically. It is important to know when a contract expires. With contracts that outlast the tenure of the person who negotiated them, this can be a challenge. A CLM system can ensure that, whether the contract is being managed by the person who negotiated it or a successor, the coming expiration or renewal point is no surprise to the contract manager.

Knowing a contract expiry is important because, as a procurement professional, it is your job to ensure that all of the value that was bargained for when the contract was negotiated is realized. And, knowing when a contract is up for renewal is important because you may not want a contract to automatically renew. You may want to allow it to expire, you may want to renegotiate it, or you may want to conduct strategic sourcing to determine what decision you will make. It's not good to be stuck with a supplier because you weren't aware of—or forgot—an important date. It's worth noting that sometimes contracts renew unless notice is given several months before the expiration date and this can trip up procurement professionals whose focus may have shifted to newer priorities.

CLM systems help procurement professionals avoid the consequences of losing sight of renewal and expiration dates.

Supply Chain Visibility

For as long as procurement has been a profession, one of the biggest sources of stress for procurement professionals is hoping that a critical delivery is made on time and wondering where in the process the order is at a given point. Today, many buyers will feel the need to call suppliers for an update on order status. Their supplier contacts will then have to research the order—perhaps making multiple touchpoints—and eventually report back to the buyers. Sometimes, the update is a guess. Sometimes, the update is a best-case scenario. Sometimes, the update can even be a lie.

It all feels very 1980s-ish. Like *the wave* in sports stadiums. Fortunately, technology is finally coming to the rescue in the form of supply chain visibility solutions.

Supply chain visibility solutions digitally track orders at various stages along the supply chain. They provide "real-time resilience tracking of physical disruptions or financial disruptions in your supply chain," says Bayer's CPO Thomas Udesen. "A bridge goes down in Singapore and we know immediately."

Supply chain visibility systems require a lot of setup to be able to provide these types of insights. Suppliers, products, freight routes, logistics providers, and orders all need to be set up in the system. But, when the success of the entire business depends on being able to meet customer demand through a dependable supply chain, the effort is well worth it.

"We have mapped the majority of our critical products, as well as all medically necessary products—those where people die if our supply chain breaks down," shares Udesen. "We know immediately if a worst-case scenario happens, and we are capable of acting on that." He, along with a growing number of other CPO's, believes that such real-time insight is becoming necessary for today's business world.

Other Solutions

In the seeming blink of an eye, the procurement technology landscape changes. Legacy companies change their names or get acquired. And, the combination of a recent rise in private equity investment and different types of people becoming interested in the procurement technology space has led to many new entrants jumping onto the procurement technology playing field.

In fact, Simfoni's Bush lists investor funding as one of the biggest developments in the procurement technology market in the past five years. "There is a massive amount of outside capital that has been injected into this industry," he says. "If you have seen some of these procurement technology maps, [they] are stuffed full of start-up companies. The landscape is massive now. There are hundreds and hundreds of technology solutions out there now." Buyers Meeting Point Managing Director Kelly Barner notes the change in the profile of the founders of these start-ups. "Most of them are being founded by people who are in IT or finance or operations and say 'This existing technology doesn't meet my needs, so I am going to solve it better,'" she says.

It would take a whole separate book—and possibly more—to cover the breadth of procurement technology solutions that exist today. But, to keep with the spirit of a book that can be read cover-to-cover in a relatively short amount of time, we will simply mention these other types of procurement technology solutions that you can look into beyond those we've described in this chapter: supplier management, supply chain collaboration, supply risk monitoring and management, and sustainability ratings and reporting.

Evolving Developments

Three evolving developments in procurement technologies include spend automation, provider ecosystems, and the expanded universe of procurement technology users. We will briefly highlight each of these.

Spend Automation

Generalized, spend automation is simply having a computer perform work that was previously done by a procurement professional. Several broad technology advancements are facilitating spend automation, including machine learning and artificial intelligence (AI).

What is machine learning? "For me, machine learning is basically teaching a machine to do the same task that you've done before," explains Chirag Shah, Executive Chairman of Simfoni. "The easiest example is probably predictive text. It's effectively putting a code in place that allows a machine to be able to build up on repetitive patterns itself. It's seeing a pattern from behavior and saying, 'There is a trend here.' Ninety percent of automation that you see today is machine learning. We, as humans, are pretty predictable and it's just pattern recognition, it's trend analysis, it's trial and error, and so on."

AI is a more advanced application of machine learning in that it is built to test its efforts and improve upon its accuracy. "The really true AI is where a computer is drawing connections from disparate sources of data and pulling them together in ways that are initially random but, over time, can become smarter because the machine is almost able to test for itself the validity of its output," according to Shah. "It's exactly like a child. A child learns by trial and error, doing things and saying 'Oh, that didn't work,' then doing something else [and saying] 'that works,' then doing more of that and getting better at it. And, AI is driven on the same principles."

Machine learning and AI are increasingly being deployed as part of procurement technology solutions. Does this mean that, in the near future, computers will be negotiating and making supplier selection decisions without any human involvement whatsoever?

Most experts tend to think that AI-driven procurement applications will issue prompts and make recommendations more so than making decisions, at least in the short term. "If you ask me in the next five years, it will still be recommendation-driven," believes Shah. "Going back to the child [metaphor], we don't let our children actually make decisions, they make suggestions: 'Dad, can I do this? Dad, can I do that?' We still supervise. We generally think it takes 18 years before people can be mature enough to make decisions for themselves. I think we'll approach it the same way with our computers."

That being said, technology developments over the next two decades will likely force a shift in the activities that procurement professionals are involved in. The technology-driven shift will dovetail with the shift being spurred by the previously mentioned BPO-related developments. "When you start to look at data analytics, the applications for AI, and the applications that are going to be coming in the next few years, it's going to change the roles" of procurement professionals, predicts Bill Michels, Vice President of Operations Americas for the Chartered Institute of Procurement and Supply. "The tactical roles and the transactional roles will probably disappear over time."

What will the new roles of procurement professionals be after this technology-driven shift? They will "all be strategic roles about managing relationships across the supply chain and integrating the supply chain," says Michels.

Provider Ecosystems

Even though the trend of going for *all or nothing* with procurement technology has reversed with the resurgence of best-of-breed options, organizations still need multiple pieces of technology—not just one type of solution. So, best-of-breed providers who address different aspects of procurement technology have teamed up to form what may be called *provider ecosystems.*

When a client of one type of solution discusses a need for a different type of solution, solution providers can refer those clients to preselected partners with whom they have developed a synergistic relationship. "[For example], if you want to start with supply chain risk monitoring and move to procurement analytics, riskmethods and Sievo are going to play nice together," explains Buyers Meeting Point's Barner. "You see all kinds of companies referring to who would have been competitors in their marketing materials, in their blog content, in interviews, on websites. I think that's been a very powerful thing because it creates a very viable alternative to the traditional platform option."

Expanded Universe of Procurement Technology Users

As you read earlier in the chapter, a technology like CLM is as much an everyday tool for the legal department as it is for procurement. That is the case with other solutions as well while procurement technology grows to cover more of the touchpoints between procurement and stakeholders.

"Gone are the days that you would put spend analysis and eSourcing in place and then 25 people in procurement would use them," says Barner with a bit of a laugh. "Now, it is so much more common to have everybody in the enterprise touching some piece of procurement's technology."

As the technology makes the procurement-stakeholder interaction more comfortable, it is possible that we'll see an increased delegation of what has historically been considered to be procurement department tasks. P2P is perhaps the most mature example of this principle. However, the evolution is moving toward stakeholders "accessing supplier databases, contract databases, and then, even now, self-guided buying or self-sourcing, where you give them access within certain parameters to an approved supplier network and you say, 'As long as you meet these requirements, have at it,'" Barner observes.

CLOSING REMARKS

One of the most exciting moments in sports is when a record is broken. Why do most records not last forever? Because athletes are always figuring out how to perform better than their predecessors. Whether it is through more aggressive training, better equipment, or something else, athletes in general have an insatiable quest to be the best.

This desire for continuous improvement exists in the procurement world, too. Whether it is new processes, new technologies, or new ideas, there is a constant movement toward doing things better than procurement professionals of years past. Successful procurement departments are those that leverage the optimal combination of available technologies and services in order to deliver unprecedented results for their organizations.

REFERENCES

1. Ariba. "Vision 2020: Ideas for Procurement in 2020 by Industry Leading Procurement Executives."
2. Next Level Purchasing Association. 2014. "2014 Purchasing & Supply Management Career & Skills Report."
3. Sharp, Callum. "What Is a Blanket Purchase Order?" *Procurify Blog*. Available from https://blog.procurify.com/2017/02/24/everything-need-know -blanket-purchase-orders/.
4. "P-Card Introduction and Glossary." *NAPCP*. Available from https://www .napcp.org/page/PCardIntro.
5. Morgan, Suzanne. August 1, 2008. "The Fading Reverse Auction." *Printing Impressions*. Available from https://www.piworld.com/article/reverse -auctions-being-used-less-less-printing-industry-and-8212-suzanne -morgan-114818/all/.
6. "What Is Supply Chain Optimization?" July 24, 2007. *Next Level Purchasing Association Podcast*. Available from https://podcasts.apple.com/ us/podcast/what-is-supply-chain-optimization-part-i/id267161044?i =1000020002898.

14
CHAPTER

SPECIALIZED AREAS OF PROCUREMENT: *SPECIAL TEAMS* ARE IMPORTANT

Many team sports have *situational specialists* who are players with a niche role. They are brought in by coaches to participate during specific situations. In baseball, you have *closers* who are relief pitchers, entering late in the game when their team has the lead. In American football, you have *special teams* players who enter the game only when there is a punt or a kickoff. In ice hockey, there are *enforcers* whose primary role is basically to fight the enforcer on the other team.

Procurement also has its niche situations. While most procurement teams are too lean to have a person dedicated solely to each situation, these situations call for the involvement of an individual or a team with specialized knowledge. The four specific situations covered in this chapter are global sourcing, services procurement, project management, and inventory management.

GLOBAL SOURCING

Global sourcing can simply be defined as buying from suppliers outside of your own country. It has become a quest of procurement to find and do business with the best suppliers on the planet. It is unlikely that the best supplier on the planet for every product or service you buy is located in the same country that you are. Therefore, global sourcing should be utilized, at least to some degree, by almost every procurement professional in today's world.

Global Sourcing Differences

While global sourcing certainly shares many of the same processes as domestic sourcing, there are some key differences:

- **Additional costs**—A global sourcing strategy is often used to reap the benefit from lower labor costs abroad. But there are also other additional costs for a buying organization to bear that aren't part of domestic transactions. They include multimodal freight charges, broker fees, bank fees, import/export taxes (called *duties*), and shipping insurance, to name a few.

- **Multiple sets of laws**—Global sourcing forces buyers and suppliers to choose one of three bodies of law to apply to their contract: the law of the buyer's country, the law of the supplier's country, or international law applicable under a treaty accepted by both countries.
- **Multiple currencies**—The buyer and the seller must agree on a currency to use for their transactions. While some buyers insist on their own currency for simplicity, prudent decisions consider use of the supplier's currency when the buyer's currency could possibly strengthen, relative to the supplier's currency, between the agreement and payment dates.
- **Longer lead times**—Lead times for global purchases are usually significantly longer than domestic lead times. This is due to ocean travel being slower than air travel, and customs clearance adding time not involved in domestic sourcing.
- **Languages and cultures**—If you are unfamiliar with the supplier's language or culture, you increase the risk of communication challenges, misunderstandings, and offensive or uncomfortable encounters.
- **Multimodal transportation**—While domestic sourcing usually involves one shipping mode, global sourcing involves *multimodal transportation*, which is a strategy for combining air, water, and ground transportation to get goods from the supplier to the port of the supplier's country, and then to your own country's port and to your dock.
- **Payment methods**—Global sourcing often involves payment using a letter of credit, which requires the involvement of both the buyer's and supplier's banks.

Global Sourcing Tools

Because of the differences between domestic and global sourcing, you need the right skills, knowledge, and tools for global sourcing success. Here are five of the most important global sourcing tools:

1. **The business case**—Many company executives need to be convinced that global sourcing is a smart move. A business case documenting the researched savings potential is a tool for convincing them. When questioning and analyzing the savings potential, "Let's say that you get an answer of $30,000 savings," says Dick Locke, author of *Global Supply Management*, "is that something your company can afford to walk away from?" Sometimes, analysis like this on just one contract or category is appropriate. Other times, it can open eyes to much larger opportunities within a procurement

department's managed spend. Regardless, it's important to have a broad, strategic view of all opportunities when deciding which opportunities to include in your business case. "And don't forget about opportunity cost," Locke cautions. "There may be a much larger potential savings you should be working on." Only after management reviews a well-written business case can the question to *move forward or walk away* be properly answered.

2. **Cultural research**—In Locke's opinion, learning about your suppliers' culture is critical for global sourcing success for two reasons: "One is that if you have misunderstandings, they can get in the way of closing deals. The second reason is that if you understand cultural differences, you might be able to be more demanding of a supplier in another country than you would be in your own country."

3. **Landed cost model**—In global sourcing, there are more cost components, as compared to domestic sourcing. A landed cost model helps you include global sourcing cost components, such as multimodal freight, duties, customs fees, and other factors into your analysis.

4. **INCOTERMS chart**—INCOTERMS, "define the responsibility for the buyer and seller in terms of handling and paying for customs and shipping," according to Locke. "They also define where the risk of loss transfers between the seller and the buyer." INCOTERMS are published by the International Chamber of Commerce and are updated approximately every 10 years. As of the time of this writing, there are 11 INCOTERMS. It should be noted that INCOTERMS differ from the Uniform Commercial Code's F.O.B. terms that are used domestically in the United States.

5. **Transportation time chart**—The location of suppliers influences transportation times, which influences your inventory strategy. Always know your transportation times.

SERVICES PROCUREMENT

With procurement being viewed as more and more valuable, we are seeing procurement taking responsibility for more categories of goods and services that have not historically been part of procurement's portfolio, such as facilities management, travel, information technology services, fleet management, business process outsourcing, personnel benefits, and marketing/advertising.

In many companies, getting the opportunity to be responsible for *every* dollar spent on goods and services is still challenging, especially when there are internal politics involved. Sometimes, senior management needs that little extra push to feel comfortable about reigning in spend. We found an interesting *push* in the following example.

Decentralized Responsibility for Services

We listened to a *BusinessWeek* podcast[1] called *Selling to Giants* that discusses how small companies can sell to big companies and the advantages of doing so. While the point of the podcast was to educate sellers on how to sell, certain excerpts of the podcast could serve to educate senior executives as to why the procurement department, and not end users, should be managing services spend.

For example, in the podcast, a guest expert proposed that bigger companies pay better than smaller companies and are willing to pay higher prices for products and services than their smaller counterparts; but then sheepishly added, "Maybe not always—if [the decision makers are] in the supply chain." The host incredulously asked why big companies would pay more for "that same hour of that same service." The guest then explained that small companies' procurement decisions have the built-in control of the fact that purchases take money away from the owners for the owners' personal financial needs such as funding their children's college education or even school shoes. No such control exists in large corporations where budget holders have total responsibility for their procurement decisions. The guest concluded that, company funds are treated by end users as, "just a bucket of money called *my budget*," whereas supply chain professionals are more focused on ensuring appropriate pricing.

The podcast reinforced the common belief in the profession that budget holders are not very fiscally responsible when procurement is not involved. Obviously, we have seen irresponsible behavior firsthand in companies, and as procurement leaders, were able to introduce more fiscal responsibility into those areas.

Does your management need that extra piece of ammunition to understand how the company's money is being spent? As discussed in Chapter 12 and elsewhere in this book, it is up to the procurement professional to show value.

Reasons That Services Procurement Is Challenging

We are not saying that services procurement is easy or that you can just instantly achieve success by taking over a services category. In many cases, services procurement is significantly more difficult than goods procurement. There are a few reasons why, including:

- **Many services are one-time purchases**—Whereas maintenance, repair, and operations items and direct materials are bought repeatedly, therefore giving the buyer time to understand the market, services are often bought only once to fulfill a specific need, particularly in smaller organizations. Consider things such as a plumbing repair, a website design, or exhibiting at a trade show; these will not show up in your periodic spend profile as categories to source.

- **The traditional process for some services is sending a bill without a PO**—Think of utilities, lease payments, and insurance as examples. These are all things that can be negotiated by a larger company, but often fall into the way things have been traditionally done.
- **Many services are local**—Products can be shipped almost anywhere. Because many services require the presence of a person where the service is performed, you may need a different supplier in different cities. This makes spend consolidation difficult.
- **Apples-to-apples comparisons can be difficult**—When you are buying a product, the specifications are often easy to define. In some cases, you may be getting the exact same product from any supplier. Services can be a little trickier than products, especially when they are intangible. Think about legal services; when you are in discussions with several competent law firms, deciding which one gives you the best chance of winning a patent infringement lawsuit is often a matter of subjective judgment. This is also true of other services, like those from advertising agencies, where you are buying *ideas* that you won't even get to review until the future. Of course, there are ways to qualify those suppliers to determine who might work out best but, truly, it can be a guessing game and a gamble.

Problems with Service Providers

As if the preceding challenges did not pose enough problems, there are additional and unique problems commonly experienced with services suppliers. These may include:

- Not having services finished by the date you expect
- Too heavily depending on a supplier's *key person*

On-Time Performance

When buying goods with a 30-day lead time, you can usually expect delivery in 30 calendar days. But *days* in a services quote's lead time may mean one of three things:

- **Calendar days**—Each day, including weekends and holidays, counts towards the lead time. If you place an order on July 1 and the lead time is 30 days, expect your service to be complete by July 31.
- **Business days**—Each day, except weekends and holidays, counts toward the lead time. If you place an order on Monday, July 1, and understand that July 4 is a national holiday and Saturdays and Sundays aren't business days, expect your service to be complete by Tuesday, August 13.
- **Working days**—For some services, specific supplier employees are assigned to specific tasks. *Working days* include only those days that those

specific people work on your project. If an individual works on another customer's project on a certain day, that day will not be deemed a working day nor count toward your lead time. So, if you place an order on July 1 and the individual works on your project every other business day, expect your service to be complete in late September.

Wouldn't it be easy for you and your internal customer to be disappointed if by *30 days* your supplier meant 30 working days, and you were expecting the service to be performed in 30 calendar days? When purchasing services, personally reach agreement with your supplier on the meaning of *days*, and then confirm it in writing.

Dependence on a Key Person

Performance levels for services are often determined by one key person on the supplier's team. Be it a software implementation project manager, a consultant, an equipment installer, or any other type of service personnel, that one person's success can determine the success of the service procurement.

When comparing service suppliers, learn about the key person for each supplier by asking questions. We prefer to ask these questions in person because it is too easy to provide fake answers with the lag time allowed for written responses. Here are six questions to ask the service suppliers' management:

1. **What are the key person's qualifications?** This information can help you develop a measurable comparison between suppliers.

2. **How long has the key person been employed there?** To get this information, ask for a copy of the key person's resume. If the person hasn't been there long or has a pattern of leaving a job at a consistent interval, you may be able to assess the risk of the person leaving the supplier during your project.

3. **What other projects is the key person working on?** This question can help you assess the risk of the key person being distracted from your project, which could lead to unacceptable performance.

4. **What could happen to make another project become a higher priority for the key person than our project?** Knowing the risks, challenge suppliers to give you the confidence that those risks will not occur.

5. **If the key person was to leave the company or be unexpectedly out of the office for a long period of time, who would be his or her backup?** If the supplier only has one person capable of performing for you, there is a heightened level of risk for this procurement.

6. **How do the backup person's qualifications compare to those of the key person?** Having a backup is great, but if the backup is not qualified, you can be facing just as much risk as if there was no backup.

We also like to ask about how things are handled when processes or costs go off track. In order to get the supplier's management talking even more about their services, you might ask:

- What type of conflict resolution process do you have in place?
- What is the escalation process?
- What will it be like if I don't hear from the key person by the time a deliverable is due?
- Will I have to be the *squeaky wheel* to get things done?
- After how many occurrences of late deliverables do you think that we should treat the engagement as having problems?
- What type of situation would make you want to assign a new key person to our account?

Again, asking these types of questions in person will go a long way toward truly understanding how much of a priority your company will be to your new service provider. You can't distill this stuff onto a spreadsheet, but with experience, you will be able to identify red flags that can help you identify service providers who may pose more risk than their competitors.

PROJECT MANAGEMENT IN PROCUREMENT

As organizations have grown globally, procurement is called upon to unify everyone with a common buying strategy. This requires that a leader assemble a team and coordinate the efforts of subordinate procurement staff, business unit representatives, and management. There are limited resources, specific goals, and timelines.

Does this sound like the project management discipline? You bet it does! Project management has become an essential element of successful procurement. The procurement professional must be educated in project management methods.

If you are not yet educated in project management methods and are asked to lead a project, what is the first thing you should do? If you are the manager of a project and you want to follow best practices for successfully leading that project, you need a project charter. The project charter is the foundation for the entire project. It establishes what is supposed to be accomplished.

The Project Charter

Never, never, never (did we say *never*?) start performing project tasks until you have developed a project charter. To fail to develop a project charter is lazy, and makes very real the risk that you and the team are going to be working on the wrong tasks to accomplish the objective.

Formalizing a project in a project charter gives a form of proof that someone with authority in the organization has thought through the organizational commitments (e.g., money, people, resources) to start the project, and understands that those resources must be protected from other responsibilities that may interfere with the project. A project charter accomplishes four things:

1. Establishes the project as something that the organization officially intends to do as a goal
2. Provides an official authorization for the project manager (i.e., you) to do the work
3. Confirms that management has explicitly approved the project
4. Serves as the basis on which a project plan can be developed

Take note of that last item—the basis on which a project plan can be developed. A project charter is not a project plan, in and of itself. Some people mistake it for one. A project plan is much more detailed, while the charter is broader.

The Project Plan for Simple Projects

Different projects have different levels of complexity. The less complex projects require less formal and less detailed project plans. The more complex projects require more formal and more detailed project plans. If your project is simple enough to not require an in-depth project plan, that doesn't mean that you can forgo using some of the project management best practices that are available to you. You should at least apply these three basic tips:

- **Tip 1: Use project planning tools**—The many types of project planning tools available (such as websites, software, and mobile apps) serve as great resources for keeping your project organized. You can track all of the tasks that need to be done, who needs to do them, when they will be worked on, the unit price and cost of each, and much more. You can create Gantt charts that offer a graphical way of evaluating the project (see Figure 14.1), as well as other helpful visuals. Many providers of such tools offer free trials so that you can find one that best fits your organization and its culture. These tools are generally very affordable, making it almost a no-brainer to use them when considering how much they can help you keep your projects organized.
- **Tip 2: Break down your project**—Any project is essentially a set of individual, but related, tasks that are done in order to achieve a goal within a certain time frame. When you know what the project goal is, determine which tasks need to be done to achieve that goal. Then, determine how long each task will take. This will give you a realistic view of whether or not you are capable of achieving the project goal by its deadline. For example, you

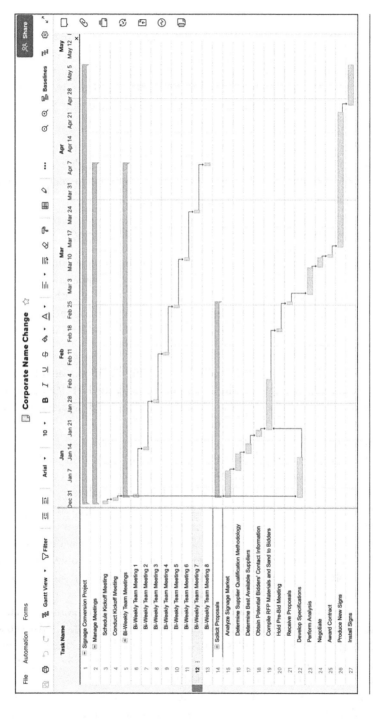

Figure 14.1 Example Gantt Chart

would not necessarily know that a goal of writing a report for your boss in one week is unrealistic unless you first determine that it will take three days to do research, three days to write the report, and two days to proofread.

- **Tip 3: Monitor progress against your schedule**—Regularly compare the tasks that you have completed at a certain point in time against the tasks that you expected to complete by that time. This will enable you to identify any adjustments required to meet your deadline.

As with any new and challenging activity, project management can be a minefield of potential mistakes. The more complex the project, the higher the likelihood of mistakes or oversights in planning. That's where a more formal project plan becomes invaluable.

The Project Plan for Highly Complex Projects

What does a detailed project plan for a highly complex project consist of? There are seven main components of a project plan, according to Diana Lindstrom, a former strategic sourcing manager for a telecommunications firm, author of the book *Procurement Project Management Success*, and currently president of Los Lobos Consulting. These components of a project plan are illustrated in Figure 14.2, and described as follows:

1. **Scope**—"The scope is the goal of the procurement," explains Lindstrom. "Sometimes, you can use the description from your RFP, RFI, or RFQ for your scope. But the big secret is that it has to be very specific and document every assumption that has been made."
2. **Schedule**—"The schedule includes a work breakdown structure; the specific steps that are required to complete the procurement," Lindstrom says. "You break down each activity into its smallest task. Then you can assign a specific amount of time it is going to take to do each one of those tasks."
3. **Budget**—Lindstrom notes: "The budget can mean different things to different companies. In some companies, if you're billing your time to specific internal projects or the business unit, the budget does become important. The easiest way to create a budget is to tie it to the schedule." She suggests multiplying the number of hours of work by the prorated salaries (perhaps including benefits) of the workers.
4. **Quality plan**—"The quality plan lays out how you're going to maintain the standards and requirements for a good procurement," Lindstrom says, noting that some examples of items that should be included in a quality plan for a procurement project include ensuring that the competition is fair and that the suppliers are qualified.
5. **Human resources plan**—"The human resources plan describes the qualifications of the personnel that you need on your team," Lindstrom

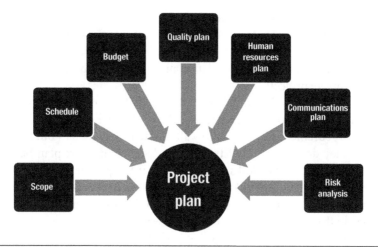

Figure 14.2   Components of a project plan

explains. "Usually, you can get the people you want if you can justify exactly why you need them. What is it that they know or do that you need? Remember to document it if you aren't allowed to use the people that you asked for; that can help you in explaining why your project is not doing as well as you thought it ought to do."

6. **Communications plan**—"The communications plan clearly describes who is on the team, who the end users are, and anyone else affected by the procurement," Lindstrom says. "It also defines the role each stakeholder has within that procurement." She notes that including titles and contact information is important as well as defining how communications will take place, citing the example of the procurement professional being the only one to communicate with bidders during the request for proposal process.

7. **Risk analysis**—A risk analysis is, "figuring out what can go wrong and how to either avoid it or fix it," according to Lindstrom. "By figuring out what can go wrong—identifying risks—we're one step ahead of Murphy's Law."

This seventh component of the project plan, procurement risk analysis, is so critical that we are going to expand upon it in the next section.

Procurement Risk Analysis

Great project managers see projects in a logical sequence of systematically executed events. Developing a procurement risk analysis is no different. "Once we've identified the risk, then we assign a level to that risk," Lindstrom explains. "You can use 1 through 10, ABC, or any other ranking system."

The final piece of the procurement risk analysis is the risk plan. "The risk plan includes the steps necessary to avoid the risk or mitigate the fallout from the risk if it does happen," says Lindstrom. "By knowing the risks, understanding how likely each one is to occur, and having a plan in place to deal with it, we're able to successfully complete projects."

Using a risk plan, as shown in Table 14.1, can help a procurement department demonstrate its value to the organization. "Most internal customers don't understand why procurement needs to follow all the steps that are laid out by the company. And they don't care," Lindstrom notes. "So, using a risk plan becomes an educational tool. It teaches folks what happens if the procurement steps are not followed. It shows them in black and white what can happen—the risk—and how procurement professionals deal with it—the plan. It shows them that procurement wants to help them do business in a less risky way."

In summary, identify risks, assign levels to those risks, determine the steps to avoid or mitigate the risks, and share the plan with stakeholders.

One of the most common and embarrassing procurement project risks is when the project falls behind schedule. The worst thing you can do as a project manager is to try to hide the delay from stakeholders and management.

In the event that the project falls behind target dates, be honest with management and stakeholders. Also, let them know why dates slipped, and what you are going to do to get the project back on track, or at least prevent it from slipping further. Though project management is usually technical in nature, human relations are what matter the most when things go awry.

If you are genuine in your communications, accepting of responsibility, and willing to learn from mistakes, you can earn leniency when you encounter challenges. If you are defensive, not forthcoming with information, or aloof, irritated managers or stakeholders can be less forgiving.

Table 14.1   Example risk plan

Risk	Criticality level	Probability	Actions to avoid or mitigate
Natural disaster affects supplier's region	High	Low	Dual source with suppliers in different regions
Supplier runs one week behind on production	High	High	Maintain sufficient inventory
One of supplier's ships is hijacked by pirates	Medium	Medium	Maintain sufficient inventory
Demand exceeds forecast	High	Medium	Ensure suppliers have plan in place to expand production
A shipment is out of tolerance and fails inspection	Low	Medium	Have rework instructions for internal techs and include reimbursement clause in contracts

INVENTORY MANAGEMENT

Inventory—finance executives hate it; operations executives love it. Whoever is responsible for managing inventory levels needs to please both finance executives and operations executives with decisions that impact inventory levels. Traditionally, inventory management has been handled by materials planning groups. However, as the scope of supply chain management changes, procurement professionals are increasingly gaining responsibility for this specialized area.

So, that brings us back to pleasing both finance executives and operations executives and satisfying their disparate interests. Is that an impossible goal? Maybe not. The key is finding the right balance in inventory levels. Finding that balance depends on mathematical formulas that you can adapt for your situation.

There are many calculations involved in managing inventory. In this section, we will cover the most basic, and perhaps also the most important. To manage inventory well, you need to be proficient at these six foundational activities:

1. Forecasting future demand
2. Deciding on minimum inventory levels
3. Determining when to replenish inventory
4. Deciding how much to order
5. Knowing when traditional formulas are inappropriate
6. Measuring inventory management performance

Forecasting is a topic that could take up several chapters by itself. Understanding trends, seasonality, moving averages, exponential smoothing, and so on, are all involved when doing a great job of forecasting. Because of the extent of the body of knowledge associated with forecasting and the fact that, even in organizations where procurement professionals are involved in inventory management, that responsibility often resides outside of procurement, we do not fully address forecasting in this book. However, it is critical to mention forecasting for any reader who wants to know what it takes to expertly manage inventory.

The other foundational activities that more commonly find their way into procurement professionals' job descriptions relate to decisions about minimum inventory, when to replenish inventory, how much to order, use of traditional formulas (or not), and measuring inventory management performance.

Deciding on Minimum Inventory Levels

Once a forecast is in place, you have quantities in mind that you need to support through a combination of new items that you buy and items held in inventory. The first question is, "What is the minimum inventory you should have on hand?"

One of the most embarrassing situations for a procurement professional who is responsible for inventory management is to run out of stock, especially if it brings certain operations to a halt. More inventory guards against stockouts. However, inventory represents costs that executives seek to minimize. You need a balance between high cost and high risk, which involves calculating the safety stock level for each key inventory item.

Safety stock is a quantity of inventory that you keep in the event of an emergency. What type of emergency? To simplify, there are two main reasons that inventory can be depleted sooner than normal: either the demand for the item increases so that more inventory is consumed than normal, or the supply of the item is delayed.

Theoretically, inventory levels should never drop below the safety stock level. In an ideal world, inventory levels reach the safety stock levels at the exact moment a replenishment order arrives. That is why it is called *safety stock*—it is there just in case something goes wrong. However, realistically, inventory will from time-to-time dip below the safety stock level before a replenishment order arrives. If you find your organization's inventory regularly dipping below safety stock levels, something is wrong.

So, how do you establish a safety stock level? Sorry, but there is no one, perfect safety stock calculation applicable to all situations or that will please all executives. You'll want more safety stock for items that are highly important to the organization, the process they are a part of, or the product they are incorporated into. You'll find resistance to holding a lot of safety stock of items that cost a lot of money. You will want more safety stock if items are not available on short notice elsewhere in the supply chain. So, setting safety stock levels requires a deep understanding of your organization, the market, and the consequences of a stockout.

One calculation that we have used as a benchmark for having too much safety stock is:

$$\text{Maximum SSL} = \text{MHDU} \times (\text{MHLT} - \text{ALT})$$

where,

> SSL = Safety stock level
> MHDU = Maximum historical daily usage
> MHLT = Maximum historical lead time
> ALT = Average lead time

The theory behind this safety stock calculation is that you will have just enough inventory in stock if two catastrophic events happen simultaneously:

1. Your supplier's lead time slips to the longest it has ever been with that supplier
2. On those days that your supplier is late, your organization uses the most inventory it has ever used

In most situations, this is probably too much safety stock to have on hand because the chances of both things happening at the same time are less than only one of them happening. So, some may view this calculation as an indicator for determining if your safety stock level is set too high.

That being said, we have to invoke the investing cliché, *past performance does not guarantee future results*. What if demand was stable in the past, but some type of external event—a competitor going out of business, a marketing campaign, or unexpected press coverage—caused demand to skyrocket overnight? Those types of things could set a new record for maximum historical daily usage.

The same could be said for supply. Just because you have a maximum lead time for your supplier's historical performance does not mean that the supplier will not have an operational hiccup that could make them exceed their worst lead time. Plus, there is always the possibility that a natural disaster could hit a supplier's region, impacting their ability to perform.

So, you can use the safety stock formula we've presented, then determine whether to adjust it downward or upward based on your own observations of the risks to demand and supply.

Determining When to Replenish Inventory

When should you place an order to replenish inventory? Well, it certainly shouldn't be when your inventory reaches or goes below the safety stock level. It should be in advance, so that the items arrive before your organization begins consuming safety stock.

After you figure out the safety stock quantity, you are ready to determine when to reorder materials for inventory. Generally, this point in time is determined when the quantity of materials in stock decreases to a certain level, called the *reorder point*. The reorder point is calculated as:

$$ROP = SSL + (QUD \times ALT)$$

where,

$$ROP = \text{Reorder point}$$
$$SSL = \text{Safety stock level}$$
$$QUD = \text{Quantity used daily}$$
$$ALT = \text{Average lead time (in days)}$$

One caution: using average lead time can be tricky. If the average is skewed by perhaps one emergency overnight shipment and, therefore, does not represent the lead time you can currently expect from your supplier, this formula may result in a situation where you do exactly what you want to avoid—digging into the safety stock. So, use your firsthand knowledge to determine if the average lead time is realistic and, if not, adjust it appropriately.

Deciding How Much to Order

When you are ready to order, what quantity should you order? Before we answer this question, we need to give some background on the components of the order quantity calculation to come. It is important to understand a couple of inventory-related costs. There are two types of costs that will factor into a calculation for determining order quantity. Those costs are inventory carrying costs and acquisition costs.

Inventory carrying costs are usually calculated as a percentage of the inventory's value. Most experts agree that the percentage is between 18 and 35 percent per year. So, how is that 18 to 35 percent determined?

First, look at all of the costs associated with inventory. This includes the cost of the facilities where the inventory is kept. It includes the utilities for those facilities. It includes the cost of the employees who are responsible for managing the inventory—not only salaries, but also benefits and other overhead associated with them. It includes things such as insurance and taxes that are associated with holding that inventory. It also includes the costs of inventory obsolescence and spoilage.

Once you determine the annual inventory costs, you divide the total of those costs by the average inventory value to come up with a preliminary percentage. To that preliminary percentage, you have to add the opportunity cost of inventory. What that means is that if the organization invested its money elsewhere in the organization rather than in inventory, what kind of return on investment (ROI) would that generate? Or, even if the organization put its money into a money market account and earned a half percent interest per year, the ROI of that capital has to be added to the preliminary percentage to come up with the final percentage.

It should be pretty clear from this discussion that the procurement department is usually not solely responsible for determining the carrying cost percentage. That job usually falls to the finance department. So, we recommend working closely with your finance department to determine specifically what your organization's inventory carrying cost percentage is. Inventory carrying cost will drive a lot of decisions regarding order quantity and timing, so it is important to get it right.

The second type of costs that impact order quantity calculations are called *acquisition costs*. One of the most common questions in procurement is, "How much does it cost to process a purchase order?" The cost of processing a purchase order is synonymous with acquisition costs. The procurement profession has been trying to figure out the answer to that question almost as long as the Philadelphia Flyers have been trying to win their third Stanley Cup championship. But, just like the Flyers have failed (sorry Philly people), the procurement profession has come up short in terms of coming up with a widely accepted number for the cost of a purchase order.

But, it's not like there hasn't been effort expended on studying the matter. Here are a few stabs that people have taken at answering this elusive question throughout the years:

- In 1994, the U.S. Environmental Protection Agency conducted a study on its own processes and revealed that some of its procurement officials had estimated the cost of a purchase order to be as high as $300, but published a conservative estimate of $94.20 per purchase order.[2]
- A 2006 report from the American Productivity & Quality Center[3] found that the cost of a purchase order differed, depending on the capabilities of the procurement department on a continuum from bottom performer to top performer. This report indicated that the cost of a purchase order ranged from $35.88 to $506.52.
- The 2006 edition of *Supply Management Handbook*[4] says, "it often costs organizations more than $100 in administrative expenses to generate a purchase order," and that, "in many firms, the cost of managing and generating a purchase order can exceed $200 per transaction."
- In a 2015 Cross-Industry Report of Standard Benchmarks, CAPS Research indicated that purchase order processing costs vary by industry from $238 in the metals and mining industry to an immense $955 in the petroleum industry, with the average being $411.[5]

Would one of these benchmarks apply to your organization? Maybe, maybe not. There are many variables, including the procurement department's capabilities, industry, organization's specific processes, systems used, and so on. If you want a number that is true to your organization, you would need to track everything involved with an order; know the salaries of each individual who gets involved in that order; amortize the price paid for systems by the number of purchase orders generated over the life of the systems; know the telecommunications and paper costs; factor in overhead costs such as facilities, supervision, and benefits; and determine any other cost inputs. The cost of obtaining such information would likely outweigh the benefits of having that information. This is an example of a situation with the potential for *paralysis by analysis*. Instead, you may want to pick a number out of the range of benchmarks that we previously cited—like $200, $300, or $350—being as conservative as you need to be to fit the culture of your organization, and just go with it.

Wow, that was a lot of background, wasn't it? To truly understand how order quantities are determined, it is important to know what each component of the equation means. So, back to the question: "How much should you order?"

This question is answered by a complex mathematical equation that determines the economic order quantity (EOQ). The equation recognizes the *tug of war* between acquisition costs and inventory carrying costs: when you order bigger quantities less frequently, your aggregate acquisition costs are low, but your inventory costs are high due to higher inventory levels. Conversely, when you order smaller quantities more often, your inventory costs are low, but your acquisition costs are higher because you are expending more resources on ordering and receiving. The EOQ is the order quantity that minimizes the sum of these two costs.

Fortunately, inventory management systems calculate the EOQ for you. If you want to understand how that number appears, or ever need to calculate EOQ by hand, you can find the equation in Figure 14.3.

There is also a chance that you may want to use a spreadsheet program like Microsoft Excel to do this type of calculation, so here is how you would perform the calculation in Excel:

1. Enter the acquisition cost per order in Cell B1
2. Enter the annual usage in units in Cell B2
3. Enter the unit cost in Cell B3
4. Enter the carrying cost percentage in Cell B4 (either use the percentage sign after your number, or enter the percentage as a decimal, like 0.20 for 20 percent)
5. In Cell B6, enter this formula:

$$= SQRT((2*B1*B2)/(B3*B4))$$

If it costs $150 in overhead per order, and you use 5,000 widgets a year, paying $200 per widget, and your finance department tells you that annual carrying costs are equal to 20 percent of the value of the goods in stock, you should order (drumroll, please) . . . 194 widgets at a time.

$$EOQ = \sqrt{\frac{2 \times ACPO \times AUU}{UC \times CCP}}$$

Where:

EOQ = Economic order quantity

ACPO = Acquisition costs per order

AUU = Annual usage in units

UC = Unit cost

CCP = Carrying cost percentage

Figure 14.3   Economic order quantity formula

When Traditional Formulas Are Inappropriate

When determining safety stock level, reorder point, and economic order quantity, we used several formulas. However, there are certain factors that make inventory management more than just a numbers game or a math exercise. Here are a few of those factors:

- **Finite product life cycles**—If a product line is going to be discontinued, you want to make sure that you don't end up with a significant amount of materials or components that will never get used after the end product is discontinued.
- **Big cheap things, small inexpensive things**—Because inventory carrying costs are expressed as a percentage of the value of items, the implication is that it is not as bad to have inexpensive stuff compared to expensive stuff on the shelf. But it is a problem if the inexpensive stuff is large and consumes a lot of space. The EOQ formula may have you ordering large quantities of physically big, but inexpensive items. The EOQ strives to consider carrying costs, but it does not factor in the cubic footage of the item. It should factor in cubic footage because it is plausible that the EOQ might result in the recommendation that you order a warehouse full of large but inexpensive items, and the facilities required to accommodate bulky items can actually increase your costs.
- **Seasonality**—The EOQ formula uses annual usage statistics. However, seasonality can swing usage like a pendulum based on the demand cycle for the end product or service. If you are in a seasonal business, EOQ could result in you ordering too often for efficiency's sake in busy times and keeping too much inventory on hand in slow times.
- **Items with a shelf life**—Some items have a shelf life. Food items are one example. If EOQ tells you to order two months' worth of inventory, but the items only last two weeks before spoiling, following the EOQ is not advisable. Items in rapidly advancing markets—like computer memory—should be treated similarly.
- **Items where suppliers offer quantity discounts**—The traditional EOQ formula only allows you to put one price in, and assumes that the price will be consistent, regardless of purchase quantity. However, some suppliers offer discounts at certain quantity thresholds. So, the traditional EOQ formula would not necessarily lead you to the next quantity discount threshold when it actually may help you save money.

Measuring Inventory Management Performance

So far, we have covered the tactical inventory management numbers dealt with by *procurement and inventory management* professionals on a day-to-day basis.

Inventory management also has some strategic numbers used by *management* to determine the organization's inventory performance.

A few of the metrics that management uses to evaluate inventory management performance include:

- Inventory turnover ratio
- Fill rate
- Months of inventory

Next we'll discuss each metric, one-by-one.

Inventory Turnover Ratio

The inventory turnover ratio indicates how well your organization is managing its purchased inventory assets. Inventory turnover is the number of times that your inventory is replenished in a year. Low inventory turnover means that you are carrying too much inventory, thereby unnecessarily restricting your company's access to cash that it could be using to invest in profit-generating activities, pay its bills, or even stay in business.

So, how do you calculate the inventory turnover ratio? Well, there are a couple of ways. Inventory turnover can be for a single item or for overall inventory.

Here is the formula for a single item:

$$ITR = US / [(BI + EI)/2]$$

where,

ITR = Inventory turnover ratio
US = Units sold in the last 12 months
BI = Beginning inventory (the number of units in stock
at the beginning of the 12-month period)
EI = Ending inventory (the number of units in stock at
the end of the 12-month period)

When calculating the inventory turnover ratio for the overall inventory, you need some financial numbers. Here's the formula for overall inventory:

$$ITR = YCIS / [(BIV + EIV) / 2]$$

where,

ITR = Inventory turnover ratio
YCIS = Your cost of inventory sold in the last 12 months
BIV = Beginning inventory value (the total value of inventory
at the beginning of the 12-month period)
EIV = Ending inventory value (the total value of inventory at
the end of the 12-month period)

You will also hear the inventory turnover ratio expressed as *turns*. People will say, "Our inventory turns 12 times per year," or, "We're achieving 12 turns." Twelve turns per year basically indicates that the organization has an average of one month's worth of inventory on the shelf at any given time. Six turns means that the organization has an average of two months' worth of inventory on the shelf at any given time. And, 24 turns means that the organization has an average of a half a month of inventory on the shelf at any given time.

Most executives think that the more turns, the better. Of course, operationally, having inventory can bail an organization out of a jam or give it an advantage over poorly stocked competitors in times of high demand.

Fill Rate

There are several variations of fill rate. We will concentrate on order fill rate. *Order fill rate* measures the percentages of orders that are filled on time. To find the order fill rate, simply divide the number of orders filled on time during a period by the total number of orders, including orders not filled on time during that same period.

In a procurement role, you could measure your suppliers' performance this way. If you also manage inventory, you should measure your inventory performance this way, as well. Whether you are managing inventory for use in production of a finished product, for resale, or for internal consumption, you can measure fill rate. An ideal fill rate is obviously 100 percent.

We mentioned that there are variations of fill rate. You can also measure fill rate by the percentage of line items filled on time. So, for example, if your organization was filling an order with 10 lines on it, and had the inventory to fill eight of those 10 lines on time, then your order fill rate would be zero percent, but your line fill rate would be 80 percent.

Months of Inventory

Months of inventory is a third type of measurement. While some organizations try to keep inventory at a bare minimum, it is common for organizations in some industries to actually want to keep a certain large amount of inventory on hand at all times.

We were once at a conference where a supply chain leader from a pharmaceutical company said that it was a goal of that organization to have 12 months of inventory on hand. Many attendees were shocked at this seemingly large number at a time when supply managers in many industries were under unprecedented pressure to adopt aggressive *lean inventory* and *just-in-time inventory* strategies. Because of strict regulation, traceability requirements, the need for consistency in ingredients, and the sole source relationships that arise out of those constraints, the speaker's industry is prone to disruptions in critical supply, thus, adequate inventory is the primary buffer against those disruptions.

CLOSING REMARKS

Because procurement has been increasingly recognized as a strategic contributor to organizational success, the scope of procurement has been growing. Procurement departments are involved in activities previously reserved for top management or other departments within the organization.

As such, procurement professionals have had to adapt to these changes, learning about new, specialized areas. With procurement continuing to evolve, having specialized knowledge in areas such as global sourcing, services procurement, project management, and inventory management will only become more important. These areas span many still untapped opportunities for the procurement function.

REFERENCES

1. "Selling to Giants." 2006. *BusinessWeek*. [Podcast].
2. United States Environmental Protection Agency. 1995. "EPA's Use of the Government Purchase Card."
3. "Procurement Benchmarks Show Wide Variation Between Top and Bottom Performers." October 4, 2006. *Supply Chain Digest*.
4. Cavinato, Joseph L., Anna E. Flynn, and Ralph G. Kauffman. 2006. *The Supply Management Handbook*. New York, McGraw-Hill.
5. CAPS Research. July 2015. *Cross-Industry Report of Standard Benchmarks*.

15

CHAPTER

PROCUREMENT Q&A: POST-GAME INTERVIEWS WITH SUPERSTARS OF THE GAME

Of all of the sports to analyze, American football is perhaps the most distinctive. Teams play only once per week, but the analysis and sports talk after the game keeps fans galvanized until the next game's kickoff.

Perhaps the most interesting component of this week-long dialogue for any given team is the infamous post-game interview with players and coaches. During these interviews, they offer up some insights that are sometimes more interesting and enduring than the game itself.

With that same spirit, we set out to interview several executives who are influential in procurement to share *post-game insights* on some of their biggest victories and lessons learned.

LOGISTICS' ROLE IN SUPPLY CHAIN PERFORMANCE WITH PATRICK COZZENS AND DAVE UNCAPHER

Patrick Cozzens is President of Modern Transportation Services, a leading provider of bulk logistics solutions. Dave Uncapher is Director of Logistics for Kalmbach Feeds, Inc.

As we have stated in different sections of this book, supply chains are unique and complex networks among businesses that deal with the procurement of raw materials, production, warehousing, inventory, transportation, and delivery of products. It is well understood that these networks are critical to businesses as they largely affect sales and profits. However, without effective, well-managed, and well-operated logistics, procurement and supply chain professionals can't help businesses gain a clear advantage over their competition. For a diagram of how logistics fit into the supply chain, see Figure 15.1.

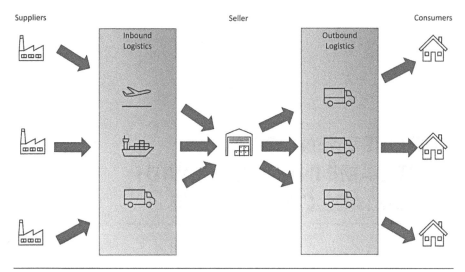

Figure 15.1   Example of logistics in a business-to-consumer supply chain

To highlight the importance of effective and reliable logistics, and how best-in-class transportation organizations function, we had an opportunity to sit down with Patrick Cozzens, president of Modern Transportation Services which was founded in 1987 with headquarters in southwestern Pennsylvania. Under the leadership and aegis of Cozzens, who joined Modern Transportation in 2006, the company has taken a holistic approach in making it one of the leading bulk materials logistics organizations. The mission of the company is to provide superior transportation solutions to their customers in the safest and most professional and efficient manner.

Cozzens stressed that "we value the safety of our drivers, employees, and customers above anything else. Nothing we do is worth hurting ourselves or others. For that reason, we live by our motto of 'Home Safe Tonight!' Regardless of the destination of our customer's shipment, our goal remains the same: get our drivers home, safely!"

The transportation industry has as many opportunities as challenges. Safety, coupled with the lack of qualified drivers, are the biggest challenges in this field these days. Any mishap on the road is harmful for the driver, vehicle, and company, as well as the customer. It adversely affects all of them physically, financially, and mentally.

Today's drivers are becoming more selective about where they want to work and often turn to private transportation companies' compliance, safety, and accountability scores[1] to help them make the decision. Drivers well know that any violations become a part of their resume. While a number of violations ultimately come down to the driver's responsibility, some are dependent on the organization, and a growing number of drivers are no longer willing to work for a company that doesn't make safety a priority. As a result, at Modern Transportation, by taking advantage of new technologies such as GPS tracking devices, electronic logging devices, and fleet dash cameras, they have been able to track their fleet in real time, monitor locations and paths, and more important, observe the speed of vehicles and their drivers' habits to increase safety. For Cozzens, being laser-focused on safety, caring deeply for the people, and proactively providing drivers' training are all high priority. "When we get every load delivered without incident and every driver home safely, we consider that day a success," he said.

Cozzens encourages employees to be creative, innovative, and motivated to improve the value the company brings to its customers and shareholders. This spirit of innovation resulted in a partnership with Automated Cargo Transport Systems.[2] Modern's support and collaboration led to the implementation of an automatic pneumatic tanker trailer unloading system with monitoring and radar-guide sensors with customer silos, enabling real-time volume readings which are accessible to customers via Modern Transportation's website. Such automated unloading of dry materials has resulted in increased efficiency, allowing the driver to hook up to an empty tanker and get another load. For customers, there is no waiting for silo capacity readings, and no overfilled silos. A win-win outcome!

"We are always seeking to uncover and develop the next innovative idea. We strongly believe that research and innovation are integral elements of environmental responsibility and sustainability," said Cozzens. In 2012, Modern Transportation was the first commercial carrier to run production lanes in tractors powered by 12-liter liquefied natural gas engines. This commitment to sustainability has resulted in a dramatic reduction of their carbon footprint. "Our collaborative relationships with our equipment suppliers, coupled with our commitment to continuous improvement, render us the perfect partner when new innovations in fuel, lubricants, or safety require real-time testing," noted Cozzens.

"To proactively plan for unexpected events and to establish strong supplier relationships have been high priorities for our company. Having a preferred customer status with one of the major travel centers and fuel providers during the recent Colonial Pipeline cyberattack[3] that took down the largest fuel pipeline in the U.S. and led to shortages across the East Coast proved to be a smart contingency plan. While our competitors may have been scrambling for fuel, our drivers were notified and able to obtain fuel, resulting in limited interruptions in deliveries to our customers," said Cozzens.

In addition to having a strong working relationship with key suppliers, Cozzens believes in the value of establishing trust and collaborating with their customers.

He indicated that they have been working with one key customer for over 25 years. However, it wasn't until Dave Uncapher came into the picture that this partnership truly blossomed. To learn more about this partnership, we then followed up with Uncapher, who is presently the director of logistics at Kalmbach Feeds, Inc. While he was in charge of procuring transportation services at his former employer, in support of his organization's goal of reducing its carbon footprint and sustainability, he started working with logistics suppliers to promote and convert to natural gas. This created a vigorous competition among Uncapher's suppliers and opened the door for those who were willing to come to the table to discuss approaches for not only addressing the goal of reducing their carbon footprint, but more important, looking at the company's newest location, various routes, and pricing structures, along with going from a cost-based to a value-based way of doing business. This resulted in establishing trust, a close customer-supplier working relationship, and ultimately opening books between Uncapher and Cozzens. By routinely meeting, reviewing progress, willingly sharing information/data, and cooperating, they found ways to unlock significant new sources of value that benefited both organizations. Cozzens highlighted that Uncapher's legacy of advanced procurement practices have remained strong even now that he has a new position in a different organization.

"In addition to focusing on and nurturing trusting relationships with our customers and suppliers, we strive to create a culture of honesty and respect with our employees where a sense of trust and mutual confidence flourishes," expressed Cozzens. He has an *open-door* policy providing an opportunity for employees to easily contact him. Promoting the use of *Modern InTouch*, a hotline feeding directly to Cozzens, has resulted in employees reaching out with their improvement ideas, concerns, and problems, anonymously.

Cozzens remembered a call from one of their drivers complaining about his supervisor, a manager of one of the terminals, as to how poorly he was treating the drivers. Apparently, this terminal was one of the high-performing locations for the company. Nevertheless, upon further investigation, it became evident that although this manager was result-oriented and contributed to the financial success of the company, he lacked interpersonal and managerial skills. Subsequently, he was offered leadership classes and one-on-one coaching sessions resulting in an improved working relationship with his staff. Morale among drivers drastically improved, and now the terminal is a much more pleasant workplace as expressed by the staff.

"We believe that by treating our customers right, having a holistic approach in improving our processes and practices, as well as having a vibrant company culture that supports, respects, and nurtures our employees are the keys to our success and a sustainable competitive advantage," concluded Cozzens.

SUSTAINABLE PROCUREMENT WITH THOMAS UDESEN

Thomas Udesen is the chief procurement officer (CPO) of Bayer, headquartered in Germany, and the cofounder of the Sustainable Procurement Pledge, a pro bono community of those committed to embedding sustainability into their procurement practices.

In Chapter 4 we discussed sustainable business and sustainable procurement. As you've read, sustainable procurement success is a huge determinant of whether or not a sustainability initiative for the whole business will succeed. As such, whoever is leading procurement is given a great deal of responsibility for driving sustainable business practices throughout the entire organization.

Does it make sense for procurement to lead that charge? Thomas Udesen thinks so. Procurement is "the function that is by far best positioned to make sure that the power we hold is used for good," he declares. "It's not a job anymore to be a procurement professional. It carries a responsibility. There is nobody better positioned to have a positive impact. We control world trade."

Despite that positioning, there are plenty of challenges to transforming a typical organization into one that is a sustainability leader. So, Udesen cofounded the Sustainable Procurement Pledge to help other procurement leaders on their sustainability journey. Doing so has helped raise awareness of the challenges so that they can be overcome with proven solutions.

"What the Sustainable Procurement Pledge ambassador community has shared with us is very clear feedback about what are their problems," Udesen says. "One is knowledge. One is maturity. One is lack of support from their leadership."

With these barriers to success, procurement leaders can get discouraged. Implementing sustainable procurement practices that have true impact can feel like a lead-off batter trying to hit a grand slam. You can't do it alone—you need other players on the same team to get on base. "Grab your friends," Udesen advises. "Find a couple of like-minded companies and do it together, because you get scale. You limit the paperwork that is required on your side with the supplier for having to answer the same questions multiple times. Industry collaborations would be my clear recommendation. Find friends, do it together. Then, you will see you get much more return for your money."

The Sustainable Procurement Pledge offers a tangible path toward the type of collaboration that Udesen recommends. "Don't reinvent the wheel," he said. "A lot of organizations maybe do not recognize the knowledge that's out there. That's, in a way, what www.spp.earth is all about. We are democratizing the knowledge. Our knowledge is there for everybody. It's free. It's just so you can move faster and benefit from members who have gone through similar experiences in the past."

Suppliers are another external constituency that procurement leaders need to collaborate with in pursuit of a more sustainable supply chain. Udesen cautions that supplier collaboration requires a well-thought-out, careful, and diplomatic approach. "You need to be honest with your suppliers about what's going to happen," he says. "But, you also need to be respectful that they may not all have reached the level of maturity that we are aspiring for them. With that, we stick around. We work with them. We will, of course, also offer knowledge and investment, as long as they are committed—and, we can see immediately if they're committed or not."

The value that this type of collaboration delivers is measured in more ways than just in an organization's carbon footprint. Looking back, "The COVID-19 pandemic showed us that sustainable supply chains are resilient supply chains," Udesen reveals. "So, the ones who had already invested in relationships were the ones with the least disruptions and the least pain. We also saw that there was a divide happening across companies and CPOs, between the ones that are committed to developing new, sustainable supplier relationships and the ones that are going back two decades—back to price only. And, I do think that we are going to see winners and losers. I'm pretty convinced that the ones who have gone two decades back in time—on a path of self-destruction—will not be around for long."

Looking forward, Udesen envisions the focus on sustainable procurement accelerating at a very fast pace—a potentially scary pace for those who are unprepared. "What we are looking at now and in the next decade is probably the biggest change management effort in the history of procurement," Udesen says "I do think that what we are now asking people to be—and how to act—differs greatly from what has worked in the 'analog age,' before digitalization and climate change. And, in a way, we are asking people to create a new identity."

Though procurement leaders are often the ones encouraging others to embrace change, some of them may be finding themselves with mixed feelings about the sustainability-driven future of procurement. "Many people, as they are moving toward this end game, are probably super nervous," Udesen expresses. "They don't necessarily enjoy the additional mandates. They don't necessarily feel that they are ready. They haven't yet built the necessary courage. They don't have the necessary knowledge right in their hands. So, we are asking them to make a step into the unknown. And, that's very uncomfortable for most."

However, with procurement all-stars like Udesen and his team being willing to take new players under their wings and offer advice, procurement professionals of tomorrow have a better chance at winning the sustainable procurement game.

CREATIVE THINKING IN PROCUREMENT WITH GREG TENNYSON AND DON HOEPPNER

Greg Tennyson held the role of CPO for three organizations: Oracle, Salesforce, and VSP Global. He is currently the senior vice president of strategy and procurement for Fairmarkit, a sourcing platform provider. Don Hoeppner held several executive-level positions for General Electric, including the position of CPO for GE Capital. He is currently the CEO of Paladin Associates, a leading procurement consulting firm.

People outside of procurement may not realize how creative of a profession it can actually be. They may envision procurement professionals engaged in dry activities, like poring over a spreadsheet of spend data; Googling prospective suppliers; or reconciling purchase orders, packing slips, and invoices.

But, procurement is a profession where creative thinking is very necessary to success. By creating unique approaches, procurement leaders can earn stakeholder buy-in, solve supplier-related problems, and save unprecedented amounts of money for their organizations.

Greg Tennyson recalled a time when he was CPO at VSP Global, where compelling stakeholders to comply with procurement initiatives was particularly challenging. The well-worn paths of pushing for executive mandates or outright begging for compliance are often unsuccessful in certain cultures such as the one at VSP.

So, Tennyson took a marketing path instead. That marketing path involved a character more likely to be spotted in a sports stadium than a boardroom. "We actually created a mascot, Moolah—a physical mascot, a big, purple, furry creature," recalls Tennyson. "And did some interesting things with change management: created a tagline, 'Spend It Like It's Yours,' which morphed into 'Fiscally Fit.'"

Tennyson is quick to point out that a purple, furry mascot isn't the template for procurement transformation at every company. He says that the key to successfully executing three different transformations as the CPO of three different companies was "doing it consistent with the culture at all three companies."

Tennyson says that corporate culture, values, and mission/vision statements must guide a procurement leader's approach to implementing improvements. "How I executed on transforming the function and driving change at Oracle was fundamentally different than how I did it at VSP; at VSP, I didn't have a vocal champion, an advocate," he said. "And that's why I partnered with the chief marketing officer to create a campaign and use video vignettes, created the mascot, created the tagline." Tennyson said that one of VSP Global's core values was to have fun, so his procurement transformation strategy had to be aligned with that core value to be effective. And it was!

Creativity doesn't have to be outrageous nor involve purple, furry mascots. It can be simply to explore supply base-related initiatives that are atypical. For example, "one other thing that I'm not sure that procurement leaders take a broad enough view of is asset recovery," observes Don Hoeppner. "When we were at GE, our view was 'Any money out the door, any payments made, were all fair game for procurement and strategic sourcing to at least get involved in.' Not necessarily to lead, but to get involved in."

The success of that broader perspective translated from GE to Hoeppner's current consulting firm, which has "developed relationships with a number of audit and recovery companies," he says. "It started with sales tax recovery." He said that the finance departments of clients often wondered if their companies were paying sales taxes when they didn't need to "so, we developed these relationships and brought in the experts and they found a whole bunch of opportunities."

That creativity that produced positive results in sales tax recovery spawned deeper investigations into value-added tax (VAT) recovery, too. "You can recover VAT on travel and living cost spent mostly in Europe and Japan," Hoeppner says. "Those countries that have high VAT rates—20 percent or more—it makes sense to identify those and apply for the VAT recovery."

Do you think Hoeppner and his clients stopped there? There is about as much of a chance of them stopping at sales and VAT recovery as there is for Carolina Panther running back Christian McCaffrey stopping when he has an open path to the end zone!

What was next for Hoeppner and his clients?—unrecovered deposits, particularly for facility-related expenses. "You hook up to the electric companies with a new lease and you have to put down a deposit," Hoeppner explains. Twenty years later when you move out of that building, the deposit is still there. But, it may not be on the books anymore for some unknown reason."

Compounding the lack of documentation is the fact that, often, the people that made the deposit and signed the original lease are no longer with the lessee. "The company moves out of the building, has maybe been bought [or] the company's name changed, and the deposit remains with the power company," according to Hoeppner. "They eventually have to turn it over to the state. There are literally billions of dollars sitting in state treasuries waiting for companies to apply to get them back."

Despite the fact that recovering deposits is a huge opportunity for bringing money from the supply base back into the organization, Hoeppner laments that procurement is rarely involved. But, a procurement department well-versed in such matters—or a consulting firm that they contract—"can recover some nice bucks," he exclaims.

Hoeppner advises procurement leaders to not let deposit recovery fall through the cracks because it's not a traditional procurement job. "Taking a broad view of what procurement really is and where it can impact a business is an important opportunity to go to the next step and be a more important part of the business," he says.

NEW MEDIA IN PROCUREMENT WITH KELLY BARNER, PHILIP IDESON, SCOTT LUTON, AND GREG WHITE

Kelly Barner is the owner and managing director of Buyers Meeting Point, a website of resources and trusted insights for procurement. She is also the head of content and brand partnerships at Art of Procurement, a procurement media organization offering podcasts, peer-led support groups, and advisory services. Prior to Buyers Meeting Point, Kelly was a hired services sourcing analyst for Ahold USA. Philip Ideson is the Founder and Managing Director of Art of Procurement. Prior to Art of Procurement, Philip was head of international procurement, sourcing, and third-party risk management for Ally Financial. Scott Luton is the founder and CEO of Supply Chain Now. Greg White is the principal of Supply Chain Now. Supply Chain Now provides a wide variety of supply chain-focused digital media, including podcasts, live streams, vlogs, virtual events, and articles.

Using the Internet to offer free digital resources to procurement professionals is nothing new. *Spend Matters* is widely regarded as the first procurement blog, started in 2005. And the *Next Level Purchasing Association Podcast* aired its first episode in 2006, years before supply chain podcasts became commonplace. To put how long ago that was into perspective, consider that the following sports teams existed during those years: Atlanta Thrashers (hockey), Seattle Supersonics (basketball) and the St. Louis Rams (American football)!

In 2009, Buyers Meeting Point was founded on a similar solid media model that remains intact today. "Buyers Meeting Point today is, in a lot of ways, what it always was," says Kelly Barner. "It is predominantly a practitioner-facing resource. We offer book reviews, webinar listings, event recommendations, and independent thought leadership."

Barner has led the media company through changes in both what it offers as well as the procurement topics that have progressed into hot-button issues. Barner says she takes cues on topics "from the C suite and from the end customer." What topics have risen to prominence in recent years that may not have been top-of-mind in 2009? "Sustainability, diversity and inclusion, risk mitigation, and innovating with suppliers," Barner rattles off in discussing the more prominent topics. Topics aren't the only thing evolving in procurement media today, however. Whereas early 2000's procurement media often revolved around *news*, news has become a secondary priority today.

What's the first priority? "It is undoubtedly and unquestionably education," contends Greg White. "If you poll listeners to podcasts or any kind of digital media, they're searching for breakthroughs. They're using what we ordinarily would have called 'downtime'—commute time, workout time, going-to-the-grocery-store time—and they are looking for insights and breakthroughs to help them get to the next level of performance, to help them solve their problems."

Also, engagement and interaction has skyrocketed compared to years past. "As more and more procurement professionals have come out of their shells and started engaging on social media, it has been fantastic for community building and meeting people," says Barner. "I think that's probably the biggest change I've seen over the last few years, is that procurement folks are actually talking now. It's no longer this like creepy, stalky 'I'm going to read your content, but not comment, and I definitely won't share it!' "

Scott Luton feels this isn't just a procurement media change, but a business culture change. "You take a couple of plays out of modern workforce management," he says. "Folks want to be heard. They want to interact. They want to share what they know. Creating forums where there is two-way conversation is really important."

Apparently, the change is being accepted in the procurement world. "It's officially okay for procurement to have a voice," observes Barner. "And people are using it. People have a lot to say! It's been wonderful! It's finally a two-way conversation."

While many of the new procurement media offerings allow procurement professionals to interact and be social, that's not where its value ends. *Social* implies *optional* and the new procurement media landscape has shown itself to be very needed in the profession. The new procurement media is filling the same need that conferences have for years: to connect procurement professionals and allow for the exchange of information with a perspective unique to them.

Supply chain publications and even general business publications will cover procurement-related stories. "But, what almost no one outside of procurement is covering, though, is that procurement perspective, which is what gives people in these roles the insight they need to do their jobs," Barner says. "So, the value of procurement media is that it takes these stories that are covered as general business or covered broadly as supply chain, and it brings them down to the level of making them actionable for procurement professionals."

That action orientation is one of the keys to success for both practitioners logging on to procurement media as well as the providers. A measurement of value is determined by "how quickly someone can engage with a piece of content and gain insights that they can take into action," according to Ideson. "When you sit and watch an hour webinar, do you actually put into practice what you learned? The vast majority of the time you do that, you don't. So, if a media site can take the content and create that into ways that make it as easy as possible for someone to take action on that, then that helps the listener, the reader, get measurable outcomes from investing the time and engaging in that content." The more Ideson talks about action-oriented content in procurement media, the more passionate he becomes. "Content without being able to take action is nothing more than just entertainment," he scoffs. "It's like sitting in front of a TV, watching a show for 30 minutes. Nobody really has the time to do that, related to procurement or their job. If you're not [providing actionable content], people aren't going invest their time in it."

While no one can dispute the value of action-orientation in the success of a new procurement media property, a difficult balancing act for serving the practitioners is determining which niche to fill and how globally relevant the content will be. Ideson has watched many media companies stand out by focusing intently on category niches or a niche like direct versus indirect materials. However, focusing too narrowly at first was a situation that the leadership of Supply Chain Now felt they had to correct. "We started out with a very tight purview," recalls White. "But, the truth is, you can't bound media. We had to realize very quickly and very early on that we're speaking to the world, arguably, the universe. We had to start to take on a more global, universal perspective because of that. We have to know a little about what's going on in India, which is one of our huge markets. Brazil is a huge market. Europe, and the UK in particular, are huge markets for us. And we have to know what their point of view is. We can't just present things with the American point of view. We are constantly reminded of that. So, the biggest learning was to speak universally."

With the evolution of procurement media, what's next? The influencers who were interviewed for this section of the book seem to agree that the future of procurement will be based around the cornerstones of live video, real-time conversations 24/7, strong opinions, and diversity of views. Some of these characteristics of the future of procurement media were accelerated by the COVID-19 pandemic in Ideson's opinion. After global in-person business shutdowns forced such a large proportion of the procurement workforce deeper into online meetings for years, "I don't think we're going to go away from that," he predicts. "There's going to be an ongoing place for media that's based around video that's all virtual and remote. I think that's opening a lot of opportunities for people to connect and collaborate with each other." Luton agrees and adds: "I think we're going to see all digital media really shift to be more focused on engaging—right there, during the broadcast— with who is consuming that content" (see Figure 15.2).

Such engagement is most likely to be stoked by influencers with thought-provoking—if not outright provocative—perspectives. "One of the things that we continually hear is that people want strong opinions," White shares. "They don't want the words distilled down or filtered. They want people to be real because it makes them feel that connection. People connect with that 'real reality.' Not 'Jersey

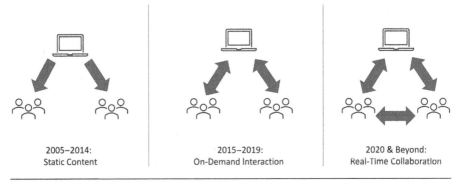

| 2005–2014: | 2015–2019: | 2020 & Beyond: |
| Static Content | On-Demand Interaction | Real-Time Collaboration |

Figure 15.2 Evolution of Procurement Media

Shore reality." Not 'Big Brother reality." Real, actual reality. What we'll see is a lot less of that producer driving the show from behind the scenes, and more people just talking about their point of view, that distinct point of view, that opinion. People love it."

A key to getting thought-provoking opinions into the procurement media landscape is to have a relentless pursuit of diversity and inclusion. "Representing a diversity of views and experiences and walks of life is so important to us," says Luton. "It's so important to . . . ensure that you're giving a voice to all the ways we define diversity, whether industry or geographically or ethnicity or you name it. But valuing diversity isn't enough. It's about taking action, which is what we're doing here at Supply Chain Now in order to amplify all sorts of points of view."

Procurement media has come a long way in the twenty-first century. Beginning with a focus on entertaining and informing, evolving to educating and now moving deeper into facilitating conversations and collaborations, procurement media has become a durable and valuable tool for keeping procurement professionals at the top of their games. And, it will likely survive longer than plenty of other sports franchises.

CLOSING REMARKS

Fans can analyze games all they want, but the players who actually pull on a uniform have the best insights into what works and what doesn't in real-life game conditions. Those players—as well as future players—can learn tremendously from reviews by the people on the field, court, or ice. We hope that as a procurement professional you've learned from what the all-stars in our profession have shared in this chapter.

REFERENCES

1. Federal Motor Carrier Safety Administration. https://csa.fmcsa.dot.gov/.
2. Automated Cargo Transport Systems. https://automatedcargo.com/.
3. Mehrotra, Kartikay and William Turton. June 4, 2021. "Hackers Breached Colonial Pipeline Using Compromised Password." *Bloomberg*. Available from https://www.bloomberg.com/news/articles/2021-06-04/hackers-breached -colonial-pipeline-using-compromised-password.

16
CHAPTER

A CAREER IN THE PROCUREMENT WORKPLACE: BECOMING A PERENNIAL ALL-STAR

Sports journalists love to do stories on *athletes gone wild*. Consider the media coverage given to Olympic swimmer, Michael Phelps, who was photographed smoking marijuana and consequently suspended for three months.[1] Or to golf legend, Tiger Woods, whose extramarital affairs with numerous women have been written about for over a decade.[2] Or to NFL receiver Antonio Brown who was sued for throwing furniture from an apartment balcony, almost killing a toddler; cited for driving over 100 mph; sued by a personal chef and personal trainer who both claim to have not been paid for their services; and accused of sexual assault, all within a span of a year or so.[3]

Fortunately, there is not that much scrutiny or publicity of the personal lives of procurement professionals. However, your behavior in the workplace must be held to a high standard. This chapter will discuss some of the behavioral characteristics of successful procurement professionals. We will then conclude this chapter by giving some advice on how to get more respect in the workplace, increase your visibility as an expert, and manage your career, so that you have the positive personal brand necessary for lifelong success in the procurement profession.

THE MIND-SET NECESSARY FOR PROCUREMENT SUCCESS

To be a procurement professional for the long haul, you need to have *thick skin*. When you are dealing with internal customers and dozens or hundreds of suppliers, things will go wrong sometimes. As much as smart procurement can help minimize the potential for problems, things will still go wrong.

Even if all of your suppliers have Six Sigma capabilities, that means that they will still produce 3.4 defects per million opportunities. One of those defects may be an order of yours! So, you need to have the personality that can withstand unexpected problems. Don't take them personally or let your emotions take over. You can't be the type that has a coronary at the slightest anomaly.

All anomalies must be fixed, though, so you have to diligently pursue resolutions. You don't handle each resolution the same way. We have seen a lot of procurement professionals make mistakes in that area.

Some suppliers chronically perform poorly and are most responsive when taken to task, military-style. Other suppliers are committed to quality and customer satisfaction, and will make corrective action an immediate priority. They don't need to be barked at, but unseasoned procurement professionals sometimes go barking anyway, which is an error in judgment.

When a problem arises with a supplier, ask yourself, "Can I get the same results in the same time frame by being collaborative—as opposed to being combative?" If so, do not rip the supplier's head off! You hurt your own reputation by aggressive behavior and may forever damage your company's relationship with that supplier.

The bottom line is that today's procurement professionals must be capable of dealing with problems professionally.

GETTING RESPECT IN THE ORGANIZATION

Having the right mind-set is a step toward more respect in an organization. However, it is not the only step. There are six actions that you can take to increase the respect you get in the workplace. Apply them all for maximum impact:

1. **Over-deliver**—You have goals for the year, right? If you reach those goals, you may feel that you've done really well. Does management share this view? Usually, managers see achieving goals as *expected* or *minimum* performance. You must exceed your goals to be truly impressive.

2. **Communicate your value**—It is great if you produce great results, but is anyone going out of their way to see how well you're doing? Probably not. You must communicate what you've accomplished; otherwise, it is likely that no one will know what you've done. Or worse, management may think that you've done nothing.

3. **Consciously develop relationships**—The best way to develop good relationships in procurement is to deliver great service. Go above and beyond the call of duty, and challenge yourself: return calls faster, give status updates more frequently, and follow up to make sure your manager and internal customers are happy. If things go wrong, apologize and show your commitment to getting things corrected.

4. **Join a board of directors**—Many trade and professional associations need talented volunteers. Joining a board demonstrates your commitment to your business, profession, and industry.
5. **Get certified**—Meeting third-party standards for excellence is objective proof of your capabilities. Certification is another external credibility source.
6. **Have an article or interview published**—If a third party wants to write about your ideas and/or success, others are more likely to notice that you do your job very well. Outside opinions increase your credibility.

Charles had an interesting and somewhat humorous experience related to that last point about having an article published. Shortly after switching employers and accepting a new procurement management role relatively early in his career, Charles was discussing with his boss a breakthrough idea that Charles had for making a procurement improvement. It's important to note for context that Charles' boss himself was new to procurement, having recently been moved from the tax department (remember our discussion of *The Island of Misfit Toys* from Chapter 3?). The boss wasn't sold on Charles' idea. He said something to the effect of "Show me something from an authoritative source like *Purchasing Today* (a popular magazine at the time) that says this is a good idea." Charles didn't have a published article at his fingertips to support his idea. However, he did immediately get to work on writing articles and soon had his first article published in *Purchasing Today*. Of course, Charles made sure his boss saw it, and he found that his ideas suddenly received much less resistance from his boss from that point forward!

Charles became the type of *authoritative source* that his boss respected. You can—and should—pursue ways of becoming an authoritative source, too. If writing an article alone isn't the most comfortable path for you, the procurement media is always seeking interview subjects. Collaborating with the procurement media can be tricky, so we'll dedicate the next section to helping you navigate that path to becoming a valued expert.

BECOMING A VALUED EXPERT TO THE PROCUREMENT MEDIA

Because there is such little guidance for procurement professionals on the topic of media relations, we will take an opportunity to provide some here. Having experience on the journalistic side of media, one thing we have noticed is that, when it comes to providing good interview material, procurement professionals, as a group, generally leave a lot to be desired.

Being career procurement professionals ourselves, this criticism is difficult to say. But it's true. However, with the following guidelines, you can become one of the most valuable resources to journalists in the procurement field, and as a result, increase your own visibility as an expert:

- **Understand your organization's rules**—Most organizations will want to review, edit, and approve an interview before it is published. Some organizations want you to get permission from a corporate communications group before you agree to participate in an article. Know what the rules are, and communicate them to your media contact as early as possible.

- **Know the timeline**—All online or print publications have deadlines. An article that is due to go to press on March 10 needs your final input far in advance of March 9. Know when your response deadline is, how long an internal review will take, and leave a little breathing room so you know how fast you need to do your part. If the publisher's deadline is March 10 and your internal review will take a week, you may want to have your part done on or before February 21.

- **Never copy and paste from a manual**—When you relax in bed at night, do you read your procurement department manual? Of course not! Why not? Because it is booooring! Writers depend on their interview subjects to make their articles come alive. If you paste your boring manual text into an email interview, the writer will likely not want to use quotes from you because it will bore the reader (i.e., their customer).

- **Use bullet points wisely**—For some reason, procurement professionals love bullet points. They can be helpful in certain documents—hey, you're reading a bulleted paragraph right now!—but if you're answering every question with bullet points, it is an indication that you're not giving a good interview. You don't talk in bullet points, so don't respond to an interview in all bullet points either. Use them only to answer questions like, "Can you tell me five keys to achieving this type of success?"

- **Write in full sentences**—Writers love to use quotes. Having your quotes used is a testament to your talent. But, if you don't write in full sentences, your quotes won't get used or, if they do get used, you won't sound very smart. If asked something like, "What are your goals for the year?" your response should be in full sentences, such as, "Our goals are focused on achieving more savings than last year, improving supplier performance, and implementing a new procure-to-pay system" rather than, "save more money, improve supplier performance, implement system."

- **Don't use abbreviations**—If you're responding to an email interview, write in the same manner that you talk, don't write how you write. For example, you may write *managing the SC* and one of your coworkers may know that you meant *managing the supply chain*. But in an email interview, if you mean managing the supply chain, write *managing the supply chain*!

- **Don't be curt**—If all of your answers are shorter than the questions, it is a red flag that you're not doing a good job as an interviewee.
- **Write conversationally**—Quotes come off best when the reader can imagine hearing your voice saying the words. Use colorful words. "When we presented our savings to management, their jaws practically hit the floor!" is so much more interesting than, "Our savings exceeded the expectations set forth by management."
- **Always be ready for the typical last question**—Many reporters close the interview with a question like, "What else might someone need to know about this topic?" This is your chance to control the direction of the interview. Have the perfect response scripted as the answer to this question because it will often be quoted word-for-word.

SPEAKING AT PROCUREMENT CONFERENCES

There are many procurement-related conferences held each year. These are hosted by professional associations, technology and service providers, and other entities. Each of these conferences has a particular challenge: recruiting enough good speakers to make the conference a high-quality experience for attendees. If your organization permits you to speak about your procurement work at conferences—and you should always verify that it does before applying to speak—it can be a worthwhile accomplishment for your career as well as a way for your organization to promote itself. What can you speak about at a conference? Here are just a few ideas:

- A problem that you and your organization solved
- An improvement that you and your organization made
- A list of keys to your organization's success
- Current trends you've observed
- Predictions about the future

There's something about preparing a speech that takes your insight into your work to a higher level. It helps you think through business logic and understand fine details that you can apply to future projects.

Conferences are also great events for expanding your own knowledge. And, when you speak at conferences, you often get to attend for free, enabling you to learn from others without having to purchase admission as you otherwise would! Other benefits of speaking at conferences include:

- Recognition as an expert in the profession
- Practice at giving formal presentations, which will likely serve you well as you seek to advance within an organization

- Meeting—and impressing—people who could become valuable members of your network
- Having an accomplishment that you can include on your resume

Before this chapter is finished, you will learn how valuable those last two benefits can be to you throughout your career.

CAREER MANAGEMENT

This book has given you a lifetime's worth of tips and techniques for high achievement in procurement—a true game plan for procurement success. Logic may tell you that all you have to do is deliver great results for your employer and you will have a successful career, but it's not that easy.

Your career, like a procurement department or a sports team, must be actively managed. You need a game plan for your career, too!

The last section of this chapter will focus on how to actively manage your career and is divided into two parts: the first part describes what to do while you still have a job to make yourself promotable, and the second part describes what to do if you find yourself looking for a new job.

What to Do When You Have a Job

Justifying Your Existence and Demonstrating Your Value

When economic times are good, there is not much concern about keeping a job. Talented people often feel secure in their roles and clear about whether they want to move on to the greener grass on the other side of the fence. Should they find themselves victims of a downsizing, they feel confident that they will easily find other gainful employment.

When economic times are bad, it is a whole different story. If you have a job, you probably want to keep it, at least for the time being. There are not as many jobs available in bad economic times. If you do leave the organization, there is the chance that the organization you join will experience downsizing. If they decide who to let go by seniority, guess who will get the pink slip?

In either economic situation, there is a commonality between how to be promotable in good economic times and how to hold onto a job in bad times. Whether an organization is expanding in a hot economy or cutting corners in a cold economy, they do what they do for a simple reason: to maximize profits. (Of course, most organizations exist to earn profits.) So, to be promotable or retainable, you have to correlate your presence with better profits.

Who will decide which procurement team member gets promoted when a position becomes available? Who will decide which procurement team member stays or goes when the organization downsizes? Will it be your boss, his or her boss, or human resources? Whomever it is, he or she should certainly know what your contribution to profitability has been. Modesty can be an admirable quality, but not when it comes to advancing your career.

Think about the cost savings you have achieved. Even if you just paged through this book, you have probably realized that we mean *real* cost savings, not cost avoidance or savings that is merely *estimated* and not based on real results. We are talking about the type of cost savings that is so defensible that you can show any finance specialist exactly how it would have been recorded and applied to the bottom line.

Once you know what your contribution to profitability has been, you need to share that in a documented format. If not sharing directly with the person who makes the who-gets-promoted, who-stays, and who-goes decisions, at the very least, share your contributions with your boss. In case you work in the type of organization where it may not exactly be politically correct to spend time on such an endeavor, work on it from home and let the person you are speaking with know that you did the work from home.

If you can convince the person to whom you are reporting cost savings that you understand and are committed to your organization's quest for profitability, and that you have a track record of being one of the best contributors—if not *the* best contributor—to profitability, you will have an advantage, especially if you can show a return on investment. In other words, if your savings exceeds your salary, it might just be a smart business decision for your employer to keep you moving up, or at least keep you around.

Build and Maintain Your Network (Just in Case)

People who get back into the workforce quickly after being displaced are often the people who leverage a network. A *network* is a group of people and associations whom you have a relationship with, and who may be able to help you in certain situations. Knowing people who are aware of job openings and/or can serve as references may be of tremendous help when you are seeking a job.

Unfortunately, a mistake that many people make is trying to build a network when they are in the desperation of a job hunt. There are several problems with that timing. First, you may need job leads and references sooner than you can meet with a decently sized network of people. Second, it can be uncomfortable to call a former coworker whom you haven't spoken with in several years and ask for them to tell a prospective employer how wonderful you are.

So, there is no time like the present to build and maintain your network. Think about the people whom you work with now and those whom you have worked with in the past, both your peers and others who may be in more senior positions. Who could you envision writing a reference letter for you at some point in the future?

Whomever it is that you want in your network, be sure to maintain contact with them. Get together for lunch, call them once in a while, email or text them, interact with them on social media—whatever. Stay in contact despite the fact that it is so easy to lose contact with friends in this busy world. You can't have too many friends.

However, including only the people you already know is not enough—you need to meet more people. You can do this the traditional way, for example, by going to networking events such as your local procurement association's meetings or national procurement conferences. If you are shy about networking in person, there is no shortage of online networks available. There are even some websites that are dedicated to procurement groups, and can be found on social networking sites. These online social networking groups represent a way to learn about other individuals' backgrounds in order to determine whether they might be someone that you want to get to know. The point is: you need to meet, get to know, and maintain contact with the people who can help you in your career.

Ask yourself, "If I became unemployed tomorrow and had a job interview, who could I allow the prospective employer to call for a reference check? Who could write a reference letter? Who could lead me to an open position?" The people who come to mind are the people whom you need to be communicating with regularly. Today, you may not know whose help you may need tomorrow. So, grow your network as soon as possible.

Distinguish Yourself

Imagine yourself in the situation where you have to apply for jobs. You don't think you'll be the only person applying for that job, do you? Of course not. With shifts to outsourcing and constantly changing economic conditions, you can bet that there will be more competition than ever for available jobs.

Maybe you have a few (or many) years of experience, but so will most of the competition. Maybe you have a college degree, but so will the competition. According to a survey that we conducted, over 75 percent of procurement professionals have a bachelor's degree or higher. So, what will you do to stand out from the competition, and how can your qualifications look better than everyone else's?

One thing that not everyone has is a procurement certification. A certification positions you as someone who has met third-party standards for excellence in the profession, as well as someone who is truly committed to procurement as a career, not just as a role you fell into. Certifications do take time to earn. Therefore, it is smart to earn them while you are employed so that you already have the credentials *if and when* you find yourself looking for work. There are several procurement certification options available. They all differ in terms of content, quality, cost, rigor, time requirements, recognition, and so on.

For example, the Next Level Purchasing Association states that its lowest-level certification can be earned in less than three months if the candidate dedicates more than four hours per week to studying.[4] The Institute for Supply Management says that the average amount of time it takes self-paced learners to earn its certified professional in supply management (CPSM) certification is approximately six to 12 months, "depending on experience and time available to study."[5]

A certification from the Chartered Institute of Procurement and Supply (CIPS) "is quite a bit different than other certifications—it's not a short program," according to CIPS' Bill Michels. "For a person coming in, it might take them 100 to 120 hours of study to get through the process. And, there's multiple exams at every level of the program. So, it would take someone, start to finish, two years."

Despite the program's long length relative to other certifications, a healthy share of procurement professionals opt for it over other choices, perceiving the challenge of the program as a strength. "I thought that [120 hours of study] would be difficult for people to do and want to do," says Michels. "But I'm finding it's not. Because of the rigor of the program—because of what they get at the end—it's been very powerful."

The time-and-effort investment of any certification is going to positively reflect on a candidate's seriousness about procurement as a career. "It's going to take a person that has a commitment to go through," notes Michels.

That doesn't necessarily mean that a certification program that takes longer to complete will be regarded as more valuable to every employer. Each hiring manager's recognition of a certification will be shaped by their own experiences and their exposure to various certifications, which can vary tremendously. So, one final thought on that matter is that certifications are not mutually exclusive; you can earn more than one if you're ambitious enough to utilize certifications as a factor that distinguishes you from the competition.

Update Your Resume

Having better credentials than your competition is most of the battle. However, you still have to communicate those credentials to prospective employers. You do this via the resume, also called a curriculum vitae or CV.

Your resume can either help you greatly increase your salary or hinder your career advancement. Here's how to achieve the former with your resume.

First, focus on the structure. An ideal structure consists of the headings: Name and Contact Information, Objective or Career Summary, Past Achievements, Professional Experience, and Education.

Then, consider the resume's length. For entry-level procurement positions, a one-page resume is appropriate. "If you have more than five to seven years of experience, then you want to have a two-page resume," according to Tonia Deal, President of Tonia Deal Consulting, a supply chain recruiting firm, during an appearance on the Next Level Purchasing Association Podcast.[6] "I will not submit a resume over three pages."

Next, ensure that the Professional Experience section is done properly. List experience from most recent to oldest. Within that section, have headings listing each company and the years you've worked for those companies. An additional, commonly ignored item that employers and recruiters like to see is a short description of those companies.

"Who is this company? What do they do? I want the annual sales," says Deal of placing company descriptions on the resume. She explains that employers like to "know the type of organization that [candidates] are coming from."

Underneath each company heading, you should include subheadings for each position you've held, accompanied by the dates that you've held those positions.

Under the position subheadings, include your responsibilities and achievements in bullet point or paragraph form.

For responsibilities, Deal indicates that she finds the following information helpful:

- The categories you are/were responsible for buying
- The annual spend you are/were responsible for
- The type of supply base you have dealt with
- The number of team members you have supervised
- The procurement organization's structure (e.g., centralized), particularly if the individual [has] been part of restructuring the company

For achievements, Deal admits, "The first thing that I will look for is numbers," such as, "Improved delivery performance by 50 percent" and "Initiated structured cross-functional global sourcing process to accelerate $20 million of annual savings."

"I love it!" Deal exclaims, when asked about a candidate's including credentials such as the senior professional in supply management (SPSM), MCIPS, or CPSM on a resume. "I like to see it right under Education." Including a certification on a resume is *critical* in Deal's opinion. "I really want to see that highlighted." See Figure 16.1 for a graphical representation of a procurement resume structure and the recommended items to consider including.

So, this concludes the first part of the Career Management section, focusing on what to do while you still are employed. If you think that you will never need this advice, we hope you are right. However, it never hurts to be prepared for risk, whether in the supply chain or in your career.

Name and Contact Info
❖ Self-explanatory!

Objective/Career Summary
❖ One or two sentences: Who are you and/or what are you looking to do next?

Past Achievements
❖ Two or three "highlights" of your career

Professional Experience
❖ Each company w/ years worked
❖ Company description, annual sales
❖ Each position within company
❖ Each position's responsibilities and achievements with numbers
  ❖ Categories
  ❖ Spend
  ❖ Type of supply base
  ❖ Number of team members supervised
  ❖ Procurement organizational structure

Education
❖ Schools attended, degrees earned
❖ Certifications

Figure 16.1   Procurement resume structure

Strategies for Getting a New Job, Fast!

When searching for a job, you will have the most success if you take a strategic approach. This second part of the Career Management section will cover several components of a strategic approach.

Determine Your Target Salary

It can be a challenge to determine the proper salary. You may think that you should aim for something in the range of what you were making in your most recent position, but what if you were underpaid? You might relegate yourself to many more years of being underpaid.

What if you were overpaid? You might learn that no one wants to hire you. This could be a painful lesson to learn as many months could pass until you realize that your desired salary is not in sync with what the market is paying, meaning you could be out of the workforce longer than you thought.

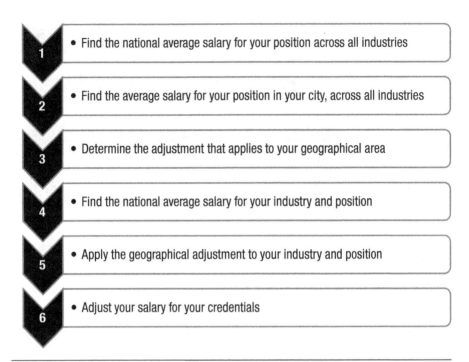

Figure 16.2   Salary benchmarking procedure

Regardless of the situation, it is important to have a methodology for bench-marking your salary. A six-step procedure designed to help you determine how your salary compares to an objective measurement is shown in Figure 16.2. Take out a sheet of paper or open a blank note on your device and number it vertically from 1 to 6. We refer to those numbered lines as Line 1, Line 2 and so on.

Step 1. Find the national average salary for your position, across all industries.

- Go to http://www.bls.gov/oes/current/oes_nat.htm
- In the tables, find the occupation title that best describes your job, either:
  □ Purchasing Managers
  □ Buyers and Purchasing Agents
  □ Procurement Clerks
- Look in the *Annual mean wage* column (second from the right) in the same row containing your occupation title to find the average annual salary for your job title
- Write this number on Line 1

Step 2. Find the average salary for your position in your city, across all industries.

- Go to http://www.bls.gov/oes/current/oessrcma.htm
- Find the city nearest to you
- Click on that city
- In the tables, find the occupation title that best describes your job, either:
  - Purchasing Managers
  - Buyers and Purchasing Agents
  - Procurement Clerks
- Look in the *Annual mean wage* column (second from the right) in the same row containing your occupation title to find the average annual salary for your job title
- Write this number on Line 2

Step 3. Determine the adjustment that applies to your geographical area.

- Divide the number on Line 2 by the number on Line 1
- Write the answer on Line 3

Step 4. Find the national average salary for your industry and position.

- Go to http://www.bls.gov/oes/current/oessrci.htm to display a list of *sectors* or industries
- Click on the sector/industry that your employer is in to display a list of more specific industries
- Click on the industry that is closest to the one that your employer is in
- In the tables, find the occupation title that best describes your job, either:
  - Purchasing Managers
  - Buyers and Purchasing Agents
  - Procurement Clerks
- Look in the *Annual mean wage* column (second from the right) in the same row containing your occupation title to find the average annual salary for your job title
- Write this number on Line 4

Step 5. Apply the geographical adjustment to your industry and position.

- Multiply the number on Line 4 by the number on Line 3
- Write the answer on Line 5

Step 6. Adjust your salary for your credentials.

- If you have earned a procurement certification, you should determine the premium that can be earned as a result. For example, our most recent research indicates that procurement professionals who have earned the SPSM certification earn 14 percent more than those who have not earned it.[7] Other salary surveys, such as those published by trade publications and professional associations, indicate the salary premium for several certifications. If you have earned a certification and identified the salary premium that applies to you, add the appropriate amount to the number on Line 5.
- If you do not have a certification with a published salary premium, add $0 to the number on Line 5.
- Write the answer on Line 6. The number on Line 6 is a benchmark salary considering your position level, the industry, the location of employment, and your credentials.

Search for Jobs

Obviously, the Internet makes it easy to search for jobs, so not much direction is required in this section, just a few tips. First, there are a few websites dedicated to recruiting procurement professionals. These are good resources because they are targeted and, unless positions are also advertised on more general job boards, may result in fewer applications for the hiring company to sift through.

Second, you can search the general job websites such as Indeed, Career Builder, Monster, and ZipRecruiter. To get the most out of your searching, understand that our profession is one that has difficulty agreeing on standard terminology.

Your search for *purchasing manager*, for example, may produce a certain number of job listings. But that doesn't mean that those are all of the jobs listed on the site for which you would qualify. Also, try *supply chain manager, procurement manager, supply manager,* and *sourcing manager.* Doing multiple searches using all of the various synonyms will maximize the number of job listings that you will find.

Interview Like a Pro

When you submit your well-prepared resume to an employer who advertised an open position and you get called for an interview, the hiring manager will want to dig deep into how qualified you are. That hiring manager will likely have three questions about you that he or she will want to explore in the interview. This section will discuss three such questions.

These are not questions that are directly asked of you—we call these Unspoken Questions. They represent what the hiring manager is asking himself or herself about you and your experience.

The first Unspoken Question is: "Was this reported cost savings real?" Most seasoned procurement professionals know that it is a good idea to include measurable results on their resumes. So, seeing lines like, "Achieved $15 million in cost savings" or "Reduced cost by 4 percent each year," on a resume is not unusual.

But hiring managers know that different companies have different standards for recording cost savings. They will want to know if those cost savings would meet the criteria for legitimate cost savings in *their* organizations. So, when interviewing, be prepared to demonstrate how those cost savings actually hit the bottom line. If you reduced your prices by 20 percent, but only had 50 percent compliance, some hiring managers will consider taking credit for the entire cost savings number to be misleading.

If you can verify how each and every dollar of cost savings you claim on your resume actually impacted your previous employer's financial statements, you will go a long way toward convincing your future procurement boss that you are the right candidate. Be prepared to defend your cost savings numbers as if you were presenting them to the CEO of the organization for which you achieved them. If your cost savings numbers are believed to be more legitimate than other candidates, it will definitely be an advantage to you.

The second Unspoken Question is: "How well did you relate to your internal customers?" Procurement managers know that procurement teams are positioned differently in different organizations. Some procurement organizations are powerful within their organizations, while others are lower on the political food chain. They want to know how you will fit into their particular organizational culture.

If you have come from a relatively powerful procurement organization, hiring managers in less powerful procurement organizations may have concerns about how you will interface with their internal customers. Will you treat procurement decisions with the kid-glove care that is needed? Will you be adept at building consensus and inspiring compliance? Will you involve end users so that they feel ownership of the decisions and support them? Or will you be perceived as an arrogant individual who fails to motivate people toward a common vision?

It is a risk to hire someone that could be a political time bomb. So, give the hiring manager comfort by asking questions about the organizational culture and how procurement fits in. Then, share real-life stories of how you were successful at working with internal customers and cross-functional teams in a similar environment. If you can demonstrate that you know how to harmoniously and effectively work with internal customers, you will increase your chances of getting the job.

The third Unspoken Question is: "What was your track record with managing supply risk?" In many organizations, continuity of supply is a make-or-break proposition. If supply is disrupted, the organization fails.

Unfortunately, many procurement professionals were brought up in a culture that has *cost savings tunnel vision*, a mind-set where they think that the only metric that matters is cost savings. Yes, cost savings will always be important, but making decisions based on cost alone to the exclusion of supplier performance or supply risk considerations is amateurish. Sophisticated hiring managers want to weed out amateurs.

So, what did you do to prevent supply disruption? Did you ever experience a supply disruption, and if so, what did you do to minimize the negative impact? What did you learn from the supply disruption and what will you do to prevent a similar situation from happening again? In any procurement interview, you should be prepared to share at least one story about how you successfully dealt with a supply risk.

Powerful, real-life stories that demonstrate your experience in these areas—as well as other areas not described here—will differentiate you from other candidates. Think through your career. Revisit in your mind situations where you succeeded, where you overcame challenges, and even where you failed. What did you do that enabled you to succeed? What would you do differently today? Be prepared to share personal stories in response to inquiries that begin with the phrase "Tell me about a time when you . . ." Have your stories prepared—and even practiced—before going into the interview.

Follow Up

Getting to the interview can be pretty tough. There is a lot of competition and relatively few available jobs. Imagine the inboxes of hiring managers, stuffed with resumes from qualified candidates, as well as from people who send their resume to every hiring employer even if the job bears no relevance to their experience.

Having your resume stand out among the others and getting the opportunity to interview is great. If you do well at the interview, you have reason to feel good, too. So, then, do you just sit around and wait for the phone to ring? Nope. Not on your life.

You should follow up with the hiring manager regularly until a decision is communicated to you. This begins with sending a handwritten thank you card in the mail as well as an email. Emailed thank you notes are standard and expected, so you need to send one. But an email alone won't set you apart from almost every other candidate against whom you are competing. There's something timeless, classy, and above-and-beyond about sending a tangible card. Then, plan on following up weekly. Some people prefer to communicate via email, others prefer the phone—therefore, your follow-up plan should alternate between the two.

Don't worry about being a pest as long as your follow-up messages are friendly, professional, respectful, and patient. Tenacity and keeping on top of things are desired character traits in procurement. You can demonstrate that you have those traits by following up.

CLOSING REMARKS

At this point, the message of this chapter should be clear: having your career go in the direction that you want requires some work. Following the steps outlined in this chapter can help to maximize your employability and ability to be promoted.

More and more executives of organizations of all sizes have learned to recognize the value that procurement brings to the fold. But, until there are no more senior managers like the one in the first chapter of this book who had yet to understand the incredible impact that a well-trained procurement department can have on the success of the organization, there is still plenty of work to do.

This book is your game plan to achieve results and to be the winner that you can be, making the procurement department your organization's *Most Valuable Player*. So, hit the field, execute the plan, and bring home a victory. Consider the two of us as your fans, passionately rooting for you from the grandstands.

REFERENCES

1. Macur, Juliet. February 5, 2009. "Phelps Disciplined Over Marijuana Pipe Incident." *The New York Times*. Available from https://www.nytimes.com/2009/02/06/sports/othersports/06phelps.html.
2. Zakarin, Jordan. December 1, 2020. "Tiger Woods' Sex Scandal: Inside His Fall from Grace and Comeback." Biography. Available from https://www.biography.com/news/tiger-woods-sex-scandal-facts.
3. Gleeson, Scott. September 11, 2019. "A Timeline of Antonio Brown's Lawsuits and Legal Problems." *USA Today*. Available from https://www.usatoday.com/story/sports/nfl/2019/09/11/antonio-brown-timeline-lawsuits-legal-problems/2284178001/.
4. "Individuals: Certification Process." *NLPA*. Available from https://www.certitrek.com/nlpa/individuals/certification-process/.
5. "CPSM Certified Professional in Supply Management." *Institute for Supply Management*. Available from https://www.ismworld.org/certification-and-training/certification/cpsm/.
6. "Purchasing Resume Perfection." March 11, 2008. *Next Level Purchasing Association Podcast*. Available from https://podcasts.apple.com/us/podcast/purchasing-resume-perfection/id267161044?i=1000023640908.
7. "Purchasing & Supply Management Salaries in 2018." 2018. *NLPA webinar*.

EXHIBITS

EXHIBIT A: REQUISITION QUESTIONNAIRE

Any time a purchase is made, there is a risk that you will not be satisfied with the product you receive. A key to getting exactly what you want is to provide the supplier with a detailed specification. Answering a few simple questions can tremendously contribute to successfully developing an effective specification.

For questions 1–13, circle yes or no. For any *yes* answers, use an additional sheet to provide as many details as possible. Remember, the more details that you provide to the supplier, the higher the probability that you will avoid disappointment with the delivered product.

1. Does the product have to be a specific color?   Yes   No

2. Does the product have to be a minimum, exact, or maximum size?   Yes   No

3. Does the product have to be a minimum, exact, or maximum weight?   Yes   No

4. Does the product have to be compatible with any other item?   Yes   No

5. Does the product have to fit in a specific space?   Yes   No

6. Does the product have to produce a certain level of output per period of time?   Yes   No

7. Does the product have a minimum time period that it has to last?   Yes   No

8. Is there a purpose for which you intend to use the product that may be different than the *typical user* of the product?   Yes   No

9. Does the product have to be attached to anything?   Yes   No

10. Will you need to reorder the product in the future?   Yes   No

11. If you do not have the product by a specific date, will our organization face an operational problem?   Yes   No

12. Are you willing to pay for a sample prior to the first multiple unit purchase?   Yes   No

13. Will you be testing the product upon delivery?   Yes   No

14. Why might you refuse the product? List as many reasons as you can. Doing so helps us make sure that we get you the right product the first time!

EXHIBIT B: NO SUCH THING AS A FREE TICKET

Susan Knox, deputy to the county executive of the largest county in Southern Texas, was an avid baseball fan and was delighted to take her retired former colleague, John Waters, up on his invitation to attend the All-Star game which was being played in their city. Waters indicated he had an extra free ticket and would meet her at the stadium the night of the game.

When she arrived, she saw Waters talking with Joe McKenzie, president of the local XYZ Telecommunication Company. She assumed that they had bumped into each other in the lobby and was surprised when she realized she was joining McKenzie in the XYZ Company's box along with Waters, his family, and their friends. Because the county was beginning to negotiate a new contract with XYZ Company, she felt especially uncomfortable when the executive sat next to her. During the game and the breaks, she found herself in the middle of a wide-ranging discussion of the future of the telecommunications industry and the county's expansion into new services.

At the end of the game, she rushed home and sent an email to McKenzie and Waters, asking for the cost of the ticket so that she could reimburse the company. Both responded that there was no cost—it was a free ticket that was part of the season privileges purchased by the XYZ Company. She felt betrayed by her former colleague and unaware that he was now a consultant assisting XYZ to secure new businesses including the one with the county. She felt she was set up and frustrated that her attempts to pay for the ticket were not successful.

Questions

1. What should Susan Knox have done?
   - Should she have left the game as soon as she found out she was at XYZ Company's box?
   - Should she have confronted Waters, indicated her displeasure for being set up, and asked for his help to discourage McKenzie from discussing any business-related topics?
   - Would the best approach have been to claim an emergency and leave the game?

2. What else could she have done when she realized that she was in the XYZ Company's box?
   - Should she have set boundaries by indicating that due to the upcoming negotiations, they could not discuss business?
   - Should she have avoided talking to and sitting next to McKenzie?

3. How should she now proceed?
   - Should she send an email to her boss explaining what happened?
   - Should she remove/recuse herself from the negotiating team?
   - Should she donate money in the amount of a ticket price to a charitable organization in the name of XYZ Company?

EXHIBIT C: EXAMPLE OF A BACK-DOOR SELLING CONVERSATION

Supplier (Maria) makes unexpected visit to ABC University to meet with a professor (Jack)

JACK: Good morning, Maria. How have you been?

MARIA: Real well. Thank you for meeting with me on such short notice.

JACK: No problem. However, I need to attend another meeting in 10 minutes. With these remote learning sessions, I have been very busy. I wish we had more time.

MARIA: No problem, that is all the time I need. I just wanted to let you know that we have a price increase coming up, somewhere around 12 percent.

JACK: Oh, well with all the recent supply chain disruptions and bottlenecks, I anticipated a price increase. You know your software and simulated programs work best for our Engineering courses. You are the only supplier for this type of software with such high quality and service. As long as I am here, if you give us the service we need, I'll back you. Just keep me out of trouble with our purchasing department!

MARIA: Well, I just wanted to tell you in person. You know I appreciate the university's business. It has been a great account for me.

JACK: I appreciate the visit. But it wasn't necessary for you to come all the way over here. We have been doing business with you for a long time. As far as I'm concerned, we are partners.

MARIA: Thank you. I knew I would have your support.

JACK: That's right. Let me make a call to Ms. Taylor, our senior buyer in purchasing. You can talk about price stuff with her. If she plays hard ball, let me know. I will make sure she approves the price increase.

MARIA: You bet!

JACK: By the way, when is your annual golf outing? Every year, I look forward to a competitive round of golf that is organized by your company.

MARIA: You are one of our VIP guests. You should be receiving an invitation sometime soon.

MARIA: I will be in touch and thank you for your time.

Questions

1. What did Jack say to Maria that can bring harm to his university?

2. Why did Jack inquire about the golf outing? Was his request appropriate?

3. What was Maria trying to accomplish as a result of this visit?

4. Why did Maria go to Jack first and not the purchasing buyer (Ms. Taylor)?

5. What could Ms. Taylor have done to prevent this visit?

6. What can Ms. Taylor do after this back-door selling episode to decrease overall cost for her university?

EXHIBIT D: SAMPLE PROCUREMENT ETHICS POLICY

Purpose

The purpose of this policy is to address legally and morally charged issues, ensuring the highest ethical standard is maintained in every aspect of all business dealings with current and potential suppliers.

Scope

This policy applies to all purchasing and company employees in all locations within (country name or names).

Policy

No employee shall use his or her authority or office for personal gain. All employees shall conduct themselves in a manner that is beyond challenge or reproach by adhering to the following requirements:

- **Integrity and honor**—Conducting business ethically, fairly, and honestly in all cases
- **Conflict of interest**—Refraining from any private business or professional activity that would create a conflict (or appearances of a conflict) between personal interests and the interests of the company
- **Abiding by the law**—Establishing and maintaining competition while complying at all times with the letter and spirit of the laws of the country and while remaining aware of contractual obligations, as well as company policies and procedures
- **Back-door selling**—Discouraging suppliers from back-door selling and preventing them from obtaining valuable company data and information
- **Confidentiality**—Protecting the property and confidential information of all parties involved in the contracting process
- **Standing by policies**—Adhering to policies and procedures that promote positive, courteous, and impartial supplier relationships
- **Competence and accountability**—Failure to comply with this ethics policy may result in severe penalties, including, but not limited to, termination of employment

EXHIBIT E: SUPPLIER RFP SCORECARD

Supplier RFP Scorecard

Project Title:		Sourcing Team Leader:	
Supplier Name:		Review Date:	
Total Weighted Score:	0		

Criteria				Criteria Weight	Weighted Score For Criterion
Cost & Value	Evaluated Items	Possible Points	Actual Score	Comments		0
	Cost & Value item 1					
	Cost & Value item 2					
	Cost & Value item 3					
Cost & Value Totals		100	0			

Quality & Safety	Evaluated Items	Possible Points	Actual Score	Comments		0
	Quality & Safety item 1					
	Quality & Safety item 2					
	Quality & Safety item 3					
Quality & Safety Totals		100	0			

Delivery	Evaluated Items	Possible Points	Actual Score	Comments		0
	Delivery item 1					
	Delivery item 2					
	Delivery item 3					
Delivery Totals		100	0			

Service	Evaluated Items	Possible Points	Actual Score	Comments
	Service item 1			
	Service item 2			
	Service item 3			
Service Totals		100	0	

Social Responsibility	Evaluated Items	Possible Points	Actual Score	Comments
	Social Responsibility item 1			
	Social Responsibility item 2			
	Social Responsibility item 3			
Social Responsibility Totals		100	0	

Risk	Evaluated Items	Possible Points	Actual Score	Comments
	Risk item 1			
	Risk item 2			
	Risk item 3			
Risk Totals		100	0	

SCORECARD TOTALS	100%	0

EXHIBIT F: INSTRUCTIONS FOR USING THE SUPPLIER RFP SCORECARD

Purpose

The main purpose of the supplier RFP scorecard is to ensure standard, accurate, and fair evaluation of the responses from all the suppliers who participate in your bid process.

Procedure

The following 10 steps can help you and the members of your strategic sourcing team to evaluate suppliers and their responses to your RFP.

1. *Prior to* receiving any responses to your RFP, you and your team members need to decide upon the criteria on the scorecard that you believe aligns with the questions addressed on your RFP.

2. You also need to decide the weight, as a percentage, for each criterion *prior to* receiving RFP responses. The weight reflects on the relative importance that each criterion holds in achieving the goals set forth by your team. Make sure that the combined weight of all criteria equals 100%.

3. Determine which evaluated items will contribute to the scoring for each criterion. It is acceptable to have as few as one evaluated item for each criterion if the sourcing team deems that appropriate for the situation.

4. Determine a scoring scheme for each evaluated item for each criterion and assign a maximum possible number of points for each evaluated item. The combined possible number of points for all evaluated items for each criterion should equal 100.

5. Using one scorecard per supplier, determine the actual scores for each evaluated item for each criterion.

6. Total the actual scores for each evaluated item for each criterion.

7. Multiply the total actual score for a criterion by the weight for that criterion. This will produce the weighted score for that criterion. Repeat this for each additional criterion.

8. Add the weighted scores for each of the criteria to arrive at the total weighted score.

9. Repeat steps 5 through 8 for each supplier.

10. The supplier with the highest score is the supplier deemed to be most attractive based on your criteria, weighting, and scoring. Before making a final selection, always apply qualitative judgment and common sense to determine if your evaluation methodology was appropriate. Any shortcomings identified should be addressed in improvements that you make to your evaluation methodology in the future.

NOTE: The supplier RFP scorecard for a supplier can be completed collectively by the sourcing team. Alternately, each member of the team can complete individual scorecards for each supplier and all scorecards for each supplier can be averaged to produce an aggregated, master scorecard for each supplier.

EXHIBIT G: CONTRACT REVIEW CHECKLIST

This checklist is designed to help you review your contracts before signing so that you avoid some of the most common procurement contract pitfalls.

- ✓ Make sure the contract has a start date, an end date, and does not automatically renew.

- ✓ Make sure all quantities include a unit of measure.

- ✓ Make sure all prices include a unit of measure.

- ✓ Make sure pricing is either expressed as fixed or that the circumstances and methods for pricing changes are specified.

- ✓ Make sure risks have been fairly allocated. Be certain that your organization is not bearing any risks that should reasonably be borne by the supplier.

- ✓ Make sure that the force majeure clause does not contain any unreasonable excuses for the supplier's failure to perform.

- ✓ Make sure that the warranty clause specifies the applicable remedy or remedies for failure and includes the time frame in which each remedy is required.

- ✓ Make sure that the time that the warranty begins is adequately specified since there are many options.

- ✓ Make sure that the limit of liability provision applies to your organization, not just the supplier.

- ✓ Make sure that the confidentiality provision protects your organization's intellectual property, not just the supplier's.

- ✓ Make sure that the indemnity provision protects your organization, not just the supplier.

- ✓ Make sure the time frame for payment and/or delivery is specified in number of days and that it is clear when the counting of those days begins since there are many options.

- ✓ Make sure how the word *days* is to be used and that it is adequately defined since there are many options (i.e., business days versus calendar days).

- ✓ Make sure that you follow your organization's policies for having contracts reviewed by an attorney.

- ✓ Make sure that all documents incorporated by reference are in the contract, including exhibits, attachments, and appendices.

EXHIBIT H: SAMPLE SUPPLIER BUSINESS REVIEW MEETING AGENDA

SUPPLIER BUSINESS REVIEW MEETING
Date

Location (if meeting in person):

WebEx Info, Zoom Call Info, etc. (as needed):

Supplier Attendees:

- Names and Titles (Sales/Account Manager, Technical Rep, Management, etc.)

Your Company Attendees:

- Names, Titles (e.g., Stakeholder(s), Quality, Buyer, Management, etc.)

Agenda:

- Your Company—Quality, Delivery, Service Review
- Supplier—Status of Quality or Service Issues
- Your Company—Invoicing or Payment Issues (Possibly Invite Accounting)
- Supplier—Prior Year Purchases
- Supplier—Current Year Purchases YTD & Status
- Supplier—Cost Savings Report

- Supplier—Performance Metrics Reports (e.g., Quality, On-time Delivery, Shipment Defects, etc.)
- Your Company—General Corporate Update
- Your Company—Specific Project(s) Update
- Supplier—Supply Agreement Extension (if applicable)
- Supplier—Commodity/Product Outlook
  - Best Practices—What are other customers doing that we are not doing?
  - Trends
  - Market Pressures
  - World Demand
  - Technology/Process Improvements
  - Pricing
- Supplier—Potential Additional Value-Added Services
- Supplier—What Can Your Company Do Better? Process Improvement Ideas
- Your Company—What Can Supplier Do Better? Process Improvement Ideas
- Both—Review of Action Items, Timelines, Next Meeting Date

INDEX

HUBZones (historically underutilized business zones) small business, 81, 84
human resources plan, 290–291
Hurricane Harvey, 223–224
Hurricane Ida, 224
Hurricane Katrina, 136, 185, 223

Ideson, Philip, 311, 312–313
incentive plan, 185
INCOTERMS, 283
information sharing during negotiation, 169
Institute for Supply Management, 325
integrity in eSourcing, 269–270
internal critical data, 106
internal customers, 14–16
  communicating timelines to, 15
  efficient service to, 4
  feedback, 16
  impatience, 15
  involving, 14
  overcoming resistance of, 122–124
internships, 55
interpersonal skills in negotiation, 174–175
interview, 330–332. *See also* career management
inventory carrying costs, 296
inventory management, 293–301
  determining replenish inventory, 295
  fill rate, 301
  inventory carrying costs, 296
  minimum inventory levels, 293–295
  months of inventory, 301
  safety stock, 294–295
inventory turnover ratio, 300–301

Japanese purchasing technique, 136
job rotation, 54

job search, 330. *See also* career management
John, Geraint, 218–219

key performance indicators (KPIs), 74
Knudsen, Ken, 166–167, 168, 169

Lamoureux, Michael, 271
landed cost model, 283
large number of suppliers, 111–112
leakage
  defined, 197
  mitigating strategies, 197–199
learning supplier's interests, 168–169
leasing *vs.* buying, 121
legal risk, 37–38
LGBT-owned business enterprise, 83
liar, 66
Lindstrom, Diana, 290–292
Live Science, 72
Locke, Dick, 282
lunch and learn meetings, 54
Luton, Scott, 311, 312, 313, 314

machine learning, 277, 278
Massetti, Michael, 202–203
matrix, 21*f*
McKinsey, 72
media, 311–313
#MeToo movement, 88
Michels, Bill, 278, 325
minority-owned business enterprise, 83
Modern InTouch, 306
Modern Transportation, 221–222
money-based goals, 6
months of inventory, 301
Myanmar, 225

National Association of Purchasing Card Professionals, 258